Multimodality and Genre

Discourse Analysis

Multimodality and Genre

A Foundation for the Systematic Analysis of Multimodal Documents

John A. Bateman
University of Bremen

First published 2008 by
PALGRAVE MACMILLAN
Houndmills, Basingstoke, Hampshire RG21 6XS and
175 Fifth Avenue, New York, N.Y. 10010
Companies and representatives throughout the world

PALGRAVE MACMILLAN is the global academic imprint of the Palgrave Macmillan division of St. Martin's Press, LLC and of Palgrave Macmillan Ltd. Macmillan® is a registered trademark in the United States, United Kingdom and other countries. Palgrave is a registered trademark in the European Union and other countries.

ISBN-13: 978–0–230–00256–2   hardback
ISBN-10: 0–230–00256–0   hardback

This book is printed on paper suitable for recycling and made from fully managed and sustained forest sources. Logging, pulping and manufacturing processes are expected to conform to the environmental regulations of the country of origin.

A catalogue record for this book is available from the British Library.

A catalog record for this book is available from the Library of Congress.

Transferred to Digital Printing 2010

Contents

List of Tables   ix

List of Figures   xi

Acknowledgements   xvii

Preface   xix

1 Introduction: Four Whys and a How   1
  1.1 Learning to walk: framing issues and analytic focus   3
    1.1.1 Why multimodality?   3
    1.1.2 Why 'documents'?   7
    1.1.3 Why genre?   9
    1.1.4 Why analysis? 11
  1.2 How can we analyse multimodal documents? 13
    1.2.1 An orientation for analysis: empirical linguistics . 14
    1.2.2 A framework for empirical analysis: the GeM model 15
    1.2.3 Structure of the book 19

2 Multimodal Documents and their Components   21
  2.1 Starting points: how to find document parts? 24
  2.2 The page as an object of interpretation 27
    2.2.1 Interpretation within document design 28
    2.2.2 Multimodal linguistics 38
  2.3 The page as object of perception 57
  2.4 Page as signal 65
  2.5 The Page as object of production 74
    2.5.1 Describing a page for design 75
    2.5.2 Describing a page for rendering 85
    2.5.3 Producing a page from intentions: automatic document generation 91
  2.6 Combining viewpoints on document parts 103

3 The GeM Model: Treating the Multimodal Page as a Multilayered Semiotic Artefact   107
  3.1 The GeM Model: the base layer 110
  3.2 The GeM presentation layers: the layout base 115
    3.2.1 Layout segmentation: identification of layout units 116

3.2.2   Realisation information 117

3.2.3   Layout structure 121

3.3   A more complicated example of layout analysis 129

    3.3.1   The parts of the Louvre 130

    3.3.2   The layout of the Louvre 134

3.4   Conclusion 142

4   The Rhetorical Organisation of Multimodal Documents   143

4.1   Rhetoric and multimodal documents: our starting points . . 144

4.2   A brief introduction to *Rhetorical Structure Theory* 146

    4.2.1   The RST rhetorical relations 147

    4.2.2   The RST rhetorical structure 150

4.3   The move to multimodal RST: the GeM rhetorical layer . . 151

    4.3.1   André's extension of RST 152

    4.3.2   Problems with traditional multimodal RST 155

    4.3.3   Multimodal relationals: subnuclear elaboration . . 160

4.4   Example analyses: rhetorical relations between layout units   163

    4.4.1   Mismatches between layout structure and intended rhetorical structure 166

    4.4.2   Explaining how to use a telephone 171

4.5   Conclusion 174

5   Multimodal Documents and Genre   177

5.1   Perspectives on genre 183

    5.1.1   Genre as social semiotic 184

    5.1.2   Genre as social action 188

    5.1.3   Genre: the need for fine-grained descriptions . . . 194

5.2   The move to multimodal genre 196

    5.2.1   Multimodal moves within linguistic and rhetorical approaches to genre 197

    5.2.2   Moving in on genre from the visual 201

    5.2.3   Cybergenres: a brief critique 209

5.3   Representing genre 217

    5.3.1   Genre typology 219

    5.3.2   Genre topology 223

5.4   The multimodal genre space 225

5.5   Illustrations of genre: tracking change 229

    5.5.1   Field guides across time 229

    5.5.2   Wildlife fact files across time 240

5.6   Discussion and conclusion 246

6 Building Multimodal Document Corpora: the State of the Art **249**
6.1 Corpus-based linguistics 250
6.2 The origin and representation of annotated corpora 252
    6.2.1 Annotated corpora: early days 252
    6.2.2 Applying XML to corpus design 254
    6.2.3 Annotation problems with complex data 260
6.3 The move to multimodal corpora 264
6.4 The GeM model as a corpus annotation scheme 267
6.5 Conclusions and recommendations 272

7 Conclusions and Outlook: What Next? **273**

Bibliography **279**

Author Index **301**

Subject Index **307**

List of Tables

1.1 The primary sources of constraints adopted by the Genre and Multimodality framework 18

1.2 The primary layers of the Genre and Multimodality framework 19

2.1 The primary Gestalt laws of perception 61

3.1 Table of page elements to be identified as base units during analysis 111

3.2 Base units of the Gannet page 113

3.3 Base units of the Louvre two-page spread 133

3.4 Extract of the correspondence between layout units and base units 136

4.1 List of RST relations with the constraints they impose on their respective nuclei and satellites 149

5.1 Extract from Orlikowski and Yates's definition of coding criteria for their investigation of genres deployed within an extended email-mediated organisational effort (Orlikowski and Yates 1994, p552). 195

5.2 Selection of the results of Shepherd and Watters' analysis of 96 websites according to their content, form and functionality scheme 213

List of Figures

1.1 A sample of varied document pages which raise, to differing degrees and in differing ways, issues of multimodal interpretation 3

1.2 An extract from a domestic gas bill that is attempting to communicate how much the consumer should pay (or not) 4

1.3 A continuum of visual-textual deployment 10

1.4 The GeM model 16

2.1 Spectrum of approaches to a document and its pages . . . 25

2.2 An example page from an early field guide book on birds . 26

2.3 Possible layout compositions according to the information value portion of Kress and van Leeuwen's 'visual grammar' 45

2.4 Examples of a diagram and a page layout that have received ideological interpretations according to Kress and van Leeuwen's framework 47

2.5 A page layout and its functionally-motivated layout clusters 55

2.6 Good continuation and bad continuation 59

2.7 Examples of pre-attentive perception at work 62

2.8 Eye-tracking results 63

2.9 Successive reduction of resolution in a page image 67

2.10 Using discriminability at different resolutions to reveal layout elements 68

2.11 Alternative visual filters applied to an extract of a newspaper page 70

2.12 Consecutive construction of an XY-tree 72

2.13 Two alternative layouts that receive the same XY-tree description 74

2.14 Construction of line segments obeying the proportionalities of the Golden Ratio 77

2.15 Examples of page layouts produced by Le Corbusier . . . 79

2.16 Grid designed by Gerstner 82

2.17 A modular grid for a more complex Gannet page 84

2.18 HTML source and its rendering in a web-browser 87

2.19 Flow of information in an XML-based document preparation scheme 89

2.20 A formatted extract from a patient information leaflet adapted from Power, Scott and Bouayad-Agha (2003, p226) together with a more simply formatted variant . . .   95

2.21 Document structure from Power *et al.*   97

2.22 Example of layout structure and its realisation on the page as developed within the DArt$_{bio}$ multimodal page generation system   102

2.23 The page as a site of cooperation and integration of distinct semiotic modes   106

3.1 The distribution of base elements to layout, rhetorical, generic and navigational elements   109

3.2 The Gannet example page repeated   112

3.3 Example of differential use of leading in the example Gannet page   119

3.4 Layout structure for the 1972 Gannet example page according to the GeM model   123

3.5 Graphical representation of the general method of correspondence used to relate layout structure and the area model in the GeM framework   126

3.6 Correspondence between the layout structure and the area model of the 1972 Gannet page   128

3.7 A page from a Dorling-Kindersley guide to Paris: description of the Louvre   131

3.8 Base units of the Louvre page shown for ease of reference using the page as background   135

3.9 Example layout positioning of the 'facade' information from several pages of the Dorling-Kindersley *Eyewitness Travel: Paris* guide   138

3.10 Layout structure for the Louvre page according to the GeM model   139

3.11 A grid for the Louvre page   140

3.12 The complex area model for the Louvre page, combining a geometric shape and a vertical grid   141

3.13 Correspondence between the layout structure and the area model for the Louvre page   142

4.1 The graphical representation of the RST analysis of the 'text': "In the event of fire, open the doors by pressing the red button. Then leave the building." 151

4.2 A multimodal rhetorical structure diagram describing instructions for using a coffee machine from (André 1995) . 153

4.3 Example labels taken from the Louvre page 161

4.4 Problematic Louvre inset 165

4.5 Fact sheet extract: features of the Bengal Tiger from the *Wildlife Explorer* series 167

4.6 Layout structure for the tiger page extract 167

4.7 Rhetorical structure for the tiger page extract 169

4.8 Mismatching layout and rhetorical organisations in the tiger page extract 169

4.9 Extract from the fact file from the *Discovering Wildlife* series 170

4.10 Instructions for setting up a phone 172

4.11 Layout structure and a corresponding rhetorical structure for the telephone page extract 173

4.12 Intended rhetorical structure for the telephone page extract 174

4.13 Three semiotic modes commonly deployed within document pages 175

5.1 The positions taken by genre in the design process according to Waller (1987a, pp298–301; Figures 9.5–9.9) 179

5.2 Two versions of *The Guardian* newspaper—one print, the other online 180

5.3 Graphical representation of the genre structures of Hasan (1984) for nursery tales and of Labov and Waletzky (1978) for narrative 186

5.4 Characterisation of the cyclic process of genre change according to Yoshioka and Herman (2000) 191

5.5 Graphical representation of the development of the memo genre as discussed by Yates and Orlikowski (1992, p315) . 193

5.6 The verbal and numerical row of Twyman's schema of 'graphic language' together with examples from Twyman (2004) 203

5.7 Constructed analysis of an example newspaper page 209

5.8 Cybergenres and their development according to Shepherd and Watters (1998) 214

5.9 Development of parallel distinct online news genres 215

5.10 Contrasting Shepherd and Watters (1998) view of cybergenres with the approach proposed within the GeM model . . 216

5.11 Network for classifying members of the factual genre family (Martin 1992) 220

5.12 An example of spatial layout constraints and a possible page solution 222

5.13 Example of overlapping genres adapted from Lemke (1999) 224

5.14 The genre space and some recognisable regions lying along its boundary 226

5.15 Two example documents that share a centre-margin organisation but which vary considerably in other respects 227

5.16 Documents that all remain within broadly typographical, linear-interrupted genres ('text-flow') 228

5.17 Documents ranging from single entry points to multiple entry points (non-linear directed viewing) 228

5.18 Four Gannet pages 231

5.19 Generalised content structure for the Gannet pages 232

5.20 The area models for the four Gannet pages 232

5.21 The contrasting associations of a common layout structure with the area models of the 1972 and 1994 Gannet pages . 233

5.22 Modal presentations of a fragment of the Gannet content structure across time 237

5.23 Mode distribution across the four Gannet pages 238

5.24 Mode distribution across the four Gannet pages shown as a continuous development 239

5.25 Three fact file entries for the Nile Crocodile 241

5.26 Composite layout presenting information about the distribution of the Kingfisher 243

5.27 Layout grid for the 2002 animal fact sheet for the Northern Gannet 245

5.28 Contrasting layout organisation taken up by the central spreads of the three editions of the animal fact files 246

6.1 Extract from the Lancaster-Oslo-Bergen (LOB) corpus . . 252

6.2 Extract from the SUSANNE corpus (slightly abbreviated) . 253

6.3 Example of XCES-conformant annotation adapted from the TEI Guidelines 258

6.4 Example of a common mark-up situation and an ill-formed XML attempt at its representation 261

6.5 Example of stand-off annotation 263

6.6   The inter-relationships between base units and the compo-
      nents of the GeM layout model 268
6.7   A GeM-style XML representation of a Gannet page show-
      ing base, layout and RST layers 270

7.1   Three versions of the tiger fact sheet image 276

Acknowledgements

Many of the results and ideas presented in this book are the results of joint development with my colleagues in the Genre and Multimodality project: Judy Delin and Renate Henschel. The project itself was funded by the British Economic and Social Research Council (ESRC) from 1999 to 2002. Former members of the project were Patrick Allen and Stewart Pleace, who also played a significant role in the project's early directions and approach.

The project also involved direct input from our design collaborators: The Guardian (Roger Browning), HarperCollins (Myles Archibald), The Herald, JET Documentation Services (Jane Teather), and Enterprise IDU (Rob Waller). We thank them for their cooperation and for making materials available to us for analysis and presentation.

In addition, the author thanks the following for assistance during the preparation of this book: Maria Brady (International Masters Publishers Ltd., London) for providing QuarkXpress files of the animal fact sheets discussed in Chapters 4 and 5 and Dr. Klimis Mastoridis (University of Macedonia Press) for pdf-files of Prof. Michael Twyman's article discussed in Chapter 5.

Finally, the author is grateful to the following for permission to quote from copyright works:

- Prof. Elisabeth André for permission to use the material shown in Figure 4.2.
- Dorling-Kindersley for permission to show the Louvre page spread from *Eyewitness Travel: Paris*, 2007, pp122-123, used in Figures 1.1, 3.7, 3.8, 4.3, 5.15.
- Elsevier for permission to reproduce Figure 5.5 from *Information Visualization: Perception for Design*, Colin Ware, Page 166, 2000, ISBN 1-55860-511-8; used in Figure 2.7.
- *The Guardian* for QuarkXPress files and permission to show the pages used in Figures 1.1, 2.11, 5.2, 5.7, 5.17.
- HarperCollins for the bird pages and extracts used in Figures 1.1, 2.17, 5.17, 5.18, 6.7.
- Prof. George Herman for permission to use the diagram shown in Figure 5.4.
- Dr. Jana Holsanova for permission to use the eye-tracking displays shown in Figure 2.8.
- International Masters Publishers Ltd. for permission to use the animal fact sheets (*Wildlife Fact File*, 1990; *Wildlife Explorer*, 1997;

Discovering Wildlife, 2002) shown in Figures 1.1, 4.5, 4.9, 5.25, 5.26, 5.27, 5.28, 7.1.

- *The Journalist* (Taiwan) for permission to use the magazine spread that appears in Figures 1.1, 5.17.
- Prof. Michael Twyman for permission to use the diagram shown in Figure 5.6.

The author offers his apologies should the rights of any further copyright holders have been infringed upon unknowingly.

Preface

This book is intended primarily (but not, of course, exclusively!) for three distinct groups of readers; each of which has its own starting points, requirements and interests. It is hoped that the focus of the book, multimodal documents, will provide a meeting point where these communities may find some useful common ground.

The first group is formed by that growing body of researchers and students who are looking for ways of analysing communication anchored in *combinations* of distinct semiotic modes—in the present case, verbal language and visual presentations such as pictures and diagrams. There is a severe deficit in re-usable methodologies for guiding such investigations; this book seeks to provide one.

The second group consists of those who are working in any particular area concerned with documents—be that design, automatic document analysis, literacy, and so on—and who are interested in seeing how other research communities are approaching issues of multimodality. Young disciplines are often fragmented and different but closely related areas of knowledge can develop in distinct research communities without, at the outset, awareness of each other's efforts. Connections across the distinct communities are then surprisingly infrequent. At a more general level, therefore, this book is also concerned with bridging some of these gaps and in further consolidation of the field. For example: what can the practical process of automatic document recognition gain from abstract semiotic analysis of document rhetoric? Or what can abstract analyses learn from image analysis? There are many such questions and also much to learn.

The last group consists of those who have already been working on multimodality and its description for some time—for those who are familiar with the ground-breaking work of Kress and van Leeuwen on the *Grammar of visual design*, of Kress on multimodal genre, of O'Toole on displayed art, of Lemke on multimodal genre topology and the like, and who ask themselves: what now? When we have already moved to a position where meaning-making is accepted to be essentially multimodal and to rely on an extended notion of genre, one which necessarily includes artefactual components of production, dissemination and consumption, what then? What consequences does this have for how we can structure future investigations into multimodal meaning-making?

This book suggests one possible direction, one which is particularly aimed at research in a 'post-Kress & van Leeuwen' world of pervasive multimodality.

1

Introduction:
Four Whys and a How

This is a book about the 'written document'—a form of communication now so frequent that it is fast coming to rival the spoken word. Written documents, from bus tickets to doctoral dissertations, from supermarket sales offers to legal contracts, assail us from every direction and in hitherto unprecedented quantities and variety. Within such documents, it was traditionally the 'written text' that played the central role, serving as the principle carrier of information. But things have changed: nowadays that text is just one strand in a complex presentational form that seamlessly incorporates visual aspects 'around', and sometimes even instead of, the text itself. We refer to all these diverse visual aspects as *modes* of information presentation. Combining these modes within a single artefact—in the case of print, by binding, stapling, or folding or, for online media, by 'linking' with varieties of hyperlinks—brings our main object of study to life: the *multimodal document*. In such artefacts, a variety of visually-based modes are deployed simultaneously in order to fulfill an orchestrated collection of interwoven communicative goals.

Whereas much is now made of the individual modes that contribute to multimodality—the text, the image, the diagram and so on—our focus throughout this book will be very much on the 'multi' of multimodality: we will explore precisely how we can characterise the *interaction* and *combination* of multiple modes within single artefacts. This is a crucial step to take. Although the meaning of multimodal documents is increasingly depicted as relying on the simultaneous orchestration of diverse presentational modes, analytic methods for handling this orchestration are few and far between. To achieve this, the book will set out a framework for analysing in detail the particular contribution that such combinations open up for a

1

document's meaning. Just as the development of *written* text significantly changed what language can do (Ong 1982), the extension now underway into multimodal documents takes this several steps further. It is precisely because of this broadening in 'modal basis' that multimodal documents are assuming their central role in information dissemination in the modern world: they can apparently do much more than verbal language alone (cf. Thibault 2001, p294). But what, precisely, is gained in the combination? How does the orchestrated combination of modes lead to *new* meanings, to a *multiplication of meaning*, to use a metaphor from Lemke (1998), rather than simple addition?

The ascendancy of the multimodal document is also accompanied and accelerated by the dramatic growth of the technologies by which such documents are produced, distributed and consumed. As a consequence, multimodal documents already exhibit a striking increase in complexity over documents of even the quite recent past. A complexity which involves not only the sheer range of modes commonly found in single documents but, and more importantly, the extent to which the employed modes are interlinked—it is their *modal density* (Norris 2004), or *co-deployment* (Baldry and Thibault 2006), that has increased so dramatically. This has already led to widespread talk of (the need for) 'multimodal literacy', of a 'visual turn' in communication, and of a, perhaps threatening, increase in the visual and non-verbal orientation of culture at large. This represents a substantial change in our awareness of the nature, roles and complexity of multimodal documents and has motivated their acceptance as intriguing objects of analysis in their own right.

But, despite an increasing openness to accept the non-verbal component of such documents as serious contributors to the overall meaning they carry, there remain substantial gaps in our understanding of how investigation can proceed. Consider for example the range of rather different document pages shown in Figure 1.1. In all cases the various areas on the page carry verbal and graphical material that is not simply placed side-by-side: the spatial placement itself carries a variety of further *semantic*, i.e., meaningful, relations between the content that is being expressed. But how can we describe these relationships?

The main task of this book is to provide a framework that can begin to unravel the mechanisms of multimodal multiplication evident in such artefacts. The model proposed is intended to allow researchers and practitioners alike to attack any example of a multimodal document with a single set of tools that can provide reproducible, and therefore evaluable, analyses of what is involved in the multiplication of meanings discovered.

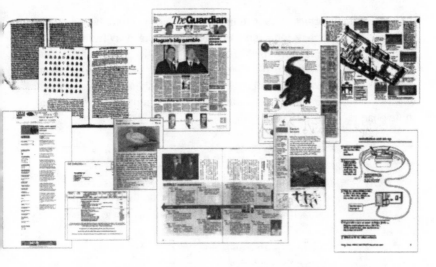

Figure 1.1 A sample of varied document pages which raise, to differing degrees and in differing ways, issues of multimodal interpretation

1.1 Learning to walk: framing issues and analytic focus

To get us started we will first set out some significant restrictions that we impose on our object of study. These restrictions will allow us to be very concrete about just how analysis in subsequent chapters can proceed. Only in this way can a sufficiently firm foundation be achieved for extension into yet more complex and challenging realms of multimodal meaning-making. Our restrictions can be set out as answers to four questions drawn with respect to the book's title. We will first ask (and answer) why we are concerned with *multimodality*, why we are concerned with *documents*, and why we are concerned with *genre*. We will see that there are natural relationships between these concepts and that their combination enriches what we can say about how such communicative artefacts work. This will lead to our fourth question: the question of why we are concerned with *analysis* at all.

1.1.1 Why multimodality?

A more explicit approach to the role and nature of multimodality is important for many reasons. Consider, as an example, the rather normal gas bill portrayed in Figure 1.2. Here we see one of the sheets of a multiple page bill that is attempting to communicate to the consumer how much is owed;

the names and identities of both company and consumer have been made illegible. Although many companies are already moving away from this kind of presentation, the layout shown remains surprisingly common (cf. Delin, Searle-Jones and Waller 2006). It manages to abuse several strong spatial cues both so that relationships between portions of the page are suggested when there should actually be none and to render relations that are intended more opaque.

Meter point reference	Meter number	Reading date	Reading this time	Reading last time	Units Used	Correction Factor	Adjusted Units 100 cubic feet	Adjusted units in cubic metres	Calorific Value	kWh
		C - Customer reading E - Estimated reading								
		R - Removed reading								
		No code - Company reading								
503~~~	0000~~~	12/01/07	6792	6608	184.00	1.022640	188.16	532.50	39.1905	5796.93

	£ p
~~ General Domestic	
Charges 20 Oct 2006 - 31 Dec 2006	
Standard energy 4600 kWh at 2.260p	103.96
Standing charge at 10.100p for 73 day(s)	7.37
Charges 1 Jan 2007 - 19 Jan 2007	
Standard energy 1196.93 kWh at 2.530p	30.28
Standing charge at 11.400p for 19 day(s)	2.17
Monthly Direct Debit Discount	8.05 CR
VAT at 5.00% on charges of £135.73	6.78
Total this Invoice	142.51
Refund direct to bank account	100.00
Balance from previous bill	117.38 CR
Payment received 03 November 2006	32.00 CR
Payment received 03 December 2006	32.00 CR
Payment received 03 January 2007	32.00 CR
BALANCE CARRIED FORWARD	**29.13**

Figure 1.2   An extract from a domestic gas bill that is attempting to communicate how much the consumer should pay (or not)

The fragment starts off with a strong statement that we are engaged with some kind of table with entries: 'meter point reference', 'meter number', 'reading date', etc. This presentation presumably more or less directly reflects the information maintained in the company's database: the fact that for a domestic consumer the meter number is unlikely to change very often while the rest of the information may is not expressed graphically and so conflates information possibly relevant for *this* bill with general, customer-identification information.

The portion of the page that lists the charges is also set out as a table. There is, however, a spatial relationship suggested between the previous line of information (with the explicit cell boundaries) and the charges. Is the previous line of information a heading for the charges? Although the columns do not line up exactly, the right-hand side of the pounds and pence subheading does lie rather close to the right-hand boundary of the 'calorific value' table cell. The visual weight of the column of costs in the lower portion of the fragment also aligns with the 'calorific value' cell, thereby strengthening a potential interpretation of 'calorific value' as a column header. Similarly, the unity of the charges information below and the consumption information above is strongly signalled by their inclusion within a single framing line running around the entire fragment—precisely as one more often finds in a table with headings. In short, we must read and understand what the words and figures mean in order to work out what is and what is not a sensible interpretation.

Focusing on the column of charges itself, this is presented according to the long tradition of bookkeeping, combining here both positive and negative figures in a single column. What is not shown is any dependency that might exist between any of the figures presented: for example, the 'VAT' row specifies that it is calculated with respect to a figure of £135.73 and it is left to the intelligent reader, again, to presume or believe that this figure is the sum given by the figures in the right-hand column up to that point. The total charge for the charging period is then presented in the middle of the column in a bold, but relatively small typeface; the bottom line is given as 'balance carried forward'. This reflects the nature of the bill as a report concerning the state of an account that is being paid by direct debit from a bank: there is no actual figure to be paid, the task of the consumer is to monitor the situation by balancing incoming automatic debits with the outgoing charges raised against consumption.

What is then interesting about this 'multimodal' document is just how little assistance it offers towards finding a sensible interpretation. It relies almost exclusively on the consumer knowing both what information is being presented and the relationships behind that information. The fact that such poorly produced documents are actually intended as the basis on which consumers should make decisions concerning the running of their accounts only exacerbates the situation. The present bill was accompanied by a proposal from the gas company that the monthly automatic debit figure be increased from the monthly £32 shown in the 'payment received' lines of the lower table. A reason for this proposal is not apparent in the document.[1] It is clear that the by now relatively long history of proposals from the field of *information design* concerning how information of this kind can be presented more effectively (e.g., Keller-Cohen, Meader and Mann 1990, Delin et al. 2006) has had little effect here.

---

[1] This is not an argument that *all* documents need to be immediately transparent to their readers: as Lemke (2002, p300) notes, there are cases where texts, for aesthetic, persuasive or attention-getting reasons, quite deliberately leave work for the interpreter to do—for example, in advertisements (cf. Van Mulken, Van Enschot and Hoeken 2005). The issue here is making sure that the effect is only produced deliberately and when intended rather than, as with the present gas bill, as an accident.

There is little technical difficulty nowadays in producing more helpful documents; the question is simply one of awareness and willingness on the part of the companies producing them. Customers are also increasingly making decisions on the basis of their impression of the companies that they deal with: and unfriendly documents are part and parcel of the entire image that a company creates for itself (cf. Waller and Delin 2003). In the chapters below, we will see how a proper consideration of the communicative intent of such documents can lead on the one hand to far more effective deployment of the visual modes available and, on the other, to a focused language for voicing critique.

Unfriendly or unusable documents—be they gas bills, video recorder instructions, legal or medical information leaflets or whatever—often have a disturbing effect: their consumers blame themselves for not being able to understand them. This brings with it broader sociological and ethical implications. As Schriver notes:

> "People's bias towards blaming themselves has potentially serious long-term consequences—perhaps leading them to believe that they are incapable of dealing with complex technology and reducing their interest in new technology. This is a serious worry in documents and technologies designed for the elderly or the physically challenged. A wider problem, however, is the real possibility that students of any age may be led to believe that they are too incompetent to understand either the subjects they study in school or the topics and technologies they must learn on the job." (Schriver 1997, p247)

Teaching consumers to critically engage with documents rather than accepting them as necessarily unproblematic by virtue of their 'authority' as documents would clearly be advantageous, but leaves open the question of just *how* this can be done or best supported.

There have been many changes in the use of visual modalities in documents over the past 50 years and the decoding tasks that readers face are becoming ever more complex. We will see in this book that it is possible to show quite concretely that the intended meanings of a document are now being distributed over a broader range of the available visual modes than was the case 30 or 40 years ago. This increase in complexity has raised awareness of the need to get presentation design 'right' in some sense, to make documents intelligible for their recipients and effective with respect to their design goals. Moreover, even when a document designer has done their job well and set reasonable demands on a reader, used the visual resources consistently, etc., it is still by no means clear that a reader will be in a position to recognise and interpret the visual modalities deployed *without appropriate training*—a concern addressed increasingly by *visual literacy* (cf. Dondis 1972, Messaris 1998, Messaris and Moriarty 2005, Seppänen 2006). Traditionally, the ability to deal with multimodal documents has been acquired implicitly—at least by successful learners. As the use made of co-deployed and interlinked visual modalities increases, however, the question must be raised as to whether we can afford to continue relying on implicit learning by 'osmosis' for multimodality. Recognition of this problem is leading ever more educationalists to concern themselves with *multimodal literacy*, now incorporated as one crucial component of a more general move towards 'multiliteracies' in education (cf. Kalantzis and Cope 2000, New London Group 2000). In this context, multimodal literacy is seen as an explicit part of the teaching curriculum, just as verbal literacy has always been. The questions being raised by these growing communities require a careful consideration of the multimodal document as a carrier of meaning that draws on visual, spatial and verbal presentational modes in combination and co-operation. This kind of meaning is locatable neither within traditional linguistic views of text *nor* within traditional views of the image. To make progress here, we need to place 'multimodality' as such very much higher on our research agenda.

1.1.2 Why 'documents'?

We have suggested something of the practical motivations for our restriction to multimodal documents above. Multimodal written documents are already assuming a central role in many areas of communication. In some areas, they have been the standard, if not the only, form of accepted communication for a considerable time.

Laws, patents, legal contracts of all kinds generally reside in written form rather than any other and some of these have long included illustrations in addition to text (e.g., patents: Bazerman 1994, p80). School textbooks have also long included, for a variety of pedagogical reasons, illustrative material (cf. Laspina 1998, Roth, Bowen and McGinn 1999, Baldry 2000); and scientific texts of many kinds have relied essentially on the co-presence of graphical material almost since their emergence as a distinctive type of text in their own right (Gross 1996). Now, web-based access to information is expanding the dominion of the written document still further.

Pages of spatially orchestrated static content in a combination of modes are the type of artefact that is currently used predominantly for advertising, education, information-presentation, and entertainment. They are delivered by a broad variety of technologies, including print processes of various kinds, with differing capabilities, and by browsers for the web as well as other devices such as personal digital assistants (PDAs), mobile phones, and access terminals (banking machines, ticket vending machines, etc.), each of which leaves its traces on the document shown. So from their sheer significance at this point in history, multimodal *documents* are a clear target for research and analysis.

There are also theoretical and methodological issues important for our restriction. For the development of much of our account in this book, we will be employing methods that originate in linguistics. Linguistics has a long history of dealing with exceedingly complex *structured* semiotic artefacts. It is within linguistics that the most finely articulated accounts of such artefacts have been proposed and where the most detailed methodological discussions concerning just how such artefacts might be studied have been tried and tested.

For some purposes, it may be possible to take broader, more inclusive views of the kind of multimodal artefact considered than we will here. In the fast-growing tradition of multimodal linguistics, for example, everything from book pages to films to art installations to museums to entire cities may be included as 'multimodal texts' to be analysed. In one recent publication, Baldry and Thibault (2006), for example, offer descriptions of printed leaflets, book pages, web-pages, film and TV advertisements; other work involves such non-traditional 'texts' as museum exhibitions (e.g., Meng 2004, Hofinger and Ventola 2004, Martin and Stenglin 2007); yet others consider painting, sculpture and architecture (O'Toole 1990, 1994, Safeyaton 2004). But when analysts move beyond the multimodal document, there are some significant dangers lurking—dangers which arise whenever linguistics is applied outside of its traditional domain of concern.

The application of linguistic frames of analysis to multimodal artefacts is in fact neither self-evident nor obviously correct and so we need to proceed carefully. Our understanding of the meaning-making potential of visually- and spatially-based artefacts is still sufficiently weak that it is relatively easy for sophisticated theories to overrun the information that we can actually extract from those artefacts.[2] This can produce analyses that are insufficiently motivated by the objects of analysis themselves. Our main path of investigation in this book will therefore be to attempt to provide a foundation for an investigative method that is sufficiently robust to advance theory empirically. And it is to make this as concrete as possible that we

---

[2] This concern with perhaps inappropriate applications of linguistics has a much broader history within many areas of study; it is inherent in the disagreements concerning whether linguistics is a part of semiotics or *vice versa* and is equally an understandable response to the 'linguistic turn' of twentieth-century thinking (cf. Rorty 1979, p263).

are restricting the kinds of objects that we consider. We believe that this focus of attention allows us, on the one hand, to push somewhat further towards a detailed account of multimodal meaning-making as such while, on the other, providing a useful set of tools for dealing thoroughly with what is still one of the most challenging and widely used types of multimodal communication. In short, we need to learn to walk before we can run.

The limitations that we will impose on ourselves for the purposes of this book and its investigations are then essentially three:

- First, the book will restrict its attention to multimodal artefacts that work with a *page metaphor*.
- Second, the book will restrict its attention to *static* artefacts. That is, we will not explore visual presentations in which elements change or move within the visual array.
- And third, the book will focus particularly on those documents or artefacts that *combine* at least textual, graphical and pictorial information in single composite *layouts*. We will not be examining purely visual graphical presentations such as paintings (cf. Arnheim 1974, Gombrich 1982*a*, Bertin 1983, O'Toole 1990).

These three restrictions together define our object of study: the kind of artefact that we have termed a *multimodal document*.

1.1.3 Why genre?

Another aspect of multimodal artefacts that considerably complicates their analysis is the question of *comparison*: when analysing an artefact such as a multimodal document, what are we comparing it with? This is important because the meanings that are being made in the document and the forms of expression employed to carry those meanings are anchored in a historical and societal context that appears considerably more fluid than that effecting verbal language. Moreover, there is little point in analysing the particular meaning of selecting to produce text that is coloured blue rather than red, or narrow columns of text rather than wide, if the technology and cultural practices responsible for the document's production were not capable of producing any other colour or any other column width.

We need, therefore, to consider explicitly the range of documents that stand in contrast at any point in the historical development of a culture. For this we will draw on the foundational notion of *genre*. Genre plays a particularly central role throughout our account of multimodality documents in three interlinked ways.

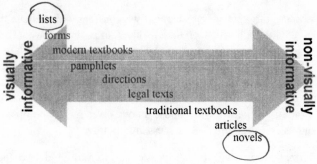

Figure 1.3   A continuum of visual-textual deployment adapted from Bernhardt (1985, p20)

First, genre is already used in an informal sense in many discussions of documents of all kinds, including those explicitly identified as multimodal. We hear increasingly often of the 'genre of websites', the 'genre of news-papers', the 'genre of homepages' and so on. It is important, therefore, to understand more precisely the sense in which this is being done.

Second, genre provides a way of theorising the range of *possibilities* open to documents. We will view genres not as a loose collection of separated text types, but as 'points', or better *regions*, in an entire space of genre pos-sibilities (cf. Lemke 1999). Considering genre in this way is an essential development because it is clear, as writers such as Fairclough (1992), Baz-erman (1994) and others have pointed out in detail, that genres can change, and can hybridise with, and colonise, one another. This requires a space within which document genres can 'move' and within which distinct docu-ment genres can encounter one another. We can characterise regions of the multimodal genre space in terms of the traces that they leave in the particu-lar forms and expressive resources employed by the documents that occupy them. It is by no means the case that all documents simply employ whatever resources are available. Bernhardt (1985), for example, proposes that types of documents can be ordered across a continuum according to how much they rely on the visual presentation modes and how much they rely on the verbal. Figure 1.3 shows this graphically: at one end of the continuum, we have documents that come close to the traditional understanding of 'pure text' with little exploitation of the possibilities offered by visual layout and differentiation; at the other end, we find documents where more extensive use of visual possibilities is regularly made.

And third, we consider the very *materiality* of multimodal artefacts, docu-ments included, to constitute a crucial component of any complete account of multimodal genre. Whereas traditional accounts of genre would have little to say about whether their objects of interest are being published in

books or in looseleaf binders or as posters, the move to multimodal genres places the artefactual nature of genres very much in the limelight (cf.
Kress and van Leeuwen 2001). Considering more carefully the physical (or
electronic) manifestations of documents relates directly to current discussions concerning the particular 'styles of interaction' that distinct artefacts
support or fail to support. For example, and very simply, with a book, the
pages can be turned and we can flick through to find particular passages
that we might be looking for; often we might remember that the passage
was somewhere on the top half of a page on the left-hand side and that it
was somewhere in the middle third of the book. With a web document,
we cannot flick through the pages in the same way, we need to scroll or
click on hyperlinks. In other words, the two artefacts offer different *affordances* (Gibson 1977) for interacting with them and these affordances can
impact on the verbal and visual forms sensibly employed in any associated
genres. Much more than is the case with verbal texts, therefore, the actual artefactual nature of a document will impact on its association with a
multimodal genre.

1.1.4 Why analysis?

Our final 'why' question concerns analysis as such: Why do we need analysis to understand multimodality? The main reason is that multimodal documents are extremely complex entities. Without detailed analysis, the mechanisms by which they build their meanings will not be revealed; we in fact
need quite detailed analysis in order to make the multimodal 'signal' being
sent out by multimodal documents visible and to avoid pre-structuring our
results with preconceptions imported from our experience with other kinds
of semiotic artefacts.

This is important because multimodal documents are in many respects
quite different from the 'texts' that are the objects of study in linguistics.

First, multimodal documents are, by virtue of certain aspects of their materiality, anchored in distinct kinds of perception—particularly spatial and
visual perception. This means that when we move to include objects of
analysis that spread their meaning over written verbal language, images
and layout, we do more than just change selection of means of expression
in the way we do when changing the wording in a text. We move to funda-
mentally different semiotic modes that exhibit very different properties (cf.,
discussions of the distinct logics of writing and of the image: Winn 1987,
Kress 2003) and which are even processed by completely different areas
of the brain (cf. Kosslyn, Koenig, Barrett, Cave, Tang and Gabrieli 1989,
Baker, Rogers, Owen, Frith, Dolan, Frackowiak and Robbins 1996). Just

what the consequences of this are for multimodal documents and their analysis is currently unknown (Kress and van Leeuwen 2001, p127).

Second, multimodal documents also rely crucially, and in a way that verbal language does not, on *technology*—be it burnt stick on cave wall or a graphics workstation. This adds a dimension to the analytic mix that still needs to be explored in much closer detail. Consider, for example, the current rise of the analysis of 'web-pages of type X' as a favourite dissertation topic among linguistics students—despite the fact that we take up in detail below that web-pages of any type are, by and large, still products struggling with a very limited technology that constrains what can be produced into stereotypical, artificial straightjackets. We might highlight something of the problem here by considering how we would react to a field of studies that chose to focus on the properties of the signal received over an early telegraph line in the 19th century, possibly sending Morse code, as if this were an interesting semiotic resource in its own right. Many of the properties observable in such a signal were *artefacts of the technology used* and never came to carry much in the way of interesting configurations of meanings. They did not come to support oppositions that could stand *in contrast* to anything and so could not be meaning-bearing. Much talk of 'new' genres can, with an appropriate view of genre, be called into question. Unless the 'contribution' of the *technological* basis is properly theorised, the object of study has not yet been made accessible.

Third and finally, multimodal documents are also, and this is a big unknown with respect to its consequences for analysis, both produced and interpreted predominantly by 'non-native speakers' or non-experts. Non-native speakers can be considered speakers who operate more 'lexically' than 'grammatically' in the following sense of Kress and van Leeuwen:

> "a mode [may be] 'grammatical' to some of its users, and 'lexical' to others, especially in cases where there is a gap between producers and consumers, and where the producer's knowledge of design and production is kept more or less secret. For most people 'smell' is a collection of distinct individual smells, often associated with specific, individual memories, and evaluated in highly subjective ways. But for scientists, perfumers, aromatherapists, etc. who produce smells, there are systems."   (Kress and van Leeuwen 2001, p113)

Many documents we study may not then be simply taken at 'face-value' as providing an accurate indication of the meaning-making potential of multimodal artefacts.

In the light of these considerations, the extent to which multimodal documents can be seen as analogous to the semiotic entities familiar to us from linguistic investigations is simply an open issue. The discourses of interpretation inherited from multimodal linguistics, design and so on, although highly suggestive and promising of insightful analyses, need to be ground more effectively in the concrete details of the objects being analysed. And, for this, we will need very explicit analysis.

1.2 How can we analyse multimodal documents?

With our 'why' questions out of the way, we turn with our 'how question' to the main task that we will take up for the rest of the book. Our concern is to articulate a framework within which it is possible to frame precise questions concerning the mechanisms by which a multimodal document goes about creating the meanings that it does. To do this we concern ourselves primarily with the issue of *how* we can analyse multimodal documents. We establish requirements for a framework that can lead to usable answers concerning how documents function. We seek, above all, to place the analysis of multimodal documents on a sound *empirical* and *scientific* basis.

This is still largely beyond the possibilities of informal discourses of multimodal 'analysis'. And sometimes this is not even their aim. For example, after presenting a sophisticated analysis of some particular multimodal artefacts, Kress and van Leeuwen state:

> "The point of this explanation is not whether we are right or not. The point is that we have used the principles of provenance and experiential metaphor to create an interpretation. We have used some arguments based on 'where such frames have been', on their cultural history, and some arguments based on 'what they literally are': separate, strongly framed off from each other, etc. In the absence of a 'grammar' to help us along, we have used, to put it another way, modes of interpretation oriented towards 'cultural studies' and 'phenomenology'."
>
> (Kress and van Leeuwen 2001, p121)

In contrast to this, we need very much to be able to say that an explanation is 'wrong', that it does not match what a document itself brings to the interpretation. Unless we can do this, we are unlikely to proceed beyond 'running commentaries' that reaffirm our starting points.

We see here a double danger. First, there is the problem that relatively superficial interpretations become obscured behind apparently technical discourse, whereas in fact the analyses may not have gone beyond what is readily available to inspection. Second, there is the further problem that applying rich interpretative schemes from other areas of study—including multimodal linguistics—may all too easily swamp the rather weak signal that we are currently capable of receiving from the multimodal artefacts themselves. Both problems contribute to the fact, as Kaltenbacher (2004) notes, that research into multimodality is still considered a less than fully respectable activity by many from linguistics and communication research 'proper'.

Boosting the strength of this signal using linguistic methods will involve uncovering, systematically and empirically, precisely to what extent multimodal documents construct meanings analogous to, and different from, those now established for language. And to do this, we must establish what aspects of multimodal document interpretation are products of historical processes of acculturation and fashion, which are strongly constrained by our perceptual make-up, and which are simply sites of conflict between intent and technological and practical capability. We need further to be able to derive on the basis of empirical evidence hypotheses for the kinds of meanings being made multimodally and to validate or refute those hypotheses by explicit testing. This is only possible with explicit analysis which keeps its interpretive components closely in check.

But establishing a sound methodological position for approaching the analysis first of multimodal documents and, subsequently, of multimodal artefacts in general, presents significant difficulties.

1.2.1   An orientation for analysis: empirical linguistics

We proceed towards a framework for this kind of investigation by building on the methods of empirical investigation pursued in linguistics. Within linguistics, fine-scaled descriptions of linguistic phenomena, the data, are examined in order to build theories of how those data work. We select linguistics because there is no doubt that it is with language that we have now amassed the greatest experience on how complex semiotic artefacts can be structured to carry meanings.

To pursue investigations that lead us further in understanding how multimodal documents 'work', we need first and foremost to be able to state testable hypotheses concerning the relations between their forms and functions. For this, we propose the incorporation of methods of empirical study developed within corpus-based linguistics. Chapter 6 introduces this area, its origins and goals, in more depth—sufficient here is Biber, Conrad and Reppen's (1998, p4) description of a corpus as a "large and principled collection of natural text". Checking hypotheses against such collections brings substantial advantages in comparison to 'armchair'-theorising, including the fact that one is confronted with how language is actually used rather than relying on intuitions or artificial examples.

In traditional, non-multimodal linguistics, the use of such linguistic corpora has established itself to be of central importance. Corpora support both the initial search for linguistic patterns, which can then be worked into theoretical analyses, and the subsequent verification of predictions that those analyses make concerning expected linguistic patterning. If the predicted linguistic patterns are actually found to occur in the data, then the analysis is supported; if not, then the analysis is shown to be wanting. Only with an empirical anchoring of this kind can similar progress be made towards understanding multimodal documents.

Empirical corpus-based methods therefore offer a sound basis for achieving the kind of empirical anchoring for analysing multimodal documents that we require—one that is sufficiently systematic, and which exhibits sufficient rigour, to support empirical investigation. Applying empirical corpus-based methods to multimodal documents should make it possible to ask detailed questions of such documents in a way that leads to predictive theoretical analyses.

1.2.2 A framework for empirical analysis: the GeM model

In order to develop corpus-based approaches to multimodal documents where we can uncover just what multimodal documents are doing *in their own* terms, and not in the terms inherited from investigations of language, we need a strong foundation for making the organisation and contents of multimodal documents visible. That is, we require a model that is strong enough to support hypothesis building and analysis, and which also provides an appropriate framework for the construction of multimodal document corpora. The scheme we propose for this is the main result of the project on which this book is based—the GeM project ('Genre and Multimodality')—and is accordingly called the GeM model.

The GeM model defines several layers of description for multimodal documents. Our claim is that these layers are the very least that are required to do justice to such documents—there are certainly more, but without the layers we describe, basic components of almost any multimodal document will be left out of the picture. As we will also show in Chapter 6, the formal specification of the layers defined by the GeM model provide the basis for the construction of a corpus of multimodal documents conforming to the most recent recommendations and standards for linguistic corpus design. This is why we believe that the account developed contributes directly to our stated goal of furthering empirically based research into multimodal meaning.

A schematic overview of the model as a whole is given in Figure 1.4. We see documents formed by configurations of social practices shown in the centre of the diagram. Particular multimodal artefacts are produced with particular forms and with the help of particular production technologies, or tools, for their construction. Documents are then produced 'on' a particular *canvas* that is to carry the artefact physically. We employ 'canvas' as a technical generalisation to refer to whatever medium is adopted as substrate for the artefact at issue. This could be paper of a particular size (and thickness, absorbency, etc.), or a monitor screen (of a particular size and resolution), or an animal skin (of particular texture), and so on.

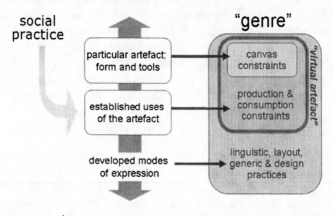

Figure 1.4   The GeM model

Whatever substrate is selected for an artefact's canvas brings its own constraints with it—such as, for example, enforcing fonts to be above a certain minimum size to avoid the characters bleeding into one another due to high absorbency, etc. Possible forms are therefore constrained by the particular 'canvas'. Forms are also constrained by the technology that is used to produce the artefact. Certain printing presses may only be able to print columns of a certain width, or use a particular restricted range of colours, etc. Certain brushes for painting characters may only allow a particular size of character to be produced, and so on. These restrictions are not strictly imposed by the canvas, but by how the artefact is brought to life on the canvas. Finally, forms are constrained by their intended uses: if the document is to serve as a quick reference guide, then certain forms (and canvases) will make better choices than others.

Combining these three sources of constraint on forms gives rise to what we term the *virtual artefact.* Viewed from the outside, i.e., without going into the details of the physical substrate, production technology, and consumption requirements, it may be difficult to disentangle just which constraints are due to what source. And, indeed, there can be redistributions among these three sources without the form of the final artefact changing. For example, early newspaper press technology was not able to produce columns of arbitrary width: columns needed to be short enough both to fit on a particular device and to avoid having their type thrown out by that device's high-speed rotary action (cf. Hutt 1973, p43). At that time, the constraint on form was a production constraint. Similarly, the use of a particular size of font was a canvas constraint, owing to the lower quality of paper that was available. Nowadays, columns can be of more or less arbitrary width and the fonts used could be very much smaller: but the established *use* of the newspaper has brought into being a sufficiently strong (and functionally motivated) tradition that the outward form of the newspaper has not changed nearly as much as the technology and material used could in theory support. The newspaper is then, in our terms, a 'virtual artefact' in which the final form is constrained by a *combination* of physical, production and consumption constraints.

We therefore see documents as being created and used within a configuration of constraining influences. Our view of these aspects of documents is particularly inspired by the model of document description developed by Waller (Waller 1987*a,b*). Although centered broadly on typography and design, Waller draws extensive parallels and connections with linguistic models of communication and so already went a considerable way towards providing a model compatible with the other layers of linguistically motivated description that we include. Briefly stated, the GeM model extends and replaces those of Waller's layers concerned with linguistic description, while adopting and further specifying the layers of his model responsible for capturing design and layout. This results in two broad areas: (i) features describing aspects of the conditions of production/consumption of the document including its physical manifestation, and (ii) features concerned with the properties inherent in the document being analyzed. The constraints of the first area are summarized in Table 1.1.

Taking the conditions of production for multimodal artefacts seriously as this suggests enables a more realistic appraisal of the precise motivations and reasons for the appearance of documents. Design is often described as a compromise between many competing and sometimes conflicting constraints and these need to be brought into any discussion of the functional motivation of the resulting artefacts. This issue is equally relevant for all professionally produced multimodal documents. Such documents are typically subject to stringent production constraints ranging over the provision of material, time pressure for decision-making, conforming to the generic design constraints, and so on. Such constraints can make themselves felt in the smallest details of a document—for example, page layout can be a

Canvas constraints	constraints arising out of the physical nature of the object being produced: paper or screen size; fold geometry such as for a leaflet
Production constraints	constraints arising out of the production technology: limit on pages, colors, size of included graphics, availability of photographs; constraints arising from the micro-and macro-economy of time or materials: e.g. deadlines; expense of using color; necessity of incorporating advertising
Consumption constraints	constraints arising out of the time, place, and manner of acquiring and consuming the document, such as method of selection at purchase point, or web browser sophistication and the changes it will make on downloading; also constraints arising out of the degree to which the document must be easy to read, understand, or otherwise use; fitness in relation to task (read straight through? Quick reference?); assumptions of expertise of readers

Table 1.1   The primary sources of constraints adopted by the Genre and Multimodality framework

result of negotiations between publisher and advertisement companies and not a matter of strictly functional design at all, or the need to produce a particular length of headline may restrict linguistic choices right into grammar and vocabulary.

The technology used to produce a particular multimodal document can also impose its specific footprint on the artefact as a whole—for example, as print technology changed, newspapers began to use color, but in different ways as the technology developed; analyzing the use or non-use of color images at that time needs to include consideration of this boundary condition. Not being aware of the production constraints always opens up the danger of over-interpretation because more design freedom, and hence more controllable resources for making meaning, are assumed than are actually available.

Since all of these social practices and their particular contributions to the production of a document are subject to constraints of the types we have suggested, we group these constraints together to give our extended notion of genre, shown to the right of Figure 1.4. Traditional, non-multimodal views of genre would concern themselves primarily with the bottom row: a social practice employing particular modes of linguistic expression; we open this up both to include the other semiotic modes available and to take into consideration the artefactual nature of multimodal documents.

Content structure	the content-related structure of the information to be communicated—including propositional content
Genre structure	the individual stages or phases defined for a given genre: i.e., how the delivery of the content proceeds through particular stages of activity
Rhetorical structure	the rhetorical relationships between content elements: i.e., how the content is 'argued', divided into main material and supporting material, and structured rhetorically
Linguistic structure	the linguistic details of any verbal elements that are used to realize the layout elements of the page/document
Layout structure	the nature, appearance and position of communicative elements on the page, and their hierarchical inter-relationships
Navigation structure	the ways in which the intended mode(s) of consumption of the document is/are supported: this includes all elements on a page that serve to direct or assist the reader's consumption of the document

Table 1.2   The primary layers of the Genre and Multimodality framework

Each source of constraint (canvas, production, etc.) may bring restrictions for the concrete forms that may appear in the artefact itself. In order to isolate the effects of genre constraints, therefore, we need to be able to characterise the concrete forms and contents that are found in multimodal documents in sufficient detail to make genre variation visible. This characterisation is given in terms of the particular semiotic modes deployed within a document—e.g., in terms of the verbal (linguistic), visual (graphical, diagrammatic, etc.), and layout (composition). We summarise these main descriptive layers of our account in Table 1.2. This offers a framework for the layered decomposition of any multimodal document that can be used directly for multimodal corpus annotation.

1.2.3   Structure of the book

The layers of our model guide the overall structure followed in the rest of the book.

In Chapter 2, we take up the issue of just how a multimodal document is to be 'taken apart' analytically. We cannot analyse a multimodal document and ask how the particular configurations and inter-relationships between its component parts carry or reject particular meanings if we cannot recognise those component parts accurately. We then build on this in Chapter 3 and present a detailed synthesis that provides the *visual* or *presentational* layers of the GeM multimodal document model: here, in particular, we motivate the composition of the layout structure and present some examples of its application.

In Chapter 4, we turn to the kinds of meanings carried by the layout structures. For this we employ a detailed model of the rhetorical organisation of documents. It is increasingly accepted in document design that design should be informed by an applicable account of rhetoric; Schriver goes so far as to describe document designers as 'practicing rhetoricians' (Schriver 1997, p332). But precise accounts for just how one can engage with this notion of the rhetorical organisation of design in anything more than intuitive terms are rare. Here we show how one explicit treatment of rhetorical organisation developed in text linguistics and computational linguistics, Mann and Thompson's (1988) *Rhetorical Structure Theory*, can be applied to multimodal documents. This then makes up the rhetorical layer of the GeM multimodal document model.

In Chapter 5, we take up the issues of relating documents to one another so as to bring the infinite variation possible at the level of individual documents under control. We propose here a strong organising framework in which bundles of reoccurring properties, be they verbal, graphical or some combination, are associated with the 'generic type' of a document—i.e., with its *genre*. For this, we need both to introduce the relevant approaches to genre that have been developed in non-multimodal contexts and to show how these can be beneficially extended to cover the multimodal artefact. This provides the necessary foundation for understanding the genre structure of the GeM model.

In Chapter 6, we change gears and present the technical instantiation of our analytic framework as an approach for corpus design. To motivate this, we set out something of the history of 'annotated' corpora in linguistics, some of the tools and techniques that have been developed there, and then go on to show the more recent growth of multimodal corpora and where the GeM model fits into this development.

Finally, in Chapter 7, our conclusion, we briefly review the account that we have presented and identify what we see as necessary steps for the future.

2

Multimodal Documents
and their Components

In order to move from a descriptive approach to multimodal documents towards the more analytical stance motivated in the introduction, we need to fix the 'lower' levels of the overall model—these are the levels which make direct contact with what can be seen on the pages of the documents we analyse. As O'Toole puts it for the semiotic artefacts of art:

> "the first priority of any description which is intended to contribute to a shared discourse is what can actually be perceived as present in the 'text' of the work itself." (O'Toole 1994, p213)

Securing access to what can be perceived as present—primarily, in our case, spatially arranged configurations of *document elements*—is of considerable importance for the entire enterprise of performing revealing analyses. A methodologically sound and well specified decomposition is critical because it provides the foundation for everything that follows: analysis builds on the parts identified and discusses their combination into larger 'meaning-carrying' elements.

Recognising reliably just which elements are being used on a page and how they are being related is by no means an easy or obvious step—although it is too often treated as if it were. There are some significant methodological issues lurking which need to be explicitly problematised: whenever an analyst is free to select, invent or ignore elements on the page at will, with little more in the way of justification than that they appear significant (or not), it remains difficult to move beyond anecdotal interpretation. It is crucial that elements are brought to our analytic attention regardless of whether we as analysts thought, intuitively, those elements to be significant or not. That is, we need to overcome the selective blindness that applying a pretheoretical interpretation of what we *think* is happening on the page can bring.

An appropriate framework for recognising document parts needs to provide substantial constraints for the analyst's decomposition of a page into units. The decomposition process must be made as reliable and as *reproducible* as possible. The configurations of elements and their formal properties that we discover during this phase then provide, to adopt again terms from O'Toole,

> "a multidimensional space of shared points and lines and planes which we might see as the common denominator of potential meanings. ... Topologists call this multidimensional space the 'backcloth' against which the 'traffic' of further meaning-making moves."   (O'Toole 1994, p230)

We need precisely this backcloth, and the particular *design features* that it provides in the case of multimodal documents, to ground all subsequent interpretation.

That documents *do* have parts that are worth finding is beyond any reasonable doubt. Established results show that page elements and their organisation strongly influence how readers interact and interpret the documents that contain them. Several areas of research have contributed to this. Particularly detailed investigations of how readers interact with documents and how that interaction is influenced by layout and composition decisions are undertaken in *usability studies* (cf., e.g., Wright 1980, Wright 1995, Schriver 1997, p445 onwards, p473, Nielsen 2000, Nielsen and Loranger 2006). If, for example, the document is an instruction manual, then the usability of that manual can be evaluated according to how easily its readers can actually carry out the instructions given in order to achieve desired ends—e.g., to record a TV programme on some recording device. Similarly, if the document intends to inform the reader of some information, the document can be evaluated in terms of how much of the information being imparted is actually perceived, understood and remembered by the reader.

Studies of this kind have shown that the overall layout and composition of documents influence readers' uptake of document content and intent in many ways; effects range over the broad interpretation of how items in a document such as pictures and text are related to one another right down to many more fine-grained differences in comprehension and ease of use within typography and formatting (e.g., Bransford and Johnson 1972, Hartley 1994, Wright, Lickorish, Hull and Umellen 1995, Sless 1996, Lentz and Pander Maat 2004); we will mention several of these fine-grained effects in more detail below. Since changes in low-level properties of page composition *systematically* influence how readers interact with those pages, we know that document readers are led to particular interpretations rather than others by the documents themselves. Such results demonstrate the existence of particular cues that readers are recognising, and responding to reliably, that trigger their observed behaviour. This gives important insights concerning both the parts into which our documents should be decomposed *and* the properties that those parts must be assigned in order to explain observed variations in document interpretation.

In some ways we can see our starting point as similar to that which faced linguists throughout the first half of the twentieth century: how to decompose the units of interest for analysis into their natural, i.e., motivated and demonstrably present, sub-units. There are many ways of breaking up a document, just as there are many ways of breaking up a sentence, and some of those ways may be useful and insightful and others not. We need then some guidelines and direction in order to proceed. Taking this step carefully uncovers several different communicative tasks that elements on a page regularly fulfill; these tasks, or functions, cannot be simply lumped together and pulled out of a hat as required. Indeed, this is one of the main problems that previous approaches to this issue exhibit: the motivations for the elements proposed are often drawn from differing levels of abstraction with differing purposes.

We also face a problem still very much with us in linguistics at the beginning of the current century: what is the unit that we are decomposing? In linguistics there has been considerable movement more recently away from the 'sentence' to consider entire 'texts'. Multimodally, we must raise an analogous question: we have talked of document parts, but just what is the 'whole' that these 'parts' are parts of? This is not as straightforward as it might initially seem. Even for a printed document, where we can get the whole of the document into our hands, so to speak, there are important questions about the units that we consider. Do we consider just the physical unit of a page or, if the layout so indicates, do we consider the two-page spread? Or, a further alternative, if we are in a magazine and a single article runs over several pages, do we consider *that* to be the unit whose parts we consider? The situation becomes much worse when we turn to new media and consider websites: what are the boundaries of a website? For all of these questions, we will see that having a multilayered set of descriptive resources for describing just what is going on will prove essential. Only then can we work towards answers that may be generalised across all the documents that we choose to consider.

2.1　Starting points: how to find document parts?

This chapter will consider how we can go about identifying and describing the elements that make up documents and their pages—i.e., decomposing a document into its *component parts*. There are, in fact, many such frameworks already in existence—which should come as no surprise given the centrality of the issue of document parts for building analyses. Somewhat more surprising perhaps is the fact that these frameworks are still mostly unconnected with one another. They have been developed within several distinct research and development communities and accordingly draw on a variety of perspectives and pursue somewhat differing goals. Each, however, offers beneficial pieces of the entire picture.[1]

A major aim of this chapter will be to place these disparate approaches into a common overarching framework. This will allow us to see what each approach brings while organising its contribution with respect to others. It will also allow our own synthesis of perspectives to be placed on a firmer theoretical *and* practical foundation so as to provide a scheme that is strongly supportive of detailed and reliable empirical analysis, comparison and critique of multimodal documents, of whatever their type.

Contributions particularly useful for meeting these requirements can be found in the fields of design, multimodal linguistics, document understanding, and automatic document generation. We will begin, therefore, by setting out what we can and cannot take from these disciplines. We then in the chapter following turn to the explicit account that we have developed for capturing those components of multimodal documents which provide the expressive resources necessary for those artefacts to carry meaning. The discussion here begins with a consideration of how each perspective on page decomposition has *construed* its object of investigation: i.e., the 'page' as such. At one extreme, we have approaches that set the page against the social and individual context of the production of its containing document; at the other extreme, we have approaches which set the page against the social and individual context of reception of that document. Between these two positions, we see a continuum of possibilities, suggested graphically in Figure 2.1.

Along the path from document production to reception, our discussion will stop at four points that have received focused attention from at least

---

[1] There have already been calls for closer cooperation between some of the perspectives we discuss. Both van Leeuwen (2004) and Waller (Waller 1980, 1999), for example, argue convincingly for the need for linguists to consider aspects of visual presentation, while Waller (1987*a*), drawing on the proposals of Twyman (1982), is a book length plaidoyer for those concerned with typography, composition and the visual to build on notions developed within linguistics—particularly, notions of genre and rhetoric.

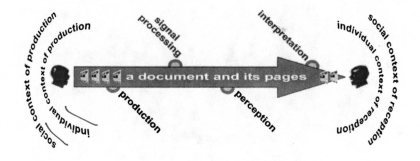

Figure 2.1 Spectrum of approaches to a document and its pages

one significant research community. For analysts of multimodal documents coming from a linguistic, semiotic or design perspective, it is here probably the rightmost perspective, that of 'interpretation', that is most familiar. We will therefore begin with this, noting some problems and open issues which establish the importance of being aware of the other approaches also. We then move progressively back from receiver to producer—i.e., from right to left in the figure.

The four perspectives corresponding to these points then construe the page as follows:

- as an object of interpretation,
- as an object of perception,
- as a 'signal' to be processed,
- and as an artefact to be 'produced'.

Each perspective concerns itself with the physical manifestation of the page and so contributes directly to the task of this chapter. We return to make contact again with the end points of the spectrum—with the social aspects of production and reception—when we discuss multimodal document genres in Chapter 5; here we are more concerned with the processing steps between these two extremes in order to locate those aspects or perspectives that we can usefully apply to the page in order to reveal its workings.

Consider, for example, the page set out in Figure 2.2, selected from a field guide on birds published in 1972. Illustrating the different approaches to be discussed, we see this page in rather different ways. First, it is a page that is to be interpreted using the vocabulary of design and the techniques of multimodal linguistics: what design features went into the page's composition

Gannet   *Sula bassana*
Family SULIDAE.   Gannets   No. 27

This great bird has the magnificent wings and flight
of a giant Gull, and a wing-span of nearly 6 ft.   It
can sight a fish from a great height while on the wing
and will drop like an arrow into the water after its
prey.   The plumage is white with a tinge of buff on
the head and neck, and dark brown, almost black,
wing-tips.   Immatures are first dusky all over, later
piebald or white sprinkled with dark spots.
Haunt   The coast and sea, and at breeding time rocky isles
and stacks, chiefly on the north and west of the British Isles.
Nest   Of seaweed and tufts of grass or thrift; on the rocky
ledge of a stack or island in a great colony with others.
Eggs   1, nearly white, chalky.   April or May.
Food   Fish.
Notes   Short and harsh.
Length   36 or 37 in (91 or 94 cm)
Status   Resident

Figure 2.2   *An example page from an early field guide book on birds* (The Observer's
Book of Birds *by S. Vere Benson, Frederick Warne & Co., 1972, p22; original drawing in colour.*)

and what communicative functions does the page thereby achieve? Second,
the page becomes an event in the visual field, which our perception delivers to us in particular ways rather than others: how then do we 'see' this
page? Third, we can measure the page as having certain 'physical' properties directly, such as patterns of light and dark, of areas of different visual
textures and so on, and can accordingly employ algorithmic techniques for
separating the 'visual signal' into those that contribute to the whole: what
do such procedures reveal about the page? And fourth and finally, we can
also consider what it would involve technically to *produce* such a page; if
we wanted to specify precisely how this page and no other is to find its way
onto paper, then we must explore techniques for document *description* that
are sufficiently finely discriminating while still maintaining a causal link to
purpose and task.

When we ask basic questions concerning what the individual elements on the page are out of which the page as a whole is made, or how these elements 'hang together' (or not), we receive several answers from these perspectives—not all mutually exclusive, but not identical either. Most important for our aims here is to find that range of answers useful for exploring just how such a page 'works' multimodally. A crucial property of appropriate answers will be that they make 'meaning-carrying alternatives' visible: they need to show us not only what is in the page but also what is not on the page *but could have been.*

In the page describing the Gannet, for example, the information could have been spread around the page in a variety of ways, broken up in differing segments, expressed in different visual modalities, etc.: what is it about this particular publication, about its particular date of publication, about its intended purpose, about the technology used for its production, about its intended readers, and so on that led to it appearing as it did?

2.2 The page as an object of interpretation

Since all the approaches considered in this chapter can be said to 'interpret' pages in some way, we need to clarify just what sense of interpretation we mean in this section to distinguish it from others. Primarily we are concerned with issues of 'functional' or 'rhetorical' interpretation—analysis that attempts to characterise just what a page is communicating and how it does so. As suggested above, this relation to pages is probably the one which is the most 'intuitive': consumers of documents interact with documents at precisely this level, although their intent is not typically analytic. The step to an analytical stance then requires that we discuss in explicit terms just how the meanings assigned to the page are supported (or not) by its physical realisation.

This overlaps substantially with the traditional concerns of document design, graphic design and now information design. There the task is both to produce documents that support their intended communicative functions and to be able to critique and improve designs so as to achieve the best results. This relies on trained sensitivity and exposure to wide ranging examples of good and bad 'solutions' to design problems. While still the best way of producing high-quality document design by far, much of the design process within this framework remains in the skill and experience of the designer. For our purposes, we need to focus on methods by which we can make the sophisticated meaning-making methods that designers are drawing on visible. Again, the situation is identical to that within linguistics: being aware of the linguistic methods by which texts are constructed is no replacement for literary text production (or even, usually, for good practical text writing, such as technical documentation). What the linguistic analysis provides is a deeper understanding of just what is happening in producers and consumers when sophisticated textual artefacts are exchanged and what properties the texts themselves must have in order to support those processes. We are looking for the same degree of understanding for meaning-making in the multimodal realm.

The analytical perspectives that we highlight in this section are accordingly drawn from multimodal linguistics as well as from graphic and document design. We briefly set out the approaches to document interpretation that these approaches support, drawing out similarities between them. We also present some of the issues that arise that make none of them alone sufficient for our needs.

2.2.1   Interpretation within document design

We will make two points of contact with document design in this chapter—the first here, focusing on issues of document interpretation for the purposes of improving design, and the second below when we come to consider document production proper in Section 2.5.1. In a sense this reflects the need within design to consider both interpretation and production as interlocking aspects of a single task. Design is best seen as a cycle of design proposals producing draft documents which are then subjected to criticism leading back to improved proposals. Thus we necessarily encounter both interpretation and production and writers describing the design process often move back and forth across the two perspectives, sometimes barely distinguishing them.

We believe that some of the techniques that we develop here can usefully feed into this cyclic process of design–critique–revision. But, to date, very little use has been made in design of the rather explicit kinds of analytic procedures followed in the linguistic or automatic analysis approaches that we will see below. This is generally a purely practical issue: developing and employing the reflexive meta-awareness that comes from theory and explicit analysis is rarely compatible with the day-to-day demands of meeting design deadlines. Where we do see clear overlaps in concern is in areas of design concerned with research and teaching. For here it is clear that a deeper theoretical apparatus can bring benefits, as long as it is also always embedded within and founded on practice. All of the approaches that we describe in this section are therefore positioned somewhere between practical description and theoretical consideration.

The Reading School

One body of work relevant here that was, from the perspective we take in this book, considerably ahead of its time is that of the Department of Typography and Communication at the University of Reading. Research in this tradition continues to this day to explore issues very much related to those we pursue here. Some basic assumptions underlying all of this work are set out by Twyman (1982), where the need is emphasised for a far more detailed theoretical and empirically motivated grasp of the visual presentation of 'language'—taking in all the graphic and typographical possibilities offered by current, previous and future technology:

> "we should engage in a serious study of verbal graphic language in much the same way as linguistic scientists have studied spoken language. We need to know much more about the language that we use and the circumstances of use. ...It seems to me self-evident that only when we know what the characteristics of verbal graphic language are can we begin to design effectively for it."
>
> (Twyman 1982, pp16–17)

This has led to a series of broad surveys of documents and the typographic and graphical resources deployed in those documents, the aim of which has been to discover how the possibilities of visual graphic language vary across time and context of use. As a research task, this comes very close to the task that we take up again in detail in Chapter 5, when we turn to multimodal genre. For the purposes of the present chapter, we draw particularly on the analytic frameworks that were developed in these surveys for decomposing documents analytically into their parts. Two orientations were particularly significant for this work. One is the weight given to the production of documents by *laypersons*—i.e., design by the non-expert or non-professional. The other is the role of changing technology bases for document production.

Non-professional design is considered significant because it is here we come the closest to 'natural' or 'spontaneous' verbal graphic language production. Just as the linguist might want to study spontaneous, unedited speech to get a sense of how the language 'really' is, i.e., before it is channelled into particular preregulated—and thus perhaps artificial—shapes and forms, the researcher into verbal graphic language can try to ascertain just what the implicit knowledge of graphical/visual organisation in a society is. Walker (e.g., Walker 1982 and Walker 2001) accordingly includes surveys of *letters*, both handwritten and typed, as examples of lay design that can reveal the norms and conventions of visual language.

This orientation is also linked to technology because it is only quite recently that the full range of multimodal document design possibilities has become available for the layperson. As a consequence we now see a much broader range of documents being produced by those untrained in document design. Discovering the decisions made in such documents presents an exciting and very new area of research that will need to draw on a range of research methodologies. For example, psychological experimentation into the kinds of spontaneous decisions made by untrained 'information-givers' when presenting information multimodally is only just beginning (e.g., van Hooijdonk, Krahmer, Maes, Theune and Bosma 2006) but already promises to take our understanding of 'spontaneous multimodal utterances', and consequently of multimodal meaning-making, significantly further.

The influence of technology was also a prominent issue in several of the surveys carried out by the Reading group for other reasons. One was a parallel interest in the historical development of verbal graphic language as document production has changed over time and another was specifically commissioned analyses of the potential (or otherwise) of emerging online information presentation systems for information dissemination. The systems analysed included services where videotext is transmitted along with television signals for display on regular TV screens (e.g., Ceefax, Prestel and similar offerings) and were, at that time, severely limited with respect to their typographic and multimodal possibilities. The research question was then one of considering just how information could be presented with such a restricted graphical mode. This was termed the 'graphic translatability' of text (cf. Twyman 1982, p21 and Norrish 1987): that is, to what extent could graphically sophisticated versions of some document be presented on systems of reduced capabilities in such a way that their information-content and organisation would nevertheless be recoverable by a reader.

Although the battle lines in this area of investigation have moved almost beyond recognition over the past twenty years in that the overwhelming majority of the technical restrictions of those early online text presentation systems have disappeared,[2] the *analytic tasks* that had to be carried out are just as important and relevant today. In order to characterise just what may or may not need to be preserved when changing representation form, it is advisable to take stock of what is being used in the first place. With this in mind both Twyman (1982) and Walker (1982) present components of a framework for documenting the verbal graphic language employed in documents in a way that was independent of whether the documents analysed were produced as traditional printed documents, handwritten, typewritten, videotext and so on. This common form of description could then support

---

[2]Which does not mean that the *systems* have disappeared: systems, just as other products, exhibit considerable inertia once developed (cf. Norman 1988).

generalisations concerning both the typographical features relied upon by distinct classes of document and the constraints exercised by varying technological processes for document production.

Twyman's contribution to this framework focused mainly on narrow typographical features (i.e., properties of characters including typeface, spacing, colour and so on) and a classification of document types according to their combination of text, images and graphics; we will see more of the discussion of typographical features in Chapter 3 and of the discussion of document types in Chapter 5 on genre. Walker's contribution takes this further, drawing on Crystal and Davy's (1969) characterisation of linguistic and paralinguistic levels so as to construct a 'checklist' of document properties to be used for comparisons. Visual graphic language is described here (Walker 1982, p104) according to a document's physical make-up (e.g., typewriter, print, the kind of paper used and so on: i.e., in our terms, the production and canvas constraints), its spatial articulation (e.g., the spacing between words, lines, indentation, margins and the like) and its graphic articulation (e.g., modifications expressed by underlining, punctuation, initial capitalisation and so on).

A further refinement of the approach is pursued by Norrish (1987) in order to provide a more fine-grained analysis of the larger scale *structure* of collections of documents. For this, Norrish sets out a hierarchical view of documents in which structure is captured in terms of nested sequences of typographical categories. These categories start with an entire document, such as a journal or a book, and progressively break the document down into subcomponents such as paragraphs, lists, notes and so on. Each of these components receives a particular description concerning the typographic features employed. These include the kinds of checklist features proposed by Walker and, in addition, places their occurrence within a structural representation of the document as a whole. Problematic with the approach, however, is its combination of several kinds of information which, logically, do not belong together—in particular, the physical distribution of information across pages and the functional organisation of that information. Conflating these is then less than ideal because generalisations are easily obscured. The approach also fails to describe the precise spatial articulation of pages in any generic way. The model as a whole is therefore still more focused on textual presentation with relatively limited coverage of the spatial possibilities of pages.

Despite these drawbacks, the approaches developed by Twyman, Walker and Norrish nevertheless represent a landmark in multimodal document analysis. Much of the development that we pursue in this book can be seen as following the same path that they define and for many of the same reasons. Their commitment to an explicit analytic method for setting out the particular structures and realisational forms employed in multimodal documents is still rarely found in other areas of design.

Schriver

The most detailed introduction and overview of the field of document design as a whole is still probably that given by Schriver (1997) and we will return to positions that she sets out in many places in this book. For our immediate aims in this section, however, we pull out of Schriver's description aspects particularly concerned with how *designers* see the process of document interpretation—although, as we shall see below, Schriver's account also leads directly into issues of production, too.

Schriver follows a line of argument in document and information design that sets out as a basic premise that designers need a good understanding of how readers interpret the documents that those designers have produced. The main goal is to produce *user-oriented documents* which support the activities and requirements of the documents' intended consumers. This builds on modern research into reading and comprehension, extending it to the case of the multimodal written document. From reading comprehension, for example, it is well known that prior knowledge (cultural, specific, genre-related, etc.) plays crucial roles in forming interpretations of received material (cf. Spiro 1980, Wright 1980, Wilson and Anderson 1986, Winn 1989, 1991, Hegarty, Carpenter and Just 1991, Ollerenshaw, Aidman and Kidd 1997, and many others). It is therefore problematic to produce documents as if their readers were passive receivers of some straightforwardly coded message.

This variability in potential interpretation on the part of readers presents serious problems for appropriate design: it is not straightforward for designers to predict just how their designs will be received. In general, a document is improved when its design employs information structuring that corresponds to, or supports, the knowledge its users can reasonably be assumed to have and when the reader's short-term memory for interpreting language and layout in combination, for example in tables, is not stretched too far (cf. Wright 1970, Wright and Barnard 1978 and Schriver 1997, pp274–275). All of these issues can be incorporated to motivate better design decisions and so need to be brought into the design process: waiting until the document has been produced before testing for usability is often too late (cf. MacDonald-Ross and Waller 2000).

Explicit awareness of the fine-grained functional consequences of design decisions therefore plays a central role in current professional design. To support this, Schriver sets out several ways in which particular selections of design features—layout, spacing, fonts and so on—can be used to increase the rhetorical and communicative 'impact' of a document on its interpreters. These design features are carried by *text elements* (Schriver 1997, p342), which are Schriver's way of defining the parts that go to make up pages. Schriver suggests two kinds of text elements that we distinguish here as 'simplex' and 'complex'. First, there are simplex elements that "often depend on their genre (e.g., reports have executive summaries, online help has procedures ...)" and which serve as individual, isolatable elements of page design (Schriver 1997, p343). Second, there are configurations of such elements on the page which Schriver terms *rhetorical clusters*. These are defined as follows:

> "By *rhetorical cluster* I mean a group of text elements designed to work together as a functional unit within a document. Rhetorical clusters act as reader-oriented modules of purposeful and related content. They are comprised of visual and/or verbal elements that need to be grouped (or put in proximal relation) because together they help the reader interpret the content in a certain way."
> (Schriver 1997, p343)

Identifying such rhetorical clusters is then one of the basic steps proposed by Schriver for 'seeing the text', for describing and analysing what goes into a page design.

Schriver suggests several particular examples of rhetorical clusters, such as 'illustrations with annotations and explanations', 'body text with footnotes' and 'procedural instructions with visual examples'; we will see other examples below. As can be gathered from these, a rhetorical cluster can be quite extensive in scope and will often include smaller-scale clusters within it. Schriver suggests that an explicit consideration of this kind of organisation can contribute substantially to turning design and design interpretation into a more analytic enterprise—and this, in turn, should render design more 'teachable'.

Applying this to our Gannet example, the approach appears quite natural—up to a certain point. For example, we have a body text with particular paragraph styling, some headings and subheadings and an itemized list (cf. Schriver 1997, p343). This body text is itself perhaps part of an 'illustration with annotations' cluster—or is the illustration within the body text cluster? In any case, we can see that as readers it appears straightforward to interpret the page by deploying such standardised interpretive frames:

> "We can think of a document as a field of interacting rhetorical clusters. If the document is well designed, the clusters orchestrate a web of converging

meanings, which enable readers to form a coherent and consistent idea of the content."   (Schriver 1997, p344; original all in italics)

More or less intuitive analyses of this kind can generally be produced on demand by a document's readers. This therefore provides us with a good starting point for interpreting multimodal written documents but needs to be taken further in at least two respects.

First, recognising a rhetorical cluster presupposes that we have interpreted the contributing elements to stand together in some particular functional relationship. We need to be able to open up this account so that we can explore *possible* clusters on the basis of a document's layout without having already recognised their function. If we can only find clusters when we know the function of the cluster, the account is in some respects circular. Although this is less of a problem for interpretative analysis, we want to reach a position where we can lay bare the process of interpretation itself. This requires being able to specify identification criteria for elements so as to provide a reproducible scheme for exploring interpretations and for asking which interpretations a document supports and which it does not.

Second, there are many fine details of design which are not readily assimilable to a rhetorical cluster. In the Gannet page, for example, what exactly is happening in the itemised list in the lower portion of the page? That it is an itemised list is clear, but its precise form of expression is unusual by today's standards. The entry for the Gannet's eggs is particularly strange; we repeat the approximate layout here:

Eggs   1, nearly white, chalky.   April or May.

This appears almost to be working towards a single line table in which we have three 'columns': the object considered, the appearance of the object, and the time of occurrence of the object. We see something similar to this in the second line of the page also. In both cases, simply stating that we have an itemized list, or a table, or something else, would be to miss the details of the particular case; this appears to be a tentative spatial transition towards the very explicit tables that we will see in some further example bird field guides that we analyse in Chapter 5. Since we want to explore how meanings are being made (or not) multimodally and how these practices develop over time, it is important to capture this and all other relevant levels of detail so that we can consider their contribution to *establishing and changing* applicable conventions of interpretation.

Reading 'into' graphical materials

We must also address here an issue that we will raise at several points in the current discussion. When considering the possible parts of a multimodal document, we have to take an explicit position with respect to the extent, if at all, that we will be prepared to 'read into' the pictures and graphical materials on the pages we analyse. In the case of the Gannet, there are naturally resonances between the information portrayed in the drawing and the text—this is also particularly relevant for the genre at hand because the drawing is intended to capture some of the essential features of the bird. With the more informal approaches that characterise design, this is again usually done 'on demand', particularly when there is something 'striking' about the visual information; here accounts examining the use of pictorial rhetoric, visual metaphors, etc. provide many illuminating examples (cf., e.g., Forceville 1996).

For our starting point here, however, we will be more concerned to *restrict* this possibility. This is in order to rule out at the initial segmentation stage of analysis the considerable flexibility in recognised 'parts' that would otherwise ensue. This is not to say that it is impossible, or not valuable, to segment visual material in the ways required to describe how the detailed content of an image can interact with other components of a document and its interpretation and, indeed, we will return to issues involved here when we discuss more of the relationship between text and images in Chapter 4. But for the present we seek to minimise the variation that will be found across analyses and so do not want parts appearing, or not, depending on what strikes the analyst's eye.

There have been attempts within design to render this particular area of meaning-making more accessible to analysis. For example, Gaede (1981) suggests a scheme by which designers can systematically explore alternative rhetorical relationships between visual and verbal components so as to produce designs that are more effective and interesting; a similar proposal is made by Marsh and White (2003, p661) with respect to their own, independently derived, set of text-image relations. In general, the role of rhetorical relationships of these kinds has been considered particularly with respect to their consequences for the uptake of messages, including advertising messages: examples of studies in this direction include, for example, Phillips and McQuarrie (2004) and related work.

These approaches do not, however, provide us with direct means for identifying parts of multimodal pages, although we can draw some lessons from them. Problematic is that they rely on an intelligent reader or user who is able to draw out the particular connections required to make the rhetorical combination—such as, for example, contradiction or analogy—work. As an illustration of this, Gaede begins his discussion with an example of using his library of visualisation methods to explain the method behind a cigarette advertisement consisting of a verbal component at the bottom of the advertisement stating "I'd go miles" and a visual component showing a cowboy sitting back against a barn, loosely crossing his legs and lighting up a cigarette (Gaede 1981, pp10–12).[3]

The clue to the interpretation is claimed by Gaede to be the fact that the reader of the advertisement can quite clearly see a hole in the bottom of the cowboy's shoe. This then falls under Gaede's category of 'visual causal/instrumental relations', since the 'I'd go miles' is the *cause* of the 'hole-in-shoe'. This visual-verbal rhetorical figure then is one possible means of increasing the 'attractiveness' of the visual presentation as a whole (cf. Gaede 1981, p253), although whether or not this is actually so appreciated by readers remains a matter of debate (e.g., Van Mulken 2003).

Important here is that whereas in *isolation* we would have no more motivation to pick out the hole in the shoe as we have for picking out some of the holes in the walls of the barn behind the cowboy or the third large wrinkle from the bottom that can be seen in his left trouser leg, in *combination* with the verbal text it is quite likely that we need to recognise the hole in the shoe as a 'part' of the presentation.[4]

We can consider this in a similar way to searching for linguistic constituents, particularly by applying the notion of *dependence*. Clearly, if we remove the third wrinkle from the trouser leg by some visual processing trickery, nothing much will change in the interpretation of the advertisement; if we remove the hole in the shoe, however, the interpretation is radically changed if not destroyed. This is then one way in which combinations of messages across modalities can conspire to require that particular document parts be recognised rather than others. We will propose below, after we have seen several more approaches that have been taken to segmenting the visual content of images in a document, and particularly those of Kress and van Leeuwen (1996) and Royce (2007), that parts should only be recognised when there is direct evidence of this kind for a combination across modes.

---

[3]The original advertisement discussed by Gaede is in German, but the loose translation given here is sufficient for present purposes.

[4]A similar observation is made by Stöckl (1997, p128, p138) in his criticisms both of attempts to demarcate the structural units of images and equally of attempts to extract components of argumentation directly from visual representations. Stöckl also provides several pointers to older work that has grappled with precisely this issue and come to very similar conclusions.

There are also visual *qualities* of the images used in layouts that are significant for those layouts' interpretation but which are not readily isolatable as distinct 'elements' or parts of an image. 'Lines of force', 'movement', 'gaze' and other invisible directions in images serve to direct a reader's attention and so also contribute to how readers are navigating a page, grouping elements together or not as they go (cf. Dorn 1986, pp145–153). In this sense as well, therefore, simply characterising an image as a unit by itself, or some of the identifiable elements in that image, may not yet fully cover the information that we will need in order to characterise how a layout is functioning (or not). This also relates to some of the properties of images described in multimodal linguistics by Kress and van Leeuwen (1996) which we will see below.

Returning, then, to our Gannet drawing, we actually need very little in the way of segmentation: the image simply shows a gannet, on a cliff edge, with some other birds flying below. More of concern for the designers of this particular field guide to birds were evidently some of the visual qualities of the Gannet—for example, the textual "The plumage is white with a tinge of buff on the head and neck, and dark brown, almost black, wing-tips"—is also in evidence in the drawing (cf. Chapter 4). The only 'part' that the document depends on being present in the drawing is a gannet, or gannets. A drawing showing no discernable gannet would clearly support a very different range of interpretations for the relation between the drawing and the rest of the document.

Conclusion

There is very much more to be said about design and the techniques that designers employ when interpreting and critiquing pages of designed information. For our purposes here, however, we need to focus on those tools of the trade which can feed directly into the kind of reproducible empirical investigations that we want to develop for multimodal documents. Motivations for this step, even for designers, can readily be found. As mentioned above, Schriver suggests that the skills involved in successful design could be made much more readily 'teachable' if we could articulate more explicit accounts. A further motivation is to be found in document critique. Despite training and considerable skill, designing documents remains a difficult task—and, accordingly, it *can and does go wrong*. As Wright (1998) tellingly observes:

> "... it is not surprising that instructions may sometimes fail to communicate; but it is surprising that writers have difficulties recognizing these troublespots ... When reviewing written advice given to the elderly, Epstein (1981) con-

cluded, 'The people who produced the leaflets are all more or less convinced that they have turned out a good product. The four experts on information design whom we consulted were of a different opinion.'"   (Wright 1998, p46)

We already saw in our introduction with the gas bill an example where professionally produced documents do not appropriately show their readers how they are to be segmented into meaningful elements; below we will see many more such cases. It appears that working with purely intuitive interpretations of, for example, an allocation of clusters or of a rhetorical figure, is *not* guaranteed to reveal (and correct) problems—even in design.

2.2.2 Multimodal linguistics

Within multimodal linguistics, there have been several attempts to find more analytical methods for investigating multimodal artefact interpretation. As we shall see, it has been relatively natural for linguistic accounts that focus on linguistic function rather than on form to broaden their attention to artefacts other than verbal 'texts', construed narrowly.

A prime example of work of this kind is that of the social semiotic tradition developed by Halliday and colleagues, called *systemic-functional linguistics* (commonly abbreviated as SFL: Halliday 1978). Work within this direction of research makes the following, general assumption.

> "A multimodal and social semiotic approach starts from the position that visual communication, gesture, and action have evolved through their social usage into articulated or partially articulated semiotic systems in the same way that language has."   (Kress, Jewitt, Ogborn and Tsatsarelis 2000, p44)

And, building on this, ground-breaking work by Kress and van Leeuwen (1996) on a linguistics of the visual image and by O'Toole (1994) on a linguistics of art has certainly revitalised earlier semiotic and philosophical attempts to achieve a broader understanding of the relations between meaning in language and other semiotic modes (cf. Barthes 1977a). Many researchers working within the SFL tradition now include a variety of multimodal artefacts—multimodal documents among them—in their domains of interest (for overviews see, e.g., O'Halloran 2004c, Kaltenbacher 2004, Martinec 2005, Royce and Bowcher 2007).

Systemic-functional approaches investigate how texts in general are articulated to show their appropriateness for particular situations of use, or contexts. Moreover, 'text' as such is construed as an essentially *semantic* unit, rather than one defined by its external appearance or surface realisation. It is this starting point that has made it natural to consider extensions of the framework to apply to semiotic artefacts more broadly.

SFL captures the appropriateness of texts to context in terms of three interacting but distinct functional domains: the representational domain, the interactional domain and the 'text-organisational' domain. These domains are referred to as *metafunctions* because they are essentially 'generalised' functions that hold whenever a linguistic unit is constructed: any linguistic unit, such as a clause, can be analysed *simultaneously* according to the work it does to represent the world, the work it does to enact social relationships (e.g., asking questions, evaluating entities, etc.), and the work it does to contribute to an unfolding text or dialogue. The presence of this work is not dependent on what particular meaning is being expressed.

Multimodal SFL analysis sees visual presentations as subject to the same generic functional requirements as other communicative artefacts. Such artefacts are accordingly already presumed to manage meaning-making in the three metafunctional domains. A photograph, for example, may present simultaneously a representation of something occurring, an interpersonal appeal to the viewer (as when a character in the photograph looks directly 'out of' the picture at the viewer), and a textual organisation whereby some things are made more salient in the composition (by visual prominence, position, selection of subject-matter, etc.) and others less so. *Combining analyses from distinct functional perspectives in this way is a technique* well developed in linguistic accounts and it is likely that we will see increasingly revealing analyses drawing on this particular aspect of meaning 'multiplication' for multimodal artefacts also.

Within this tradition, the principle approaches that have been applied to multimodal documents so far are, in addition to Kress and van Leeuwen (1996), those of Baldry and Thibault (2006), Royce (2007), and Lemke (1998); we will see more of these below. In addition, a related but rather different course has been taken by O'Halloran in a series of detailed studies of *intersemiosis* between the visual modes of verbal language and *mathematical formulae* (O'Halloran 1999a,b, 2004a,b). Since this has not been a prominent feature of the multimodal documents that we have analysed so far in our own studies, we will simply set a place marker: whenever the account proposed here moves to consider documents of the kind that O'Halloran has analysed, we will need to extend the descriptive layers present to include the areas of meaning O'Halloran has identified.

There are also several explorations into the multimodality of documents pursued within text linguistics, since texts more obviously raise issues beyond the linguistic mode construed narrowly. Although this has generally been seen as something very much on the edge of text linguistics 'proper', a long-standing concern with classifying text types has led to several attempts to extend this practice for multimodal artefacts (cf. Spillner 1980,

Kitis 1997, Stöckl 1998, 2004*a*, Blum and Bucher 1998, Straßner 1999, Fix and Weillmann 2000, Eckkrammer 2004). We do not provide an overview of this work here because its utility for our purposes in this chapter is unfortunately limited: these linguistically-informed accounts do not generally problematise the actual identification of the page elements upon which their analyses are built. We do see, however, the general model that we develop as one way of bringing these diverse investigations together in the future.

Towards a 'Grammar of Visual Design'

In multimodal linguistics at large, the most important and influential position is without doubt that articulated in Kress and van Leeuwen (1996). In this work, the main concern was to set out a systematic map of the territory for multimodal visual-based communicative artefacts, to provide a 'grammar' of the possibilities of meaning-making available that applies to all forms of visual presentation. The starting point for their approach is again the fundamental assumption of SFL that communicative artefacts, including those that are the results of visual design, can be characterised along the dimensions defined by the three SFL metafunctions. Kress and van Leeuwen then provide within each metafunctional domain an explicit 'grammar' for the kinds of meanings found in visual artefacts. Such visual design grammars take on a particular task: they need to set out detailed 'systems of choice' that show the abstract range of meanings that can be selected from in their metafunction. This is itself a significant claim and raises an entire range of challenging issues concerning the organisation of meanings in different semiotic modes. For the ideational metafunction, for example, Kress and van Leeuwen propose a decomposition of visual messages into elements analogous to the division of linguistic clauses into processes, participants in those processes, and the circumstances of occurrence of those processes. Then they suggest a classification of such visual configurations that is similar, but in some interesting respects different, to the classifications found in functional linguistic interpretations of grammatical configurations. In particular, they define *narrational* visuals and *conceptual* visuals—the former visually depict some action (Kress and van Leeuwen 1996, pp73–75) and the latter some kind of classification or analysis (Kress and van Leeuwen 1996, pp88–89, p107). This way of decomposing visuals is also adopted by, for example, Baldry and Thibault (2006, p122) in terms of *visual transitivity frames* and Royce (2007, p73) in terms of combinations of *visual message elements* (VME's) that we will say more about below.

For the interpersonal metafunction, Kress and van Leeuwen set out possibilities for evaluating the visual material depicted in terms of inter-relationships between that material and the viewer: visual properties such as the direction of gaze of any people depicted in the visual (e.g., looking at the viewer, looking away) or the relative angle, or tilt, of the camera (e.g., looking up at, down on) are suggested to construct particular interpersonal relationships involving relative power and engagement or appeal. Many of these suggested meanings have been the explicit focus of theory and experimentation: for example, the relation between camera angle and power is explored in Tiemens (1970), Mandell and Shaw (1973) and others, the effect of 'point-of-view' depictions of 'direct gaze' has been related to visual perception and its natural focus on where potential interactants are looking by Solso (1994, pp136–137), and the effects of apparent viewing distance on interpretations of social distance are examined in Meyrowitz (1986). A useful overview of these results is given by Messaris (1997, pp34–52), who also demonstrates that there is still considerable need for more detailed investigations of precisely how these dimensions of variation are to be interpreted in context; viewers' assumptions or knowledge about depicted scenes are already known to influence significantly the extent to which particular visual choices are available for taking on particular interpretations.

The meanings that we have sketched here from both the ideational and the interpersonal resources generally involve components *within* images; this raises again the possibility, perhaps even the necessity, that we mentioned above of extending segmentation of multimodal documents to include 'internal' parts of the graphic material. Ideationally, therefore, the drawing in our Gannet example is clearly a 'conceptual' visual used primarily as an opportunity to present visually some of the physical properties of the Gannet's appearance and habitat rather than to show action. The elements of the drawing are then the bird, its identifiable parts, and the circumstances of its sitting on a cliff top. Interpersonally, Kress and van Leeuwen's account would pick out the facts that the Gannet is not 'looking' out of the picture (i.e., there is no 'appeal' to the viewer, as might be seen in pictures of seals in campaigns against seal hunting), that we are dealing with a colour drawing rather than a photograph (with associated claims of reality/non-reality), and that the picture portrays the bird slightly below the viewer.

Although it may at some stage, and for some purposes, become useful and beneficial to regularly decompose images in this way, for our current more restricted goal of determining a baseline segmentation for multimodal documents, we will follow the line suggested above and only recognise any such putative parts *if they are picked up cross-modally*—e.g., if they are also mentioned in an accompanying text or in explicit labels in the document and so on. For the Gannet page we have the cross-modal resonances given by the conceptual visual of the drawing, classifying the bird and depicting attributes of its plumage and its location just as does the text ("the coast and sea" and "rocky isles and stacks"). This gives us a systematic and operationalisable way of deciding whether a part or part-quality is to be included in the first round of segmentation or not.

For the analysis of pages that we are pursuing in this chapter, however, it is the resources that Kress and van Leeuwen develop for the *textual metafunction* (Halliday and Matthiessen 2004, Chapters 3 and 9) that are the most significant. The meaning-making resources here drive principles of organisation that are intended to be relevant whenever analysing pages for their *composition* and so present tools for analysing the combination of material within a single semiotic product—such as a page. Kress and van Leeuwen propose three main areas of meaning-making potential within the textual metafunction: information value, salience and framing.

Both salience and framing are seen as scales running from high to low. High salience indicates that an element draws attention to itself in some way, usually by deploying one or more of the perceptual features that we will discuss more closely in Section 2.3 below. A high degree of framing corresponds to maximal *disconnection* between an element described and the other visual elements in the visual artefact; a low degree of framing corresponds to maximal *connection* between the element described and its surrounding elements. Standard framing devices include lines separating regions on a page, empty space, discontinuous areas of colour, particular recognisable shapes that create boundaries, and so on. In our Gannet example, it is primarily whitespace and the differing texture of the text and the drawing that provides (generally rather weak) frames.

The question of precisely what 'entity' is carrying these meaning-making alternatives—a composition, a part of a composition, a visually-recognisable element, etc.—is quite important for securing a robust analysis. Kress and van Leeuwen's description suggests that the categories of salience and framing may apply to entire compositions and to individual elements in a composition; for example, a single element may be strongly disconnected from its surrounding elements or, alternatively, we could talk of an entire composition as being strongly framed because all of its elements are disconnected from their neighbours. With salience it is not quite so clear what its application to the composition as a whole would mean, although its application for individual elements appears natural enough.

The remaining area of meaning potential, information value, is considerably more complex and, despite broad acceptance among those working in this particular multimodal tradition, is also more problematic. The possibilities for a composition to attribute information value are first classified into two alternatives: *centred compositions* and *polarized compositions*. Centred compositions are proposed to be recognisable by virtue of some distinguished element appearing in the centre; conversely, polarized compositions are recognisable by virtue of no element appearing in the centre (Kress and van Leeuwen 1996, p224). Applying this classification reliably also requires issues of salience to be considered: a centred composition is likely to exhibit an overall perceptual balance for example (cf. Arnheim 1982).

Kress and van Leeuwen distinguish two cases of centering: *circular*, where non-central elements are distributed spatially around the centre, and *triptych*, where non-central elements lie predominantly on a vertical or horizontal axis passing through the centre. Both of these are further classified according to whether the involved composition is a *margin composition* or a *mediator composition*. In a margin composition, the non-central elements are similar so that an impression of symmetry is created; in a mediator composition, the central element is intended to provide a bridge or, in some sense, to 'mediate' between dissimilar non-central elements.

The role of the mediator composition in the account as a whole is somewhat uncertain in Kress and van Leeuwen's description because it shows relations both with centred compositions and with the polarized compositions that we discuss next. The defining difference appears to lie in the symmetry and similarity of the non-central elements. When non-central elements are not identical or 'near-identical', as Kress and van Leeuwen write, then they can be mediated between in both polarized and centred compositions.

The main subclassifications of polarized compositions involve two simultaneous possibilities. The first, taken directly from linguistic accounts of the textual metafunction, Kress and van Leeuwen denote by *given-new*; the second, they call *ideal-real*. Both distinctions impose a differential interpretation on non-central elements, regardless of whether or not a central element is also in the composition. The given-real distinction applies to the horizontal axis; the ideal-real distinction to the vertical axis. Kress and van Leeuwen claim that at least one of these distinctions *has to* apply (Kress and van Leeuwen 1996, p224). The terms 'given', 'new', 'ideal', 'real' therefore label particular spatial regions of a visual artefact that can be identified under certain compositional conditions.

Putting all of the combinations together results in the kind of 'visual grammar' required, analogously to that commonly developed for linguistic units. Just as a grammar of the possible combinations determines which particular configurations of structural elements may combine in, for example, a clause, Kress and van Leeuwen's description defines possible decompositions of a visual artefact. The combined definitions in fact define just 8 possible composition 'structures'—9 if we add the distinction of vertical *vs.* horizontal centre-margin triptychs, which is entailed but not explicitly enumerated in Kress and van Leeuwen's grammar. These structures are set out in Figure 2.3.

Which of the possible compositional layouts should apply to a specific page is determined by the constraints that distinguish margins from other elements i.e., margins should be 'similar'. Non-similar elements are then not margins and must be labelled either with 'given'/'new', if they lie along the horizontal axis, or with 'ideal'/'real', if they lie along the vertical axis. Summarising, we can describe the possibilities in terms of (i) the presence or absence or a polarization along the vertical or horizontal axis or both, (ii) the presence or absence of a central element, and (iii) the similarity or difference of the non-central elements, giving rise to a center-margin composition if they are similar and given/new, ideal/real otherwise.

As mentioned above, this approach has been very influential and there are many analyses being produced using it. There are, however, two significant sources of difficulties. Kress and van Leeuwen are concerned to establish a link between compositional choices and ideological import; in Kress and van Leeuwen (1998), for example, they interpret newspaper front pages in terms of the items that are placed in the 'ideal' position and those that are placed in the 'given' position of the front page directly in terms of statements about ideological values thereby attributed to the material so presented. This is a natural continuation of the approach found within social semiotic views of language in general: first, it is assumed that there is a fundamental connection between the forms of language (and when generalised multimodally, to all semiosis) and the contexts of use of those forms; second, since contexts of use are structured ideologically according to their cultures and subcultures of use, we have a link between, on the one hand, the forms that are used and their patterning and, on the other hand, ideological configurations.

This line of research is taken the furthest in *Critical Discourse Analysis* (CDA: Fowler, Hodge, Kress and Trew 1979) and it is against the background of their long-standing involvement with this tradition that Kress and van Leeuwen's (1996) connection of compositional zones with ideological significance should be seen. Within CDA and related approaches, there are now many results throwing considerable light on the mechanisms of ideology construction and maintenance via the use of language (cf. Fairclough 1989, van Leeuwen 1993, Martin 2000, Martin and Wodak 2003,

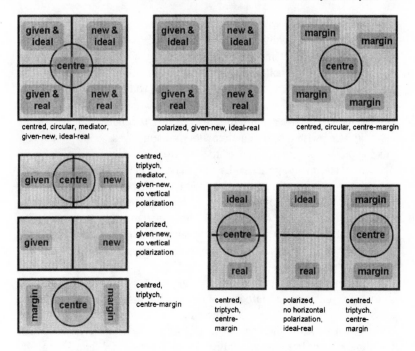

Figure 2.3   *Possible layout compositions according to the information value portion of Kress and van Leeuwen's 'visual grammar' (Kress and van Leeuwen 1996, pp223–224)*

Bloor and Bloor 2007). And, as with other areas, this is now being taken in the direction of multimodal analyses, bringing in considerations of the ideological import revealed by detailed analysis of the use of multimodal resources as expressions and enactments of ideology (e.g., van Leeuwen and Kress 1995, Müller 1997, Knieper and Müller 2001, Lassen, Strunck and Vestergaard 2006).

The connection between compositional zones and ideological import drawn by Kress and van Leeuwen is, however, unusually direct. It is unlikely that such an unmediated link between a spatial region and regular ideological interpretation can be constructed—and, indeed, if we apply Kress and van Leeuwen's categories directly to the layouts used as illustrations in this book, it is often difficult to locate generic meanings where attributions such as 'ideal' or 'real' provide significant insight. This notwithstanding, the assumption that these categories can be transparently applied is already widespread.

We regard this as particularly problematic for our current purposes in that Kress and van Leeuwen's characterisation has not received the same kind of empirical evaluation that would normally be expected of a linguistic account. Analyses built using it remain overwhelmingly 'discursive' and are equally difficult to verify or to disprove. Consider, for example, Kress et al.'s (2000, pp42–59) otherwise very illuminating and valuable discussion of the use of diverse semiotic modes in a secondary school science lesson dealing with the human circulatory system. Kress *et al.* paint a convincing picture of how pupils need to deal with a complex multimodal semiotic discourse involving the verbal discourse of the teacher, the teacher's actions and gestures, diagrams drawn on the whiteboard, pictures and verbal explanations in textbooks, and even a plastic anatomical model like a partial skeleton used by the teacher to show anatomical relationships. The multimodal competence presupposed by such situations is considerable and justifies far closer attention being paid to the development of the necessary skills.

As part of the analysis, however, we are informed of a particular utilisation of visual semiotic information in which a diagram is drawn for the class on a whiteboard in order to show the circulation of blood around the body and the role of the heart in this process. After some development, this diagram reaches a state similar to that depicted in Figure 2.4(a). In order to characterise this diagram and its contribution to the unfolding discourse, Kress et al. (2000, p52) first decompose the drawing into parts and then assign these parts functions according to the framework of Kress and van Leeuwen. Neither step is sufficiently problematised. The 'top' of the diagram is taken to include the heart and lungs, while the 'bottom' of the diagram includes the organs of the body. This is then further assumed to be polarized both horizontally and vertically giving rise to the layout composition shown in the upper-left of Figure 2.3's possibilities.

Just why this layout should apply rather than any other is unclear; one might have supposed that because the discourse is about the heart, the heart should occupy the central part of the diagram (rather than an 'upper' part of the diagram), but apparently this is not so. The heart is accordingly assigned to the space of the 'ideal'; the organs that 'use' the blood are assigned to the 'real'. The diagram is therefore set up as realising abstract semiotic categories in terms of ideologically loaded visual composition rather than, for example, 'iconically' recreating the spatial alignments found in the body.

Although the evidence for this interpretation coming from the diagram itself is somewhat thin, one might draw on the fact that the body does contain organs that use the circulating blood and which are nevertheless situated above the heart. No such possibility is suggested by the diagram and so

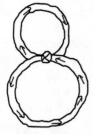

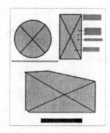

(a) Redrawing of the diagram of blood circulation discussed by Kress et al. (2000, p47)

(b) Layout composition of a page in a biology textbook discussed by Baldry and Thibault (2006, p82)

Figure 2.4   *Examples of a diagram and a page layout that have received ideological interpretations according to Kress and van Leeuwen's framework*

a schematization (cf. Herskovits 1998) has been enforced that could be argued to be more in line with a semiotic reconstruction than iconic verisimilitude. Whether or not we find further evidence in this direction, the sense in which the heart and lungs are "presented as the idealized or generalized essence of the information" (Kress and van Leeuwen 1996, p193 or Kress and van Leeuwen 1998, p193) remains questionable.

A more explicit ideological reading of the same kind is given in an analysis by Baldry and Thibault (2006, pp71-90), drawing extensively on Thibault (2001), of some biology textbook pages from the late 1950s. Our discussion here relates to the page layout shown in schematic form in Figure 2.4(b). This page contains upper left a circular drawing (as if viewed through a microscope) of some frog blood cells and upper right a rectangular and labelled view of some human blood cells. The lower part of the page is taken up with a large view of the capillaries in a frog's foot. Baldry and Thibault inform us that:

> "amphibia are positioned as being lower on a 'perfection' scale ... and this would motivate their positioning in the overall visual space with respect to the more highly-valued human case."   (Baldry and Thibault 2006, p82)

The image for the amphibian blood is then again described in terms of an interpretation of its position according to Kress and van Leeuwen, i.e., "ideal/given, salience: median, importance: high"; similarly the image for the human blood, i.e., "ideal/new, salience: high, importance: high". Here both horizontal and vertical assignments are far from self-evident. For the assignment of amphibian's blood to *given* and human to *new*, we need apparently to see 'new' as corresponding to 'highly-valued' on some scale of perfection; similarly, the capillaries in the frog's foot shown in the lower portion of the page is somehow to be seen as *real* in contrast to the blood cells (both human and frog) shown in the upper portion of the page.

But there are many stories which could be told here: the frog's foot is at the bottom because feet generally are at the bottom, or the frog's foot is at the bottom because the picture is much larger and so would look unbalanced if presented at the top, or the human blood is shown on the right because the labels of the diagram (called callouts) are on the right and it would lead to confusion to have these in the middle of the page midway between the picture of the frog's blood and the human blood, or the human blood is on the right because developments happen in time and cultures that read left-to-right commonly put time running left-to-right (note: this is *not* the same as a reading in terms of given-new), and so on. How do we distinguish a post hoc rationalisation from an analysis?

It may be the case that there is a common design principle at work, one in which the form and parts of an entity are allocated to the ideal, higher-position on a page and the function and use of that entity (e.g., here, blood transportation and circulation) is allocated to the real, lower position on the page. Then we could explore if this allocation recurs over some sizable proportion of documents of particular genres and cultures. This kind of empirical analysis is rarely presented, however, and so it is not yet possible to say what, if any, role is being played by these placements within the page.[5]

When we apply Kress and van Leeuwen's scheme to our example Gannet page, we find several of the problems that we have just highlighted. There is a general problem concerning precisely which of the 9 possible composition layouts applies to the page and, even if we make an assignment, there remains considerable uncertainty about just what is what. First, however, we can note that there does not appear to be any horizontal polarization involved on the page and so we can ignore this possibility. Then, if we take the position that there does not appear to be an obvious centre, we are required to consider vertical polarization; but what is the top?

First, it may be plausible to treat the drawing of the Gannet as the top—which would mean that this is the 'ideal' and the text is the 'real'. This would align well with one of the motivations for using a drawing here: draw-

---

[5]Interestingly, Baldry and Thibault (2006, p189) go on to reject the given-new scheme as defined by Kress and van Leeuwen themselves when they discuss the moving image; from our current perspective, several of the critiques they bring at that point are already relevant for static multimodal documents also. And, in a similar vein, Knox (2007) rejects the ideal-real distinction when applied to the vertical dimension of web-pages. Taken together considerations such as these argue for making functional interpretation far more sensitive to genre than has typically been the case—we take this up in Chapter 5 below.

ings are actually still the preferred visual representational form in books for the serious bird expert and are intended precisely to provide the "idealized or generalized essence of the information". For this we need to know, however, that the 'title' information that appears even more to the top than the drawing is, for some reason, not to be taken as the ideal.

Alternatively, we might consider that we do have a centred composition after all, with the large body of text in the middle of the page taking up this role. Then we have a triptych with the picture taking up the 'ideal' as before, the list of points at the bottom taking up the 'real', and the text functioning as a bridge between them; as we shall see below in Chapter 3, particularly Section 3.2 and Figure 3.3, evidence for this triptych reading can in fact be gained from the typographical decisions made in the page. Alternatively again, given the extreme salience of the drawing—easily the most salient element of the page—this may be considered the central element, and all the text below is the 'real' and the Latin name of bird and family at the top is then the 'ideal'. Here the drawing mediates between the ideal scientific categorization and the detailed description of how instances of this category carry out their lives.

One can consider each of these analyses useful in that they invite particular stories to be told about the functioning of the elements on the page; each of them could be bolstered with argument and used for detailed interpretations of the different status of the elements combined by the page composition. But for our present purposes we must regard this as a problem rather than a solution: first, we have no basis for deciding between the suggested analyses and, second, it is far from clear that the attribution of idealness or reality does any work for explaining the particular design of the page at issue—particularly as this page, as with many such pages from the 1970s and before, is an example of what we will term below a *text-flow* dominated set of pages: that is, the text and its supporting typography is dominant. Dominant here means not that it is more prominent or ideologically significant, but that it is the semiotic resources of textual typography—paragraphs, bulletted lists, headings, etc.—that determine how the document's content is distributed on the page not spatial-visual considerations.

The main point to be taken away from these examples is that we need to exercise considerable caution when developing our analytic tools. Although the allocation of ideologically-charged characterisations (such as 'ideal'/'real') can be used to make suggestive interpretations of artefacts, it can equally lead to statements whose validity is difficult or impossible to assess. In positive cases, interpretation will generally require gathering evidence from all available sources, from the language deployed, the patterns of connection created across text and image, and from the context and genre of the artefacts analysed (cf. Martin and Rose 2003, pp255–262 for a good example of this). In less positive cases, we find direct statements of the form: 'image X is in top-left position and so is given and ideal' followed by ideological interpretations of what is ideal, what is the norm, and so on. Typically such statements are made when the interpretation sounds plausible for the particular case at hand and omitted without comment when not.

Linguistically-based discursive interpretations of multimodal documents of this kind also tend to manifest a further unfortunate property. Although, on the one hand, they suggest ways in which documents are highly orchestrated pieces of multimodal meaning-making with rich and diverse relationships between elements, on the other hand, they are less able to show where such documents might not be effective, or may even mislead. The detailed analysis offered by Baldry and Thibault (2006, pp71–90) of their biology textbook, for example, suggests an illuminating picture of how 'waves of thematic periodicity' help construct the text by growing a rich web of interconnections back and forth across modalities. But the pages discussed are actually minor multimodal disaster zones, with conflicting and haphazard deployment of visual-rhetorical resources resulting (arguably) from unresolved tensions between the content structures to be expressed and the visual-typographic means available for expressing them. These rather important properties of the pages analysed (particularly for the genre of textbooks) go unremarked and so, presumably, unnoticed.

Analyses of this kind therefore provide detailed running commentaries on the grammatical, visual, graphical and spatial resources that are employed across the contributing modes, bringing out patterns of resonance and similarity across these, but still fail to get substantially beneath the surface. As *heuristics* for exploring the organisation of pages, frameworks such as Kress and van Leeuwen's and Baldry and Thibault's have certainly been valuable: they raise questions of detail and of connections across modes, situations and practices that are essential for framing our multimodal analyses. But we also need to characterise the starting points for analysis—the 'parts' of the pages that we analyse—with considerably more precision. In many analyses being produced currently, whatever meaning the multimodal object under investigation might be making can no longer be heard: it is 'known' that it is adopting a given-new/ideal-real organisation (unless it obviously is not) and the subsequent analysis proceeds on this basis. But if we have already assumed that we know the function or intention of a document and its parts, how can we explore whether that function is 'actually' communicated by the artefact itself? Establishing a more reliable foundation for analysis is therefore crucial.

There is very much more to investigate here because most of the concrete analytic procedures suggested by Kress and van Leeuwen and others clearly *do* have a basis in objectively analysable properties of the artefacts they analyse. The sight vectors that decompose the ideational meanings made in an image can be shown to provide relevant clues that readers/viewers use in their readings of that image. The vectors created by visual weight and shape configurations in an image—as we will see more of below—are also known to contribute directly to how an image is perceived.

There are also psychological studies that demonstrate the reliable and recurrent influence of where information is placed along the vertical and horizontal dimensions. Meier and Robinson (2004), for example, show that a word like 'happy' when presented to experimental participants on a computer screen is reliably recognised faster if placed in the upper part of the screen than when placed in the lower and, conversely, a word like 'sad' is recognised faster when placed in the lower part of the screen than it is in the upper. Similar results have recently been obtained with appropriate *facial images* rather than words (Coventry, Lynott, O'Ceallaigh and Miller 2008). There are also results across cultures that indicate that 'higher' on the page correlates with increasing quantities (Tversky, Kugelmass and Winter 1991), whereas things which are lighter will also be naturally higher than things which are heavier. Results are found for the horizontal axis also. For example, experiments have shown that participants that read left-to-right respond to large numbers faster when those numbers are placed on the right than when they are placed on the left; smaller numbers are responded to faster on the left than on the right (Dehaene, Bossini and Giraux 1993).

Such results are seen as exhibiting the SNARC effect (spatial-numerical association of response code). There is much debate as to both the cause of this effect and the categories for which it holds. In general, it is presumed to be a consequence of the Simon effect, where a response to a stimulus is faster if that stimulus 'corresponds' in some way to the spatial position of the stimulus regardless of whether there is any meaningful connection between stimulus and position (Simon, Acosta Jr., Mewaldt and Speidel 1976). In the case of the numbers, we have a congruence in reading direction and counting order or magnitude. The precise relationships are still unclear however and research continues (cf. Ito and Hatta 2004).

Certain other 'increases', in particular the direction of time, are known to be preferentially shown left-to-right rather than right-to-left. Tversky et al. (1991) report very suggestive findings of this nature even for children who come from cultures with right-to-left reading systems but who themselves are too young to read. What this might mean for culturally-specific inter-pretations of the visual semiotic is currently difficult to say.

The issue is therefore not whether such properties of images exist: they clearly do. The issue is far more one of what they *mean*. The reaction time experiments strongly suggest that a process is operating by which di-mensions in harmony are perceived faster than dimensions that compete or conflict. This holds for both the vertical and the horizontal dimension. The further step of relating horizontality to 'given-new' and verticality to 'ideal-real' is a considerable leap. We may be able to find effects that match up particular dimensions with the spatial dimensions available on a page: such as increasing value, visual weight, size with left-right, or 'happier', 'lighter' *vs.* 'sadder', 'heavier' with top-bottom. In both cases there are links to be made with embodied perception. To what extent, 'happier', 'lighter' can subsequently be reliably aligned with 'ideal' is an open question—doubly so in that the meaning intended for 'ideal' is itself very flexible.

It may be more appropriate here, therefore, to consider the distinctions proposed by Kress and van Leeuwen far more strictly in the manner that grammatical categories are interpreted. This is the source of the analogy they rely on when adopting 'given-new' and so may actually be more ap-propriate than the ideological interpretation. In that case, then, given/new, ideal/real, etc. become technical labels that do not in themselves bring a concrete, readily verbalised meaning to the interpretation. Stating that an area of an image or a page is allocated to the 'ideal' portion of the spatial array is then doing no more than to draw a contrast between the portion of the image that is *not* ideal, i.e., 'real', and noting that this distinc-tion is available for carrying meanings. This uses them analogously to a non-ideologically interpreted grammatical label (such as Subject or Direct Object)—i.e., just as a name for the position within the image. The *func-tional interpretation* of these areas in particular contexts of use remains to be done and it is here that a more empirically grounded analysis of a broader range of multimodal documents is essential.

For this, we need to expand Kress and van Leeuwen's proposed crite-ria for recognising spatial configurations so that a polarisation into distinct spatial zones can be reliably ascertained, and independently characterise the use that is made of these zones on the page. Then, rather than assuming directly that we have a link to some ideological notion of the ideal, we will be able to see how designers of such artefacts are drawing on the spatial resource in distinct genres and for distinct purposes. We may also then be able to investigate more effectively the role that positioning on the page serves: does it lead to particular interpretations rather than others? Until this is probed experimentally with systematically varying compositions, we will not be in a position to say much more.

Baldry and Thibault's 'transcription approach'

Another prominent approach to multimodal artefacts, including multimodal documents, is that of Baldry and Thibault (2006). This overlaps to a certain extent with the approach of Kress and van Leeuwen, adding several touches of its own within a broadly Hallidayan metafunctional division of the artefacts analysed. Baldry and Thibault have also been more concerned with time-based multimodal artefacts, although they do not draw any particular distinction in their methodology when looking at film or video and when looking at page-based artefacts and so this focus will play less of a role here.

Analysis for Baldry and Thibault centres on providing a multimodal *transcription* of the artefacts analysed. This is very similar to the basic position for empirically based work that we set out in Section 1.2.1 of the introduction and to which we return in more detail in Chapter 6 below. Transcription entails providing more or less sophisticated 'labelling', or description, of each element found in a multimodal artefact. These descriptions are pitched at several levels of abstraction—for example, from the perspective of each metafunction—and, when combined, are intended to show how the various modal contributions to a multimodal artefact work together to create the perceived meaning of the artefact as a whole. Clearly, the more that the descriptions selected reveal about the working of the artefact, the more useful or appropriate they are judged to be.

For the concrete task of identifying the elements of multimodal artefacts that are to receive transcriptions—page compositions included—Baldry and Thibault propose a notion of 'cluster' that is very similar to Schriver's (1997, p343) rhetorical cluster defined above.

> "Our use of the term *cluster* refers to a local grouping of items, in particular, on a printed or web-page (but also other texts such as manuscripts, paintings and films). The items in a particular cluster may be visual, verbal and so on and are spatially proximate thereby defining a specific region or subregion of the page as a whole. The items in a cluster are functionally related both to each other and to the whole to which they belong as parts."
>
> (Baldry and Thibault 2006, p31)

Just as with Schriver's clusters, Baldry and Thibault's identified units are often intended to capture re-usable fragments for fulfilling particular discourse purposes: so-called *mini-genres* (Baldry and Thibault 2006, p42, p113). In both Schriver's and Baldry and Thibault's cases, therefore, we see a nexus of presentational and functional issues: a cluster is spatially localized and at the same time that localization serves a function for the intended reading of the text/page/document.

As we have already seen something of above, Baldry and Thibault apply a rich array of tools and constructs from systemic-functional linguistics to construct analyses for the artefacts that they study. Clusters, for example, are grouped together to form *phases*, as defined by Gregory (2001), collections of units that exhibit homogeneity of features—linguistic, graphical, spatial, etc.—and it is these phases that serve to communicate the intended meaning (Baldry and Thibault 2006, p47). The features themselves are taken from all the modes at hand and are seen as collectively providing the semiotic resources by means of which meaning is made: this Baldry and Thibault term the *resource integration principle* (Baldry and Thibault 2006, pp18/9).

The ability to combine various semiotic resources is seen as one of the compelling functional reasons for the existence of multimodal artefacts at all. Meanings made concisely in one mode can be exported and re-used to enhance meanings made in other modes. This is similar to the concept of 'multiplying meanings' proposed by Lemke (1998) mentioned in the introduction and to O'Halloran's (1999*a*) notion of *intersemiotic metaphor*. All of these theoretical constructs suggest that configurations of meanings made with one mode can beneficially contribute to meanings made in other modes—not by simple addition of 'more' meanings of the same kind, but by bringing together meanings that are essentially *different* in nature.

On precisely the aspect of finding and identifying those page elements that contribute to an analysis, however, Baldry and Thibault provide surprisingly little detail. Clusters are assumed to be recognisable but the appeal to visual properties remains informal and discursive. There is even talk at one point of 'derived clusters', which appear to be constructed by assuming the reader to read a page in a particular order, putting elements together in a way that reveals the function of the page (Baldry and Thibault 2006, p28). This takes the conflation of presentation and the function of presentation that we identified as a problem above for Schriver's account of clusters even further. If we are to analyse whether a document is effectively orchestrating its diverse modal presentations, we cannot assume too quickly that a particular function is served even by spatially 'connected' or proximal collections of elements—let alone elements that are not so connected. We need crucially to break into the interpretation circle in order only to posit clusters when they are potentially really 'there' in some fairly strictly defined sense. That is, we must adapt both Schriver's and Baldry

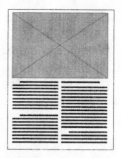

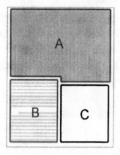

(a) Layout of a page from a 1972 textbook on Canada

(b) Functionally motivated clusters
for the page

*Figure 2.5   A page layout and its functionally-motivated layout clusters (Taken from
R. Howard et al. A new history of Canada. 2: Fishermen and fur traders.
Éditions format, Montreal, p128.)*

and Thibault's definitions to pick apart the presentational claims and the
functional claims.

We have already seen some of the problems arising for our Gannet example from this perspective when we illustrated Schriver's use of rhetorical
clusters above, so here we take another example from the same year of publication: 1972. Consider the layout shown in Figure 2.5. The left-hand part
of the figure shows the original page composition. The filled box in the
upper half of the page is a colour drawing; the rest of the page is filled with
lines of justified text. Where are the clusters here?

The 'correct', i.e., the functionally intended, clustering is as shown to
the right of the figure. There is little to support this visually, however. We
might argue that the knowledge that a caption for a figure is being given
(after reading the text) is then sufficient to posit a *derived* cluster serving
the particular mini-genre of picture-plus-caption, but when we conflate the
visual evidence and the functional evidence in this way, we hide part of that
very processing that must go into our decision. For the book series from
which this example is taken the captions of drawings and maps are identified solely by their position in the first line of text following or preceding
the graphic, the presence of a number and the selection of an italic font.
This realisation is carried out perfectly consistently throughout the book
and so can be learnt: but our point here is that its recognition is *not* strongly
supported by the layout decisions made.

There is then here an analogous lack of clues to that observed for the gas
bill we discussed in the introduction (cf. Figure 1.2). In Kress and van
Leeuwen's terms we could say that there is a very weak connection (loose

framing) between the drawings and their captions, which leads to misreading because the caption is too easily grouped with the paragraphs of running text. Moving directly to discuss clusters is then assuming that we have already done the work of recognising the functionally relevant groupings on the page. But in general this task can present considerable difficulties. We can apply semiotic integration, or multiplication, to derive the correct meanings, but we also need to have recorded in our analysis somewhere that this step was complicated by deficits elsewhere.

Baldry and Thibault themselves write of the need to consider 'scales' of clusters, where smaller clusters are grouped inside larger clusters, and where larger clusters provide 'integrating contexts' for the smaller ones. As a consequence:

> "Smaller-scale units are *not* simply smaller parts or building blocks in larger wholes. Leakage across levels is part of the way in which a hierarchy of meaningful units and relations functions in discourse."
>
> (Baldry and Thibault 2006, p144)

We can operationalise this for our present purposes as follows.

Clearly, in the Canada book layout shown, we should only consider as clusters the blocks shown to the right of the figure. But we cannot simply put this together out of the parts that are available to us perceptually as the clues of spatial proximity and framing are too weak. It is then, as explicitly suggested by Schriver above and now by Baldry and Thibault, the participation of elements in a rhetorical strategy that motivates their inclusion within a single 'cluster' and not merely the perceptual cues. Indeed, if we could not recognise a rhetorical strategy for linking them (an 'integrating context') in the present case, then we would have few grounds for including them within a single cluster. The cluster at issue here is then to be more properly understood as expressing or carrying the particular *rhetorical strategy* (cf. Chapter 4) of combining a figure with a caption that is very common in particular *genres* (cf. Chapter 5).

Although this provides a path forward where more appropriate analyses can be proposed, the achieved combination does not alter the fact that there is an important difference to be drawn between the functional interpretation and the physical support that a document provides for functional interpretation. Only then are we able to draw attention to situations where, on the one hand, there is a functional intent that certain identified layout elements function as captions and, on the other, those elements fail to be grouped in terms of their layout configuration with the layout elements to which they 'belong'. A simple allocation of visual clusters on a combined visual-functional basis is not sufficient for this as potential mismatches are already resolved in the analysis; we again need a more differentiating account.

2.3 The page as object of perception

In this section, we move away from the informed understanding of what a document is trying to communicate that we commonly see in interpretative approaches to multimodal documents and try to intervene in this process at an earlier stage. In order to be an artefact that can provide information at all, a page must *first be perceived* by its readers: that is, readers must interact with the page as an object of perception in their visual field. Whereas the approaches of the previous section took the perceived page for granted, here we are concerned with just how that process works—how do we get to the state of 'having seen' a page?

This question makes the entire field of visual perception relevant to issues of design and page interpretation. From this perspective, we focus on precisely how readers obtain 'information' from the page through their perceptual systems. Many cognitive models have been proposed which are intended to reproduce the kind of processing, and processing decisions, that are observable in humans when decomposing a page into its component parts. We can see this analogously to auditory phonetics, in which subjects can be asked whether they perceive two sounds as distinct or not, or two words pronounced differently, as different or not. For the page, we can consider whether particular elements are seen to be similar, whether they are grouped together, whether they are perceived as salient (e.g., seen 'first') or not, and so on. The principles of perception are accordingly well known in professional design. If elements are to be made prominent, then this can only be done within the bounds of the human visual system; similarly, if elements are intended to be grouped together then their human readers have to be able to perceive this. Visual perception and design go hand in hand.

A further rich source of data about the perception of documents is inherited from psycholinguistic studies of reading comprehension. This has led to detailed and, by now, established design recommendations involving preferred line-lengths, sizes of fonts, contrast of fonts and background, and much more. Comprehension studies have also made it clear that it is beneficial for design to strive for both content and organisation compatibility between information in memory and the information presented in a document (cf. Wright 1980, p186). There are also processing differences to be observed depending on the *delivery channel* of the document: for example, whether a document is presented on paper or on a computer screen makes substantial differences for effective design (e.g. Dyson 2004). All of

these contributing factors need to be considered when predicting how readers will interact with multimodal documents. However, in this section, we
focus on just one particular aspect of cognitive processing—that of visual
perception—since this is central for our goal of decomposing documents
into their parts.

Gestalt perception

A good example of the relevance of perception for design is Schriver's
(1997, p314) analysis of a layout spread (i.e., two pages functioning as
a single visual unit) for a multilingual instruction text for a stereo. The examples relevant to the discussion are shown in schematic form in Figure 2.6
where we can see two versions of a possible layout. In the version on the
right, a perceptual principle known as *good continuation* has been violated
in order to show how this has a significant effect on the manner in which
a page as a whole is perceived. Good continuation in a page layout causes
the visual system to perceive spatially distinct elements as being connected,
or even as being the *same* element occluded by something else that has got
in the way.

We see this in Figure 2.6 as follows. The example page as a whole consists of one large graphic of the stereo running across the centre of the
page; this graphic does not include any language-specific information and
simply illustrates the stereo and the locations of actions to be performed on
it. The four vertical blocks on the page then provide the detailed textual instructions related to the stereo in each language covered. The designer has
intended each column to be grouped as a single continuous sequence of instructions running from the top of the page to the bottom. The instructions
within each column then refer to the stereo shown in the central graphic
by means of numbers labelling the components shown: this has become
a common genre for multilingual instructions since the design and layout
can remained 'fixed' and different language versions can be slotted in as
required.

This intended grouping is favoured far more by the layout on the left,
in which alignment of the text blocks' left edges provides 'good continuation', than on the right, where there is no alignment. The lack of continuation means that perceptually there is a much reduced tendency to group
the components together. In the latter case, a reader would have to look for
further clues that the lower half rectangles are connected with their corresponding upper half rectangles, perhaps by virtue of continued enumerated
lists or by the choice of language. This reiterates the important point that
we have now seen at several places in the discussion: as with both the

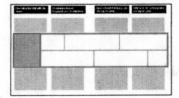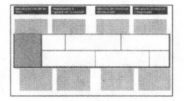

Figure 2.6   Good continuation (left) and bad continuation (right); an example adapted from Schriver (1997)

Canada history book page that we saw above in Figure 2.5 and the gas bill of the introduction, although a reader *may work out* that the lower halves continue their upper halves, there is little in the layout itself supporting this perceptually.

Principles of perception therefore play a significant role for layout and layout decomposition. When some larger scale element, such as a text column, is temporarily interrupted by some other element, such as an embedded headline or a picture, appropriate continuation can nevertheless communicate directly that there is a single document 'part' at issue. Readers generally take this in their stride and are more likely to attribute the interruption to information *layering* in space: that is, one element can stand 'in front of' another. This property cannot be predicted without knowledge of the human perceptual system: it is not simply a deduction about how a reader might 'work out' how the page is to be seen.[6]

The area of perceptual psychology that has contributed most to our understanding of these aspects of visual perception and their relevance for design is Gestalt Psychology (Koffka 1935, Köhler 1947). The Gestalt school psychologists developed several 'laws' of pattern perception which appear to be implemented by the human visual system. Demonstrations that the laws hold are found in enumerable and completely reliable examples of visual perception or misperception and underlie most well-known 'visual illusions'. The seven essential Gestalt laws are shown in Table 2.1.

In most cases, these laws combine during perception to strongly direct interpretation in one direction rather than another. The case of 'good continuity' above with the stereo instructions brings together at least continuity, similarity, and closure; the Canada book page in turn combines at least proximity and closure. More information and many visual examples demonstrat-

---

[6]In this respect, claims such as those of Ittelson (1996) that processing markings on surfaces is completely different to processing real-world scenes are probably overstated: there are clearly differences, but overlaps also.

ing the effectiveness of these laws are given by, for example, Ware (2000, pp203–213).[7]

Pre-attentive perception

There are also additional features of perception that can play a significant role during layout perception. Certain objects are well known to attract attention either due to their intrinsic form (such as human faces) or due to perceptual properties (such as a distinctive bright colour). All of these can be used in layout and document design in order to direct perception and decomposition. For understanding this aspect of page perception more exactly, it is useful to know about attributes of the visual field which are *pre-attentive*: i.e., that are distinguished at very early stages of perception before higher-level processing has starting identifying and classifying what is being seen. Pre-attentive distinctions are available as *direct perceptions* and so naturally provide the strongest layout cues of all. If, for example, something is bigger than something else, or of a different colour, or is similar to a set of other objects with one small addition, then this grouping is part of how the visual field is seen and does not need to be 'interpreted' by the viewer.

Something of the force of these pre-attentive discriminations can be seen in the examples shown in Figure 2.7. Here, in all but the last two boxes (labelled 'juncture' and 'parallelism'), we see examples of pre-attentive processing at work. Look, for example, at the upper left-hand box, 'orientation'. What we directly *see* when looking at this box is a collection of vertical lines and one that is not vertical. We do not have to examine the individual lines and ask ourselves which ones are vertical and which ones are not—this information is *already part of how the image is perceived*; that is, the information that there is one line whose orientation differs from the others is directly and unavoidably present in our perception. The remaining boxes illustrate this phenomenon for other aspects of visual processing that are also available pre-attentively. Only when we come to the last two boxes do we have to actually scan the image carefully in order to discover that, in the first case, there are two lines which do not meet and, in the second case, there are two lines that are parallel.

We also have pre-attentive access to, for example, comparative line widths and lengths, co-linearity (alignment), colour and spatial position

---

[7]A nice online collection of examples of 'named' visual illusions, complete with original references, has been compiled by John Andraos (2003) available at: http://www.careerchem.com/NAMED/Optical-Illusions.pdf (last accessed January 1, 2008).

Proximity	Objects which are closer together are generally assumed to belong together.
Similarity	Entities in the visual field which are perceptually similar are assumed to be grouped together.
Continuity	Entities in the visual field will be built out of perceived parts assuming continuity and smoothness rather than sudden changes of direction. This is one way in which 'connectedness' is constructed; connectedness itself is, however, an extremely strong perceptual principle for assigning grouping.
Symmetry	Shapes which are symmetrical about an axis provide a much stronger impression of a single, contained object than when the boundaries are not symmetrical.
Closure	Whenever a recognisable contour in the visual field is closed, i.e., forms itself into a continuous loop, then this is generally seen as dividing an 'inside' from an 'outside' and the inside is perceived as an object. Without further information, it is then difficult to see the 'outside' as an object—e.g., as an object with a hole. Moreover, the perceptual system will generally *assume* continuity and closure: thus, if there is a partially obscured continuous shape, then the perceptual system will assume that the shape is closed and the unseen part of the shape is simply 'behind' some obscuring object, not that there is a gap in the shape.
Relative Size	When sharing a common area of the visual field, smaller areas are generally seen as objects placed in front of larger areas, which are seen as the background.
Figure-Ground	Somewhat similar to the last 'law', but rather more general in application, perception generally divides perceptions into elements (figures) which are picked out from some background (ground). Several visual illusions work with this principle: i.e., under unusual circumstances, just what is taken as figure and what is taken as ground can be reversed: e.g., the well known 'Rubin's Vase' illusion (Rubin 1921), where either a vase is seen against a background or two silhouettes face one another. In one case, the figure is a vase and in the other the figure is two faces.

Table 2.1   The primary Gestalt laws of perception

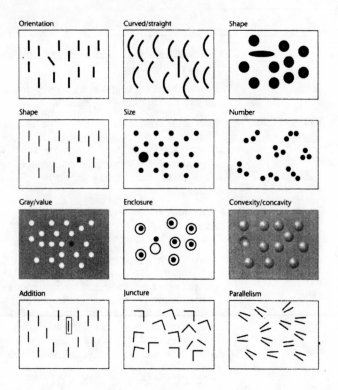

Figure 2.7   Examples of pre-attentive perception at work. Taken from Ware (2000, p166; Figure 5.5); used by permission of Elsevier

itself, as well as to several motion-dependent features of the visual field, which are not so relevant for us at present, such as direction and flicker (cf. Ware 2000, pp165/6). An important consequence of the existence of such features is that designs need to be sensitive to the fact that certain features of a layout will be 'accessed' by readers regardless of intention—whenever a layout employs pre-attentively available visual features, readers will register these (not necessarily consciously) and build them into their interpretations of relations on the page. Visual presentations that make use of pre-attentive features will directly indicate particular decompositions of layout parts rather than others. Effective design must ensure that whatever interpretations readers are led to are ones that *support* the intended interpretations of the page rather than undermining them.

Figure 2.8   Eye-tracking results from the Holsanova et al. (2006) study; used by permission of the author. The tracks show the points of fixation during the first
minute of exposure to the spread. We also see the paths between fixation
points and, indicated by the relative size of circles, the duration of the fixation. The large filled circle lower right in each image shows for reference
what the size of a one-second fixation would be.

Reading paths

Visual perception is also by no means a passive affair of simply being subjected to patterns revealed by pre-attentive processing. It is now well established that vision is a process of *active construction* on the part of the
reader. The eyes gather information necessary for constructing a visual interpretation by rapidly moving between points of fixation; moreover, those
points are themselves selected by the perceptual system *so as to gather
information* effectively for constructing hypotheses. That is, if the visual
scene is still unresolved concerning what it is showing, the eyes are directed towards points that pre-attentive processing predicts will contribute
maximally to the disambiguation of interpretations.

Nowadays we can readily observe this process of selecting points of fixation by employing *eye-tracking* technology. Devices of this kind produce
a record of precisely where readers' eyes are directed while they process a
document, noting points of fixation in sequence so that these can be analysed. This kind of research is gaining in significance because it can be
used to determine actual reading paths—i.e., the reading paths that are genuinely used by users of a document rather than what a designer may have
predicted or what users might themselves report. It also shows relations *between* elements—i.e., the paths that readers follow around a page from element to element. This gives a useful method for exploring both traditional
views of prominence in visual images and more recent semiotic predictions
of salience such as those described above by Kress and van Leeuwen.

A good example of what occurs during such an experiment is shown in Figure 2.8, taken from a study reported by Holsanova et al. (2006). This study is additionally relevant for us here because it also has the goal of empirically evaluating some of the proposals made in semiotic and linguistically-informed analyses of documents. In particular, the study examined whether evidence could be found for Kress and van Leeuwen's claims concerning reading order, prominence and framing for newspaper layouts. To do this, the principles and possibilities set out by Kress and van Leeuwen were translated into a collection of assumptions concerning reading behaviour. The actual reading behaviour of experimental participants was then investigated using eye-tracking methods.

The results obtained were mixed. For example, the classification of the right-hand side of the page to new, salient information (cf. Figure 2.3) was translated into a reading path assumption that this location in the spread would be attended to early in the reading process: this was not the case; however, an assumption that information would be sought higher on the page before examining lower positioned information was confirmed. Headlines and pictures attracted attention as expected and a certain reliance on framing could also be seen. There was no evidence that readers scanned the entire page or visual field before making decisions concerning what to read.

Reading paths are also now known to be susceptible both to the knowledge that a reader has concerning how a visual image/page is to be interpreted and to the purpose the reader has in using the image/page. Another of Holsanova *et al.*'s results was that advertisements (pre-attentively available due to colour and texture differences) were often *not* on the reading path despite theoretical 'salience': readers have evidently already learnt to ignore them—which is certainly not what advertisers will be wanting to hear. The relationship between reading behaviour, visual prominence and semiotic value is clearly complex and there is a pressing need for further investigations of this kind. When we add into the layout mixture graphics with clear 'eye-flow' qualities of their own, salient size, colour and font decisions, framing of distinct functional elements (such as, e.g., navigation bars and content areas; cf. Naumann, Waniek and Krems 2001), connecting lines and so on, it becomes very difficult to predict precisely how readers will interact with the information on offer.

More accurate description of how readers actually scan pages can contribute significantly to our accounts of interaction with multimodal pages. Discussions of reading paths in semiotic and linguistic approaches to multimodality are still too often unclear concerning the methods by which paths are ascertained (e.g., O'Halloran 1999*a*, Guo 2004). Since it is perfectly possible even for designers to guess wrong (Schriver 1997, p317), intuitive analysis is certainly inadequate. When subjected to validation by eye-tracking, many sources of traditional wisdom are currently being refined or relativised to particular types of documents, types of design and circumstances of use. For example, readers from cultures with a left-to-right writing system are generally considered to use what is in design called the *Z-pattern*, moving right from the optical centre, back to the left edge and then again right towards the lower right-hand corner. This is the pattern expected when there are no sources of distraction/attraction on the page. More recent studies of web-pages suggest, however, that web-page readers now adopt a quite different pattern; Nielsen (2006) in particular presents results where the areas readers actually see on web-pages are markedly different to those that simple evaluations of prominence or newsworthiness might suggest. Significantly, the right-hand portion of the page (which according to both traditional wisdom and Kress and van Leeuwen's page compositions should be the most significant, prominent and newsworthy part of the page) is frequently *ignored*. This is certainly not immediately consistent with an ideological reading as new and salient information.[8]

In general, we need to separate where readers are actually looking on the page from the notion of *intended* reading path: only the latter can be designed. Good design will encourage readers to adopt the intended path. Designers make regular of this to achieve successful layouts and employ a sophisticated and trained sense of how particular images and other features of a page can direct the reader's attention (for an illustrative discussion and many examples, see Dorn 1986, pp145–153). There is much more to learn here concerning just how these interactions between visual qualities and functional interpretations of layouts proceed. We also need to work with models that can accurately predict reading paths on the basis of visual input and examine how knowledge of various kinds further influences this (cf. Yarbus 1967, Itti and Koch 2001, Schill, Umkehrer, Beinich, Krieger and Zetzsche 2001, Lentz 2005). Relatively little is to be gained by proposing reading paths intuitively.

2.4 Page as signal

In this section we move a step further away from human interpretation of the pages under analysis. Although it may appear strange to talk of the page

---

[8]It does, however, suggest a particularly important role for *thematic* organisation in the sense of Martin (1992), thereby supporting Djonov's (2007) recent application of thematic organisation to websites.

as a 'signal', this view is actually precisely analogous to the treatment in linguistics of speech as an acoustic signal that can be analysed instrumentally. Just as it is possible to describe the acoustic features of a speech signal in terms of its component frequencies, energy, etc., we can do the same with the 'visual signal' that a page produces. We can then apply *signal processing techniques* to this signal just as we can to sound.

This approach is explored most actively in the research and development community concerned with *document recognition*. This very active area is, in many respects, a logical outgrowth of earlier efforts to automate the acquisition of information from printed documents available in paper form by optical character recognition (OCR). This technology, now available with most scanners, is used to process the visual input signal so as to derive from the patterns of dark and light on the page the actual characters used in a document. An obvious motivation for this development was the fact that it is much more convenient (and much less wasteful of computer memory) to represent the characters directly. When stored as internal computer codes, we can edit the scanned text with text editors, run spell checking and correction programs over it, re-format the text and so on. None of this is possible with a simple representation of the 'picture' seen.

The relevance of this for our current concerns is the subsequent interest of the document recognition community in going considerably further than simply recognising the characters on a page. Currently the goal is to produce full document recognition, including layout analysis, in order to show which bits of a document belong together and which not. That is, rather than simply returning a string of characters that might involve the text body of the page as well as headings and figure captions simply placed (if we were lucky) in the sequence they were encountered on the page, document recognition now attempts to recognise the *structure* of a page also. This means that any text recognised is appropriately allocated to elements such as figures and captions, headlines with body text, multiple columns of an article, and so on.

This direction of research is given considerable extra impetus by the obvious commercial relevance of providing automatic recognition procedures of this kind. Decomposing a page appropriately supports several tasks currently under investigation including:

- information *extraction*, whereby only parts of documents relevant for some query are retrieved by a search engine,
- automatic document reformatting, or *re-purposing*, where a document's layout is altered to fit different sizes and types of displays (consider, for example, the problems of sending a large scanned page

to someone who has to view the result on a mobile phone with a small display),

- automatic document *classification*, where depending on the kind of document that is found, that document can be routed to different groups of potential readers—this latter capability relies on the close relationship between layout and genre.

The primary goal of this research area is to provide fully automatic capture of scanned documents where the output is a structured representation of the distinct elements on the page. This is clearly very similar to our aims in this chapter and so it is worthwhile considering the progress and techniques that have been developed in this field.

Visual processing filters

Although the precise principles by which signal processing of this kind is performed will not be our concern—detailed overviews of the range of approaches taken can be found in, for example, Dori, Doermann, Shin, Haralick, Phillips, Buchman and Ross (1997) and Okun, Doermann and Pietikäinen (1999)—we can illustrate some of the mechanisms involved very simply. We begin with the approach set out in Reichenberger, Rondhuis, Kleinz and Bateman (1995), where we discussed several alternative renditions of a page in order to consider relations between intent and form. In this study we also needed to find more objective ways of determining potential carriers of functional relationships so as to avoid the problems of conflating function and visual clues discussed above.

Figure 2.9   Successive reduction of resolution in a page image (from: Reichenberger et al. 1995)

One of the primary methods that we suggested for finding such elements was to progressively reduce the *resolution* of a representation of the page as an image. This procedure removes detail from the page since, for example, instead of representing a page with a matrix of 1000×1000 dots, we reduce the resolution to 100×100 dots. Each 'dot' of the reduced image must then do the job of 100 'dots' of the unreduced image, which can be achieved in several ways, for example by taking the average of the 'brightness' of the 100 dots in the original. The idea behind such a procedure is that it makes visible larger visual groupings of elements on a page. We have seen above in our introduction to visual perception that grouping elements in close proximity has important effects on processing and is also used in computational models of perception (cf. Sarkar and Boyer 1993). Making this grouping 'visible' was then seen as a useful step towards uncovering the *visual* decomposition of pages into parts. The result of a succession of such reductions in resolution is shown in Figure 2.9. Here we can readily see that what is revealed visually is the larger layout 'blocks' of the page.

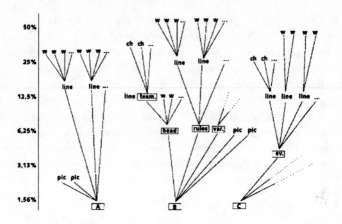

Figure 2.10   Using discriminability at different resolutions to reveal layout elements (from: Reichenberger et al. 1995)

We then suggested further that the granularity at which certain elements became indistinguishable suggested particular candidates for consideration as elements of the page. This is shown in the graph of Figure 2.10. Here the vertical axis shows the resolution (100% is full resolution) and the entries in the graph show at which scale particular elements can be distinguished from one another. Thus, at the lowest resolution, 1.56%, we can only barely distinguish the large blocks labelled A, B and C in the rightmost rendition of Figure 2.9. As the resolution increases, more details become visible, first various pictures, then blocks of texts (labelled according to their subject matter in the graph), then lines and finally individual words.

This simple mechanism therefore provides a first indication of how we can find elements of a page that are in some sense really 'there' without appeal to functional interpretations.

To make the process of document recognition more reliable, research has revealed a host of techniques that go beyond simple reductions in resolution. These have progressively included principles of visual perception so as to lead to decompositions that correspond ever more closely with those made by readers. We can easily show the principles involved here since most reasonably sophisticated image processing software nowadays already provides processing options for images that can be considered as ways of getting at *perceptually* relevant 'views' of a page. These processing options are termed 'filters' in that they operate like a filter used with a camera, changing the colour balance, the degree of sharpness, etc. of the image received. Filters also have a precise mathematical definition in that they perform a specified transformation of the information provided as input to produce a corresponding output. A simple filter might, for example, remove all the colour information or reduce the resolution of an image in the manner seen above.

More sophisticated filters can locate places where there are sudden changes in image quality, such as brightness, look for places of homogeneous visual 'texture', and much more. Figure 2.11, for example, shows what might occur with a combination of resolution reduction and 'contour' finding of this kind when applied to a newspaper page that we will use as an example at several places below. The figure shows how these different filters make particular features of the page more or less visible. That these differences are more visible to us in the diagram also means that they are more accessible to automatic recognition. If we have a generally gray area and within that a much darker, almost black area, then this can be automatically segmented as a distinct element. More generally, if we have two areas that are each relatively homogeneous along some dimensions but different from one another along others, then we have good grounds for distinguishing them as distinct page elements.

We see this in the example shown in Figure 2.11 in several respects: the upper filter view on the right (a) provides evidence for a segmentation of a central element as well as several bordering headline elements; the lower right filter view (b) also shows a clear distinction between the homogenous lines of text and the line drawing (a cartoon) in the middle of the text; and filter (c) in the middle at the bottom picks out element boundaries, including in this case the columns making up the main body of the article.

There are also useful issues to be discussed concerning just what *kind* of structure is (a) made visible by such a process and (b) most useful for

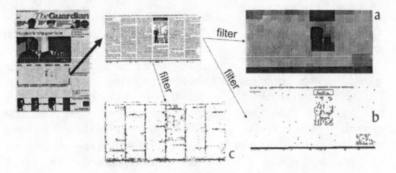

Figure 2.11   Alternative visual filters applied to an extract of a newspaper page

document recognition. Clearly one aim is to bring these together. In document recognition, the goal is to find the so-called *logical structure* of the documents processed. Logical structure corresponds approximately to the rhetorical clusters of Schriver and similar organisations of page elements discussed above. The main idea is that logical organisation captures the dependencies and connections between the *content* expressed on a page without recording details of visual layout, formatting and so on. Within document analysis, documents are accordingly considered from two perspectives, which we will also build on substantially below:

- first, documents are seen in terms of their content, captured in the logical or semantic organisation, and
- second, documents are seen in terms of their *geometrical* properties, which include positioning information of blocks and details concerning typeface and font size for text and line widths or other visual features for graphics.

Both perspectives admit of structuring: logical structure captures conceptual organisation and, according to some authors (e.g., Doermann, Rosenfeld and Rivlin 1997), intended reading order, while geometric structure includes layout.

Once we can combine visual processing filters that give us candidate elements on the page, we can proceed further to consider their inter-relationships, working from geometric structure towards hypotheses concerning their logical structure. When one element is geometrically completely contained within another, as in the central cartoon shown in the newspaper page for instance, then we have a clear indication of a structural relationship in the content also. More complex is when we have a collection of elements within some area that may need to be inter-related, such as the columns within an article as shown in the figure.

XY-trees

A common technique for automatically capturing structural relationships within collections of layout elements is provided by *XY-trees*. XY-tree construction works by successively searching for clean divisions of the page along the horizontal and vertical axes, cycling down through ever smaller portions of the page as necessary until the page is exhausted and no further decomposition is possible. On each cycle, the process translates each visually distinguishable block on the page onto either its horizontal (X-axis) or vertical (Y-axis) extent. If, after doing this, there is a 'gap' left anywhere on the axis being considered, i.e., an interval where no blocks have been mapped to, then it is possible to divide the portion of the page being considered at that point. Dividing the page is represented by growing 'nodes' in the XY-tree—each node corresponding to an area on the page that can be segmented from the others. This process then repeats, considering each of the divided sections of the block as its own unit for further decomposition.

A concrete illustration of this process in action is shown in Figure 2.12, where we consider the very simple layout for the Canada book that we used above in Figure 2.5. The initial step is always to consider the entire page as the first area to be decomposed and to look at the X-axis (i.e., horizontally); this initialisation step is recorded in the XY-tree by growing the tree's root node (labelled 1 in the figure). The X-axis runs across the page and so we consider the horizontal extent of all the elements found on the page, mapping these onto the horizontal axis (shown at the bottom of Figure 2.12(a)). Since the drawing at the top of the page and the columns in the lower half of the page together occupy all of the horizontal axis, we can find no point of separation. This means that we cannot find any segment of the X-axis that is 'unoccupied' for this page area and so cannot split the page along this axis at this time. To record this fact, the XY-tree 'grows' a single node (labelled 2 in the figure) descending from the root of the tree. The number of child nodes descending from any node in an XY-tree represents the number of parts that we can decompose a page area into at that point: here there is only one node, indicating no further decomposition.

We then continue down to this node in the tree and consider whether we can make a clean split of units on the *Y-axis*—that is, running down the page. In this case, we map the *vertical* extents of each element on the page to the corresponding axis in order to see if there are any segments of the axis left uncovered (Figure 2.12(b)). This time there is a gap to be found:

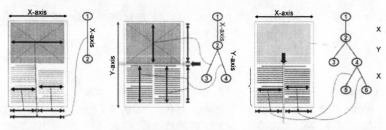

(a) X-axis cut: no un-
occupied space and so
no tree division

(b) Y-axis cut: division into top
and bottom halves

(c) second X-axis cut: division
of lower half into columns and final tree

*Figure 2.12   Consecutive construction of an XY-tree for the page layout shown in Fig-
ure 2.5 above*

the drawing in the upper half of the page and the overlapping text columns
in the lower half do not overlap and so a gap is left on the Y-axis between
them. This means that it would be possible to extend an uninterrupted line
of whitespace horizontally between these two portions of the page at the
point indicated. To represent this division into two sub-areas of the page,
we grow the XY-tree further; each division of the XY-tree means that there
is some continuous whitespace between the areas represented by the nodes
with respect to the part of the page represented by the parent node. In this
case, we have two child nodes: one corresponding to the vertical extent of
the drawing (labelled 3 in the figure) and the other corresponding to the
vertical extent of the text columns (labelled 4).

Next we consider each of these two nodes in turn and *their* possible partitions, this time cycling back to consider the X-axis. The first node, corresponding to the drawing (labelled 3), is complete: it has no further subelements and so is a 'terminal' node, or leaf, of the tree. We can derive this
information automatically whenever (a) a node in the XY-tree has only a
single child node and (b) *that* child node also has only a single child node.
When there is no branching twice in a row, this means that we have considered possible decompositions for a particular area of the page from both the
X-axis and the Y-axis; no further information can be obtained by repeating
the process and so we can consider the area as indecomposable.

Turning to the node corresponding to the two text columns (labelled 4),
we can see that this node can be split. When we map the horizontal extent
of the two columns onto the X-axis, we find an unoccupied portion of the
X-axis between them. This means that the region can be split neatly by
running an uninterrupted line of whitespace up between the columns. Note
that this was not possible on the first cycle through (Figure 2.12(a)) because

at that point we were not considering the area of the page corresponding to node 4 but rather that corresponding to node 1—i.e., the entire page, including the drawing. So we now obtain two further nodes, one for each text column (labelled 5 and 6 in Figure 2.12(c)). We could take the process further and, when considering the Y-axis again, divide each of the columns up into lines, but for present purposes the illustration is probably sufficient.[9]

This manner of representing the layout of pages works well for regular compositions and has been used in a broad variety of automatic systems. Combined with other techniques, it shows how an abstract representation of page layout can be derived relatively easily. Adding additional information concerning how large the whitespace gaps between blocks must be before they are considered, i.e., incorporating Gestalt considerations of proximity, is one way of directing the tree construction process to respect more accurately the groupings of elements on the page that would be perceived by a human reader.

The need for this can be seen clearly in the two alternative layouts shown in Figure 2.13. Because the process of XY-tree construction always begins with the X-axis, layouts (a) and (b) both receive the *same* XY-tree description as shown to the right of the figure. In both cases the simple procedure finds a 'gap' on the X-axis and so can grow the XY-tree on the first cycle, even though it is arguable that for layout (b) it is the much larger gap on the Y-axis that should be given priority perceptually. Incorporating Gestalt considerations here would allow distinct trees for (a) and (b) to be constructed. The tree shown on the right of the figure would then only hold for layout (a); the tree for (b) would need instead to group node (1) together with node (2) and node (3) together with node (4).

Further extensions concern the *kind* of information on the page that is accepted for motivating divisions: the 'Modified XY-trees' (MXY) of Cesarini, Marinai, Soda and Gori (1999), for example, trigger divisions off connecting 'lines' and similar explicit framing visuals, thereby incorporating another range of perceptually significant criteria within the general approach. Extensions implementing such additions are now available for the XY-tree technique and are used both for comparing different layouts and for automatically learning and classifying layouts typical for particular kinds of documents (e.g., Cesarini, Lastri, Marinai and Soda 2001, Mao, Nie and Thoma 2005)—a task very relevant to the discussion of multimodal genres that we take up in Chapter 5.

---

[9]If we were to continue, however, note that the caption of the figure would be the first child node of the node corresponding to the *right-hand text column* (node 6 in the rightmost tree) rather than being related to the drawing as functionally intended. This clearly illustrates, therefore, how the visual and the functional descriptions can diverge.

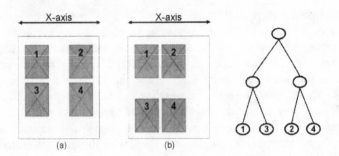

Figure 2.13   Two alternative layouts that receive the same XY-tree description

2.5   The Page as object of production

Our final point of call switches perspective entirely and looks at pages as multimodal artefacts to be *produced* rather than analysed. This is now a well-established mode of analysis in many fields of study. Attempting to 'produce' something that exhibits precisely those properties of some arte-fact being investigated usually requires a good understanding of just what the principles underlying those properties are: that is, we try and achieve a better understanding of just why some object is as it is by considering how we could instruct some 'system' to create precisely that object rather than any other.

The notion of 'describing' a product to be produced rather than actually producing the artefact in question is relatively straightforward. It corre-sponds, for example, to the use of musical notation: the sheet music pro-vides 'instructions' for performers to produce the intended result. Similarly, and moving closer to design, architectural plans can be considered as quite explicit instructions for constructing buildings corresponding to those plans. In both cases, we can see that the production process can itself be rather complex. The approach can also be taken at various levels of abstraction and here we will address three: production in design, production for the presentation of existing content, and production for the automatic creation of new designs, including content. A unifying feature of the accounts that we select for discussion is the use that they make of technical devices that make the production process *explicit*. This is again in service of our primary aim in this chapter: achieving reliable and reproducible analysis.

For production in design, we will restrict our attention to one particular technological 'aid' developed in the design process that has already con-tributed to how document pages are constructed for many years: the *grid*. This grew from experimental proposals in the 1920s and had, by the 1950s and 60s, become firmly established in practical design. Our discussion will show something of the motivation for this construct and how it still plays an extremely significant role in professional design. For the next level of abstraction, we move on to a formal notion of production in a very restricted sense. We describe this as *rendering*, i.e., the process of taking a specification, or 'description', of what precisely is to be on the page and actually making a corresponding page appear. The particular kind of descriptions we focus on are so-called *annotation languages* (or *markup languages*) used both for the description of web-pages and for an increasing range of professionally produced print documents. Annotation languages give precise 'instructions' to a technical device, such as a web browser, to produce pages that conform to the instructions given. Making those instructions sufficiently precise to distinguish any page from another tells us much about just what information has to be included.

Finally, we address production in a completely different area—one taken from the field of computational linguistics: *Natural Language Generation* (NLG). NLG plays an analogous role for entire texts as speech synthesis plays for phonetics (cf. Matthiessen and Bateman 1991, p52): that is, texts are produced fully automatically according to some specified model stating general principles of text construction and subsequently evaluated to see if they indeed function as coherent messages fulfilling the communicative functions intended. Taking this one step further, just as with sounds and texts, we can now equally look at a *page* in terms of how it would be produced—exploring what kinds of specifications give us sufficient detail to reproduce exactly one page rather than another. There are several examples of such investigations within NLG and we examine these to see what they can tell us about the parts necessary for documents and those parts' properties.

2.5.1 Describing a page for design

There are naturally very many ways of designing pages of information. We focus here on those approaches that are more codified, since our purpose is to develop reproducible methods for decomposing pages during analysis. The more that these methods remain intuitive and uncodified, the less they support our task—despite the fact that skilled designers can produce extremely effective designs by such means. It may be argued that there is also a continuum of types of documents arranged according to the information to be presented and the purpose of that presentation. The more detailed and complex the information to be presented becomes, the more 'help' intuition is going to require. In this sense, then, providing reproducible methods is also relevant for the design process as such and is not exclusively a matter of theoretical analysis.

We can illustrate various opportunities for increased codification that have been pursued in design by reference to the 'procedure' for design set out, albeit informally, by Schriver (1997, p341). This procedure consists of the following steps:

1. Take an inventory of the content elements the document requires.
2. Organize the text elements into rhetorical clusters.
3. Measure the actual print/display area.
4. Divide the print/display space into columns and rows.
5. Evaluate the elements within each rhetorical cluster in terms of the minimum and maximum space they will require.

We have already introduced some of the terms involved here above. The content elements of the first step relate to the material that is to be presented, whether verbal or graphical (cf. the *content structure* of Table 1.2 in Chapter 1). Separating this out explicitly as Schriver does here reflects the design situation in which content comes from various sources and needs then to be brought together at the design stage; this is usually the case with professionally produced documents. The rhetorical clusters of the second step were discussed in Section 2.2.1 above. Measuring the display area available contributes to the production/canvas constraints discussed in the introduction. It is, however, step (4) that is of particular relevance to us in this section: dividing the display area into columns and rows. Although this may appear as simple as step (3), it actually hides considerable complexity and there is an extensive literature in design theory and practice concerning how such divisions are to be made.

The key notion here is the *grid*, a system for design that has become so widespread that it can with some justification be said to represent the 'usual' case. Essentially a grid does precisely what Schriver says, dividing an area into columns and rows, but the manner in which it does so is both flexible and subject to a variety of more or less sophisticated constraints. The notion has its origins in early 20th-century art movements that concerned themselves with the issue of decomposing and compartmentalising 'space' in general; several of these also saw themselves as searching for new styles more in tune with what was perceived as an increasingly technologically-centred era which, accordingly, required more 'technologically' appropriate design.

This new sense of design also came to influence graphic design by translating visual space into page space. Whereas it is straightforward to divide a page arbitrarily into columns and rows, it is by no means straightforward to ensure that the resulting patterns support appropriate designs. Those proposing grid-like representations for design were also, therefore, very much concerned with achieving the *right kinds* of grids—that is, grids that might be varied and dynamic while also being aesthetically successful. And here designers drew directly on traditions for discovering aesthetically appealing divisions of space going back to antiquity.

The Golden Ratio

One particularly influential collection of early design strategies drew on the *Golden Ratio*. A Golden Ratio is formed by dividing a line segment into two unequal parts such that the proportion of the line segment as a whole to its longer part is equal to the proportion of the longer part to the shorter part. Dividing any line in this way always results in the *same* proportion. The value of this proportion was first calculated approximately by Euclid, and is nowadays written as φ after the Greek sculptor Phidias. φ is a number like π which cannot be written out in full: it begins 1.618033988749895...

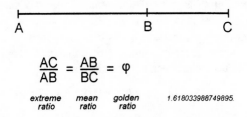

$$\frac{AC}{AB} = \frac{AB}{BC} = \varphi$$

extreme   mean   golden   1.618033988749895.
ratio   ratio   ratio

Figure 2.14   Construction of line segments obeying the proportionalities of the Golden Ratio

Figure 2.14 shows graphically the proportions involved in forming the Golden Ratio. From this we can find its value quite simply by setting the length BC in the diagram to one and solving the resulting quadratic equation for the length of AB. The precise value of the ratio is accordingly given by the formula:

$$\frac{1 + \sqrt{5}}{2}$$

The process of constructing Golden Ratios can be repeated endlessly in either direction—i.e., making ever smaller decompositions or ever larger extensions, each obeying the Golden Ratio principle. Building on the fact that the proportionality has a constant value, we can obtain larger segments by repeatedly multiplying by the factor φ or smaller segments by repeatedly dividing by the factor φ. In the diagram of Figure 2.14, for example, we can readily see that the length of the longer segment (AB) is φ times the length of the shorter segment (BC). Similarly, the length of the entire line (AC) is φ times the length of the longer segment (AB). Extending this, we could then multiply the length of the entire line by φ to give a corresponding new segment including the old line in golden proportion. This may be repeated indefinitely.

Early proponents of the use of the Golden Ratio in design argued that many works of art over the centuries, including architectural works of the ancient Greeks and Egyptians, directly reproduce proportions compatible with the Golden Ratio (cf. Ghyka 1977). This was suggested to explain their aesthetic qualities by bringing together art and nature: the Golden Ratio was also being claimed at that time to occur in many natural objects— probably the most well known example being the divisions in a snail's shell. This led to suggestions that the ratio was indicative of some fairly deep patterns inherent in the world; spatial relationships respecting the ratio could also then be expected to be perceived by human's as 'natural' and, hence, aesthetic at some fairly deep processing level.

The Golden Ratio has several interesting properties and has attracted artists and mathematicians alike. It is closely bound up with the Fibonacci series, another mathematical construct claimed to occur in nature. The Fibonacci series is a sequence of numbers in which each element is made by adding together the two elements preceding, i.e.:

1 1 2 3 5 8 13 21 34 55 89 144 233 377 610 987 1597 ...

Interestingly, if we then *divide* each element by the one before, we obtain another series of numbers that quickly converges to the Golden Ratio. With the series above, therefore, starting with the first two values, we obtain 1 (one divided by one); for the next two, we obtain 2 (two divided by one); for the next two, we obtain 1.5 (three divided by two); for the next two, we obtain 1.666...(five divided by three); and so on. By the time we reach 1597 divided by 987, we obtain the value 1.618034448...—already approximating φ to five decimal places. The same holds for any sequence that is constructed using the same procedure as the Fibonacci series: that is, *regardless* of what two numbers we start with. This means that any two consecutive elements from a Fibonacci-like series can be taken as the dimensions of a *Golden Rectangle*, i.e., a rectangle whose length and breadth conform to the Golden Ratio.

Layout: decomposing space

Several designers began experimenting with decompositions of space that explicitly respected principles derived from the Golden Ratio. Tschichold (1996, originally published in German in 1948), for example, presents extensive discussion of the 'ideal' form for the print area, margins, etc. of books and argued that many of the classic works of print over the ages have conformed to proportions explicitly derived from the Golden Ratio and related constructions. Similarly, Le Corbusier (1951) derived a method for producing aesthetically appropriate layout from a particular selection of proportions obeying the Golden Ratio. His original aim was to find a sequence of measures which could guide architectural decisions of scale and proportion. He accordingly produced particular variants of sequences of Golden Ratios, which he termed rules of proportion. Combining these linear rules along the horizontal and vertical axes then produces a grid of Golden Rectangles. These Golden Rectangles in turn provided Le Corbusier with the raw materials for an unlimited collection of grid 'layouts'. He called this system for spatial design the *Modulor* and subsequently applied it across both architectural and graphic page designs.

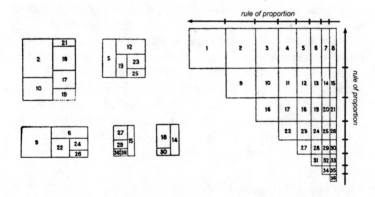

Figure 2.15   Examples of page layouts produced by Le Corbusier according to the system set out in his Modulor (based on Le Corbusier 1951, p91)

Figure 2.15 shows a collection of spatial divisions derived by Le Corbusier according to the Modulor. Here we can see on the right-hand side the variable grid of rectangles formed by combining the rules of proportion vertically and horizontally together with example layouts on the left-hand side formed by piecing together rectangles selected from this grid. Le Corbusier believed that such layouts provide aesthetically appropriate control of spatial distribution and asymmetry—although the final decision was always to be taken by the designer in the face of concrete design requirements.

Structures such as this subsequently became the mainstay of several approaches to page design in the second half of the twentieth century. They were taken up and promoted by page designers particularly in Switzerland (cf., the International Typographic Style; e.g.: Müller-Brockmann 1985, Hollis 2006), and Germany (cf. the Bauhaus; e.g.: Tschichold 1996) and came to be known as *grid-based design*; further discussion, examples and references are given by, for example, Schriver (1997, p108, pp339–341), Hurlburt (1978), Roberts and Thrift (2002) and Elam (2004).

We can see from this short historical diversion that there is far more to achieving an effective grid than simply dividing pages up arbitrarily into columns and rows. The spaces created by a grid for positioning visual and verbal elements within a page are often required to reflect additional aesthetic principles of spatial decomposition so as to improve the quality of the document produced. The flexibility of the grid is also increased still further by its manner of use. Designers look at a well-designed grid as providing *guide lines* or *heuristics* for positioning material, not as a rule book. Material is then actually placed very flexibly against a grid, respecting in all cases the intuitively perceived results of fine adjustment. Moreover, not all areas of a grid need to be filled and so some pages may leave particular spaces empty whereas others do not—all within the same grid system adopted for the publication at hand. As emphasised in most introductions to designing with the grid, therefore, it may (some authors even write 'should') not be possible in a well designed document for a reader to even recognise that a grid has been used—this, as we shall see in a moment, makes knowledge of the grid's application relevant for us here so as to avoid possible skewing of our analyses.

Types of grid in common use

Several distinct kinds of grids are in common use and it is useful to recognise these whenever possible. One helpful classification is provided by Samara (2002), who distinguishes manuscript grids, column grids, modular grids, and hierarchical grids, as well as several more or less standard deviations or even 'violations' of the more usual grid make-up. We will see these grid classifications below in terms of a progressive increase in the intrinsic complexity of the *virtual artefact* created.

The *manuscript grid* is the least constraining form of grid. This simply lays down the printing area of a page by specifying a single spatial block

within which material must be placed. This is probably the best characterisation of our Gannet example page (cf. Figure 2.2). When considering all
of the pages from the book from which this page is taken, there is relatively
little regularity of precise vertical placement apart from the material of the
titles and the upper edge of the picture. The precise vertical boundaries
for the text, pictures and summaries of habits and habitats depend mostly
on the amount of information to be given. In addition to the overall grid
structure, grids nowadays also commonly specify where on the page fixed
elements, such as page numbers, running heads and so on, are to appear.
For the Gannet page this would include the name of the bird and its technical name in Latin and the species to which it belongs, all in the upper
portion of the page.

The *column grid* is the logical extension of the manuscript page to include two or more vertical blocks within a single page. The space between
the blocks is called the *gutter*. This is, again, a very traditional form of
layout for printed documents, particularly books. It has been employed
for hundreds of years and continues in widespread use to this day. Our
Canadian textbook example from Figure 2.5 is a simple example of a two
column grid in which both columns are of equal size; newspaper layout is
also most simply specified in terms of column grids, and typically employs
6, 7 or 8-columns per page: this offers more detail on our observation in the
introduction that newspapers are designed with respect to a virtual artefact
involving columns. The placement of the picture in our Canadian example
also illustrates the role of the grid as a guide rather than as a rule: the picture
does not have to be squeezed into a single column if its size and prominence
does not warrant this. In our example, the picture runs across both columns
horizontally. More complex column grids allow the columns to be of unequal widths, or not to occupy all of the vertical extent of the page. There
is also a distinction to be made concerning the relation *between* columns,
text flowing through a grid may be added into columns in various ways and
'parallel' columns have been used for centuries for 'parallel texts' such as
translations or annotations.

When there is also reoccurring placement to be described vertically as
well as horizontally in columns, we move to what is most usually brought
to mind when referring to grids, the *modular grid*. In grids of this kind,
vertical and horizontal lines intersect to create spaces on a page where material can be placed: these spaces are called *modules*. A typical grid is then
seen as consisting of a two-dimensional array of regularly shaped modules.
The idea behind the notion of the 'modular' grid is that similarly shaped
spatial containers are made available for a variety of material: the material
can be swapped in and out, or around, within the page in a modular fashion.

Modules can also be grouped together to give larger *spatial zones* which may then carry material too large for a single module. The horizontal lines of the grid are termed *flowlines* and these help guide the eye when scanning horizontally across the page. Again, complexity can be introduced by varying the vertical and horizontal proportions of the modules. Many pages designed using this kind of grid employ the vertical alignment provided by the horizontal lines more or less loosely, filling in columns as far as is necessary for a particular block of text.

The final type of grid described by Samara is the so-called *hierarchical grid*, which appears to be applied to any grid that does not fit straightforwardly into the modular form—the designation 'hierarchical' is not used in a mathematically precise sense. Hierarchical grids include cases where different portions of the page are subject to differently scaled grids or where differing grids are brought together on the same page. Various kinds of hierarchical grids are named and used by other authors, particularly varieties of 'interlocking grids' where two or more grids overlap; examples here range from relatively straightforward combinations of two-column and three-column grids (cf. Dorn 1986, p172) to the Swiss designer Karl Gerstner's highly complex six-column grid superimposed over a four-column grid described in Hurlburt (1978, p59).

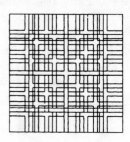

Figure 2.16
Grid designed by Gerstner

This latter grid, shown in Figure 2.16, supports designs with equally sized two, three, four, five and six column layouts and so is particularly flexible.[10] There are also ever more examples nowadays of grid-like structures that incorporate curves and other transformations of basic rectangular grids and so the story is by no means over as far as grid-based design is concerned.

Hierarchical grids and these other more varied organisational schemes can become arbitrarily complex. Applying the regularity that they allow may move beyond the regularity that readers of a document can perceive. This may also be the case when, for example, a modular grid is defined at a very small scale, i.e., with extremely small modules. In such cases the distinction between a grid proper and a traditional layout, or 'makeup', sheet that provides a fine-scaled raster of lines for orientation during design disappears. The virtual artefact created is not then necessarily perceptibly

---

[10]The entire horizontal width is given by Gerstner as 58 units; the other column-divisions, each with 2 unit gutters, then have widths of 28, 18, 13, 10 and 8 units respectively. ($2 \times 28+2$, $3 \times 18+2 \times 2$, $4 \times 13+3 \times 2$, $5 \times 10+4 \times 2$, and $6 \times 8+5 \times 2$)

different from the unconstrained page. With more constraining grids, the essential problem for layout design is the tension that arises between more or less fixed grids and variable content.

The grid and virtual artefacts

The overall purpose of using the grid in design is therefore more subtle than simply dividing pages up into rows and columns. It attempts to provide an overall pre-attentive *impression* of regularity, rhythm and identity of layout across the pages of a document without necessarily making the reader aware of those regularities explicitly. Schriver describes the use of a grid as 'unifying the visual field' so as to provide a structured and rhythmic set of perceptual cues that enable readers to see relationships between presented material more clearly (Schriver 1997, p339). Such relationships include degrees of relatedness, of relative importance, of reoccurring similarity, and so on; that is, for Schriver and most other users of the grid, the grid becomes a tool for supporting the recognition of functionally motivated, or *rhetorical*, relationships rather than 'merely' providing aesthetically acceptable arrangements. Under this view, grids have to be carefully constructed and selected so as to fit both their content and the intended purpose of the resulting document. Here again, significant training and practical experience is essential for effective use.

Our present analytical requirements are less severe, however. We need to be aware of grid-based design primarily in two respects. First, the techniques developed for grid-based design have now become very sophisticated. We can therefore usefully consider to what extent these techniques can contribute to our own analytic apparatus. Samara (2002), for example, describes the 'anatomy of a grid' as providing the basic parts of the page— which has been exactly our aim throughout this chapter. Second, documents constructed with the help of a grid are, to use the terms of the model we are developing here, constructed with a *virtual artefact* (Chapter 1, p16). The very purpose of a grid system is to establish a virtual artefact within which the deployment of spatial resources is constrained to reproduce particular patterns of spatial placement over and above the constraints that the physical page alone provides (cf. Waller 1987a, Chapter 7).

The requirement of conforming to the proposals that a grid makes may then overrule, or redefine, some of the strategies and interpretations for design that might otherwise apply. This means that we must be careful not to assume that there is more freedom of choice in the design decisions made than was actually the case. This is particularly important when considering interpretations of page decompositions such as those proposed by Kress and van Leeuwen (cf. Figure 2.3): such models assume that placement is relatively free, that the canvas within which design proceeds is simply the space on the page. When a grid is being used, design proceeds with respect to the virtual artefact of space-plus-grid and so we must consider how design within the grid influences or is influenced by such arrangements.

The vast majority of professionally produced documents now employ some form of grid, even if the particular proportions adopted for the measurements between grid lines often no longer correspond to the earlier proclaimed principles of aesthetic design. The regularity imposed by a well chosen grid will itself usually, as Schriver states, provide an impression of order that aids the user of a document considerably. Consider, for example, Figure 2.17: since we suggested above that only a basic column grid would be sufficient for our example Gannet page, we show here a grid that might have been used for a related page, one taken from a more recent book of the same generic type. We will examine the precise contrast between this and our older Gannet page in detail in Chapter 5 below—here we are concerned only with the layout of the newer page as an illustration of a grid at work.

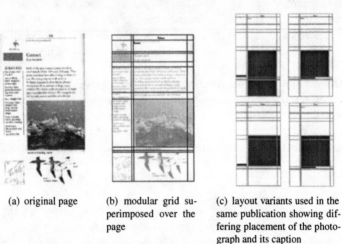

(a) original page

(b) modular grid superimposed over the page

(c) layout variants used in the same publication showing differing placement of the photograph and its caption

Figure 2.17   *A modular grid for a more complex Gannet page from 1996 with variants used in the same publication (Holden, P.* Birds of Britain and Ireland. Collins Wild Guide. *London: HarperCollins, 1996; used by permission)*

On the left of the figure we see a reduced version of the original page; even at this scale it should be clear that we are dealing with a rather more diverse layout than that used in the older Gannet page, including pictures, a column of 'facts' concerning the bird on the left-hand side, various maps and pictures along the bottom, icons and so on. Figure 2.17(b) shows a corresponding modular grid superimposed over this page. Many of the re-occurring elements on the pages of this book are fixed in particular grid positions; Figure 2.17(c) however shows various other options taken up in the book for the main photographs and their captions—which do vary slightly in their positioning. These pages appear to be formatted within the grid depending on the proportions of the photograph and the quantity of information to be accommodated in the left-hand fact column. Any conclusions drawn for the relative position of picture and caption in isolation would therefore need to be treated with caution.

The regularity and relative formal simplicity of the grid has made it a natural mechanism for automating and assisting design regardless of its possible aesthetic contributions. Early systems for automatic layout based on the grid include Feiner (1988) and there are now some very sophisticated results further in this direction being reported (cf. Jacobs, Li, Schrier, Bargeron and Salesin 2003). Modern professional layout software strongly encourages the specification of grids for aligning elements incorporated on the page, but it remains the task of the designer to decide just which grid proportions are going to be appropriate for any work at hand.

2.5.2 Describing a page for rendering

When we are discussing page production, we need to bring in from the outset some notion of the technology used in that production—whereas sounds are produced by a biological entity, pages are produced artificially and require technology, even if it is relatively simple technology such as a quill on parchment, or burnt sticks making marks on a cave wall. Each of these modes of production leave their traces in what is possible for the resulting artefact. Given a particular technical 'apparatus', however, we can describe how a particular document would be achieved with that apparatus.

As technology has developed further, it has become possible, indeed necessary, to specify more about the document being produced than the preferred spatial alignments and spatial regions that we see in makeup sheets and grids. It is necessary to include specifications of the appearance of content as well as that content's placement. This has gradually led to a considerably more complex set of tools for capturing how a document is to be 'produced'. The underlying mechanisms here rely on the notion of *document description languages*: these are special notations that are used both to describe the logical organisation of documents and to constrain how the documents are to appear on the page or screen.

The origin of this direction of development is to be found in publishers' attempts to achieve more sophisticated ways of managing the documents they were producing. Publishers wanted to be able to specify the overall logical organisation of a publication—for example, its division into chapters, sections, subsections and paragraphs—without also committing to any particular presentational style. This would allow the 'same' book to be readily adapted for a variety of publishing styles: for example, producing chapter headings differently, positioning page numbers differently, dealing with endnotes rather than footnotes, producing the first letter of the first paragraph of each chapter in a larger form, and so on. Moreover, once the logical organisation is available, a publisher might produce quite different documents, such as one that pulls names out of a larger document to produce an author index, without having to retype the content.

To support these kinds of manipulation of documents it was necessary to develop ways of storing documents in electronic form in some other way than as an image. As mentioned above in our discussion of automatic document analysis, it is clearly of more utility to have the contents of documents available as sequences of characters rather than as images of pages and, moreover, to explicitly capture additional information concerning the *logical structure* of the document also. This led to the development of the Standard Generalised Markup Language (SGML: Goldfarb 1990, Bryan 1988), the origin of all subsequent markup languages, the language of webpages, HTML, among them; SGML is now also an international standard for document markup (cf. International Organization for Standardization 1986).

SGML raises the distinction between *presentation* and *logical* organisation of documents—which we have already seen utilised in our discussion of automatic document analysis above—to *the* basic architectural principle of its system of representation. This supported the re-use of valuable content, which was already by itself sufficient reward to push many publishers towards SGML-based publishing. The division of information into content and layout, or between logical and presentational organisation, received a dramatic further boost with the emergence of the World-Wide Web. Since no two people might have their web-browsers set to exactly the same size, the idea of separating logical content from presentational form adopted as a basic principle for SGML was instantly applicable and in considerable demand. By writing a document-description file, a writer could produce content and not worry about how exactly a web-browser might finally get this content onto the screen. For this purpose, the full-blown publisher-oriented capabilities of SGML turned out to be too complex and the very much reduced version known as HTML (Hypertext Markup Language) was developed instead.

Straightforward web-pages are accordingly created by providing an HTML document that is displayed, or *rendered*, by a web browser. Importantly for the metaphor being constructed here, the HTML file is not itself the document that is perceived and interacted with by its readers: the HTML file is a set of *instructions* that are interpreted by the web browser in order to produce the final result. In this sense, the HTML file considers a document as an object-of-production: the description given is of how the document is to be produced by the supporting technical apparatus (of the web browser in this case). We can see an example of this in Figure 2.18: on the left-hand side we have the source HTML, and on the right-hand side how this would be rendered in a (very small) web browser.

```
<h1>An example of an
HTML header</h1> <p>This is a
paragraph with some <em>emphasised
 words</em> in it.</p><p>And this
is another paragraph.</p>
```

> **An example of an HTML header**
> This is a paragraph with some *emphasised words* in it.
> And this is another paragraph.

Figure 2.18   HTML source and its rendering in a web-browser

There is here no direct relationship between the distribution of characters in the source file and their layout as rendered in the formatted result. In the source file, the angle brackets enclose so-called HTML *tags* that give *instructions* to browsers concerning how the material they contain is to be displayed. In a properly formed HTML document, opening tags (e.g.,) are matched by corresponding closing tags (e.g.,). The property identified by the tag holds for the extent of the document lying between the open and closing tag (which may then itself hold further tags describing other features); we will see more of this kind of representation and its modern counterpart when we return to multimodal corpora in Chapter 6.

An increasing range of documents, and almost all professionally produced documents, are nowadays created using some variant of this approach. Rather than a 'direct' rendering of the document and its pages by, for example, pasting paper content into the areas suggested by a selected grid or makeup sheet, the writer or designer instead produces (either directly or indirectly via a software design tool) a set of instructions for where content is to appear and in what form. The intended document is therefore described as a set of elements and relationships that contains enough information for a rendering tool to produce the final pages. Widely-used professional tools such as Adobe InDesign[11] or QuarkXPress,[12] as well as simpler programs such as Microsoft Word, provide visually-based interfaces that give the designer the impression of moving content around a makeup sheet and of applying appearance styles: these operations are translated internally into sequences of instructions. This book was itself prepared in a further description language used for rendering: the freely available system LATEX.[13]

Simple document description languages, such as HTML, provide a very basic repertoire of instructions for describing pages. Designers of web-pages were understandably never satisfied with this. If one leaves it to chance how precisely a page is to appear, then one is also placing considerable trust in the web-browser. This is a resounding piece of evidence in favour of multimodal meaning. If a designer has put work into producing a well designed document for electronic presentation, he or she does not then want a web-browser to take that document and to render it in some completely different way. This unwillingness to place ultimate faith in the web-browser and its decisions led, first, to a considerable range of arbitrary extensions to HTML for controlling layout and formatting (which we will not discuss further here even though the majority of web-pages are still produced in this way) and, second, to a further cycle of development of markup languages where the particular *presentational* aspect of the document-as-product specification was given considerable attention.

As a direct consequence of this further cycle, we now have available extremely detailed models of documents that include precise specification of their elements, those elements' properties, and their interrelationships.[14] These models are embedded in the sophisticated view of document production given by the eXtensible Markup Language, XML—the successor to HTML (and, gradually, SGML too). In this view, the division between content and presentation is taken to its logical limit. XML descriptions contain no implications whatsoever for presentational style. In order to make this logical content visible at all, one needs to specify exactly how the logical elements of an XML file are to be rendered visually building on detailed document models. The overall scheme, which we will return to

---

[11] http://www.adobe.com/products/indesign

[12] http://www.quark.com/products/xpress

[13] http://www.latex-project.org

[14] The main body responsible for these schemes is the World-Wide Web consortium (W3C) and a large number of largely voluntary design groups are actively pursuing proposals and specifications. Specifications that achieve a high degree of support in the community become W3C recommendations and, from there, gradually work their way into implementations of web-browsers and other tools.

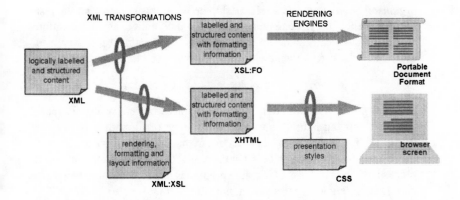

Figure 2.19   Flow of information in an XML-based document preparation scheme

below in Chapter 6 as a basis for multimodal corpus design, is depicted in Figure 2.19.

Document preparation begins on the left of the figure with the creation of some information that is structured with content-related labels. This is then moved towards rendering by *transforming* the document automatically according to an XML *Stylesheet Transformation* (XSL); such transformations are also expressed as XML documents by using a special set of defined tags and structuring constructs. The results of such transformations are further XML documents whose tags and structure express specifically how particular parts of the document are to be presented on the page or screen. One standard set of tags for this purpose is given by the XML *formatting objects* standard (XSL:FO). There are several rendering engines, i.e., special programs, that can interpret the instructions given in a formatting objects document so as to produce printed pages, for example via Adobe Acrobat's portable document format (pdf). Another standard set of tags are given by the current XML-compatible version of HTML: documents of this kind can be displayed on a computer screen, using other rendering engines such as web-browsers. For this latter case (the lower path in the figure), there is an additional possibility of specifying further constraints concerning how the elements of a document are to appear. This is achieved by means of HTML *Cascaded Style Sheets* (CSS), a style language developed specifically for web documents.

As a very simple example, the originating XML document might specify that some block of content is an 'abstract' for the article that that document represents. Note that this is first and foremost an aspect of *logical organisation*: it expresses a relationship between this content and the rest of the content in the document, it does not itself commit to any presentation choices. Let us call the tag in the original XML document that identifies this content 'abstract', then the document would contain somewhere:

...`<abstract>`some text`</abstract>`...

Then, an XSL transformation might be defined to convert an 'abstract', whenever this tag is used, into a particular type of formatting object, let us call this for present purposes a 'block' so that we do not have to consider the rather more complex objects that the XSL:FO standard actually defines; blocks have their own set of possible properties and organisation which are concerned solely with presentation, not with content.

The XSL transformation would therefore also typically add some attributes to any block corresponding to an abstract by saying that it belongs to some particular *class* of blocks, e.g., a 'salient, single column paragraph'. This formatting object document may then either be passed to a rendering engine for printed documents, where the block-element might be produced as a paragraph set-off in some way for prominence, or to a web-browser. In the latter case, we may also have an HTML style sheet that specifies particularly how blocks of the identified class are to be treated. For example, the class may call for a particular typeface, a particular type size and weight, and a particular kind of 'box' behaviour including indentation, margins, borders and printing direction (e.g., left-to-right, etc).

Although this process may appear at first glance somewhat complex, the benefits become evident as soon as a document is to be reformatted or adapted for multiple purposes. Moreover, if there are several documents, for example, a book series or a website with many pages, then much of the style information can be reused many times; updating the look of the entire book series or website is then very much easier since all the information concerning presentation styles is grouped together independently of content. It is also much easier to maintain different *views* of a website in parallel: for example, versions for users with varying interests, abilities or problems (such as reduced vision, colour blindness, etc.). These powerful features taken together are rapidly making the document preparation path shown in Figure 2.19 a standard model for document preparation in general.

These mutually interacting schemes together provide extremely fine-grained specification languages for describing document presentation and layout. They include, for example, schemes for how to describe characters and their formatting, schemes for how areas of the page are to be decomposed and positioned with respect to other areas with margins and spacing (*area* or *box models*), and schemes for how pages are to be organised as wholes (*page models*). We will use some of these constructs further below, although they have not all reached the same level of maturity. Character models, for example, are already quite complex and allow explicit specification of the expected properties of fonts, such as size, weight, typeface and so on, as well as properties required by internationalisation, such as reading/writing order (left-right, left-right, top-down, etc.) and more complex spatial configurations where individual characters may be constructed out of spatially distributed subcomponents, as found in several Asian writing systems. In contrast to this flexibility, the currently standardised page models have not reached a comparable level of sophistication and only include a few straightforward grid forms with fixed areas: e.g., header, body, foot and margins.

Considerable development effort is currently being expended to push these specifications towards the kind of sophistication found in the print industry, where there are substantially more sophisticated treatments available. This lag is one reason why most web-pages still remain relatively simple typographically. But it is now only a matter of time before the standards being jointly developed by the electronic and traditional publishing industries make their way into web-browsers also. Accounts of document parts for multimodal document analysis should not attempt to re-do the considerable quantity of excellent work that has gone into the definition of these standardised descriptions.

The most important issue for the current chapter is then simply that such models exist and that they are extremely detailed in particular ways. Our own approach will therefore be to maintain an 'open' point of connection with such emerging standards so that we can use as much, or as little, of the detail of their specifications as is required for analysis purposes in the areas that they cover. We will see this in more detail in the next chapter. But these descriptions do not cover all that one needs when attempting multimodal analysis. What needs to be done, therefore, is to bring the considerable detail that is available within the areas of rendering and document description together with other areas of necessary description which are not yet so detailed. This is one goal of the combination of presentation layers that we are pursuing in our GeM model.

2.5.3 Producing a page from intentions: automatic document generation

The work reported in the previous subsection has its origins in a combination of concerns from the publishing industry and the emergence of the

World-Wide Web as a major distribution medium for all kinds of information. In this subsection, we see work on document description that has developed in the context of a completely different set of concerns: Natural Language Generation (NLG), an area of computational linguistics that explores how we can construct computational systems that automatically produce natural language texts on the basis of non-linguistic source data, *communicative goals*, and communicative context (cf. Bateman 1998, vander Linden 2000, Reiter and Dale 2000, Bateman and Zock 2003). This is also relevant for our current purposes because there has long been an awareness in NLG that producing text alone, i.e., monomodal texts, is of rather limited utility. The kinds of documents that most benefit from automatic generation—i.e., instructional texts, weather reports, user-tailored health reports and many others—all typically combine pictures, text and graphics in precisely the ways that are typical for multimodal documents.

NLG differs markedly from the simple automatic presentation of text in, for example, search results in a web browser, or text messages in automatic bank machines, etc. in that its fundamental research goal is to fully capture the *flexibility* of natural language production. Texts are therefore to be produced on demand that are appropriate both for their particular intended readers and for their contexts of use: texts are different if they are designed for the expert or for the novice, if they are to explain or to inform, if they are to be understood in a hurry or at leisure, and so on. The flexibility that this requires means that NLG has to concern itself with issues that arise substantially *earlier* in the production processes than is required when rendering, since there is no pre-existing text to be rendered: the NLG system must itself *create* that text. As a consequence, the problems to be solved in automatic natural language generation overlap significantly with those faced by the human speaker/writer when producing texts. Building an NLG system is then another way of constructing theoretical models of how real speakers/writers produce the language that they do.

The descriptions of documents explored in NLG then go beyond those required for page rendering in several respects. Whereas rendering need only concern itself with levels of abstraction already very close to the page to be produced, NLG begins before we have made many of the decisions to which rendering could apply. Typical decisions to be made during multimodal NLG concern the modality that is to be selected in order to express some information—e.g., graphic or textual (cf. Arens and Hovy 1990, André and Rist 1993)—and the ways in which the 'argumentative', or rhetorical, relationships that will fulfill the communicative goal being addressed can be expressed. The major theoretical tool for capturing this latter collection of issues is that of computational *Rhetorical Structure Theory*. We discuss this and its precise application to multimodal documents in Chapter 4 be-low. Here it also becomes relevant precisely because this kind of description has sometimes been used in order to decompose the parts of pages to be generated—i.e., to define document parts. Although, as we shall quickly see, this turns out not to be an appropriate approach, it is still nevertheless useful to know precisely why this is the case since it helps us pull apart the functional and layout perspectives that we have seen conflated above in definitions of rhetorical clusters.

Rhetoric and layout

As one of the simplest possible examples of a rhetorical relationship, con-sider a BACKGROUND relation. This expresses the fact that some subsidiary piece of information is being provided so that the reader or hearer has a more in depth understanding of some main piece of information. This could be expressed, in a monomodal text, by some kind of conjunctive phrase such as 'This is because...' or similar. However, it can also be expressed in a layout decision to place two pieces of information in close proximity to one another on the page, perhaps with one larger and more prominent than the other in order to also communicate which is the main piece of information being communicated and which is the subsidiary in-formation. This exhibits the trade-off between visually-informative and visually-uninformative information presentation that we saw characterised in detail by Bernhardt (1985, p29) according to genre (cf. Section 1.1.3, Figure 1.3).

Further rhetorical relations are ELABORATION, where a topic is further developed, and JOINT, which groups together several distinct pieces of in-formation as contributions to a single topic: ELABORATION might hold, for example, between the main body of text on our Gannet page and the list of additional facts presented in the lower part of the page (cf. Figure 2.2), whereas JOINT would hold *between* those individual additional facts. Here again, we see a difference in page composition, i.e., in the elements of the page, that might also be described by the rhetorical distinctions holding between parts of the page.

Early systems for 'generating' multimodal pages accordingly took their account of *rhetorical* structure, which was already present and being relied upon to produce the natural language texts anyway, and used this to produce *layout* structure also (cf. the discussion in Section 4.3.1 in Chapter 4). The two were assumed to be isomorphic, or perfectly aligned. However, more recently it has become clear that we still need an account of just what kind of layout and layout elements are going to be found in any generated page *independently* of any rhetorical structure that is assumed.

Power *et al.*'s 'document structure'

One well-developed account in this area that proposes a further layer of organisational structure to mediate between abstract rhetorical organisation and the kind of units visible in layout is that of Power, Scott and colleagues (Power et al. 2003, Power 2000). ICONOCLAST Power *et al.*'s account includes, on the one hand, a structured representation that captures the rhetorical import of a communicative artefact in terms of rhetorical relationships of the kind just introduced and, on the other, a *differently* structured representation that captures the elements of that artefact as far as its layout is concerned. The principal application area from which Power *et al.* draw their examples is that of 'patient information leaflets'. Patient information leaflets provide information concerning medicine, usually accompanying the medicine when sold, and are increasingly subject to legal and other constraints that determine just what information is to be presented and in what form (Bouayad-Agha, Scott and Power 2000).

An example of the concerns Power *et al.* raise can be seen in the contrast shown in Figure 2.20. Here we see well the need for an additional layer of structure that is closer to the layout decisions to be made than the rhetorical structure. The text extract on the left of the figure is the text in its original published form; that on the left is how it would need to appear if presented as running text—both extracts are shown within boxes to frame them more clearly. Power *et al.* present many detailed examples of this kind that show an important dependence between the layout selected and the wording. Particular attention is drawn to changes in punctuation, use of capitalisation, and direct *grammatical* integration of quite different elements into the unfolding text. In this case, for example, we see the list of reasons presented as a simple continuation of 'since'—this would not be possible in the running text version which requires instead the forward-looking 'the following' in order to set up sufficient textual structure to house the reasons that follow.

Crucially for Power *et al.*, it would not be possible to change the layout substantially without also have to change the linguistic form of the texts. These examples show again and again a trade-off between a verbal expression of rhetorical relationships ("since", "however", "so", etc.) and layout in the form of itemised lists, paragraphing, and so on. This demonstrates that decisions concerning the segmentation of the layout structure must have been made *prior* to finalising the purely verbal content, thus going against the more traditional view within NLG where issues of formatting

In rare cases the treatment can be prolonged for another week; however, this is risky since • The side-effects are likely to get worse. Some patients have reported severe headache and nausea. • Permanent damage to the liver might result.

In rare cases the treatment can be prolonged for another week; however, this is risky for the following reasons. First, the side-effects are likely to get worse; some patients have reported severe headache and nausea. Second, permanent damage of the liver might result.

Figure 2.20 *A formatted extract from a patient information leaflet adapted from Power et al. (2003, p226) together with a more simply formatted variant*

and layout were seen as a relatively simply final step in producing a document: a kind of 'pretty printing'. Explaining and simulating the additional flexibility that is evidently required in document production is then the main task that Power *et al.*'s new layer of *document structure* takes on. Final layout and formatting decisions are made on the basis of document structure, not of rhetorical structure. The process of producing the layout structure is then where flexibility can appear. Essentially, a rhetorical structure is 'translated' step-by-step into a layout structure while allowing certain deviations between the two to occur so that the latter is not necessarily an exact copy of the former.

Power et al.'s definition of document structure draws centrally on the linguistic treatment of *punctuation* proposed by Nunberg (1990). Nunberg's approach is to define a phrase structure grammar for punctuation precisely analogously to that used in syntax. This grammar defines possibilities for combining smaller 'punctuation units' to give larger 'punctuation units'— for example, *text-clauses* may be combined in order to yield *text-sentences*. 'Text-sentences' are demarcated by initial capitalisation and a final full-stop, while 'text-clauses' are demarcated by semicolons, commas, etc. Special rules take care of cases where multiple punctuation marks are entailed logically but fail to appear in the surface text: for example, combining two 'text-clauses' ending with semicolons might produce a 'text-sentence' ending with a full-stop; special rules then make sure that the logically predicted sequence ";." is replaced by a single full-stop, i.e., the redundant semi-colon disappears.

For layout Power *et al.* take this further by building on a tradition in linguistics which sets out units of a *graphology* in precise analogy to 'phonology': that is, units of smaller scale are progressively combined into larger units from letters and words right up to paragraphs and pages. Crystal (1979), for example, sets out no fewer than fourteen such units arranged hierarchically with respect to each other and 'horizontally' across to units of other linguistic levels, such as phonology, grammar and semantics. The manner in which these units interrelate with each other is, however, left somewhat under-differentiated. In Power *et al.*'s account, Nunberg's formal approach is extended to the following 6 abstract levels; units of a higher-numbered 'rank' are made up of elements of a lower rank:

0	text-phrase	3	paragraph
1	text-clause	4	section
2	text-sentence	5	chapter

Hierarchical structures can then be built out of these elements, which may in turn be expressed via concrete layout elements such as itemized lists, paragraphs discriminated in particular ways, sections and subsections. The resulting structures then show a clear relationship to the views of document 'logical' structure that we saw in Norrish's approach (Section 2.2.1), in the machine-readable document and automatic document analysis communities (Section 2.4), and to the document markup approach shown in the previous subsection.

One important difference, however, is the explicit relationship drawn to rhetorical purpose. With this structuring possibility available, creating a document proceeds in the simplest case by progressively descending through a rhetorical structure, allocating parts of that structure to ever decreasing 'ranks' of document units: first chapters, then sections, then paragraphs, and so on. With reference to the two alternative versions of an extract from a patient information leaflet given in Figure 2.20, we can see the process as follows. A rhetorical analysis of the content to be expressed would include information stating, for example, that there is some kind of CONCESSION between prolonging treatment and increased risk, some kind of EVIDENCE between the increased risk and *both* (indicating a JOINT relation) the side effects and the liver damage, and some kind of ELABORATION between the side-effects getting worse and some patients reporting headaches and nausea. Producing the document structure needs to allocate this rhetorical content to a document structure unit.

The right-hand version is quite straightforward. Here a 'text-paragraph' is selected as starting point, which is subsequently decomposed into a sequence of 'text-sentences' (with initial capitalisation and final full-stops), some of which are further decomposed into 'text-clauses' (with semi-colons). The grouping of the reasons under a JOINT relation is signalled by the explicit textual conjunctions 'First' and 'Second'.

The left-hand version, in contrast, selects as starting point a 'text-sentence'—i.e., the entire content to be expressed is placed within

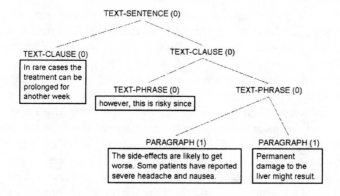

Figure 2.21   Document structure adapted from Power et al. (2003, p227, Figure 8)

a single document structure sentence. This requires a more complex treatment that extends beyond the simple creation of a hierarchy offered by recursive-descent. The document structure corresponding to this version according to Power et al.'s model is shown in Figure 2.21. Here, assigning ever-smaller rhetorical units to increasingly lower rank document units proceeds without problem until we reach the second TEXT-PHRASE node in the tree, which dominates two PARAGRAPH nodes. The resulting text shows that we need to invoke PARAGRAPH nodes here because we have two bullet items, each of which contains sentences. But this should not be permitted because paragraphs are at a higher rank than text-phrases.

To cover this eventuality, the model additionally specifies a *logical indentation level* (Power et al. 2003, p226). A higher-ranking unit can then be included within a lower-ranking unit only when its indentation level increases. This indentation level is not, as Power *et al.* emphasise, intended as a literal physical indentation but as a 'logical indentation' where some real content-based division of units is to be expressed. Just how this is realised physically on the page is left open—it may be visually presented in a variety of ways, all that is required by the model is that the logical structure is perceptually recoverable.

Returning to the current example, we can see that the logical indentation level of the problematic higher-ranking child nodes is increased relative to the parent TEXT-PHRASE node: thus we have two PARAGRAPH(1) nodes instead of simple PARAGRAPH(0) nodes: the number in parentheses indicates the logical indentation level. This enables the model to capture the fact that the left-hand, original patient information leaflet appears to have both sentences and paragraphs occurring *within* a single sentence. This is managed by moving structural information out of a purely linguistic realisation (e.g., 'first', 'second'), where such a realisation would not be possible, and into a corresponding layout realisation (e.g., an itemized list employing bullets).

This establishes a clean formal specification and also leaves sufficient information for visualisation to consider when rendering the document structure as layout. The lowest nodes are paragraphs, and have many of the formatting properties of paragraphs. But they are also logically 'subordinate' to their surrounding text and are displayed (in this case) physically indented with respect to the text around them. The model then captures both these sources of constraint for the layout options actually taken up and provides, on the one hand, a link between the rhetorical communicative organisation of a document, via the relation to rhetorical structure and, on the other, a way of flexibly relating this to a range of fine-detailed variation in wording and layout.

In the examples seen so far, the flexibility allowed between rhetorical structure and document structure has nevertheless remained relatively simple. Power et al. characterise this formally as a *homomorphism* between the rhetorical structure and the document structure—that is, it is possible for the document structure to omit details included within the rhetorical structure but not to *add* structure that differs from that of the rhetorical organisation. This supports the case where a more deeply structured rhetorical structure might be presented in a document as a relatively flat sequence of paragraphs—as typically occurs, for example, when the rhetorical relations are being expressed linguistically in terms of conjunctions.

Bouayad-Agha, Power and Scott (2000) pursue this further, presenting evidence that the relationship between rhetorical structure and document structure has to be more flexible still. In particular, they propose that an additional operation of *extraposition* has to be allowed by which complex chunks of rhetorically organised material are extracted from their position in a rhetorical structure and presented separately as their own independent document elements. This may be done for reasons of continuity, where some particular components of the rhetorical organisation are moved 'out of the way' of some other development in order for a more fluent rendition.

Although precise motivations for such a realisation step still require further investigation, Power *et al.* see this divergence between rhetorical organisation and document structure in many respects as a consequence of the *linearity* of language. The content that language delivers is rarely linear and so a variety of techniques and linguistic resources allow the order in which information is presented to transcend its one-dimensional delivery in time. Both text structures and sentence structures in probably all languages admit of special constructions that can 'lift' material out of its regular position for reasons of emphasis or other text structuring requirements. This is then precisely the kind of operation that Power *et al.* and Bouayad-Agha, Power and Scott see operating on rhetorical structures in order to produce non-isomorphic and even non-homomorphic layout representations. The mechanisms that Power *et al.* set out allow them to pursue the classic natural language generation methodology of producing variations according to a collection of constraints and evaluating the appropriateness of the generated result. But they only take us so far towards our goal in the present chapter of achieving a suitable starting point for page description. In particular, their treatment of layout as an extension of linguistic units is not yet general enough in one respect: it is still very much entwined with textual realisation.

The document structure that Power *et al.* define is, in fact, only a treatment of one particular aspect of a document's organisation: that which applies to what we term *text-flow* layout. The entire apparatus should only step in when it has been decided that some part of a document's logical content is to receive a textual realisation: once this decision is made, we can derive a 'document structure' for that fragment in the manner described. It does *not* capture, however, the situation where a page may consist of multiple layout elements—for example, it is quite possible to find pages in which there are two or more layout elements, *each of which* exhibits a 'document structure'-like organisation. These layout elements are then related to one another within the page but not in terms of 'text-paragraphs' or the like.

We find this problem in most approaches that take the linear text as a starting point. There is in such approaches a marked lack of recognition of the *spatiality* of the page. In all text-flow based models of layout, written language is seen as running text set out on the page and is assumed to operate within the same linearity as one-dimensional, perfect (i.e., abstract, idealised) speech. But the very setting out of language in the spatial medium of the page makes essential contact with another set of semiotic resources: those of the *space within which the writing appears*. Text-flow based models miss precisely this modal contribution of the spatial medium (cf. Waller 1990).

We can see this clearly with one typographic resource that already stands very much at the meeting point of text-based and layout-based methods: the *table*. Tables in multimodal documents demand a shift to the visual-spatial and it is for this reason that they are discussed by almost every research direction that concerns itself with layout and typography. Lemke (1998), for example, sees the table in precisely this sense of enabling a multiplication of meaning from the textual and spatial; Baldry (2000) and Thibault

(2001) develop this point similarly; Wright (1970) discusses the usability issues that arise from the modal multiplication; and Hurst (2006) addresses how tables are best to be recognised automatically and described formally including adequate treatment of their spatial meanings. It is also with respect to tables that Power *et al.* begin to recognise most clearly that their text-based approach to layout may have reached its limits (Scott and Power 2001).

Tables are such transitional objects because they make contact both with linguistic concerns, in that their entries are often condensed elliptical forms relying on their embedding context of use to explain them, and with spatial concerns, by capturing patterns of similarity and difference in terms of functionally distinguished portions of the visual field. They therefore incorporate and subvert visual resources for textual development reasons, achieving at the same time preferential modes of access to their visual elements—e.g., running horizontally across rows or vertically in columns, etc. Despite the textual or numeric content of many tables, their organisation and functionality is not then completely reconcilable with a text-flow model.

Extending beyond the table to the page as a whole makes these spatially-related functions of page elements more prominent still. A necessary complement to the approach to document structure set out by Power *et al.* is therefore to see documents and their pages primarily as *visual units* rather than textual. This has been suggested by several authors (e.g., Baldry and Thibault 2006, p192, Lemke 2002, p310) and is also the position taken in Bateman, Kamps, Kleinz and Reichenberger's (2001) multimodal natural language generation system: DArt$_{bio}$, to which we now turn.

The DArt$_{bio}$ approach to document layout

The patient information leaflets that were the target for the natural language generation work of Power et al. (2003) described in the previous section are predominantly textual. These are then similar to our original Gannet page used in this chapter and as such are examples of text-flow documents. The starting point for our previous work on natural language generation reported in Bateman et al. (2001) was quite different:DART$_{bio}$ here we examined magazine pages combining a far broader range of multimodal combinations. This demanded from the outset an approach in which layout structure is derived not from the text but from the page as a visual entity that is acting as a unit of communication in its own right.

The overall strategy was however similar to that of Power *et al.* The generation system had the purpose of producing multimodal pages by transforming a rhetorical structure capturing the 'rhetorical plan' intended for the generated result. And, again just as with Power *et al.*'s account, we had also previously come to the conclusion that such generated results could not simply follow the organisation of the rhetorical structure. A visually oriented layout structure also needs to be decoupled from notions of rhetorical organisation. In fact, we found similar 'extraposition' mechanisms applying not to elements such as itemised lists, indented paragraphs and the like, but to entire layout segments, containing running formatted text, pictures and combinations of these. The precise details of these mechanisms (cf. Henschel, Bateman and Delin 2002, Bateman and Henschel 2006) are less central for our current purposes than the nature of the page elements that were developed. These showed many similarities to those developed in the approaches to documents that we have considered above where the page is essentially a visual 'signal' to be decomposed and analysed: in developing the DArt$_{bio}$ system, rather than working 'out' from punctuation, we therefore defined layout structure by decomposing the page *visually* in the manner illustrated in Figure 2.10 above .

Within this framework, a page is successively decomposed into visually motivated areas of spatially-related content. Each such area can be characterised in terms of its prominence for the page as a whole. The same characterisation was then to be used for generation, but in reverse. An example of this kind of layout specification and its correspondence with the fragment of the page that it represents is shown in Figure 2.22, which shows a small portion of a page generated from a database of artist biographies (Hüser, Reichenberger, Rostek and Streitz 1995). The annotations on the decomposition lines refer to the extent and type of the material that is presented within each element as well as the relative prominence of each element within that layer of structure. Thus, for example, for the first decomposition of the entire page fragment we have the annotations "1p:20" and "54w:80", which indicate that the former page element contains 1 picture (1p) and is to take up around 20% of the available space, while the latter contains 54 words (54w) and is to take up around 80% of the available space. The arrows connecting the elements also indicate intended reading paths and dependencies in the content of the material presented within each element. This kind of structure was then converted into an 'area model' of the kind that we mentioned above when discussing page rendering: the various properties of the sub-areas holding the picture, the body text and so on were derived from a mixture of resolving the constraints specified in the layout structure and various 'default' options, such as settings for the size and kind of typefaces used.

This example also shows a notion of 'extraposition' at work serving to decouple rhetorical organisation and layout. Whereas in the rhetorical or-

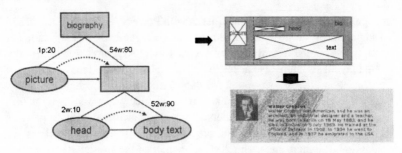

Figure 2.22   Example of layout structure and its realisation on the page as developed within the DArt_{bio} multimodal page generation system (Bateman et al. 2001). Here: ovals are terminal page elements, rectangles are non-terminal page areas, dashed curved arrows mean 'refers to', straight arrows mean 'followed-by', and straight connecting lines indicate decomposition.

ganisation the photographic material is a relatively unimportant ELABORA-TION of the artist that the biography concerns, for the purposes of presenting a more interesting visual representation, this element is extracted in the transformation to a layout structure so that it is encountered first on the reading path. In our studies of magazine pages we found three kinds of extraposition at work. First, the presently illustrated kind of extraposition, where an element is made more prominent than its position in the rhetorical organisation might suggest; second, a demotion, where some material is presented as more minor than might have been expected (leading, for example, to presentation as a footnote in a text-flow element or as a smaller boxed layout element in a magazine page); and third, as a segmentation of the page where particular elements related rhetorically are pulled apart and presented as more or less equal page contributions. All of these then relied crucially on a deployment of *space*, involving spatial proximity, framing for separation, and relative salience for expressing desired degrees of relative prominence.

Whereas this account of page layout went a considerable way towards allowing flexible design, it also opened up significant problems. Most difficult was the question of how to select an appropriate transformation of rhetorical organisation into layout organisation. Since the process was clearly so flexible, it required considerably more sources of constraint than were then available. This led directly to the line of research followed up in this book: we consider it essential to have a far more exact understanding of *genre* in order to predict precisely what kinds of transformations from rhetorical organisation into layout organisation are going to be appropriate for particular documents and which not. We return to this question, therefore, first in our account of multimodal genres in Chapter 5 and then again from the empirical perspective that we take up with multimodal corpora in Chapter 6.

2.6 Combining viewpoints on document parts

We have now followed the path from document interpretation to document production through a broad variety of frameworks and models that are currently being pursued. We have seen how each of these addresses particular aspects of what can be considered the 'basic parts' of documents. We have argued throughout the chapter that providing sound means for determining these elements of a page or document are crucial. Identifying and describing them in a reproducible way is a prerequisite for all that follows: for carrying out empirical investigations of the processes of interpretation, for critique, and for comparing and contrasting different approaches to presentation. All of these kinds of study are only as reliable as the reliability of the notion of document part that they assume.

The approaches taken within natural language generation to the problem of producing complex multimodal pages that we saw in the previous section lead us to consider two complementary perspectives from which to view what is happening within a multimodal page.

The first sees graphic design as 'macro-punctuation', in the rather narrow sense of an extension of text-based typography or formatting. This is clearly relevant for text-centred contributions to layout but is also sometimes adopted as a model for page design in general. We consider this to be a vestige of earlier monomodal approaches to documents where the linear notion of 'text-flow' is taken as basic and all more challenging layouts are seen as deviations from this. This is a position that is also perpetuated by the current state of document rendering technology—which is well developed for linear text but less so for more free spatial compositions.

Starting from language and its forms and structures in this way has always been more 'natural' for those focusing on text. It respects a traditional response to restricted multimodality coming out of linguistics, one which considers punctuation and its extension into basic formatting as *paralinguistic* phenomena. A good characterisation of the page seen from this perspective is the following description of the 'semiotic systems' of the printed page proposed by Matthiessen (2007, pp24/5):

- Language, written (with the potential for being read aloud in spoken language)

- Visual paralanguage: font family, type face ("style"), layout (graphic design)
- Visual (pictorial) semiotic systems defining images of different kinds: drawings, paintings, photographs, maps, graphs, charts, and so on.

This decomposition aligns with the model of layout structure of Power *et al.*. Visual paralanguage is often seen in terms of punctuation, especially in written codes such as that for English where punctuation is taken as an indication of intonational phrasing. Similarly, type face characterisations, such as bold or italics, can also be related to emphasis required in the text, which may in turn call for a distinct intonational prominence or effect and so is a modification of the linguistic meaning being conveyed.

The second perspective for viewing multimodal pages moves on to consider pages as essentially visual entities and document design as a process of visual decomposition. We argue that this direction is equally valid and, indeed, essential for capturing the meaning resources of multimodal pages. While this is relatively clear for larger page elements of the kind seen in our discussions of automatic document recognition and visual perception above, we can also see it extending and overlapping with areas previously claimed by 'super-punctuation' approaches. Thus, although text-flow elements organise their content into typographically signalled structures, they may *also* to a greater or lesser extent contribute to the visually communicated structure of the material presented. In this sense, just as accounts of language, its graphological form, and punctuation can consider visual elements to function paralinguistically, we can also consider certain textual elements and formatting options to be *paravisual*.

When this occurs, rather than signalling meaningful distinctions using the spatial possibilities of the visual semiotic systems of similarity/difference, proximity/difference, and grouping/nongrouping directly, a multimodal artefact may also achieve similar meanings *indirectly* by co-opting the possibilities of text-based typography and formatting. Itemised lists, for example, combine exactly the two perspectives set out here. Visually, the bullets of the list and the list as a whole's distinctive spatial framing present elements that are perceptible regardless of character-based typography. One might not know what the rendering in an itemised list means, but it would hardly be possible not to perceive the spatial segmentation expressed. Tables also, as discussed above, are archetypal examples of this dual functionality.

Both itemised lists and tables should therefore be interpreted as contributions to a particular aspect of the multimodal page that we, following Waller, term *access structure*. Elements functioning to carry access structure provide perceptually supported points of access to a document for its readers. Even paragraphing, when effective, works similarly. The use of punctuation within text blocks *can* play this role, but is not require to. Visual decomposition therefore reaches down within written language and contributes to the interpretation of the material deployed there in a way that is not dependent on the linguistic or 'logical' meanings being presented.

This is clearly a continuum, with some text-typographic elements able to take on a stronger role visually than others. Many punctuation marks, such as full-stops, commas, dashes, quotation marks, etc. are for example *primarily* character codes whose interpretation relies on familiarity with the code. Even though the value of some punctuation elements, such as a full-stop, may also be due to their iconic relationship to 'relatively free-space'— thereby leaning towards providing access structure-like visual elements— we can nevertheless set up a general difference in the semiotic contributions of the elements being discussed: whereas a sentence unit is expressed by a typographical convention, itemized lists combine elements into distinctive spatial configurations. The visual decomposition from the starting point of the page does not rely on familiarity with the typographic/punctuation code at all but is a result of visual/spatial processing.

This independence of the two perspectives active on the page makes it clear why the use of text-typographic resources within the visual written mode does not necessarily have to carry 'paralinguistic' information at all. Selecting a particular colour font for some word in a text in order to show a connection between that word and a topic is not paralinguistic in any traditional sense: we simply have the visual mode carrying an additional piece of information that could only be brought inside the text with a, possibly out of place, circumlocution. One example of this kind is now extremely common: the use of colour and/or underlining to indicate hyperlinks in web-pages. This information is not part of the verbal message being expressed by the text: at best it may represent a possible rhetorical link with something related to the text. Moving up to larger scale elements on the page, the relation to linguistic information becomes more indirect still.

Allowing both perspectives is then necessary for capturing a fuller range of possibilities. In general, text-flow page elements are just one kind of possible 'part' that can be found in a multimodal document. Within such elements, the kind of regularities reported by Power *et al.* apply. Other page elements may contain pictures, graphic material, tables and so on. Any element on the page may then *combine* elements of these kinds. How these elements are related to one another needs then to be captured by an extended organisation of layout structure similar to the models developed

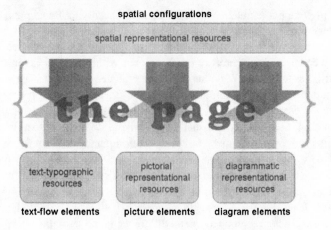

Figure 2.23   The page as a site of cooperation and integration of distinct semiotic modes

for automatic layout recognition, page rendering and visually-based generation, and not by extensions of text-formatting methods.

A large part of the specific value of multimodal documents therefore comes from the capability to act as *sites of integration* for several rather different semiotic modes. The contributions of these modes inter-penetrate each other and allow a distinctive multiplication of the potential available. These distinct contributions as well as their combination within the page is suggested graphically in Figure 2.23. Although there are many points of overlap, and semiotic 're-use', we have seen that there are also important distinctive contributions to be done justice to.

The individual mechanisms for identifying these contributions and the document parts that carry them that we have discussed in this chapter have been designed primarily to address the questions arising within the individual approaches and research communities concerned. Our main task now is to show how we can draw on all of these perspectives to achieve a well-specified, extensible characterisation of document elements sufficient for a broad range of analyses. Although our own approach is best placed within the emerging tradition of multimodal linguistics, particularly in our orientation to genre (Chapter 5) and the commitment to 'transcription' from corpus linguistics also argued for multimodal documents by Baldry and Thibault (2005, 2006), we have now seen that many of the existing accounts in this tradition fail to problematise sufficiently the critical initial step of demarcating the parts of a page. In the next chapter, therefore, we set out the explicit process of page description that we adopt.

3

The GeM Model:
Treating the Multimodal Page
as a Multilayered Semiotic
Artefact

Our goal in this chapter is to finally combine the various perspectives identified so far in order to articulate an account of document parts that is *sufficiently well-defined to support reproducible analyses.* Since the entire
purpose of the account presented throughout this book is to place multimodal analysis on a firm empirical footing, our specification needs to be
sufficiently explicit to provide detailed guidance to an analyst confronted
with a page or document to analyse. This should not be driven first and
foremost by our interpretation of what we think such elements are doing.
We have seen in the previous chapter how this readily leads to the recognition of elements motivated more to support an interpretation than by the
data being analysed. Such pretheoretical interpretations can be useful during initial stages of analysis, but they need to be bolstered empirically to
support tighter hypotheses and more robust results concerning multimodal
meaning-making.

The overall aim therefore is to work towards functionally supportable
hypotheses by means of sufficiently fine-grained formal details so as to allow empirical investigation, verification and refutation. This means getting
deeper into our multimodal documents so as to pull apart just how the elements of a page are functioning and to reveal what the breadth of possible
variations and meanings might be. When too little constraint is taken from
the concrete documents that are being analysed, then the preference for one
analysis over another remains essentially subjective and is not supportive
of empirical evaluation.

We identified towards the end of the previous chapter two broad directions from which the page as such has been approached. One starts more from language, particularly text, the other starts from the visual impression of the page as a whole. We also saw earlier in that chapter, discussion of distinct perspectives that may be taken on pages: structural, visual perceptual, functional interpretation, logical content and more. Bringing these distinct levels of analysis together leads us towards an explicit treatment of any document as a *multi-layered semiotic artefact*. Each layer of the description of a page artefact tells us something different about how the page is being constructed.

The particular layers that we have isolated in our investigations so far as being crucial for getting analysis started were set out in the introduction (cf. Table 1.2). To recap, we can also characterise the principal layers of the model in terms of the types of elements that they identify as follows:

- the GeM base: the basic elements physically present on a page;
- layout base: the layout properties and structure;
- rhetorical base: a detailed account of the rhetorical relationships between the content expressed by elements on a page and their communicative purpose (cf. Chapter 4);
- navigation base: the elements that contribute explicitly to navigation and access in the page, supporting 'movement' around the document in various ways (cf. Chapter 6);
- genre base: a representation of the grouping of elements from other layers into generically recognisable configurations distinctive for particular genres or document types (cf. Chapter 5).

Each layer defines it own 'basic' set of units as well as relations and structures defined over these units. The relations *between* layers are first of all left open to empirical investigation. We do not impose prior to analysis any particular inter-layer relationship beyond the simplest assumption that some configurations of units in one layer might be expressed in terms of some configuration of units within other layers.

The starting point for analysis is provided by the GeM base layer. This explicitly labels all the units actually occurring on the page that can be called upon subsequently to take on particular roles or functions within other layers. The GeM base identifies, in a sense, the basic 'vocabulary' of elements that any particular page deploys to carry its meanings. Because of this foundational role, we need to describe this layer before discussing any of the other components of the model where more interpretative work is done. In the next section, therefore, we define the GeM base in detail.

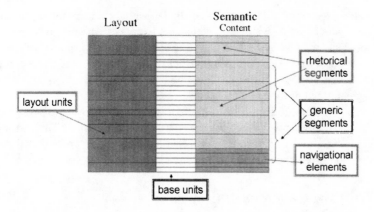

*Figure 3.1   The distribution of base elements to layout, rhetorical, generic and naviga-
tional elements*

The role of the GeM base with respect to the other layers in the model
is suggested graphically in Figure 3.1. The units identified within the GeM
base are shown running down the centre of the diagram. To the left of this
column, we see the layout units; to the right, we have rhetorical segments,
generic segments and navigational elements. As the diagram suggests, a
rhetorical unit may consist of some collection of base units: there is no
one-to-one relationship. This holds similarly for generic and navigational
elements; in general, these can be made up of any number of base units.
These right-hand groupings are all part of the 'semantics' of the page analysed. Base units are interpreted as either rhetorical units or as navigational
elements, not both—i.e., they do not overlap. A unit functioning in the
rhetorical organisation cannot simultaneously function within the navigation base; a more detailed characterisation of this relationship is given in
Section 6.4. In contrast, particular combinations of rhetorical units and
navigation elements can function as generic segments within a genre structure. We will return to these content layers in subsequent chapters: they are
all concerned with providing functional interpretations for the elements on
a page.

Our main focus in the present chapter is on the *presentational* information of the GeM model captured by the layout layer. It is here that we
characterise just those elements that carry and participate in the perceived,
or perceptible, visible document structure of any page. This draws particularly on the distinct approaches and criteria for establishing document parts
that we discussed at length in the previous chapter. In order to be perceived

on the page, base units must also be aligned with the presentational units in the layout column; again, the relationship here does not have to be one-to-one. One function of the layout units is precisely to provide *a site of visual integration* for the distinct functionalities carried by the other layers. It is there that we find structures that range over, for example, both rhetorical segments and navigational segments.

Throughout our discussion, we will use our Gannet example page from the previous chapter to illustrate the constructs we introduce. Then, to conclude the chapter, we present a rather more complex example that shows the framework being applied over a broader range of page phenomena.

3.1   The GeM Model: the base layer

The purpose of the base layer is to identify the minimal elements which can serve as the common denominator for interpretative and textual elements as well as for layout elements in any analysis of a page or document. Everything which can be seen on each page of an analysed document should *be assigned to some base unit.* That is: the collection of base units identified is comprehensive and provides those units that can be talked about later; it provides a means of establishing what is available on the page for discussion independently of how that discussion subsequently proceeds. This is the first step towards achieving full coverage of what is being analysed. As analysts, we are not permitted at this stage to leave components of the page out of consideration because they do not intuitively appear central or relevant.

For the documents that we have examined so far a relatively short list of base unit candidates has been found sufficient. More extensive empirical work may require the addition of new types or further subdivisions among the existing types, but for current purposes we can restrict attention to the categories set out in Table 3.1. These categories are labelled in terms of their functions in order to help the analyst locate them: the actual distinctions assumed by the base layer are actually very much more restricted—in effect we simply identify and label them as 'units', regardless of further possible interpretations. That is, from the base layer alone it is not possible to distinguish between a unit that is, for example, a 'header' and another that is a 'footnote'. Labelling of this kind belongs to genre-specific functional interpretation, and so would be premature at this point taking us beyond what is directly visually/perceptually supportable.

Note that we already make one simplification here for our present purposes concerning the 'textual' content of pages. Since we do not describe any detailed *linguistic* analyses in this book, we only identify in the base

Recognised Base Units

sentences	headings	titles	headlines
icons	table cells	list items	list labels
footnote label	items in a menu	page numbers	running heads
emphasized text	floating text		

- sentence fragments initiating a list
- footnotes *(without footnote label)*
- photos, drawings, diagrams, figures *(without caption)*
- captions of photos, drawings, diagrams, tables
- text in photos, drawings, diagrams
- horizontal or vertical lines which function as delimiter between columns or rows
- lines, arrows, polylines which connect other units

Table 3.1   Table of page elements to be identified as base units during analysis

layer orthographic sentences and sentence fragments that will be picked up later in, for example, the layout layer or the rhetorical layer. For some analytic purposes it might be essential to include *grammatical* analyses of the text contained in a document: to support this the base units would be extended to include orthographic words just as is usually done with computational corpora—we see examples of this in Chapter 6 below. Similarly, for reasons set out in the previous chapter, we restrict our decomposition of visual material. Both simplifications allow us to concentrate on the *combination* of information across modes that we will discuss in our example analyses below but are in no way intended to prevent finer distinctions being drawn should they be necessary for particular purposes. Moreover, nothing changes in the overall model when such additions are made—we simply have either a finer set of distinctions in one of the layers or the inclusion of further, independent layers of analysis. One design criterion for the framework developed here is precisely that its layers be open for extension.

In effect, we use the base units to declare the highest degree of *granularity* that is to be adopted in the analyses of the other layers. Units described within the other layers may be 'larger' than the base units—in that they may join base units together as realisations, or expressions, of units in those other layers—but they should not be 'smaller' than base units. That is, no other layer should break a base unit into smaller parts. We will see something of the technical motivation for this in Chapter 6; here we simply use this as a way of being very explicit about just what is being analysed.

This 'atomicity' of base units entails some particular ways of treating the units we encounter on the page. For example, individual sentences divided by a page or column break need to be marked as *two* base units rather than a single orthographic sentence because, as we shall see below, they are divided into distinct *layout* units. If we did not divide them but included the sentence as a single base unit, then the layout units would have to divide a base unit in two, which is not allowed since it would require us to find some way of getting 'inside' the atomic base units. Similarly, the captions of figures, tables etc. are always marked as extra base units, as are potential contributions to framing interpretations such as horizontal or vertical lines. Vertical lines which serve to separate columns in newspapers and horizontal lines which serve to separate paragraphs are all accordingly identified as base units.

Figure 3.2
The Gannet example page repeated

We can apply this to the Gannet example presented in Figure 2.2 above as follows—we repeat the page here as a 'thumbnail' sketch for ease of reference. Working down the page from top to bottom, we have the five labels or headers made up of text fragments that occur before the picture: these base units correspond to "**Gannet**", "*Sula basana*", "Family SULIDAE.", "Gannets" and "No. 27". The next base unit is the drawing itself, which, for the moment, we will not decompose further. Then we have the four base units provided by the orthographic sentences of the main text, followed by the seven list labels "Haunt", "Nest", "Eggs" etc. and the eight text fragments of the list items themselves. The complete list is shown for reference in Table 3.2.

At this stage, it is generally better to be over-cautious and, if in doubt, to separate the units so that they are available for later layers. Here, for example, we might consider whether the top portion of the page consists in fact of three blocks of text, one on the left, one in the middle, and one on the right rather than five separate units. This kind of consideration is better placed in our discussion of the layout of the page, however, and so we do not need to consider it here. If we had already grouped elements at this stage, this would reduce our flexibility later and so is less desirable.

In general, the base layer has a flat structure: i.e. it consists of a simple list of elements. It is up to subsequent analysis to provide additional structure, grouping, functional labelling and interpretation. As we will see in more technical detail finally in Chapter 6, the use of a flat list at this stage is a useful way of allowing differing layers of analysis to impose very different kinds of structure without confusion. If we already have structure imposed on the base units, then other layers of analysis are forced to deal

1	Gannet	9	The plumage...	17	The coast... Isles.
2	Sula Basana	10	Immatures ... spots.	18	Of seaweed...
3	Family Sulidae.	11	Haunt	19	1... chalky.
4	Gannets	12	Nest	20	April or May
5	No. 27	13	Eggs	21	Fish
6	drawing	14	Notes	22	Short and harsh
7	This great bird...	15	Length	23	36 or 37 in (...)
8	It can ... prey.	16	Status	24	Resident

Table 3.2   Base units of the Gannet page

with this also—which may not be appropriate. Our only task at this stage is, therefore, to identify the types that are to be included in the list.

There is, however, one particular generic class of cases where we do require some additional structure among the base units themselves and allow base units inside other base units. This is used in the following situations:

- emphasized text portions in a sentence/heading
- icons or similar pictorial signs *within* a sentence
- text pieces in a diagram or picture
- multimodally supported parts of a diagram or picture
- arrows and other graphical signs in a diagram or picture
- explicit references to other parts of a document occurring within a sentence
- menu items in an interactive pop up menu
- dynamically appearing pop up 'labels' provided by mouse-over behaviours on web-pages

The use of embedding within base units preserves the essential unity of a unit as a whole while still making available for subsequent analysis particular, well-specified portions of that unit.

For example, any text portion which is differentiated from its environment by its layout (e.g. typographically, background, border) should be marked as a base unit because it is likely that this will need to be picked up as a layout or navigation element. Whether it constitutes a separate unit in the main level of the base units list, or an embedded unit inside another base unit, depends on the extent to which it can be 'moved' around the page without disrupting the content.[1] Thus, if we had a fragment such as:

> Adult has *white plumage* with, in breeding season, *faint yellow-pink tinge*; usually looks pure white at distance.

---

[1] This could be handled 'simply' by breaking up the orthographic sentence into words (or even characters) and allowing the layout or navigation layer to do the grouping: for our present focus, however, this would lead to an explosion of base units that we can just as well avoid.

the phrases in italics are identified as two separate base units embedded within the base unit for the sentence as a whole: there is no sense in which we could consider these portions of the unit as having a 'life of their own' on the page. One embedded base unit of this kind in our Gannet page is unit 3, which has a subunit for 'Sulidae' since this is typographically distinguished from its surroundings by its small capitals.

Similarly, menu items in an interactive pop up menu are marked as base units embedded *within* the unit which is clicked on to open the menu. Each of the menu items may play an independent role in the navigation layer and so can be usefully identified at this stage. This also applies in headings where the chapter/section numbering portion of the heading needs to be marked as an embedded base unit to make it available for the navigation layer. For example, in a fragment such as:

> **4.3.2 Modal Adjuncts**

the section number "4.3.2" is an embedded base unit in order to allow the navigation structure access to it.

Finally, in a fragment such as:

> *You will need to fit battery packs as described on page 6.*

the expression 'page 6' is also usefully marked as a base unit for the purposes of describing document navigation and access structure. This allows us to identify what Paraboni and van Deemter (2002) define as *document deictic expressions*—i.e., expressions that explicitly express and support navigation and access operations within a document.

These considerations often need to be combined within single sentences. We see this well in the following example taken from a set of operating instructions for a telephone:

> For **Multi-Redial**, you can then press ▼ or ▲
> (see below) to scroll through the last five

This base unit includes no less than four embedded base units: one for the typographically emphasised **Multi-Redial**, one each for the two icons pointing up and down, and one for the document deictic reference "see below". We will see more complex examples taken from this genre of page documents in Chapter 4 below.

3.2 The GeM presentation layers: the layout base

When we have set out in our list of base units all the elements that are actually to be found on a page, we then proceed to characterise the page in terms of how what is visually perceptible provides the material expression for meaningful distinctions via *layout*. For this we need to capture not only the individual elements but also their layout grouping and spatial proximity, their mutual spatial relationships and their particular layout and formatting properties. These aspects of a page's make-up are placed in what we term the *layout base*.[2]

For this layer of analysis, we argued in the previous chapter that it is important to give the visual aspect of the page a particular priority, as it is through this that any user of the page necessarily comes into contact with the page's content and organisation. The visual make-up of the page is delivered in many respects pre-attentively and is not an option for the user to ignore or focus on as they will. This also extends to the spatial relationships between visually perceptible elements and so these also naturally provide additional direct input to any process of interpretation.

A starting point here is to see configurations of visual elements that are discernibly placed together on the page as clusters of some kind *regardless* of their functionality or 'reader-orientedness'. Only when we have this view is it possible to go on to functional analysis and critique. Conversely, we cannot place elements together as a cluster simply because we believe that they are functionally 'related' in some way: this must be supported by the spatial configurations in evidence on the page. We have seen that *visual* clustering and *rhetorical* clustering do not necessarily align, even in well designed documents, and so it is important to address these perspectives separately.

To capture the visual clustering, we define the layout base as consisting of three main parts: (a) layout segmentation—identification of the minimal layout units, (b) realisation information—typographical and other layout properties of the basic layout units, and (c) layout structure information— the grouping of the layout units into more complex layout entities and deter- mination of spatial relationships. We now explain these three components in detail. What unifies them is that they are all essentially related to visual perception. The layout base is deliberately restricted as far as possible to structures that are directly available perceptually: in this sense, a particular

---

[2] The layout base exhibits similarities with representations developed in the Document Analysis community, such as DAFS, DIF, and so on. Setting out an explicit comparison would take us too far afield for current purposes unfortunately.

layout base description of a page should be a valid target for an automated recognition procedure.

There are places, as we shall see, that this distinction is less watertight than might have been thought. It is known, for example, that knowledge concerning a multimodal presentation can influence perception at a surprisingly early stage. Examples of this range from very basic perceptual responses shown in 'change blindness' experiments where, once the change is known, it is very difficult to recapture the original state of 'blindness' (McConkie and Currie 1996), to more sophisticated interaction with designed presentations such as maps and charts (cf. Lowe 1993, Egan and Schwartz 1979, Hegarty 1992). It may not be possible, therefore, to distinguish perfectly between a perceptual stage and a subsequent interpretation stage. We propose, however, that it is nevertheless useful methodologically to adopt the distinction for getting empirical analysis started.

3.2.1   Layout segmentation: identification of layout units

For the layout layers we focus on just those elements which are perceptually salient when a reader encounters a page, or page spread, as a whole. Certain distinctions are available very early: for example, that between predominantly textual blocks and predominantly graphical blocks. Designers can 'play' with this distinction in various ways—for example, by using very large typographical realisations or particular shapes of typographical material to achieve graphical effects—but for present purposes we can see this as a 'manipulation' of the distinction at issue rather than as counter-evidence to its adoption. We therefore see here three broad classes of layout elements: typographic, graphic, and composite.

The graphic elements are identified as individual layout units which may possess internal structure, either by using elements such as textual labels or by displaying features which are picked out in other modes—most particularly the verbal—in the way described in the previous chapter. We return to these kinds of relationship in Chapter 4; here we can simply note that they are identified as contributions to the layout structure.

For the typographical contribution, the situation is somewhat clearer. Although in typography the minimal layout element (in text) is the glyph, in the GeM model we are primarily concerned with macro-typographical and formatting effects at a more global level of a page. Our basic level of description then revolves around the typographical paragraph rather than the glyph since, as demonstrated in the automatic document understanding community, paragraphs are often recognisable as individual elements on the basis of textual homogeneity and weak framing from their surrounding textual context. We accordingly consider the paragraph as a basic 'layout unit', one which combines certain visual properties, that we will define more closely below, and characteristic text-flow properties. Unless there is some particular need to do so, we will not consider sentences within paragraphs as contributions to layout—paragraphs are often sufficient perceptually. If there are further salient details within paragraphs, we adopt these as further layout units of various kinds; for example, we also pick out for marking as layout units highlighted text pieces in sentences as described above as well as text fragments within illustrations.

All such units should in any case be available as base units—a primary motivation for including them as separate base units was precisely so that the layout layer could pick them out and characterise their contribution to a page's layout. Therefore, if we swap orthographic sentence for paragraph, we can also take Table 3.1 as providing a list of possible layout units. Whenever we find an item of these kinds on the page, we give it a label unique for the page or document and add it to an 'inventory' of layout items to be explained.

Finally, composite layout units are 'non-terminal' elements in a layout structure: that is, they serve a grouping and generalisation role so that we can describe how larger portions of a page are working together in terms of their layout. We will see how these function below.

3.2.2 Realisation information

The second part of the layout base then goes further beyond what is recorded in the GeM base layer so as to identify the particular forms that are employed within the identified layout units. Following common linguistic usage, we say that each layout unit specified in the layout segmentation has a *visual realisation*.

As already suggested, the most obvious difference in realisation is the mode that has been used—the verbal or the graphical/pictorial mode. Following this distinction, the layout base differentiates between two kinds of elements: textual elements and graphical elements. These have differing sets of attributes that describe their particular layout properties.

For the textual elements, we need to characterise the narrow typographical features employed. This is already a well-understood area of design and so will not be particularly highlighted in our discussion here. Very briefly, when describing the use of type in a document, we need to specify the typeface (Times Roman, Helvetica, etc.), the style of type (normal, italic, bold, etc.) and the type size (usually measured in *points*, 1/72nd of an inch). We also add in here the colour of the letters and an increasing range of graphical effects that nowadays find application, such as shadows, glows, and 3D textures. Following Walker's (2001, p26) use of terms from Twyman (1982), we can consider these properties as *intrinsic* features that "reside in the characters themselves and, particularly, in the system that produces those characters". The reference to the system used is important as it makes clear that the technology employed determines the status of the particular graphical feature considered. Thus, in online documents, colour is simply an extra intrinsic feature of the characters displayed, whereas in older print technology, colour would have been part of a more or less elaborate manipulation of the printing process and so would be considered *extrinsic*.

Extrinsic features also include properties of typographical display that come about by manipulating the space 'around' the characters. In this area we need, for example, also to specify the distance between successive lines of print, technically called *leading* (rhyming with 'sledding'), since this influences the perceived texture of a block of type enormously and is a determinant of visual discrimination. Leading is also usually measured in points. A more complete specification of font use in a block of text is then traditionally written with a *pair* of numbers, e.g., '12/14pt', which means that a 12pt typeface is being used with 14pt between the successive baselines of type—therefore leaving 2pt extra (made up by the leading) between lines. As Schriver (1997, p261) usefully explains, this terminology can be confusing since by convention "10-point leading" and "10 points of leading" mean completely different things: the first refers to the distance between baselines (thereby including one line of type) and the second refers to the actual *extra* distance that is inserted *between* lines.

Whereas leading is concerned with vertical layout, we may also need to indicate how characters and words are stretched out horizontally. There may be more or less space between characters (termed *kerning*) and the characters themselves may be stretched or squeezed. The former has always been available in traditional type-based print, while the latter only really became a possibility that can be productively employed in normal document design with the advent of computer-based typesetting. Again we see technology moving previous extrinsic features to become intrinsic. Although both of these kinds of horizontal manipulation are important for professional document design, we will not refer to them further here unless they become both especially prominent visually and important for distinguishing layout elements that we are working with.

These ways of characterising typographic design decisions made on the page were developed with respect to traditional print technology, going back several hundred years. Both the '10pts of leading' used for vertical spacing and kerning were originally managed by literally inserting thin strips of printer's 'lead' between the lines of type or between characters. Nevertheless, despite the completely different technological basis that is now responsible for getting pages onto paper or screen, the traditional vocabulary still provides a good way of describing and distinguishing the design options that are available in modern document design. The techniques and effects that they describe are all basic tools of the trade for influencing the visual perception of the basic organisation of pages (cf. Schriver 1997, pp283–288 and Waller 1990).

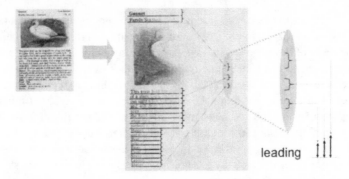

Figure 3.3   Example of differential use of leading in the example Gannet page

We can illustrate something of their continuing utility by drawing attention to the three distinct leadings used in our Gannet example; this is suggested graphically in Figure 3.3. Measuring the distance between lines in the Gannet page, we can discern three distinct regions on the page. The top lines of text are the furthest apart, the middle block are less far apart, and the bottom block is the closest together of all. The arrows on the lower right of the figure show the relative size differences. This shows that selection of leading and type size is still one of the ways that document designers manipulate typographic realisation in order to signal implicitly to the reader divisions of the page into elements and those elements' respective importance and inter-relationships.

We can then start characterising textual layout elements with specifications of the following form, which give the values of particular attributes depending on the type of layout element in question:

```
layout element                      layout element
    type: textual                       type: textual
    xref: L1.3                          xref: L1.4
    font-family: times                  font-family: times
    font-size: 11                       font-size: 10
    font-style: normal                  font-style: normal
    font-weight: normal                 font-weight: normal
    color: black                        color: black
    case: mixed                         case: mixed
    leading: 14                         leading: 12
```

The 'xref' attributes of each element identify which particular layout elements we are dealing with: the numbering and its correspondence to the base units of the page will be shown below in Figure 3.4. The first layout element shown here refers to the main block of text on the page; the second refers to the single block covering the additional bird information given in the lower portion of the page. We can see that the font information specifies that the text realisations are identical apart from the size and leading. Separating this realisational information from the particular layout elements making up the layout layer segmentation makes it possible to capture generalisations by grouping all the layout elements that share a realisation within the same specification.

Generalisations are also captured by the hierarchical structure defined over the layout elements. The information concerning the second layout unit, L1.4, is therefore 'inherited' by all its subordinate layout elements. These elements are those expressing information about the Gannet's 'haunt', 'nest', etc. in the lower part of the page (see Figure 3.4 for clarification). For these all that that needs to be expressed concerning their typographical realisation are the *deviations* from what was inherited from L1.4. We describe this below when we introduce the layout structure in detail.

Layout elements also specify the properties of embedded textual base units that are typographically highlighted against their environment in this way. These include exactly the same attributes as ordinary text elements with an extra attribute that refers back to the embedding element. The layout element explicitly notes those properties of the embedded element which make it stand out against its context (e.g., bold, italic, size, colour, etc.) by annotating these with particular values; the remaining properties are 'inherited' from its surrounding context.

The particular font attributes and values used here are for purposes of illustration only and, although useful for comparison across the texts we deal with, a more complete and standardised representation is preferable. There have been many proposals for the properties and values that could be used for this representation—those developed for the linguistically-based analysis of multimodality are relatively simple (e.g., Sefton 1990, Lim 2004), while those used in professional document design and the print industry are correspondingly more complex.[3] The actual properties and values that we will assume for the GeM model are taken from the well developed character models that we discussed in the previous chapter in the context of page rendering. These models, defined for the markup language XML and its related formatting objects and style sheet specifications, provide a well established degree of international standardisation and are being continuously extended in sophistication.

Adopting such standardised attributes also contributes to our ability to collect data since ever more documents are being produced using these description languages in any case; the properties they define for layout elements then become available 'for free'. Even if it is the case that for some particular analytic purpose a less complex characterisation (typeface, size, leading, colour, etc.) is sufficient, this should be based on a systematic simplification of the current standards. Adopting or developing further *ad hoc* characterisations that are not directly related to those standards is best avoided. We return to this issue in Chapter 6 below.

For properties appropriate for layout units realised in the visual mode there is much less agreement. Here there are proposals from each of the communities discussed in the previous chapter—such as, for example, the 'interactive meanings' of Kress and van Leeuwen (1996, p154), O'Toole's (1994, p24) 'functions and systems in painting', Lim's (2004, p236) 'system network for graphics' and many more. It will be some time still before an empirically motivated set of properties adequate for document analysis in general has been established. For present purposes, we will simply note whether the visual is a photograph, naturalistic drawing, line drawing or diagram. Further distinctions will be considered as motivated by the requirements of individual genres—for example in the area of diagrams, where we have arrows, connecting lines, and a host of other more conventional elements that must be distinguished for effective analysis (cf., e.g., Bertin 1983, Winn 1989, Tufte 1997).

3.2.3 Layout structure

Finally, we specify how the individually identified layout units are grouped together into larger elements that collectively make up the composition of

---

[3] As can be seen, for example, from current standardisation efforts such as the OASIS Open Document Format http://docs.oasis-open.org/office/v1.1/OS/OpenDocument-v1.1.pdf.

the page. For instance, a heading and the text to which it belongs form together a larger layout unit; or, similarly, the cells of a table form the larger layout unit "table". In order to capture this kind of spatial grouping of elements, we need to specify how larger segments can be constructed and positioned relative to one another. We have developed several criteria for this, such as considerations of 'framing' and 'visual integrity'. By these means layout elements are progressively grouped into larger elements´, building up a hierarchical structure with the entire page, or page spread, as the root and leading down through ever smaller elements to the smallest layout elements, those identified in the segmentation part of the layout base. The hierarchical structure itself is represented in the third part of the layout base: the GeM *layout structure*.

As discussed in the previous chapter, in Reichenberger et al. (1995) we proposed identifying visually-motivated layout chunks by progressively decreasing the resolution of an image of the page; more sophisticated methods adopted from the automatic layout analysis community could also be usefully employed at this point. The grouping into chunks can be applied in several steps, thus forming larger and larger layout chunks out of the basic layout units up to the entire document. One chunk may then come to consist of layout elements of different realisations (text and graphics). Typical layout elements will share some visual features (font-family, font-size, ...), while differing visually from their surroundings (e.g., by background colour, a surrounding box or whitespace and framing). Here we allow a very limited form of functional consideration in terms of 'what belongs together'. This is a valuable channel to segmentation that is influenced by our generic or specific knowledge of how a document is to be 'read'.

It is also useful to contrast our layout structure with the document structure of Power *et al.* described in the previous chapter. Since the layout structure is explicitly oriented towards the *visual make-up* of the page, it is naturally more 'surface-oriented' than document structure and differs from that structure in that

- it reflects the production and canvas constraints which the realisation of a given document structure is subject to (decisions about pagination, columns, margins, hyphenation, etc.);
- it includes navigational elements—layout elements which are not derived from the content, but which serve to guide the reader through the document (e.g. page numbers, pointers, running heads, titles);
- it specifies the position of layout elements on the page.

For our Gannet example, the layout structure is then relatively straightforward although, as mentioned above, there does remain some indeterminacy

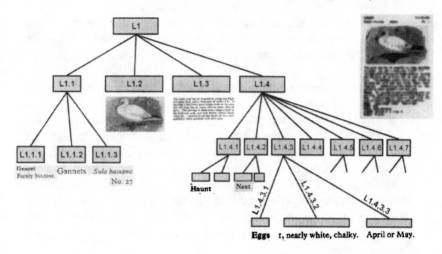

Figure 3.4   Layout structure for the 1972 Gannet example page according to the GeM model

at the top of the page. Differential texture (cf. Figure 3.3) and application of segmentation procedures such as the XY-tree, give us four bands running horizontally across the page. Moreover, if we proceeded by reducing resolution and filtering for areas of similar texture and layout element properties, we arrive at three layout units running across the top band of the page, just above the drawing: one consisting of the base units 1 and 3, one consisting of just base unit 4, and one on the right consisting of base units 2 and 5. Whether this is what the designer intended or not is a separate question—one which we will return to in more depth in Chapter 4.

A layout structure for the entire page is then given in Figure 3.4: the low resolution starting point for the visual decomposition is shown upper right in the figure. We also use here portions of the original page to indicate the base units to which the layout elements correspond. The structure shows that layout units are typically grouped into collections which are then themselves grouped into larger collections still. Each collection consists of elements showing some kind of commonality in the features of its member elements. This is the main criterion employed in the present case. For example, the three elements of the header are grouped together because of their consistency in type face selection, size and leading; an alternative would have been to maintain these separate sub-elements (L1.1.1–L1.1.3) as direct descendents of the page. The material at the bottom of the page is also grouped together into a single layout element (L1.4); again homogeneity of texture (type face, leading, size) is the main cue here together with a rather weak framing separating it off from the main text body. Within this element, the individual elements are identifiable by virtue of the list headers in bold.

Each layout element has associated with it the particular properties that characterise it: that is, for the text elements, we have information about type face, leading, size and so on and, for the image, information about the type of drawing that is involved. Generalisations about groups of elements are made by moving the shared properties and values upwards in the layout structure. Thus, for example, the fact that all of the items in the final list of the page (L1.4.1-L1.4.7) exhibit the same formatting and typographical features is captured by placing this information on the parent element L1.4. This then also expresses that the sub-elements are *visually* similar: whether they are also similar in intent is then a question addressed when we deal with the rhetorical layer.

We use the layout structure and its units to identify and group *visual* elements while the 'content' of these elements is provided by the base units of the base layer. We can therefore set up associations between layout units on the one hand and base layer units on the other. Considering, for example, the single layout unit in the centre of the page, L1.3: this is a paragraph of text. The orthographic sentences of this paragraph do not, however, contribute individually to the layout—they simply follow the text-flow determined for paragraphs. The sentences are nevertheless identifiable in the base layer. We therefore have an association between the single layout element, L1.3, and the set of base units 7–10 (cf. Table 3.2).

The layout structure captures the overall visual dependencies and realisations evident on a page but does not yet fully determine the page or page segment layout. Further information is required about the actual position of each unit in the document (on, or within, its page). For this, we introduce the *area model*. This serves to determine the position of each layout-element in a way that abstracts beyond the specifics of individual documents. As we have seen with respect to grids in the previous chapter, pages often partition their space into sub-areas. Whereas this need not always be done when designing pages, if a page exhibits grid-like properties for the reader when interacting with the page, then we certainly need to capture this in our initial analysis layer. There is a further relationship to be seen here to the XY-trees that we introduced in the previous chapter; these are also determined by the relations recoverable on the page rather than by design intent. We leave the precise connection between these constructs open at this point: it is to be expected that as the methods available for inducing XY-trees become more sophisticated, they will become candidates for the automatic detection of area models: until that is the case, however, we need to allow the analyst to determine the structure to be used. The simplest area model is a generalisation of the modular grid specification and partitions page space into sub-areas. For instance, a page may be designed in three rows—the area for the running head (row-1), the area for the page body (row-2), and the area for the page number (row-3)—arranged vertically. The page body space may itself consist of a number of columns arranged horizontally. These rows/columns need not be of equal size. For the present, we restrict ourselves to rectangular areas and sub-areas, and allow each area to be arbitrarily divided further into sub-grids, each with their own dimensions. We will also see below some cases where the area model does not consist solely of a rectangular grid: in general, we can imagine any shape serving as a guideline for positioning layout elements. This style of document layout is becoming increasingly common in modern documents mainly because it is as straightforward for computer-supported design systems to align text and other elements along curves as it is along straight lines.

Each page grid has a single root, which structures the document (page) into rectangular sub-areas in a table-like fashion. The sub-areas defined by an area model then provide abstract locations for specifying where particular layout elements or groups of layout elements are positioned on the page. A location of a layout element is sufficiently determined by saying in which cell of which area/sub-area it is to be placed. In addition, the layout elements located within an area are assumed to be aligned vertically with each other with respect to their left edge and horizontally at the top of their row. If this is not the case, then it is necessary to provide 'offset' values to record the discrepancy: these can either be explicit numeric values or abstract qualitative values like 'right' or 'centre'. The relationship between layout structure and area model is suggested graphically in Figure 3.5.

We have found the separation of layout structure and area model useful in our analyses for three main reasons:

- First, it is quite possible for minor variations in the precise placement of layout elements to occur for genre-specific, canvas or production constraint reasons without altering the hierarchical organisation of the layout structure; separating the two levels of information makes it easier to recognise the commonality. This is related strongly, just as was the grid, to issues of the virtual canvas used in a document. The area model is an essential part of the definition of such virtual canvases.

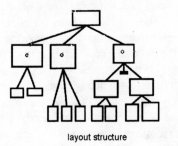
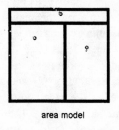

layout structure   area model

Figure 3.5   Graphical representation of the general method of correspondence used to relate layout structure and the area model in the GeM framework

- Second, the separation allows us to state generalisations over the physical placement that are inconvenient or difficult to express at the level of individual layout units. For example, one major function of the area model is to allow us to specify alignment relations over quite diverse configurations of layout units on the page: as we saw in the previous chapter, such alignment can be a significant factor in the assessment of good continuity and the forming of layout elements. These alignments are naturally captured by the area model specification.

- And finally, we also use the area model to explore Gestalt properties of the page layout as a whole. Properties such as centering and polarisation, as proposed by Kress and van Leeuwen (cf. Chapter 2, Section 2.2.2) may be pursued in terms of area model configurations. Polarisation may be indicated by grid modules that are arranged so as to provide more or less symmetrical 'sites' for positioning layout elements that serve rhetorically distinct purposes; centering by more complex grids with defined central and non-central (margin) areas for alignment. We will see cases of these below.

Although this covers an extensive range of documents, there are still two problematic cases that do not fit into the layout structure presented so far:

- **Insets:** Layout elements can displace or intrude into the space of other layout elements.

- **Separators:** Certain graphical elements (lines, arrows) do not always fit into a grid structure, but instead serve to indicate column or row separation—thereby 'showing' the area model explicitly in the page design.

For *insets* their content forces the content of the units that they are inset against to *flow* around them. In the GeM model both the inset and the relative 'background' are made to be 'child' elements of a single parent layout segment. To determine the precise location of the inset, the height and the width of the inset as well as its alignment inside the parent element's space have to be explicitly given. A second, slightly different situation occurs when the inset layout element intrudes into the space of another layout element without displacing it. The latter element does not need to be a textual flow-object. One example for this is when text intrudes into the empty space surrounding illustrations, and the background-colour of the illustration is the same as the background colour of the text. Here both layout elements are siblings in the layout structure and have their own locations in the sub-area associated with their parent. These locations are adjacent. Thirdly, one element may appear *in front of* another, obscuring its content; in this case the layout structure treats them as if they were separate and places them within a stack of area models arranged in the third dimension orthogonal to the page; we will generally omit this complexity in our discussion here however.

Separators are two-dimensional graphical elements, often of type "line", that are used as delimiters between cells, columns or rows, rather than to form cells by themselves. These lines may have a variety of further attributes, such as decorations of various kinds, arrowheads (determining direction), colours, thickness and so on. We will see examples of these in the documents analysed in later chapters.

The area model of our Gannet page is relatively simple and does not employ very much of the flexibility that we have now introduced—nevertheless its thorough description belongs to a full analysis of the genre and so we will conclude our account of the layout structure of this Gannet page with its area model. As suggested with respect to grids in the previous chapter, an appropriate area model in this case is a straightforward *manuscript grid*. Moreover, because we are trying with an area model to describe what was actually done in the design of a page rather than expressing guidelines for design, we must also specify the precise height of the horizontal bands running across the page. There is also structure to represent within these bands: in particular at the top of the page, where we have at least three layout units.

The lower portion of the page is also interesting in that despite a partial resemblance to a table in some respects, this is not supported visually for the lower part of the page as a whole. There is no regular alignment in the vertical dimension of 'cells' as is the case with tables. Instead we need here a typographical *flow rule* of the following form: for each element, take the

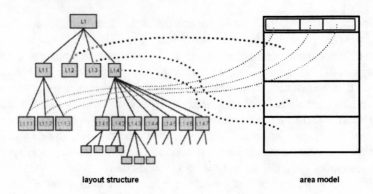

layout structure   area model

*Figure 3.6   Correspondence between the layout structure and the area model of the
1972 Gannet page*

first sub-element as a label (in bold) and separate it with whitespace from
the second sub-element; if there are further sub-elements, separate these by
whitespace also. Since the whitespace is dependent on the actual text that
is present rather than any text-extrinsic spatial organisation, the positioning
remains within the typography and is not to be captured in the area model.

The correspondence relation between the layout structure of this page, as
set out in Figure 3.4 above, and an appropriate area model is shown in Figure 3.6. This shows that the area model in the present case has rather little
alignment to capture apart from the overall margins of the page; certainly
within the itemised list at the bottom of the page there is no discernable
alignment and so there is no reason to impose a stronger area model. The
lower part of the area model accordingly consists of a single 'cell' for the
layout chunk corresponding to the entire list occupying layout unit L1.4;
the layout within this cell follows from a combination of paragraph text-
flow properties and whitespace insertion as suggested in the rule above.
This forms part of the generic information given for the seven subordinated
layout elements and so is captured as a generalisation in the *parent* element L1.4 rather than being repeated for each paragraph. It is then a matter
of further empirical investigation to investigate how widespread, in terms
of genres, production, designers, etc., this particular technique of framing
layout elements is. Its resemblance to primitive spacing techniques when
using a typewriter cannot, however, be overlooked, which already serves to
'position' the page generically.

This also serves as an interesting illustration of just how quickly things
have changed. The page, published in 1972, is clearly straining at the production and consumption constraints holding at that time. The units of

the page operate primarily within the narrow typographic mode, relying on text-flow for distributing its layout elements around the page, but with deviations (such as those seen in the spacing required within L1.4) that will in later documents be taken up entirely within the spatial mode. Then we will see explicit spatial information being taken up in the area model rather than relying on typographic 'rules' in the layout structure. The present page is, for this reason, very much in a transitional stage as our detailed analytical decomposition makes clear.

3.3 A more complicated example of layout analysis

Now that we have seen what kinds of parts a document page can be decomposed into, we conclude the chapter by illustrating the framework on a rather more complex multimodal artefact. This shows more of the model being put to work. As in most illustrations of analyses pursued in this book, we will not be examining differences in linguistic phrasing or similarly fine-grained distinctions in the visual images. Our task is to find the 'significant' elements of the pages that are able to provide a solid basis for supporting subsequent multimodal analysis that brings out the additional semiotic value of the multi-modal *combination* being acted out on the page.

This next example is taken from a very different kind of document to that of the Gannet page, a travel guide—in particular one of the Dorling-Kindersley guides to Paris. The page itself is not primarily based on text-flow and so already forces us to use more of the GeM model than was the case with the Gannet page. The Dorling-Kindersley series are well known for their lively layout style and so provide a useful counterpoint to the Gannet example: as their promotional information on the back of the book states: "The guides that show you what others only tell you", indicating at least informally that significant use of the visual and layout possibilities can be expected. This allows us to illustrate a range of further properties that are necessary for describing document parts.[4]

The discussion of this example demonstrates how all the pages that we discuss in this book are initially analysed in order to provide their parts and the relationships between those parts. This is what provides the basis for the further, more detailed, more abstract and, hopefully, more revealing analyses that follow. Since we will not be able to address all of our subsequent examples at the same level of detail, the example here will be rather

---

[4]Somewhat fortuitously for our current purposes, another page from a different Dorling-Kindersley guide book is analysed by Kong (2006, p230) from the perspective of image-text relations. A comparison of the analyses is quite instructive.

fine-grained so as to make it as clear as possible what is being done and why. The analyses of layout structures in the examples in later chapters will in comparison be somewhat abbreviated, although it is important to stress that for any complete analysis all the steps described for this next example are being carried out in precisely the same manner. The abbreviation in later examples is solely for exposition purposes and should not be taken as an indication that the *analysis* can be so abbreviated.

3.3.1   The parts of the Louvre

The page at issue is set out for reference in Figure 3.7. It is a two page spread printed in full colour. The function of the pages of this book are to give visitors to Paris information about sites of interest, including historical background and practical tips for their visit. Within this collection of information, there is little that is clearly much more important for the visitor than other facets, and so the resulting design reflects this by presenting an essentially 'random-access' document in which information can be selected in any order. Within this, however, there are particular organisations and access strategies supported. The analysis will now clarify this.

First, as in all analyses, we establish the base units for the visual unit being considered, in this case the two-page spread as a whole. For this first illustration of a complete analysis, we present this step in much more detail than will be followed in subsequent examples in the book. Even here, however, we will make a number of simplifications to shorten the exposition. In particular, as defined above and listed in Table 3.1, we know that a full base unit list should actually include all the sentences that occur in the texts of the pages analysed *as separate units*. This is in order to support subsequent linguistic and textual analyses. However, since we will not be carrying out any linguistic analyses, we will leave this level of description to one side, grouping all sentences that occur into paragraphs in order to focus more on the layout description.

In addition, the boxed inset for the 'Visitor's Checklist' upper right introduces a considerable number of base units of its own because of its free mixing of icons, text fragments, and both bold and italic highlighting of information. This information could also have been presented visually drawing more on the resources of a table—the information presented is in fact a simple list of 'attributes' (e.g., various telephone numbers, opening times, admission charge, etc.) and their values. Some of the attributes are identified by icons, others by bold italicised text. In fact most of the text apart from the initial attribute 'Map', identifying where in the main map provided in the book the Louvre is to be found, and the following information about

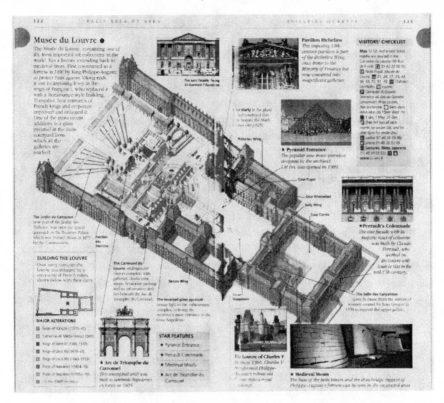

*Figure 3.7   A page from a Dorling-Kindersley guide to Paris: description of the Louvre
(Eyewitness Travel: Paris, 2007, pp122-123); used by permission*

tickets is in italics. Two extracts from this list (one from the beginning; the other from the end) that shows the contents of the inset in close-up are the following:

Map 12 E2. Automatic ticket booths are located in the Carrousel du Louvre (99 Rue de Rivoli). 🔲 *01 40 20 50 50.* 🅜 *Palais Royal, Musée du Louvre.* ▬ *21, 24, 27, 39, 48,*

▬ *Lectures, films, concerts (01 40 20 55 55).* 🔲 🔲 www.louvre.fr

Here we can see how what is essentially a single text paragraph is sprinkled liberally with visual icons. In a complete list of the base units for this page, therefore, each of these attributes and values would receive its own base unit. We omit this detail here because the paragraph in fact operates entirely in the text-flow typographic mode and so does not extend our discussion of layout at this point.

That the layout of the inset does *not* use spatial cues is, however, interesting in its own right; indeed, this non-spatial presentational form for table-like information in which a sequence of attributes and their values is presented as continuous text receives some rather harsh words in Twyman (1982). But for the present case, it can be argued that there are some good reasons for taking this solution rather than using a table. First, the inset contains only supportive 'enabling' information for the visitor rather than factual information about the building or site being visited, which is the main rhetorical focus of the page: this non-prominent rhetorical role then requires that the information presented should not become too dominant in the page layout. Second, many of the pages in the book contain insets of precisely this style and form: the reader therefore can readily become acclimatised to this presentational strategy for this book and, indeed, for the entire series of books produced by the publisher in this genre. And third, much of the function of defining the *access* structure for the information in this inset that would be communicated spatially within a table is here effected in any case by the visually prominent icons. The regular order adopted for the information presented across the pages of the book further supports this access structure.

The inset therefore functions rather well for precisely its current communicative purpose: further information of a detailed (e.g., phone numbers) or generic (e.g., is there food, wheelchair access, and so on) nature can be accessed by the reader if he or she requires it, *without* having that information at all prominent or accessible on the page when the reader does not require it. In a sense, this treatment makes information available on demand in a manner entirely analogous to hyperlinks in a web-page: the practiced reader is able to ignore the information until it becomes useful, and then to locate the required component with some efficiency. We will return to questions of the relation between communicative intentions and selected layout in Chapter 4, but we can already see from this example how it is essential to consider layout decisions and the deployment of visual-spatial resources with respect to the rhetorical purpose and genre/production constraints of their contextualising documents rather than in isolation.

Turning now to the rest of the spread, Table 3.3 sets out the base units for the remaining parts of the page. This is similar to the listing we gave above for the Gannet page, but with additional information concerning the *type* of material found in each unit—i.e., whether the unit is a photograph, icon, text and so on. This is not strictly necessary for base units because the information is in any case properly maintained in the layout structure—

U001	T	Musée …	U040	D	A.d. Triomph	U079	L	connector
U002	I	reversed 1	U041	I	star	U080	T	Sully Wing
U003	I	semicircle	U042	T	A.d. Triomph	U081	L	connector
U004	T	the Louvre	U043	T	paragraph	U082	T	Cour Carée
U005	D	the Louvre	U044	T	Denon Wing	U083	L	connector
U006	T	The Jardin	U045	L	connector	U084	T	Cour Napoléan
U007	T	paragraph	U046	T	glass pyramid	U085	L	connector
U008	L	connector	U047	L	connector	U086	p	the Louvre
U009	B	framing	U048	B	coloured	U087	T	Charles V
U010	T	Building	U049	T	Star features	U088	T	paragraph
U011	T	paragraph	–	–		U089	I	semicircle
U012	d	Louvre plan	U051	I	star	U090	B	coloured
U013	T	Alterations	U052	T	entrance	U091	T	Checklist
U014	I	square	U053	L	horizontal	–	–	
U015	T	1515–47	U054	I	star	U093	T	checklist
U016	I	square	U055	T	Colonnade	U094	P	Colonnade
U017	T	1560	U056	L	horizontal	U095	T	Colonnade
U018	I	square	U057	I	star	U096	I	star
U019	T	1589–1610	U058	T	M. moats	U097	T	paragraph
U020	I	square	U059	L	horizontal	U098	L	connector
U021	T	1610–43	U060	I	star	U099	T	The Salle
U022	I	square	U061	T	A.d. Triomphe	U100	T	paragraph
U023	T	1643–1715	U062	P	P.Richelieu	U101	L	connector
U024	I	square	U063	L	connector	U102	P	M. moats
U025	T	1804–15	U064	T	P.Richelieu	U103	I	star
U026	I	square	U065	T	paragraph	U104	T	M. moats
U027	T	1852–70	U066	T	Cour Marly	U105	T	paragraph
U028	I	square	U067	L	connector	U106	T	Paris
U029	T	1989	U068	T	paragraph	U107	L	frame
U030	T	Pavillion	U069	T	Richelieu W.	U108	T	122
U031	L	connector	U070	L	connector	U109	T	Tuileries
–	–		U071	P	pyramid	U110	L	frame
–	–		U072	I	star	U111	T	123
–	–		U073	T	entrance	U112	L	connector
U035	P	E. Facade	U074	T	paragraph	U113	T	paragraph
U036	T	E. Facade	U075	L	connector			
U037	T	Carrousel	U076	T	Cour Puget			
U038	L	connector	U077	L	connector			
U039	T	paragraph	U078	T	Cour Khorsabad			

Table 3.3   Base units of the Louvre two-page spread.
Key B:box, D:drawing, d:diagram, I:icon, L:line, P:photograph, p:painting, T:text.

it is helpful here for identifying just which unit is being talked about in each case. For subsequent reference, we also number the units and label them with the prefix 'U' in order to distinguish them from units introduced within other layers; the numbering generally runs from top-to-bottom and left-to-right although nothing follows from this.[5] Even with all the textual contributions collapsed to the granularity of paragraphs, this explicit description makes it clear that there are a considerable number of units to be considered in this spread. Nevertheless, identifying and listing them is quite straightforward and simply follows the rules for individuating units described above.

This list of base units labels the elements on the page so that we can discuss both their typographic realisation and their participation as meaning-carrying elements at other levels of analysis. For ease of reference, and again only for purposes of illustration for this first detailed example, we set out in Figure 3.8 the Louvre page showing graphically precisely where the most prominent base units are to be found. This lets us see directly which unit corresponds to which part of the page as this may not always be completely clear from our descriptions in the table, which have been abridged in order to save space.

3.3.2 The layout of the Louvre

The next stage of analysis is to identify the layout units and to organise these within an appropriate layout structure. Here we look for primarily visual groupings that can be motivated perceptually. In the present case, this combines proximity and separation, similarity (e.g., the repeated motif of photograph, bold header and text paragraph), connection (expressed explicitly by connecting lines), framing (with boxes and colour), relative size and closure.

Visual and spatial prominence let us start naturally with the 3D drawing in perspective of the Louvre. This 'brings with it' several closely associated elements: including the text and title upper-left, because of its wrap around behaviour with respect to the left edge of the drawing, and the smaller callouts surrounding the drawing, because of their connecting lines and proximity. No collection of these latter elements can themselves be organised

---

[5]The page number and running heads of the two pages are the last units listed (apart from an additional connecting line and the text paragraph associated with unit U046 that were left out on the first run through the numbering process!). There are also some gaps in the numbering—this is because of a contrastive analysis of the layout that we carried out with respect to this page and an earlier version of the same page from the 1993 edition of the guide. The units that occur in both versions have the same numbers. We do not discuss this contrastive analysis here, however.

Figure 3.8   *Base units of the Louvre page shown for ease of reference using the page as background. Some of the labels for the connecting lines have been omitted here to improve the readability of the diagram.*

into larger configurations because of their mutual lack of proximity (apart from to the drawing) and whitespace framing. The first larger, composite layout element to be formed is therefore that consisting just of the drawing, the overview text and the callouts.

We can distinguish some further detail among the callouts, however, by applying considerations of similarity and difference. On this page there are in fact three classes of callouts. The first class is made up of single bold type text fragments, naming parts of the building: e.g., 'Pavillon des Sessions' (U030), 'Denon Wing' (U044), 'Cour Puget' (U076)—all shown ringed in Figure 3.8 for ease of reference. The second class consists of a combination of a text fragment in bold type within a text paragraph, as in U006 and U007 (on the left, halfway down the page):

> **The Jardin du Carrousel**, now part of the Jardin des Tuileries, was once the grand approach to the Tuileries Palace, which was burned down in 1871 by the Communards.

This is an example where we require an embedded base unit for the bold segment as described above. Other units showing this structure

layout unit	base units	children	layout unit	base units	children
L1.1.1	*composite*	L1.1.1.1– L1.1.1.14	L1.1.1.3a L1.1.1.3b	U037 U039	– –
L1.1.1.1	U005	–			
			L1.1.1.4	U044	–
L1.1.1.2	*composite*	L1.1.1.2a L1.1.1.2b	L1.1.1.5	*composite*	L1.1.1.5a L1.1.1.5b
L1.1.1.2a	U006	–			
L1.1.1.2b	U007	–	L1.1.1.5a L1.1.1.5b	U046 U113	– –
L1.1.1.3	*composite*	L1.1.1.3a L1.1.1.3b			
			and so on		

Table 3.4   Extract of the correspondence between layout units and base units

are U037+U039, U046+U113, and U099+U100 (moving left to right below the central drawing). These first two classes of callout are not distinguished spatially, however, and so there is little motivation for giving them a distinct status in the layout structure.

This gives a grouping of base units into layout units as begun in Table 3.4. And, with these layout units defined, we can add in further information concerning their realisation. We have already mentioned the 3D drawing of the Louvre that constitutes L1.1.1.1. We also have the bold type small text of the 'a' units in the table and the normal type small text of the 'b' units that make up all the small callouts. This is how we capture the generalisation that there are two subclasses of callouts being considered here: L1.1.1.2, L1.1.1.3, L1.1.1.5 and so on that contain a header, and L1.1.1.4 and so on that do not. These distinctions are also supported by considering other pages of the book where the first class is sometimes present without the other. The bold elements in these callouts give more weight to the information being given and also strengthen their role as access elements.

The third class is more complex and requires composite layout elements combining photographs/graphics, a bold type header and a descriptive paragraph. In contrast to the previous class, the header here is not grammatically integrated into the paragraph. An example is the Pavillon Richelieu callout consisting of U062, U064, U065 connected to the Louvre drawing with the connecting line U063 (righthand page, upper left). We capture the internal structure of these more complex elements with specifications of the form:

layout unit	base units	children
L1.1.3	*composite*	L1.1.3a L1.1.3b L1.1.3c
L1.1.3a	U062	–
L1.1.3b	U064	–
L1.1.3c	U065	–

There turn out to be three variants of this class also: the form shown in this table, which also applies to the layout elements corresponding to the group {U086, U087, U088} (righthand page, lower left); the form identical to this apart from an additional base unit corresponding to a star icon, as shown in the groups linked to the photographs or drawings: U071, U094, U102, U040; and the isolated case U035 and U036 (lefthand page, upper right).

This latter case is interesting in that it represents one possible weak spot in the layout: it is actually just an unattached picture with caption. Its structure is different to all the other picture+text combinations, it has no connecting line indicating that it is a callout and, when we come to look at its contents, we find that it actually depicts a part of the Louvre that is on the mid-right-hand side of the page rather than anywhere in the vicinity of its own units. There are enough signals present to identify its distinct status but it is questionable whether this would be visible at first glance to a reader. This means that we could find misreadings at this point—leading, for example, to a potential visitor approaching the Louvre from the north (which is following convention in this case also towards the top of the page) and being surprised not to see the part of the building depicted in U035: 'the East facade'.

The key to its interpretation is only found in the context of the book as a whole. In the introduction there is a description of how the diagrams and complex spreads presented in the book are to be read. And there we find the explanation (itself presented as a callout with reference to a miniature example of a typical page):

The facade of each major sight is shown to help you spot it quickly. [p7]

This works well on many pages of the book precisely because in their case another layout structure is more likely. We can see this clearly from Figure 3.9, where a collection of these alternatives taken from other places in the book are shown.

Most of these pages construct a layout structure in which it is most likely that the photograph of the facade is one of several components combining with the *overview text* and not with satellitic callouts. The three examples to the left of the figure all have the facade photograph to the right of the overview text: this is the situation illustrated in the book's own explanation given above. The two examples in the central column show a further variant

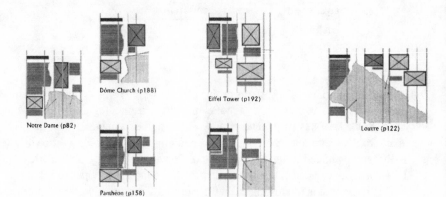

Dôme Church (p188)

Eiffel Tower (p192)

Notre Dame (p82)

Louvre (p122)

Panthéon (p158)

Arc de Triomphe (p208)

Figure 3.9   *Example layout positioning of the 'facade' information from several pages of the Dorling-Kindersley* Eyewitness Travel: Paris *guide. Text elements are shown by horizontal lined areas, graphics and photographs by diagonally lined rectangles; the facade photograph of each page is shown as a dark rectangle and other photographs and graphic material as light rectangles.*

(not explained in the book's introduction), where the facade photograph is *inset* within the overview text. In these cases both photograph and text fall under the title for the text/page and so there is no problem with creating a single layout unit including both the text and the facade photograph.

In our Louvre page, however, shown to the right of the figure, we see the problematic configuration caused by the facade photograph being 'pushed away' from the overview text by the intervening central drawing of the Louvre as a whole. This almost explicitly sets up a framing in which the facade photograph is grouped with the other photographic callouts rather than with the overview text. Given that such new groupings can always arise by chance when elements are moved around a page design, it is virtually impossible to guarantee that such unwanted side-effects are ruled out. We will see several more examples of this in a range of different document types in our analyses in later chapters.[6]

Even though we suggest here that the layout of the current example encourages a misinterpretation, strictly speaking we can only really provide

---

[6]There is also the question of whether it is even worthwhile ruling them out—for example, if the cost of checking for them is high and their consequences for readers low. Here we are simply drawing attention to methods for revealing them; the separate question of what, if anything, should be done about them, we will leave for later.

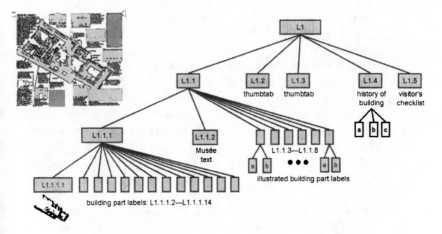

Figure 3.10   Layout structure for the Louvre page according to the GeM model

this kind of analysis when we have *first* provided our explicit account of the intended communicative functions of the layout elements. That is, in this case, we need to characterise the function of the layout element expressing the facade in order to recognise that it needs a different treatment to the other layout elements giving photographic information about the Louvre. Otherwise there are no grounds for rejecting its inclusion within the same layout element. This level of information will be provided by the GeM rhetorical structure layer and so we will return to this and several more extensive examples of potential misinterpretations in our discussion in Chapter 4. For now we simply note that the explicit characterisation of the layout structure we have given makes it difficult to overlook such problematic cases—which is one strong motivation for providing it.

The next layer of layout structure for the Louvre spread as a whole is then to add in the loosely attached 'Visitors' checklist', 'Star features' and 'Building the Louvre' insets, the navigation marks upper right and upper left, and the page number and section information. The complete hierarchical layout structure for the spread that results is shown graphically in Figure 3.10. Again we omit here some of the finer detail discussed above in order to reduce the complexity of the diagram. We also show in the upper left of the figure a view of visual prominence on the page as suggested by filtering that supports the layout provided.

The full specification of these layout units includes information about how they are realised, or physically expressed, on the page. We have already mentioned some of these features above: the titles associated with texts and photographs are in bold, for example. This information also, as suggested, allows us to draw out similarities and generalisations across layout units that are not expressed in terms of the hierarchical layout structure. Such similarities often capture the fact that distinct layout units are serving a similar rhetorical function, even if they are not clearly members of some overarching layout element. Thus, for example, we in fact can identify two distinct classes among the sibling layout elements accompanying the drawing of the Louvre, and three distinct classes among the siblings accompanying the layout element above this. Since these classes are not expressed spatially, it would not be appropriate to add this generalisation into the layout structure itself.

Now we have to specify the final aspect of the layout organisation by defining the area model for the spread that captures just *where* the layout units are positioned on the page. In this case, we will proceed in two steps as the layout is relatively complex in this respect. To begin, the layout is essentially centered without polarisation. That is, the elements of the page are spread around the central element given by the drawing of the Louvre. There is no top-bottom or left-right organisation beyond the minimal structuring imposed by the Western default reading path. Picking up again comments from the previous chapter (cf. Section 2.2.2), we do not see here any particular additional utility in providing this with a given-new or ideal-real interpretation at this point—indeed, it appears to be *access* and *navigation* information that provides the strongest functional motivations in this genre. It is not the case, however, that the page exhibits no symmetry since the virtual canvas of the spread conforms to a grid in the manner described in Section 2.5.1 of the previous chapter.

This grid is suggested in Figure 3.11; it offers three columns for each page of the spread, organised symmetrically across the central binding and with the outer column slightly narrower than the inner two. The fact that this is a true grid, rather than an opportune alignment of the 'extra information' insets on this page, can be ascertained by examining the other pages of the book—particularly those spreads which are mostly textual. In these cases there is an explicit 6 column spread, often with framing lines separating the columns. From the book as a whole we can also determine a two column grid superimposed on the three column grid: this is the orienting line shown in the middle of each page in the figure. The two-column variant is used for those pages

Figure 3.11
A grid for the Louvre page

which present an introductory text for an entire section: the paragraphs of these introductions are then set in two columns rather than in three columns, clearly showing their different communicative function. This grid organisation is a common feature of this entire series of travel guides. For the current spread, then, we have a straightforward *column grid* in operation, despite the superficial impression of freedom given by the additional placement of elements around the Louvre drawing.

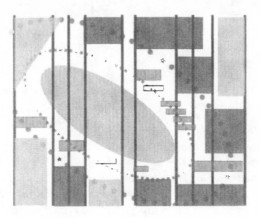

Figure 3.12   The complex area model for the Louvre page, combining a geometric shape and a vertical grid

Combining these two contributions give us the complex area model shown graphically in Figure 3.12. This composes the vertical grid with a centralised geometric figure with two 'rings' running around it: an 'inner' ring and an 'outer'. This illustrates one of the more advanced grid-like organisations that we suggested in the previous chapter: rather than a rectangular grid defining horizontal and vertical alignment possibilities, we have here the geometric shape approximating to the shape of the Louvre outline defining two concentric bands of alignment possibilities. These bands provide approximate placement opportunities for selected layout elements which can then be pushed left or right according to the virtual canvas constraints imposed by the vertical grid. Allowing several of these elements, particularly those combining photographs and text, to be slightly wider than the vertical grid's modules adds even further to the impression of a 'free-ranging' layout supportive of the centralised organisation while still ensuring that elements are spread relatively uniformly over the page area.

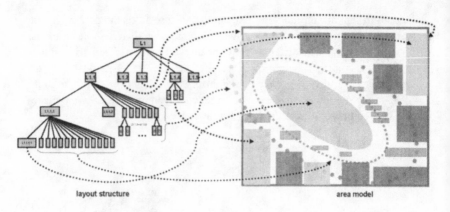

layout structure   area model

*Figure 3.13   Correspondence between the layout structure and the area model for the
Louvre page*

The last step is then to bring the layout structure and the area model
into correspondence. This is shown graphically in Figure 3.13 in the same
manner that we did above for the Gannet page. This captures sufficient
spatial detail to keep apart the distinct functional contributions made by the
various elements, which in this spread are considerable. In particular, we
are able to distinguish elements that share functionality by virtue of their
spatial proximity and grouping (layout structure) and those elements that
can be identified by virtue of their specific placement within the area model
(i.e., central, inner or outer ring).

3.4   Conclusion

In this chapter we have defined and illustrated the 'lowest' layers of the
GeM model. Specifications here decompose any page-based multimodal
document into parts and explicitly state how these parts are organised visually to create a layout structure for the pages of the document. All of the
layers of analysis of the GeM model that follow, assume that the base and
layout layers are in place as described here.

4

The Rhetorical Organisation of Multimodal Documents

We have seen in the previous chapter that it is possible to characterise aspects of the typographical, visual and spatial organisation of multimodal documents by decomposing them into various kinds of 'parts' exhibiting particular properties and structures. At several points in the discussion we needed to refer to the function or purpose of those parts and their spatial combinations. All multimodal approaches assume that *combinations* of elements are meaningful—combinations signal meaningful relationships between elements that would not be available to those elements in isolation. To reveal the workings of this process, we need to define methods for exploring how configurations of elements take on significance over and above their spatial proximity or visual similarity or difference. This is the task begun in this chapter.

One common approach to describing the functions communicated by a combination of distinct elements on the page is to employ notions of *rhetorical organisation*. We saw something of this above in our discussion of automatic document production, particularly multimodal natural language generation (Section 2.5.3). Now we take this further and develop the next, more directly meaning-related component of the GeM model: the *rhetorical structure layer*. By means of a fine-grained theory of rhetorical structure, we can identify a broad range of meaning relations that can hold between and within page elements. In particular, we will see that rhetorical relations provide a powerful descriptive mechanism for laying bare just what meanings are carried by collections of elements in spatial juxtaposition within documents.

There has been widespread acceptance that some kind of rhetorical analysis can make an important contribution to our understanding of how multimodal documents mean for some time (cf. Lemke 1983, Thibault 1990, Schriver 1997, p322). There is still a considerable way to go, however, before such analysis can become both *detailed* and *analytically reliable*. To move us in this direction we adopt one particular account of rhetorical organisation called *Rhetorical Structure Theory* (commonly referred to as *RST*). RST is one of the most explicitly developed and frequently used of currently available linguistic approaches to explaining textual coherence. We will argue that extending this approach to encompass multimodal rhetorical organisation provides just the analytic hold that we require. The underlying intuition is that just as segments of a text contribute to that text's coherence in systematic and specifiable ways, so can segments of a multimodal document, involving pictures, diagrams and texts, be related in an analogous manner also.

4.1　Rhetoric and multimodal documents: our starting points

The categories and techniques of traditional rhetoric (cf. Simon 1978, Harrell and Linkugel 1978) have frequently been applied in multimodal analysis (cf. Gaede 1981, Durand 1987, Forceville 1996, Messaris 1997, Van Mulken 2003, Amouzadeh and Tavangar 2004, among others). In such work, we see rhetoric in its old sense as the 'art of persuasion'—i.e., it is considered how multimodal documents achieve particular persuasive or attention-getting effects on their readers (as, for example, in advertisements). The use that we will make of rhetoric here is somewhat different. We are less concerned with an analysis of visual *persuasion* than with an analysis of communicative 'effectiveness' as such. We want to develop an account by which we can identify the particular functional contributions made by the elements of a document to the intended communicative purposes of that document as a whole—and we want to do this regardless of mode and as reliably as possible.

These aims show several similarities to those of accounts of the relations between image and text. Some approaches here also draw extensively on traditional rhetoric (e.g., Marsh and White 2003), others draw on extensions of relations originally proposed in linguistic treatments of 'connection'— both grammatical (cf. Martinec and Salway 2005, Kong 2006) and discoursal/semantic (cf. van Leeuwen 1991), and others still draw on Barthes's (1977b) seminal semiotic work on text-image relations (cf. Schriver 1997, pp412-428). Combinations and extensions within and across all of these approaches are common. This entire area of research is very relevant to our aims in this chapter, but space precludes a detailed comparison and critique of proposals at this point. Instead we will highlight just one very general reoccurring problem common to all current discussions.

This problem consists in the fact that the organisational structures proposed are typically *single relations between elements*: for example, between a picture and the text functioning as its caption, or between a map and its legend. Although it is generally assumed that these relations can also hold between 'collections' of elements, precisely how such collections are to be identified remains unaddressed. As a consequence, analyses collapse to a listing of text-image relations drawing together any elements, and any collections of elements, on a page that 'appear' connected. There will almost always be very many such relations to find, but simply pointing them out is insufficient. Precisely our aim of distinguishing the effective from the ineffective (not to mention the downright wrong) remains untouched by such procedures. For this we need a far more explicit and, above all, constraining notion of *structure*.

This need for structure, which we will demonstrate in our examples below, is also the reason why we cannot draw on one further type of approach to relating information across modes now commonly pursued—that based on so-called multimodal *cohesion*. The notion of 'cohesion' is taken from linguistic models—such as Halliday and Hasan (1976)—and provides a scheme that brings different elements of a text into relation independently of any structural organisation that that text and its elements may exhibit. Cohesion sets in whenever the *interpretation* of one element depends on another regardless of structure. Standard linguistic examples are reference, lexical repetition and other lexical semantic relationships, such as hyponomy. Thus, for example, a text that introduces 'a dog' and then subsequently refers to 'the animal', 'the dog', 'it' and so on can be interpreted as establishing a web of cohesive *ties* that cross-cut the structural aspects of the text.

When applied multimodally, cohesion-based approaches generally consider the verbal and graphical modes to be contributing more or less equally to a jointly constructed communicative inter-relationship. And, as with the linguistic views of cohesion, such a relation can hold across units independently of 'structural' organisation amongst the elements of the page. In these frameworks it is therefore relatively common to find individual phrases from a larger linguistic text being brought into connection with individual image elements somewhere else on the page. Analyses of this kind have been pursued in many multimodal explorations that start from text linguistics (cf. Spillner 1982, Royce 2007, Habel and Acartürk 2006, and others) and can become extremely sophisticated. Stöckl (1997, 2004*a*), for example, develops an account that combines notions of cohesion, aspects of Gaede's work, approaches to style within German text linguistics, and the visual semiotics of Barthes and others in order to carry out a detailed empirical investigation of the textual-visual 'style' of advertisements. Approaches of these kinds often tell us useful and interesting things about the pages analysed but, without structure, their capability to go beyond surface descriptions is severely limited.

A further final problem with all previous approaches in this area is that they are essentially informal: there is no guarantee inherent in the methodology that will force a designer to find flaws if he or she does not look for them. And, as documents become ever more complex, being sure that all the 'invoked rhetorical clusters' or element combinations are indeed rhetorically appropriate and motivated becomes a complex task in its own right. It is then, in the last resort, not clear whether such accounts take us much further than the informal application of traditional rhetorical categories or skilled design practice. With our application of Rhetorical Structure Theory, we aim to sharpen our analytic tools considerably.

4.2   A brief introduction to *Rhetorical Structure Theory*

Rhetorical Structure Theory (hereafter RST: Mann and Thompson 1986, 1988) is one of the very few approaches to rhetorical 'effectiveness' that has a sufficiently explicit view of discourse structure to make strong claims about adequacy and appropriateness. It began its life as an attempt to explain the coherence exhibited by everyday normal texts. This coherence presents something of a mystery. Although natural texts apparently achieve communicative goals of various kinds and exhibit properties of 'well-structuredness', i.e., they are made up of parts which 'hang together' more or less well as arguments, as presentations, as stories, and so on, they achieve this *without* necessarily signalling the intended relations between their parts explicitly. They therefore regularly communicate *more* than is superficially there.

Consider, for example, the textual sequence:

He explains things well. He'll make a good teacher.

In order to understand why these sentences have been produced as a 'coherent' sequence, we need to see them as being related in some way. In particular, unless we can see that what is actually being communicated is most likely something very close to:

Because he explains things well, I think he'll make a good teacher.

we will simply not have understood what has been said. The first sentence is being given as *evidence* for the statement made in the second sentence. The kind of 'additional' meaning at issue here is then by no means an extra optional 'reading between the lines': it is a necessary component of having understood the text at all.

Mann and Thompson describe this phenomenon as one in which certain sequences of textual material make *additional assertions* over and above those explicitly made in the text itself (Mann and Thompson 1985, 1986). Moreover, these assertions have an essentially *relational* character—for example, in the present case, the additional assertion is precisely that of the evidence relation *between* the first and second sentence.

We can readily find other such sequences where different relations need to be asserted in order to explain the observed coherence of the sequence as a whole. For example, in the text extract:

The lorry veered off the road. The brakes had failed.

there is an overwhelming tendency to see the second sentence as an *explanation* for the first, even though there is no explicit linguistic cue, such as 'because', to show this. Another kind of relation commonly asserted implicitly is the temporal *sequence* that holds between sentences in simple narrative. Uncovering just how many of these kinds of relations there are and what range of meanings they cover is therefore an important aspect of explaining text coherence.

4.2.1 The RST rhetorical relations

Non-linguistic approaches to text interpretation are often ready to accept that we know that there is, for example, an explanation relationship holding between some segments, or a sequence, etc. because this 'somehow' makes the text make sense. Linguistically this is extremely problematic. If readers or hearers of texts were to consider an open-ended set of hypotheses based on their overall knowledge of the world for each pair of sentences encountered, finding interpretations would demand a considerable investment of reasoning power. The speed, reliability and consistency of the interpretations that people in fact make when understanding text do not support such an unconstrained approach. Developers of linguistically-informed approaches to discourse, RST included, therefore argue that there must be a body of particular discourse-related information that constrains just how parts of a text can be related to one another. Readers and hearers are then guided efficiently to a narrow range of possible alternatives building on a variety of clues which *are* present in the text.[1]

RST has been one of the most significant theoretical and practical advances in recent years towards making this kind of meaningful patterning accessible to linguistic analysis. On the basis of a sample of natural texts, Mann and Thompson originally defined a set of around 25 *rhetorical relations*. These relations, now termed *classical RST*, are set out and defined in detail in several papers, most prominent of which are Mann and Thompson (1986, 1988) and Mann, Matthiessen and Thompson (1992). Crucially, relationships of this kind also hold between larger portions of text; they are not exclusively relations between individual sentences. This leads to a *recursive* definition of rhetorical structure: rhetorical relations relate not the individual sentences themselves, but the *rhetorical intent* of the text portions over which the rhetorical relations hold—and these can correspond to individual sentences, units smaller than sentences, and larger units, such as when one entire segment of a text may serve to explain, or elaborate, some other extended segment. The particular sequences of text corresponding to such segments are termed *text spans*.

The structure is also recursive in that each part, beginning with the text as a whole, is organised internally in the same way: namely, as a dependency structure where one of the subparts is seen as the most important, or *nuclear*, component at that level in structure, and to which the other subparts, called *satellites*, stand in a dependency relationship. The importance of a nuclear element is defined in terms of its contribution to the rhetorical goals of the text as a whole. Each rhetorical dependency relation between a nucleus and its satellites is associated with specific assertions that capture the intention lying behind the relation. These intentions define *applicability conditions* that govern the situations where the relation may occur.

Two kinds of rhetorical relations are defined: *asymmetric* relations, where only one of the related rhetorical units is singled out as the rhetorical head, or nucleus, and *symmetric relations*, also termed *multinuclear*, where all of the related units are considered equally important. Examples of multinuclear relations are *contrast*, which draws a relation between two equally important elements, and *sequence*, which brings together an arbitrary number of elements into a temporal or other organisational sequence. In neither case can we pick one of the related elements arbitrarily as being more important than the others. A listing of the main RST relations along with the

---

[1] The state of the art in formal descriptions of this view is the model described in Asher and Lascarides (2003). See also Danlos (2007) for a useful comparison of several distinct types of discourse structure.

ASYMMETRIC RHETORICAL RELATIONS (abbreviated)

Relation Name	Nucleus	Satellite
Background	text whose understanding is being facilitated	text for facilitating understanding
Circumstance	text expressing the events or ideas occurring in the interpretive context	an interpretive context of situation or time
Concession	situation affirmed by author	situation which is apparently inconsistent but also affirmed by author
Elaboration	basic information	additional information
Enablement	an action	information intended to aid the reader in performing an action
Evaluation	a situation	an evaluative comment about the situation
Evidence	a claim	information intended to increase the reader's belief in the claim
Interpretation	a situation	an interpretation of the situation
Justify	text	information supporting the writer's right to express the text
Motivation	an action	information intended to increase the reader's desire to perform the action
Cause	a situation	another situation which causes the nuclear situation
Result	a situation	another situation which is caused by the nuclear situation
Preparation	text to be presented	text which prepares the reader to expect and interpret the text to be presented
Purpose	an intended situation	the intent behind the situation
Restatement	a situation	a reexpression of the situation
Solutionhood	a situation or method supporting full or partial satisfaction of the need	a question, request, problem, or other expressed need
Summary	text	a short summary of that text

SYMMETRIC RHETORICAL RELATIONS (MULTINUCLEAR)

Relation Name	Span	Other Span(s)
Contrast	one alternate	the other alternate
Joint	(unconstrained)	(unconstrained)
List	an item	a next item
Sequence	an item	a next item

Table 4.1   List of RST relations with the constraints they impose on their respective nuclei and satellites (cf. http://www.sfu.ca/rst/01intro.html)

main messages carried by the nucleus and satellites of each relation is given in Table 4.1.

4.2.2   The RST rhetorical structure

A complete analysis of a text then consists of a hierarchical rhetorical structure defined by rhetorical dependency links between structural parts. The smallest parts of the structure correspond directly to portions of the analysed text. The structure is not allowed to reorder these portions or to leave portions out, which is a strong constraint on the kinds of rhetorical analyses that may be considered.[2]

We can illustrate this very briefly with the following constructed text:

> In the event of fire, open the doors by pressing the red button.
> Then leave the building.

The RST analysis of this text is illustrated in Figure 4.1 using the standard graphical representation employed for RST structures; horizontal lines denote text spans, vertical lines identify nuclei, and curved arrows show the rhetorical relations. Here we can see that the analysis first divides the text into two 'text spans': the CIRCUMSTANTIAL information that defines 'an interpretive context of situation or time' (cf. Table 4.1) and the rest. This rest is then itself recursively divided further in terms of a SEQUENCE (first one thing, then another). The first element in this embedded sequence itself consists of an ENABLEMENT, where some subsidiary information is provided (e.g., in this case: 'by pressing the red button') that can make the performance of the action expressed in the nucleus (e.g., 'open the door') easier or possible. The second element of the sequence is the simple text span directly demanding the action of leaving the building.

A text is deemed coherent and 'well-formed' according to RST when it is possible to construct at least one single overarching hierarchical rhetorical structure for the text as a whole. This structure must obey the organisational principles set out by RST, most important of which are the applicability conditions defined by the theory for each rhetorical relation. If no such single structure can be found, then the text is considered problematic in some sense—perhaps due to be being written by a language learner, or bad editing, or just poor composition. Most natural texts, however, will support at least one complete analysis and uncovering that analysis—i.e., making the rhetorical relations involved explicit—has been found to be a significant step towards understanding how texts achieve the effects that they do.

---

[2]Some indeed consider this to be *too* strong (cf. Danlos 2007, Wolf and Gibson 2005).

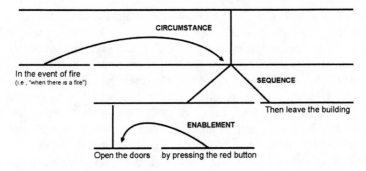

Figure 4.1 The graphical representation of the RST analysis of the 'text': "In the event of fire, open the doors by pressing the red button. Then leave the building."

RST is nowadays used for a variety of tasks, ranging from linguistic text interpretation to computational applications in language production and automatic analysis. The approach continues to be developed by text linguists, who have applied it to a much broader range of texts and languages than the original starting point of Mann and Thompson. Examples and further pointers can be found on the RST website (cf. Table 4.1) and in introductions (cf. Bateman and Delin 2006, Taboada and Mann 2006a,b). In short, the account has proved itself to be a stable and solid contribution to our understanding of textual organisation and so offers a good foundation for the further extension to multimodal 'coherence' that we now take up.

4.3   The move to multimodal RST: the GeM rhetorical layer

One aspect of the theory that RST deliberately leaves open is the selection of minimal analytical unit—i.e., just what the *text spans* that appear at the leaves of a rhetorical structure can be. Mann and Thompson state that this may vary depending on the purposes for which an analysis is undertaken; it may be fixed as sentences, as grammatical clauses, or as entire paragraphs. This freedom turns out to be useful for us here because it suggests the possibility of completely different kinds of 'text span': in particular, we can explore the use of spans that are not made up of text at all but which consist of *graphical* elements that also contribute to a text's overall coherence.

The starting point for this direction was work on multimodal information presentation systems. Such systems automatically present information coordinated across several modalities, typically combining speech, text, diagrams and animation (cf. Maybury 1993, Bunt and Beun 2001). Most significant of early research here was that of André and colleagues (André 1995), who explored from the outset multimodal extensions to Rhetorical Structure Theory for coordinating information presentation. This basic approach was subsequently adopted by many researchers and has been widely incorporated in document production systems (such as, for example, Feiner and McKeown 1993, André and Rist 1993, Stock 1993, Rutledge, Bailey, van Ossenbruggen, Hardman and Geurts 2000). Surprisingly little of the original RST specification needed to be changed and, since then, this approach has shown itself to offer a valuable angle on how the various components of multimodal documents can be combined. In this section, therefore, we sketch this extension and then draw attention to some of the problems still needing to be resolved.

4.3.1   André's extension of RST

In addition to providing a model that could explain the coherence of connected texts, a further intention behind Mann's original formulation of RST was to contribute to computational text planning systems that could be used for automatic natural language text generation. As we saw above in Section 2.5.3, RST has indeed since established itself as one of the standard mechanisms adopted for this purpose. This use of RST relies on an interpretation of the applicability conditions defined for each relation as formal definitions of *plan operators* in the sense of formal planning in Artificial Intelligence (cf. Sacerdoti 1977). Such planning starts with a goal to be achieved, which is then successively refined by the automatic planning process into a sequence of actions that progressively move the world from some initial state to a state in which the desired goal has been achieved.

The states used in communicative goal planning typically involve states of affairs in the world and beliefs held by the speakers and hearers. The 'plan operators' then specify the *effects* on beliefs that particular types of actions and utterances bring about. Particular plan operators are selected according to their contribution to reaching the target goal. For text planning, therefore, communicative goals are broken down recursively into 'smaller' goals until these 'subgoals' reach a granularity appropriate for expression through single linguistic utterances. Each such utterance can then be produced as a step towards achieving the overall communicative goal of the speaker.

One can consider the hierarchical goal-subgoal structure created as a result of this process as corresponding to a completed RST tree with particular constraints attached to the leaves concerning the content and form of the linguistic material to be generated at those points. This use of RST is described in detail by Hovy (1993), and accessible introductions can also be found in, for example, Bateman and Zock (2003) and vander Linden (2000).

André (1995) took this basic approach and extended it for the automatic generation of multimodal presentations. In such systems rhetorical planning was used to combine both verbal and graphical elements into coherent multimodal documents. The constraints specified at the leaves of the RST structures created were accordingly assigned additional information for determining not only the content to be expressed but also the *mode* of that content. An example taken from one of the first systems developed using this mechanism is shown in Figure 4.2.

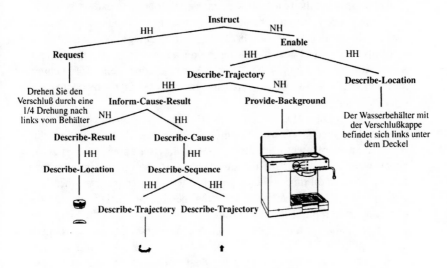

Figure 4.2   *A multimodal rhetorical structure diagram describing instructions for using a coffee machine; here: removing the cap of the water reservoir (André 1995, p55, Figure 3.10); used by permission of the author*

In André's variant of rhetorical structure we see some slightly different organisational principles to those adopted in traditional RST. The graphical notation is also slightly different. Each node in the tree can have two kinds of descendents, marked in the figure as HH ('Haupthandlung': main activity) and NH ('Nebenhandlung': supporting activity) (André 1995, pp42–43). This can be seen as a generalisation of the notions of nucleus and satellite introduced above, a generalisation made necessary by the fact that the plan tree does not only describe rhetorical relations. It also includes both 'larger scale' planning steps that need to be performed before the refinement into smaller goals reaches levels describable in terms of rhetorical structure as well as 'non-rhetorical' goals (in particular, *intentional goals* and *attentional goals*) that are also structured in terms of HH and NH relations.

The plan shown in the current example is part of a more complex presentation concerned with instructing a reader how to fill the water reservoir of a coffee machine. The overall communicative plan is then one of describing a sequence of steps that will enable the desired action to be performed. For the coffee machine explicitly modelled by André, this included four actions: lifting the lid, unscrewing the reservoir cap, pouring the water in, and putting the cap back. Each of these then requires communicative subgoals that instruct the reader how to carry them out. The extract shown in the figure concerns the second activity, namely removing the cap. It starts with the communicative goal INSTRUCT, first breaking this down into two subgoals: the central goal of getting the reader to turn the reservoir cap a quarter-turn to the left ("Drehen Sie den Verschluß durch eine 1/4 Drehung nach links…"), and a further supporting goal to ENABLE the reader to carry out that turning action.

A supporting ENABLE subgoal is clearly a good rhetorical choice for improving the effectiveness of the resulting document and one way of providing such an enablement is to make sure that the user knows where the cap is and what to do with it. This latter subgoal is itself accordingly refined further into several more specific enabling actions: in particular, there is a description of the precise movements that need to be carried out with the cap in order to remove it (DESCRIBE-TRAJECTORY) and of the precise location of the cap (DESCRIBE-LOCATION). The first of these is produced entirely graphically, the second by an accompanying text. Both are considered equally important for enabling the reader to carry out the top-level action and so are both designated HH.

The graphical presentation of the trajectory for moving the reservoir cap is particularly interesting and shows much of what we have seen above for RST analyses of text also being applied to combinations of graphic elements. First, supportive *background* information is presented in terms of a drawing-in-perspective of the coffee machine as a whole. Then, with respect to this background information, the nuclear content of informing the reader how to bring about the desired action (INFORM-CAUSE-RESULT) is itself broken down into a presentation of the cause (i.e., turning the cap to the left and then lifting it—a sequence of two DESCRIBE-TRAJECTORIES) and a supportive, satellite description of the result (i.e., the DESCRIBE-LOCATION representing the cap being positioned above and separate from its position on the coffee machine). Just as with a rhetorical description of a monomodal text, if the reader in the present case recognises the rhetorical relations holding between the graphical elements shown, then he or she will also have been enabled to carry out the nuclear action of removing the cap. Although each of the leaves of this tree, i.e., the corresponding 'spans', could instead have been expressed linguistically, presentations of *movement*, *paths* and *locations* are particularly well suited to the graphical mode. The final addition that André's approach brings is then precisely this possibility of selecting presentation modes for the spans presented. Thus, whereas a leaf of the RST tree may have been planned to require the *content* 'the cap is separated from the coffee machine', André's system is free to express this either verbally or graphically—for example by:

André's system does not in principle, moreover, restrict the kinds of presentation modalities that may be applied: she herself mentions the possibilities of language, graphics, animation, and 'mixed' presentations. Dedicated graphics modules are then responsible for producing and presenting the details of any graphic content selected and for physically laying out the rhetorical spans on the page or screen (cf. Section 2.5.3 and Section 5.3.1).

André discusses several further issues crucial for complete multimodal presentation generation and interpretation. These include, for example, the various kinds of 'anaphoric' relations (i.e., co-reference) that can hold across modalities, criteria for particular choices of modality, extensions into hypermedia, and several more. Each now has its own body of literature and is being actively pursued within the automatic multimodal generation research communities involved. While important, discussion of these would take us too far beyond the concerns of the present chapter. Our focus is precisely the utility that André demonstrates for treating multimodal compositions as *rhetorically* organised structures that combine modal contributions in the service of achieving communicative goals. Taking this further, and integrating it within our overall approach to multimodal documents, is therefore a useful step towards more detailed analytic treatments of such documents.

4.3.2 Problems with traditional multimodal RST

Although the multimodal extension to RST begun by André and colleagues has been very effective in describing the coherence of multimodal presentations, there are still some problems and gaps in the account when taken as a generic description of rhetorical function in multimodal documents as a whole. This has led us to make several further revisions of the account that, on the one hand, allow us to deal more effectively with a broader range of naturally occurring multimodal presentation issues and, on the other, make more contact with other approaches to multimodal coherence being pursued in other traditions.

The first concern to be raised is fundamental: it asks whether RST is an appropriate theoretical position for dealing with multimodality at all. As we saw above, RST was developed for traditional linear text and so, if one wants to apply RST to multimodal documents, new issues arise. There are substantial differences between how language is processed by speakers and hearers and how visual images are processed by their 'readers'. Both in terms of the component systems of the brain and in terms of the kinds of information that is perceived, we appear to be dealing with radically distinct semiotic modes. Kress (2003), for example, describes the difference between the mode of language and the mode of the image in terms of affordances, and argues that the two modes in fact support two distinct kinds of 'logic':

> "... whether I want to or not I have to use the possibilities given to me by a mode of representation to make my meaning. Whatever is represented in speech (or to some lesser extent in writing) inevitably has to bow to the logic of time and of sequence in time. The world represented in speech or writing is therefore (re)cast in an actual or quasi-temporal manner. The genre of the *narrative* is the culturally most potent formal expression of this. ... Whatever is represented in image has to bow, equally, to the logic of space, and to the simultaneity of elements in spatial arrangements. The world represented in image is therefore (re)cast in an actual or quasi-spatial manner." (Kress 2003, p2)

It is then by no means self-evident that the rhetoric of the one mode is at all comparable to the rhetoric of the other. And, consequently, it is not obvious that language and multimodal presentations can really be placed together under the same view of 'rhetorical' organisation.

This potential gulf in the foundational logics involved is then somewhat at odds with the fact that the generalisation of RST to multimodal presentations has traditionally involved rather little change to the basic framework. It appears possible for many documents to be assigned a rhetorical interpretation with relative ease. The fundamental question, *can* there be a rhetorical structure for a visual presentation, is then assumed to be answerable positively. We will suggest below that the reason for this discrepancy between the very different modes of representation involved and an apparent compatibility at the level of rhetorical organisation lies in the particular semiotic mode that has developed for 'page-like' presentations. According to Schriver (1997, p332), document designers are actually composing artefacts that are *intended* to function rhetorically—and when they do not achieve this, the resulting documents are judged less effective examples of good design. The *combination* of text and images within single 'page' layouts is therefore subject to what we will term *page-flow*—a semiotic mode that builds on distinct contributions and which *is* susceptible to rhetorical organisation.

A further motivation for considering RST as a basis for this kind of multimodal description is then the fact that RST analyses are *not* linear in the sense that they rely on a time-based development of verbal expression. Unlike some approaches to discourse which are very well suited to modelling the turn-by-turn development of a text or dialogue—such as, for example, Martin's (1992) *conjunctive relations* that van Leeuwen (1991) also applies to multimodal elements—RST looks at the text as a 'finished product'. That is, RST considers all the parts of a text as if they were simultaneously available for inspection. This has led to the framework receiving criticism as an effective treatment for verbal text, but it is precisely this feature of its design that makes it ideal for considering the simultaneous *visual* presentation at hand in multimodal text.

In addition, there are many points of *partial* overlap between the relations proposed by RST and other, independently derived accounts of image-text relations—such as those of Schriver, Barthes and others. In most cases such relations can be straightforwardly recast as traditional RST relations by accepting one constituting partner to be in a graphical mode rather than textual. The visual and verbal appear often to be quite comparable with respect to their rhetorical capabilities when brought together in the service of text-image combinations. It also appears that the relationships between text and image drawn in the Barthian tradition are not on their own sufficient for incisive analyses of how multimodal documents are functioning or, possibly more useful, not functioning. This is itself suggestive evidence that rhetorical accounts have an important role to play in dealing with multimodal communicative artefacts. RST is then certainly a promising approach for taking this further.

Nevertheless, even if a broad notion of rhetorical structure of the kind formalised in RST is assumed to be applicable to multimodal documents, there are further problems that need to be considered. Here we set out four that are particularly important and which have not been sufficiently addressed previously. The last of these leads to an extension of the framework that we have made in the GeM model and which we describe in more detail in the subsection following.

First, conventional RST builds on the sequentiality of text segments. Relations are only possible (with some minor exceptions) between consecutive segments/spans—this is the sequentiality assumption. With multimodal documents, the mutual spatial relations between the segments change from relations in a one-dimensional string-like object to relations over two-dimensional regions. This replaces the temporal logic of sequence with the spatial logic of simultaneity as Kress notes. Segments can therefore have not only a left and a right, but also an upper and a lower neighbouring segment; and, in general, one can imagine neighbouring segments in any direction. The simplest solution for applying RST to such documents while still maintaining its sequentiality assumption would be to impose a reading order on the documents' segments. This could then be used as the sequence required for the RST structure; a similar position appears to be adopted, for example, by Stöckl (1997). We saw in Section 2.3 above, however, that it is by no means straightforward to predict reading paths accurately and so the entailed reduction of the spatiality of the page to a temporal sequence is questionable. A more appropriate generalization of the sequentiality assumption, which we will adopt here, is to accept the spatiality of what is being analysed. For this, we restrict RST relations to pairs (sets) of document parts (segments/spans) which are *adjacent in any direction*. This can then be expressed with respect to our area model: spatial contiguity is present across area model cells when they are adjacent and within cells when elements are spatial neighbours.[3]

Second, the independent prominence of graphics in multimodal documents often makes it difficult to decide upon nuclearity in multimodal relations. Even when a graphical illustration is used, in some sense, to *rephrase* a text passage, it can be difficult to decide which of the two segments—the illustration or the text passage—is nuclear and which is the satellite. This is a particular problem of graphics-text relations brought about by the distinct *kinds* of information contributed by the distinct semiotic modes. It appears that we can actually find all combinations of image-text nuclearity assignments: for example, if we have an INTERPRETATION rhetorical relation, we know that there *will be* a nucleus and a satellite as stated in the definition, but we cannot state in advance which of those will be expressed as text and which as image: both are possible. To deal with this, therefore, we allow both assignments of nuclearity as necessary for individual cases. Moreover,

---

[3]In actually occuring documents one can find layouts where the rhetorical structure is obviously in conflict with this adjacency condition. Our hypothesis here is that this is generally possible, but that in such a case an explicit navigational element is required in addition so as to signal a rhetorical relation holding between the separated layout units.

we will use the *multinuclear* RESTATEMENT relation rather more frequently than previous approaches have in order to avoid forcing arbitrary nuclearity assignments.

Third, it has also been noted in previous approaches extending the notion of rhetorical structure to multimodality (e.g., André 1995, p49) that single illustrations can readily serve more than one purpose in one document and may therefore stand in an RST relation to more than one document segment/span at a time. This is often the case in instruction manuals, for example, where one and the same illustration can serve simultaneously (a) to identify a certain part of an object and (b) to show a certain action to be performed, or—another example—serve to identify several parts of a single object. Reusing a span at several places in a single RST structure is not permitted by the framework. André's (1995) solution is to extend RST structure to include acyclic graphs and not just tree structures—which is a considerable change to the framework. Taking this step means that most of the criteria by which alternative RST analyses can be distinguished from one another and motivated are no longer applicable. The view of structure resulting is then too weak to constrain document design and critique in the way that we are targeting. We prefer therefore to maintain a strict tree notion for the rhetorical structure of a document in order to maintain tighter criteria for evaluating whether an analysis may hold or not.

The *apparent* re-use of an image in more than role in a rhetorical organisation we then analyse in two ways. First, it may be the case that what is in fact being referred to, or used, in an image is not the image at large but particular elements in the image (cf. André 1995, p23). In which case, it is not true that the 'same' element is being used in more than one place in the rhetorical structure: instead particular *views* or *extracts* of the image are being presented. Second, an image is more susceptible than segments of texts to systematic 're-readings', by which a perspective shift is imposed on the image. We consider each perspective shift to provide a further possible element that can be placed in a rhetorical structure tree: thus, some material is 'transformed' to provide distinct instances, each of which can stand in a distinct position in the rhetorical structure. This means that we maintain the tree-like hierarchical organisation of the RST analysis by specifying and refining just what it means for elements to be the 'same' or not.

Finally, the fourth problematic area for a multimodal RST concerns the entire notion of what a multimodal rhetorical analysis can adopt as its minimal unit of analysis. Whereas for text analysis spans are generally restricted to clause or clause-like phrases, rhetorical relations holding across distinct semiotic modes open up several further significant possibilities, that we now describe.

4.3.3   Multimodal relationals: subnuclear elaboration

When we analyse documents that are freely combining semiotic modes in terms of the 'rhetorical' relations that hold the elements together and combine them into larger structures, it is often the case that these elements do not respect the criteria for minimal units adopted in traditional RST analysis.

We already see this in its simplest form when we consider 'macro-punctuation' such as that discussed in Section 2.5.3 above. For example, in the following extract we have a list with an initiating sentence fragment:

In the box are:
◇   three cordless handsets
◇   the base unit
◇   a mains power lead with adapter

Such renditions require a complex set of layout units, even though an alternative would have been to expressed the entire sequence within a single sentence. Instead of this, we need to divide the segment into an initial sentence fragment and a collection of similarly structured pairs of elements, each pair including the itemising diamond and a further sentence fragment. We need to be able to express how these layout elements come together at some level of description.

Combining them within a single a multinuclear JOINT relation would be one possibility. This would allow us to express on one hand the diversity of the form of expression, captured in the layout organisation of text-flow and, on the other hand, the unity of the expression, captured as a single rhetorically organised sequence of text-parts. But this is not supported by the original RST framework since the elements related are non-clause-like *fragments* of sentences and so cannot occur in verbal text as independent rhetorical 'messages'.

A further, more difficult set of cases occurs in the widespread style of attribute-value tables. In contrast to macro-punctuation, this cannot be treated adequately from the perspective of text-flow and requires further relationships to bind component elements together. For example, in the following:

Juvenile	Grey-brown, flecked becoming whiter, adult plumage after three years.
Nest	Mound of seaweed on bare rocky ledge.
Voice	Harsh honks and grating calls at colony.

we need to capture in what sense the layout elements distributed spatially across a cell-like area model combine to construct a rhetorically coherent message. Again, neither "juvenile" nor "mound of seaweed" and so on are elements that would traditionally be accessible in an RST analysis.

More difficult still is the common case of callouts where a diagram picturing a certain object may also include a variety of text labels identifying the object and its parts. We have seen several documents containing such compositions already; consider, as an illustration, the two extracts from our Louvre page of the previous chapter shown in Figure 4.3. Here again we have distinct layout elements that are related in some sense and whose connection is a necessary part of understanding the combined message, but the contents of these elements would not traditionally be singled out in an RST-style analysis.

Figure 4.3   Example labels taken from the Louvre page

All the examples given here have in common that they express states, or static relationships between two objects or between an object and a property such as identification, location, possession, or predication. In a purely verbal linear text, such relations are commonly expressed by clauses of 'being' or 'possession'; e.g.:

Juveniles *are* grey-brown, flecked becoming whiter
This part of the Louvre *is* the Cour Khorsabad.

In a traditional RST analysis, each such clause would accordingly constitute *one* undivided RST segment. In our examples, however, the two constituents of the relational clauses are broken out and appear as separate layout units, possibly even in differing modes. It is their mutual arrangement on the page plus possible extra graphical devices (such as the connecting lines in Figure 4.3) that expresses the relation between them. They then need to be combined by the reader to find the intended message precisely as do individual text spans in a verbal text.

Some of the particular issues involved with the combination of graphical elements and labels have also been addressed by Thibault (2001, pp305–306). Thibault argues that it is not possible to reduce the meaning of such composites formed by a label and what is being labelled to any one of the semiotic components considered separately. There is a relationship of 'co-contextualisation' between them in which each modality contributes in its own way—the verbal component classifying (*typological-categorial*), the graphical component showing gradients, regions and shape (*topological-continuous*). When combined in the relationship of label-and-element, an inter-modal mutual transfer is supported by which information expressed verbally may be 'added to' the information expressed visually, and *vice versa*.

Thibault also suggests that the function of the 'linking' element standing between label and labelled, typically a vector shown as a line or arrow, is analogous to a clause involving the copula 'be'. The precise relationship is, however, difficult to locate. Thibault accordingly argues for a more schematic notion of 'elaboration' that is "superordinate to both attribution and identification" (Thibault 2001, p308). The connecting line then has a primarily textual function that brings the linked elements together.[4]

Moving in a similar direction, the proposal is made for the GeM model in Henschel (2002) that we capture these kinds of composite visual-verbal configuration by extending the rhetorical layer. We have therefore added the following five relations drawn from Halliday and Matthiessen (2004) to the set of more broadly rhetorical relations described above:

Identification	assertion of identity
Class-ascription	relation between an object and its superclass
Property-ascription	relation between an object and something predicated of that object
Possession	relation between possessor and possessed
Location	relation between an object and its spatial or temporal location

These constitute further possible parts of the overall multimodal rhetorical structure analysis for a page. They are in many ways similar to the existing rhetorical relation ELABORATION but are also distinct by virtue of their application to fragments, individual entities and incomplete propositions. We accordingly term them 'subnuclear' since they decompose what would in traditional RST remain unanalysed single units and 'relational' because they generally appear as multimodal versions of relational clauses. We also term the spans related by these relations *mini-spans* to distinguish them from RST spans proper. During our analyses we have found examples of

---

[4] Thibault also draws attention to the interpersonal and indexical functions of such connectors, which correspond in our account to navigation structure and visual perception respectively; but we will follow Thibault in considering the textual function central.

all of these relations being expressed by the spatio-visual 'label-connector-labelled' combination.

4.4 Example analyses: rhetorical relations between layout units

We have now proposed that an appropriate extension of the framework of rhetorical analysis provided by Rhetorical Structure Theory provides a natural functional correlate for the more 'geometric' layout relationships that we have seen in previous chapters. Our premise throughout was that these visual/spatial configurations are also relevant for the meanings being expressed. With a suitably explicit account of rhetorical organisation, we can take the next step in describing just what those meanings might be. Spatial proximity and layout decision cues are therefore to be related to rhetorical organisation.

To include this within the GeM model, we add a layer of rhetorical structure to the base and layout levels that we have seen so far. Within this layer, the page is seen as a rhetorical unit rather than as a visual or physical unit. This need not always correspond to a single physical page; sometimes, it corresponds to a 'spread'—i.e., a two-page unit—or even to an entire document. Rhetorical organisation is a distinct layer of organisation and brings with it its own boundaries; these do not necessarily correspond one-to-one with the boundaries entailed by other layers.

Our most general constraint is then that the elements in a document are required to find their place within a single overarching *rhetorical structure*. This structure progressively decomposes the document into smaller parts, thereby building a bridge from the 'topmost' intentions of a communicative unit, such as a text or a page, down to the individual elements out of which that unit is constructed. Multimodal pages are accordingly seen from a more 'global' perspective where, in order to identify the rhetorical function of individual elements in a page, we consider it beneficial to place such elements within the document as a whole. This enables each element to be identified in terms of its contribution to the purposes first of the rhetorical regions of an entire page and, subsequently, of an entire document.

For effective design, a document needs to provide sufficient information for its readers to be able to identify the rhetorical organisation intended. The particular textual and graphical elements deployed need therefore to exhibit a unity of selection and placement that serves the intended communicative purpose of the document as a whole. As noted at the beginning of this chapter, focusing on relationships between *individual* elements may not go far enough in telling us why a page as a whole has a particular organisation. It is necessary to consider entire *structures* of such inter-relationships and to raise questions concerning the functions that these structures fulfill. This also makes more ready contact with the notion of genre that we discuss in the next chapter.

The GeM rhetorical layer is then defined as follows. As with the other layers of the model, we define a set of units over which rhetorical relationships are to hold. This is the *RST base level*. These units are independent from the units defined at other layers and so need to be *correlated* with them, generally via the base units, in order to trace back the rhetorical organisation to the physical elements on a page carrying that organisation. This allows a flexible relationship between, on the one hand, the rhetorical structure and, on the other, the particular kinds of entities that may take up rhetorical organisation on the page, and is precisely analogous to the relation we used above between base units and layout units.

A rhetorical analysis is then a structure defined over the RST base units using rhetorical relations extended in the manner we have just described. This includes all the standard relations[5] and the subnuclear elaborating relations. The standard constraints on rhetorical structures are assumed to hold, including its strict tree-like organisation, with linear sequence replaced by spatial contiguity.

In the rest of this chapter, we show this method of analysis in action with respect to several distinct kinds of documents. The main purpose of these illustrations is: (a) to show in more detail how this relates to the layers of analysis we have seen so far, and (b) to demonstrate how this layer allows us to isolate and describe areas of multimodal design which are potentially problematic for their readers. Although we can also naturally analyse documents which are not problematic, this does not bring out quite so clearly the particular benefit of applying rhetorical techniques to multimodal documents. That is, we need to see places where rhetorical organisation and layout organisation *diverge* in order to underline just why the distinct layers of analysis are both independently necessary.

Consider, for example, the comment from the previous chapter that we left hanging concerning a potential problem area for interpretation in the Louvre spread. In Section 3.3.1 we summarised the problem in terms of the positioning of a photograph of the East Facade. We suggested that the particular distribution of photographs, text and text captions in this spread invited a misinterpretation of the role of one of the images. We noted that such a claim can only be made when a more explicit account of the rhetor-

---

[5]In fact, we use the so-called 'extended relation set': cf. http://www.sfu.ca/rst/01intro/definitions.html

ical organisation of the page is available—otherwise, we are not licensed to make statements about appropriate or inappropriate interpretations. An interpretation may only be judged as appropriate or not relative to a particular communicative intention and without a rhetorical analysis we have not specified explicitly the intentions that are at issue.

The problematic layout is repeated here in Figure 4.4. To recap, we know from the 'how to use this book'-section of the guide that the photograph of the East Facade, shown as the darker crossed rectangle upper middle in the figure, was intended to provide additional background information on the appearance of the Louvre as a whole. Using rhetorical structure, we can make this information explicit as follows. There is an overall communicative intention to describe the Louvre and one of several elaborations of this description is the graphical presentation of the appearance of the East Facade.[6] The description is therefore nuclear and the East Facade photograph is an elaborative satellite expressed in a graphical mode.

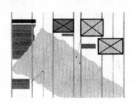

Figure 4.4
Problematic Louvre inset

When, however, we consider the layout structure and the area model appropriate for this spread, quite a different rhetorical organisation is suggested. The crossed rectangles in the figure, each representing a photograph of a part of the building, all belong to a group of similar layout elements. They are similar in size, in close proximity, and are all naturalistic full-colour photographs. The most common rhetorical correlate for such a group of similar layout units is a rhetorical organisation in which the layout units correspond either to nuclei of a single multinuclear relation (such as JOINT or SEQUENCE) or to satellites of a single rhetorical relation (such as a collection of ELABORATIONs of a single point). This means that the layout strongly suggests that all of the three photographs share a common rhetorical function.

This is not then compatible with the intended rhetorical organisation. The photograph of the East Facade should be linked with the overall communicative purpose of describing the Louvre whereas the other photographs are only related (via subnuclear elaborations) with the large drawing of the Louvre shown centre page. This very different rhetorical structure is not indicated by the layout structure.

---

[6]The precise rhetorical relation is less of concern here: it may either be a simple ELABO-RATION, an ENABLEMENT intended to help the visitor find the building, or a MOTIVATION to make the visitor go there.

The relationship between the rhetorical and layout layers required in our model is one way of capturing the general heuristic from design that similarity in layout should indicate similarity in function. The rhetorical analysis forces us to explore the extent to which any particular document manages to conform to this rule. Mismatches of this kind turn out to be more frequent than might have been thought. In the examples that we now present, we see very similar problems occurring in some rather different kinds of documents. Moreover, we can also demonstrate that the kind of corrections that a rhetorical analysis suggests are often precisely those that designers find plausible. This shows something of the value of the rhetorical analysis—i.e., it forces attention on problem areas that might not otherwise be noticed. It thereby gives a way of motivating design decisions more transparently, making those design decisions more 'arguable'.

4.4.1   Mismatches between layout structure and intended rhetorical structure

In the following examples, we consider some design issues that have arisen in documents taken from two distinct areas. In each case, we again find particular design decisions that have been made that are not entirely consonant with the rhetorical organisation that we would posit for the pages.

Wildlife fact files

The extracts of this subsection are taken from a series of information sheets on animals and wildlife that have been published by International Masters Publishers Ltd. in several forms since the 1990s. The sheets are intended for collection in order to progressively build up a comprehensive encyclopedia kept in a looseleaf binder. We will return to the genre as a whole in the next chapter; our main focus here will be on some individual layout decisions taken within one of these fact files.

Figure 4.5 shows an extract from a page presenting 'key facts' about the Bengal Tiger. This is a relatively self-contained portion of the page as a whole, which we will focus on in isolation for the purposes of our current discussion. To analyse this extract, we first carry out a layout decomposition following the guidelines and methods described in the previous chapter. This is relatively straightforward: the structure is similar in some respects to the Louvre spread in that we have labels surrounding a drawing, although the area model in this case is more rectangular. The resulting layout structure is shown in Figure 4.6: the page extract is made up of the central drawing surrounded by 6 layout elements of varying complexity. A filtered

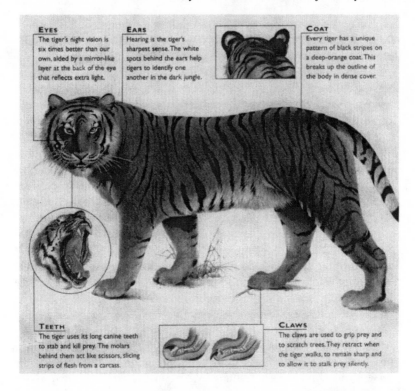

Figure 4.5   Fact sheet extract: features of the Bengal Tiger from the Wildlife Explorer *series (published by International Masters Publishers Ltd., 1997); used by permission*

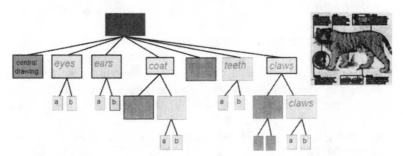

Figure 4.6   Layout structure for the tiger page extract. The light gray rectangles are text elements; the darker rectangles are graphic elements; the (a) elements contain bold subheading text; the (b) elements body text.

version of the page extract shown upper right in the figure makes clear how these elements are signalled both by framing by whitespace and the lines connecting them with the central drawing.

Slightly problematic are the rather unusual graphically augmented callouts for the teeth, claws, etc. in which a visual 'close-up' of the feature at issue intervenes between central drawing and callout text. These close-ups actually illustrate information given in the callout text and so do not simply repeat the visual information of the central diagram: the teeth picture illustrates the tiger with its mouth open (so we can see the teeth), while the claws picture shows an analytic CONTRAST between claws in their retracted and extended states. Whereas we can make a reasonable argument for the layout elements concerning the claws to be linked as part of a single layout element, this is not plausible in the case of the teeth. The visual and the text are simply too far apart to create any impression of a single layout element. Here the work of connection is carried entirely by the explicit connecting line. Such lines contribute to how readers 'navigate' the content of a layout but are not on their own strong enough to create superordinate layout units. As a consequence, we maintain these as distinct siblings in the layout structure rather than subordinating them to a common parent.

The rhetorical structure of this portion of the page is also relatively straightforward. We take the central drawing of the tiger to be nuclear, due to its visual prominence, and the callouts surrounding the drawing serve to identify various features evident in the drawing, such as the tiger's eyes, ears, teeth, etc.; we will designate these for present purposes simply as ELABORATIONs without dealing more specifically with the kind of elaboration at issue. Each of these features then receives additional elaborative material. Two of the callouts have a more complex linking structure as just discussed.

We also see in the case of the claws callout a typical example that we mentioned above of the difficulty in assigning nuclearity in multimodal rhetorical analyses . The sequencing entailed by the connecting lines suggests a reading path where the contrasting pictures are encountered first—but these are less than completely self-explanatory. The text then provides the necessary information to make this intelligible: the claws "retract when the tiger walks, to remain sharp and to allow it to stalk prey silently". Under this reading the claw diagram would be the nucleus of a BACKGROUND relation. Alternatively, if we took the text as nuclear, as would be more compatible with the other callouts, then the diagram ELABORATEs the text by providing an illustration: it is non-nuclear since it could easily be omitted without effecting the overall message of the page. Both the teeth and claw graphics also ELABORATE the central drawing, showing information

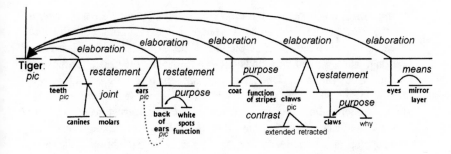

Figure 4.7 Rhetorical structure for the tiger page extract. The dashed line between the picture of the ears and the 'back of ears' shows a focusing on a particular part of a single drawing as described in Section 4.3.2.

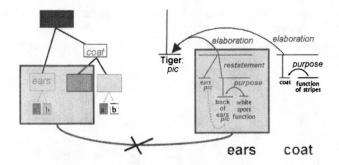

Figure 4.8 Mismatching layout and rhetorical organisations in the tiger page extract

that would otherwise not be available. We accordingly analyse the internal structure of the illustrated callouts as multinuclear RESTATEMENTs to avoid forcing unwarranted nuclearity choices. The resulting rhetorical structure is shown in Figure 4.7.

Now, despite the fact that each of the layout and rhetorical structures presented is straightforward on its own, when we compare their organisations we find a certain mismatch in the hierarchies constructed. This is shown graphically in Figure 4.8, picking out particularly the parts of the layout and rhetorical structures involved. The problem lies in the description of the function of the white spots on the back of the ears. The rhetorical structure shows that these spots are picked out graphically so that their PURPOSE can be given textually. However, within the layout structure, we see that the layout elements corresponding to these related rhetorical units are not positioned within a single superordinate layout element. In fact, the illustration of the ears is positioned within the *neighbouring* layout element concerning the tiger's coat. This has to be seen as a potential point of confusion: a reader may well consider the picture of the back of the ears as an illustration of the coat and only finds out that this is not the case after reading the accompanying text. This is analogous, therefore, to the situation with the Louvre East Facade that we described above: the layout structure misdirects readers with respect to the intended rhetorical structure.

Some evidence supporting our claim that this layout choice is less than ideal can be gained indirectly from the fact that the next edition of the same fact sheet, launched five years later in 2002, adopts a very different solution to the same design task. This solution is shown in Figure 4.9. Although the same picture of the back of the ears is used, the more recent publication explicitly separates it from the callouts for the central drawing, grouping it instead together with the text that it illustrates/restates. The link between these is also strengthened further by cross-modal cohesion, for example 'strong shoulders' are both illustrated in the picture and described in the text.

Figure 4.9   Extract from the fact file from the Discovering Wildlife *series (published by International Masters Publishers Ltd., 2002); used by permission*

The callouts of the central drawing are also reduced in complexity, containing textual descriptions but no subordinate graphics—perhaps also motivated by the potential weakness in layout structure now identified for the earlier version. As can be seen from the page shown in silhouette on the left of the figure, the simpler callouts are also well motivated by the fact that they reduce clutter and make the main message of the central portion of the page stand out more clearly than would otherwise have been the case. Altogether the layout structure of the new page corresponds much more accurately to the rhetorical intention of the segment.

4.4.2 Explaining how to use a telephone

For our next example we turn to the rather different document type of instructions for installing a household cordless telephone and its associated 'charger units'. An extract from a page from such a document is shown in Figure 4.10. Again, both the rhetorical structure and the layout structure are relatively straightforward. We shorten the exposition for this example, therefore, by briefly describing the structures involved and then proceeding directly to the contrast.

First, the layout elements of the segment include 4 main blocks, demarcated by horizontal separator lines and including explicit ordering information via large font numbers. These blocks include text, sometimes in bold, sometimes in a mixture of bold to begin and regular font to continue. In one case a line drawing of a plug being inserted into an electric wall socket is included; in another case there is a boxed text block in a much smaller type face. These layout blocks appear to occupy the left-hand column of a two column area model dividing the page approximately equally horizontally. In the upper right grid-cell is another line drawing of the 'base unit' of the telephone. Finally, there is a right-justified section heading on top of the basic cell structure and, above that to the left, a running head for this part of the instruction manual.

The relationship of the drawing(s) to the text is interesting both in terms of the layout and the rhetorical relations. In terms of layout the drawing appears decomposable into two parts, linked both semiotically and actually by the cable drawn between plug and 'base unit'. The part depicting the plug and wall socket intrudes so far into the cell of the element numbered 2, however, that for layout purposes it must be considered as part of that element. The strong horizontal alignment of the other part of the drawing, the base unit itself, and the lines of text and framing lines of the element numbered 1 also strongly suggests a layout connection. The 'NOTE' text on the right-hand side of the page is a little far from the drawing of the base unit to be assigned unequivocally to the same layout element, although the right-hand cable shown in the drawing serves as a connecting line. Least problematic is the smaller boxed paragraph under the element numbered 3: this is clearly part of that element in terms of layout. Combining these considerations gives the layout structure shown in abbreviated form to the left of Figure 4.11.

INSTALLATION AND SET-UP

Connecting the base unit and chargers

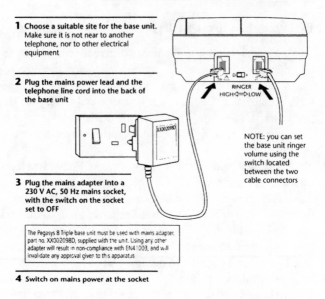

1 Choose a suitable site for the base unit. Make sure it is not near to another telephone, nor to other electrical equipment

2 Plug the mains power lead and the telephone line cord into the back of the base unit

RINGER
HIGH ⟺ LOW

NOTE: you can set the base unit ringer volume using the switch located between the two cable connectors

3 Plug the mains adapter into a 230 V AC, 50 Hz mains socket, with the switch on the socket set to OFF

The Pegasys 8 Triple base unit must be used with mains adapter, part no. XX002098D, supplied with the unit. Using any other adapter will result in non-compliance with EN41003, and will invalidate any approval given to this apparatus

4 Switch on mains power at the socket

Figure 4.10   Instructions for setting up a phone; used by permission

The rhetorical organisation of the information shown in the extract is simply a SEQUENCE. This is quite typical of instruction manuals where some aspect of the functioning of a device is first identified (here: "connecting the base unit and chargers") and then the steps to ENABLE that action are presented in sequence. Subsidiary information, of an enabling or background nature, may occur as further satellites to the nuclei of those actions. Without a further analysis of the meanings of the elements presented on the page, we can take the layout structure as directly suggesting a corresponding rhetorical organisation. We propose that this is commonly what readers in fact do: they are attempting to discern the overall and detailed communicative intent of a page of information and use the perceived layout of that page as a constraining form for likely rhetorical relations. This corresponding rhetorical structure is shown to the right of Figure 4.11. Here we can see that there is a direct one-to-one relationship between the hierarchical structure of the layout and the hierarchical structure of the rhetorical organisation.

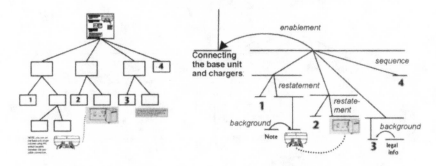

Figure 4.11   Layout structure and a corresponding rhetorical structure for the telephone page extract

Unfortunately, when we read the contents of the information expressed in these layout elements, we find that the actually intended rhetorical organisation has to be somewhat different from this. In particular, there is no direct rhetorical relationship between the text under step 1 and the drawing to its right—this drawing is actually more related to step 2. Moreover, the drawing under step 2 is actually more closely related to the actions to be performed under step 3. This can be determined by following more precisely the multimodal references across graphics and text in the distinct steps. Step 2, for example, refers to the "back of the base unit", which is only shown in the top-right line drawing; while step 3 refers to the "mains adapter" and "mains socket", which are only shown in the drawing under step 2. In addition, the main adaptor part number shown in the legal information of step 3 only appears in the line drawing of step 2. In order to successfully interpret the page, therefore, a reader needs to construct not the rhetorical structure shown in Figure 4.11 but that shown in Figure 4.12, and this is very different from that suggested by the layout structure.

It would seem then that in this case the multiple constraints imposed by the material being presented and other practical constraints on production have combined to give rise to a non-optimal design solution. For example, simply moving the drawing of the plug down in the layout to occupy the cell-space of step 3 rather than step 2 as the rhetorical organisation calls for would itself cause problems since the legal information in the inset box has also to be placed somewhere here. We can see from the intended rhetorical structure that step 3 is the most rhetorically 'overladen' part of the instruction sequence and its presentation has been 'solved' by distributing its information more broadly around the page. This has led consequently to

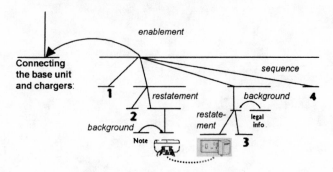

Figure 4.12   Intended rhetorical structure for the telephone page extract

a less accurate rendition of the intended rhetorical organisation, which may in turn lead to confusion on the part of the reader.

Despite this mismatch, the instructions as designed *appear* well structured and straightforward. We must, therefore, be cautious concerning the import of such appearances. It is already known from studies of textbooks that readers can be completely unaware of how poorly they have understood presented material. In such cases, 'good' design, in the sense of design that gives an *impression* of clarity, is not sufficient. Schriver discusses, for example, results from Glenberg, Wilkinson and Epstein (1982) and others concerning what they term an 'illusion of knowing':

> "Poorly designed textbooks can create more than one kind of problem for readers... at times we may overestimate how well we understand... College students... who read texts in which experimenters had 'planted' contradictions failed to notice the contradictions. Surprisingly, after having read contradictory material, students rated themselves as feeling 'very certain' they understood the text. In fact, students had overlooked the contradictions and had answered many of the comprehension questions incorrectly."   (Schriver 1997, p226)

There must therefore also be evaluations of design in terms of the *correctness* of presentations and an explicit analysis of the intended rhetorical organisation and its correspondence with layout structure is one way of supporting this.

4.5   Conclusion

In Chapter 1 we saw how Bernhardt (1985) proposed a continuum across document types concerning how explicitly the documents belonging to any given type used visual resources for the expression of their content (cf. Figure 1.3). In this chapter, we have refined this observation with particular reference to rhetorical organisation. Here again there is a continuum of relationships between text, image and layout. From any rhetorical organisation for a document, more or less of that structure may be taken up visually or textually. Some documents may use the spatial mode to bring out details of their rhetorical organisation; other might rely instead on the linguistic mode to signal that organisation. Newer documents tend to make more varied use of the spatial possibilities available to them.

We can characterise this more explicitly in terms of distinct semiotic modes that have developed for information presentation and which are now all commonly employed within multimodal documents. Figure 4.13 illustrates three such modes that are particularly relevant: one concerned with the sequentiality of text, one with temporal sequentiality, and one with spatial contiguity. This can be seen as an extension of previous discussions of how the modes of 'multimodality' combine and which modes are involved (cf. Stöckl 2004*b*).

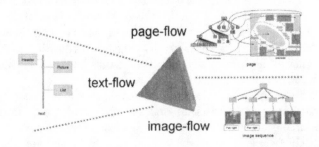

Figure 4.13   Three semiotic modes commonly deployed within document pages

As discussed in Chapter 2, the semiotic mode of linear written text is found whenever it is the one-dimensional line of the developing text that provides the basic organising scheme. Figures, pictures, diagrams tend in this mode to be situated 'near' to their referring text or to rely on explicit textual cross-references via document deixis (cf. Paraboni and van Deemter 2002). The *spatial* nature of the page does not carry significant meanings in its own right. Rhetorical organisation in this *text-flow* mode governs selection of conjunctions and other grammatical structures and extended 'macro-punctuation' (cf. Power et al. 2003 and Section 2.5.3).

A similar but semiotically distinct mode is used to organise sequences of graphical elements rather than text. We can term this *image-flow* in analogy to the linear text-flow mode. Within image-flow graphical elements are set out one after the other as found in comics and similar picture sequences (cf. McCloud 1994). The temporal sequence is used to carry a range of additional meanings over and above those in the contributing images. The relations holding between successive elements in such image-flows have been analysed from several perspectives; they also overlap with the kinds of relations that can be observed in film (for extensive references and discussion, see: Bateman 2007). We will not discuss this mode any further here, however; we simply note that such elements also commonly appear as contributions to multimodal documents alongside, and in combination with, text-flow elements.

When a document starts to utilise the full two-dimensional spatial extent of the page for expressing rhetorical and other functional organisations, we move into a different semiotic mode: one which we term *page-flow*. Page-flow can combine elements in any of the semiotic modes appearing on a page, including text-flow, diagrams, graphs and so on. It adds to the individual contributions of these elements the possibility of a *rhetorical* unity supporting the communicative intentions of the document. And so, to documents in this mode, we use the multimodal extension to rhetorical structure that we have introduced in this chapter. Without this level of description, we are not in a position to explicate many of the spatial distribution decisions taken in page-based documents—although this distribution must also be considered in terms of any canvas constraints that are applicable, such as the grids and other properties of the page.

It is also only when we have a detailed view of multimodal rhetorical structure that we can start setting out the *alternatives* for expression that are open to designers. This is one of the main reasons that we require an account of rhetoric in our overall account. In addition, we have seen how intended rhetorical organisation and the relationships communicated spatially can diverge—usually resulting in incorrect or ambiguous interpretations of the document in question. This divergence shows the necessity of maintaining rhetorical structure as an *independent* contribution to a complete document analysis.

At the present time it is an open question as to just how much of the detail of rhetorical organisation is expressible visually. If we cannot make the fine distinctions that are commonly drawn linguistically in the visual mode then we will not require the full apparatus of RST. The resources which are actually employed in any document and the ways in which they are distributed around the semiotic modes mobilised will also depend to a large extent on the type of document considered. For this we need to consider the influence of document *genres*, which we now turn to in the following chapter.

5

Multimodal Documents
and Genre

In this chapter, we address in detail the joint issues of *comparison* and *constraint*. We have raised the issue of comparison at various points in the discussion so far. Whenever we analyse a multimodal document, we need to consider the sets of documents that it resembles and the sets of documents with which it stands in contrast. This kind of comparison is of much more than academic interest: in fact, it is only *because* of this comparison that particular interpretations can be made rather than others. The overwhelming majority of constructs that we have seen in this book are elements and configurations that have, through use, *developed* the potential to carry meaning in multimodal documents: this potential is only made real in the context of actual documents standing in relations of similarity and contrast with other documents.

In short, when we see a text fragment shown slightly spatially offset in the text-flow, slightly larger and bolder than the text surrounding it, perhaps with a number before the text, this is *not* a section heading because of these features—it is (possibly) a section heading because there is an established body of documents in which this particular collection of typographical, visual and spatial properties is regularly deployed with the intention of signalling a textual division and a point of access into the navigation structure. Only then can we label this functionally as a 'section heading'. All such interpretations are dependent on the class of documents to which the analysed instance is allocated—a point recently made at length in terms of *conventions* by Kostelnick and Hassett (2003).

Allocation of this kind is part of the work of interpretation that any user of a document automatically performs. On this basis the user/reader brings appropriate interpretive schemes to bear so as to unravel what may be being meant. Well designed documents necessarily take on the task of showing the user/reader just what class of documents is relevant for their interpretation. From this perspective, the class of documents intended establishes *constraints* on document design. These constraints inform design in as far as they clarify just what signals and conventions are going to be relevant to help some user/reader select an appropriate scheme of interpretation.

 We shall argue in this chapter that a crucial theoretical construct for exploring this aspect of the meaning-making involved in multimodal documents is *genre*. The complex interplay of mutual relationships playing a role here is succinctly expressed by Lemke as follows:

> "We construct genres by construing certain sorts of semantic patterning in what we consider to be distinct texts, and we say that such texts belong to the same genre. Co-generic texts are privileged intertexts for each other's interpretation."
> (Lemke 1999)

And so when readers allocate documents to particular classes of document, those classes bring with them certain interpretive frames and expectations. These frames guide readers to make sense of what they are seeing. Moreover, seen from the perspective of document *production*, we can take the intention of creating a document that 'belongs' to one class rather than another as a mobilisation of precisely those constraints that signal that some interpretative frames are to be applied rather than others. The decisions taken during production then rely more or less explicitly on the conventions and practices established for the class of documents to which the document is to belong.

The first explicit use of genre in a detailed model of the document design process was probably that of Waller (1987*a*). Genre within this framework is very much as it is seen in linguistic work: i.e., more or less stable categories formed by restricting theoretically available design choices to particular jointly selected combinations of choices. The position that genre takes in Waller's model is shown in Figure 5.1. On the left of the figure, we see the abstract paths available for moving from design task to design solution; on the right, we see the actual paths often followed in concrete design situations. As Waller states, solutions that only consider the norms of the situation, or the intended document, may produce unusable results because attention to those documents' functionality has not been paid; conversely, solutions that only consider functionality without considering the expectations that hold for documents of particular types may equally suffer from unusability simply because the users of the document do not know which interpretive frames to apply. Appropriate solutions require a process

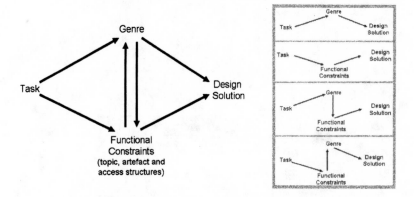

Figure 5.1   *The positions taken by genre in the design process according to Waller (1987a, pp298–301; Figures 9.5–9.9)*

of negotiation between the norms for the document type—the genre—and the functional requirements of the particular case.

Establishing just what the 'norms' of a document type are requires detailed empirical investigation. This is made doubly important because *without* such investigation it is by no means clear just what the relevant 'document types' are. Consider, for example, the two document 'pages' shown in Figure 5.2. Here we see a traditional newspaper front page and an 'equivalent' online newspaper front page; the print newspaper version is a front-page of *The Guardian*; the online version is from the equivalent web offering for *The Guardian*. Determining the appropriate classes of documents with which these pages are to be compared for interpretation is considerably less straightforward than it might seem. Their presentation here suggests, in Lemke's terms from above, that each text is potentially a 'privileged text' for the interpretation of the other; but we need to pick this apart more carefully.

Making them 'co-generic' with respect to their assumed identity as 'newspapers' certainly tells us something useful about the reasons why the two documents contain information of similar kinds: i.e., 'news'. But in other respects this view is less helpful. It does not, for example, give us a particularly accurate indication of the interpretative strategies the documents require of their readers. Interacting with a web-page is something very different from interacting with a printed page—and *not* only because of issues of hyperlinks and scrollability. As suggested by the graphical versions of the layout structures shown in the figure, we are also dealing here with two very different *spatial organisations*—and this has significant consequences.

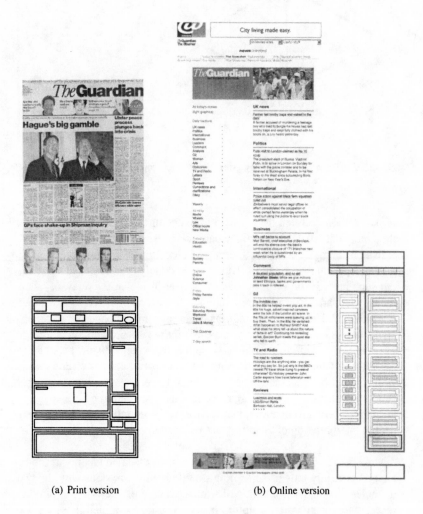

(a) Print version   (b) Online version

Figure 5.2   Two versions of The Guardian *newspaper—one print, the other online—*
each accompanied by a graphical rendition of its layout structure; both
newspaper versions used by permission

The virtual artefact of the print newspaper has developed over the past 200 years to provide a semiotically sophisticated 'access tool' for suitably apprenticed readers (for good historical overviews and accounts of news design, see: Hutt 1973, Ames 1989, Moen 1989). The distribution of news across the page and the selection of size, position and framing is well known to give readers a very clear indication of 'news value' (Bell 1998). Readers can select and prioritise their reading accordingly. This is not possible with the web-page because a very different canvas is drawn upon—that of the virtual artefact of HTML tables. Although HTML tables can 'approximate' columns, they do not allow text to flow on from the bottom of one column to the top of the 'next'; the traditional text-flow column grid of print (cf. Section 2.5.1) is therefore surprisingly difficult to achieve. The apparent grid-like structure of the web-page layout is in fact made up of single columns set out next to one another. These are, apart from some relatively weak coordinating reason for the columns being on the same page at all, *essentially unrelated.* A reader has little choice but to start at the top of each column and proceed downwards: the truely two-dimensional deployment of space within the modern print newspaper is absent.

This situation commonly leads the spatial organisation to take on different roles. For example, a central column may provide the main news items, while off-centre columns serve navigational or 'other news' roles (cf. Knox 2007). The online page is then in many respects closer generically to online offerings such as web-browser result pages and simple lists, possibly with subheadings breaking those lists down into categories. The *multidimensional* access possibilities of the print newspaper are severely reduced.[1]

Although there are many issues of design and usability to consider here, what is most relevant for our present discussion is the way in which the properties of the online newspaper align with very different sets of co-generic texts than might have originally been thought on the basis of its informal classification as a 'newspaper'. This can be problematic in several ways. For example, a reader who unknowingly applies a newspaper interpretive scheme is likely to be frustrated—perhaps without even realising it—because the artefact is assumed to have affordances that it does not.

The divisions relevant here also do not respect simple technological divisions, such as that between print and web-based delivery. There are many print documents that are also structured very similarly to this online newspaper—which makes interpretative strategies developed for those classes of documents equally relevant here. This is essentially the style of

---

[1] As we have discussed elsewhere (cf. Bateman, Delin and Henschel 2007), this is one of the reasons for a resurgence of the traditional spatial organisation for online newspapers now being successfully promoted in so-called *digital editions*.

interaction found with telephone directories and other listings of information, including some styles of newspaper from the *19th* century rather than the 21st! The success or not of the web-offering is then to be seen (a) in terms of how well this latter set of co-generic texts also meets the current-day demands and habits of presenting and receiving news, and (b) in terms of new practices for news consumption that it may facilitate.

To take this further, we need far more information concerning just what documents are relevant for comparison, and methods for determining how those documents contribute to interpretation. Without this, we face the danger that decisions in document design will either resist functional motivation or suggest functional motivations that are not relevant or appropriate for the document at hand—simply because the *actual* reason for their selection was better sought in the generic constraints of a class of documents, including historical and technological constraints, than in the particulars of the individual solution under scrutiny. A stronger position for interpretation and explanation therefore requires that we establish genres for multimodal documents. Only then we will have a theoretical framework within which constraints on the interpretations and meanings deployed in documents can be effectively pursued.

Although there is a traditional belief that genre is not amenable to precise formalisation and aids only in *clarification* (cf. Fowler 1982, de Beaugrande 1980, p196, Miller 1984), we will push for a tighter notion. We need to develop a theoretical construct which allows us to make *predictions* concerning the form and content of multimodal documents. But working with genre, and particularly developing it further towards predictive and empirically motivated explanation, requires some careful discussion. The extension of traditional notions of genre to multimodal documents is not straightforward. Just what genres there are and how they are best to be defined multimodally remains far from clear.

The main contribution to our framework for multimodal genre will therefore be drawn from precise *linguistically-motivated* accounts of genre. We consider this view of genre as the theoretical construct of choice for unravelling issues of the kind facing us here. From this perspective, genre offers a method for relating any individual document encountered to its 'generic' context by means of explicitly identifiable design decisions. These design decisions, i.e., what selection of modal resources a document makes and how these resources are related to the meanings that they carry, must be isolated by empirical analysis.

To move us forward, the chapter will first set out the current state of the art in genre as it has been applied to text and discourse.[2] We then pick out some common problems faced when moving from textual genres to multimodal genres; we will see that most of the perspectives we introduce have already been applied in investigations of multimodality, although yet again there is little contact across the particular research communities involved. We also briefly discuss work that has focused particularly on finding general classes of *visual representation* (e.g. Twyman 1979, Burford, Briggs and Eakins 2003, Kostelnick and Hassett 2003, Twyman 2004) since this often includes treatments of document pages and so contributes directly to our goal of providing an overarching account of multimodal genre as such. We then present the concrete notion of genre adopted in our framework and conclude with some illustrations of using genre descriptions in document analysis.

5.1   Perspectives on genre

The term 'genre' is widely used to label broad classes of communicative verbal artefacts. In this largely pre-theoretical sense, it has been relatively straightforward and natural to extend traditional talk of genres such as 'sonnet', 'tragedy', 'comedy' and so on in literature, into newer, multimodal realms, including the 'Western' and 'Film noir' in film, 'advertisement', 'documentary' and 'sitcom' in television, as well as newer genres still, such as 'the online newspaper' mentioned above or 'the homepage' in discussions of the World-Wide Web. Most of this discussion has not aimed at making genre function predictively and criteria for assigning an artefact to one genre rather than another remain loose.

To provide a more empirically accountable view we orientate more towards the development of genre pursued in linguistics and discourse analysis since there it becomes possible to make far stronger statements about the properties that an artefact conforming to some genre must exhibit. Two broad approaches are particularly important for us here. One of these reconstructs genre within a specifically linguistic account; we term this the *genre as social semiotic* perspective (cf. Martin 1984, Hasan 1984, Ventola 1984, 1987). The other, initiated by the influential paper by Miller (1984), is directed towards understanding communicative events in terms of their

---

[2] Although there is much significant work on genre, our discussion here will be focused solely on achieving a notion of genre usable for multimodality; a recent review of genre theory more generally can be found in Muntigl and Gruber (2005), and further introductions and discussions of schools of genre and their interactions are given by, for example, Hyon (1996), Paltridge (1997), Lee (2001), Johns (2002) and Martin and Rose (2007).

socially situated 'rhetorical actions'; we accordingly term this the *genre as social action* perspective. We will see below precisely why we focus on these two orientations; we can note here at the outset, however, that they both draw a distinction between genre on the one hand, and style, or register, on the other. We will rely on this heavily below: there are approaches where genre and style, register, etc. are not distinguished and we will argue that this reduces descriptive adequacy, making the genre classification of documents, particularly multimodal documents, unworkable.

5.1.1   Genre as social semiotic

Considering genre as simultaneously, on the one hand, a semiotically constructed social entity and, on the other, a characterisation of a class of identifiable linguistic artefacts, derives more or less directly from the view of language proposed in Halliday's (1978) *Language as Social Semiotic* and systemic-functional linguistics (SFL). Most approaches taken within this perspective on genre are aligned with this theory, which, as we have seen in previous chapters, continues to contribute actively to almost all areas of multimodal theorising.

In the systemic-functional framework language is seen as inextricably related to society, ideology and culture. The language system and its contexts of use are described at several distinct levels of abstraction, termed *strata*. These strata serve the function of successively mediating between, at the most abstract and general level, characterisations of language use as sociological, cultural and ideological phenomena and, at the least abstract level, accounts of the concrete linguistic forms, sounds and grammatical constructions employed. All of these levels of description are seen as capturing 'meaningful' contributions to a complete language event. This means that the account, in contrast to many other kinds of linguistic theorising, resists singling out any particular level as *the* level where 'meaning' is to be found. Any of the levels of the model may take up the role of constructing and carrying meaningful patterns.

This openness to considering linguistic patterns at any level of description contributed to the early development of a linguistic treatment of *register* (cf. Gregory 1967, Gregory and Carrol 1978). Register is generally defined as a particular 'style' of language use; this was taken further by several characterisations that related the concept centrally to social situation (Hasan 1973, Biber 1988, Labov 2001, Martin 2001), turning register variation into a powerful tool for exploring social and situational variation. Describing a 'style' of language use sufficiently exactly to reveal variation of this kind requires a fine-grained linguistic apparatus sensitive enough to distinguish linguistic expressions that might, more superficially, all be said to 'mean' the same thing. Accepting style as an equal partner in the process of making meanings therefore drives linguistic description to become ever more detailed.

The linguist's task in such explorations is then one of specifying as accurately as possible mutual expectancy relationships between features of the social situation and *identifiable* linguistic features of the language occurring in that situation. This has always been a central goal of systemic-functional linguistics and has played a significant role in shaping the theory overall. It will also play a central role in our move to multimodal genre. Since we will need to make the features by which we can define genres as 'identifiable' as possible, we will need a descriptive apparatus that is sufficiently sensitive to disentangle alternatives—just as is the case with grammar and other areas of linguistic analysis.

The final move to genre within the SFL account was taken as follows. Whereas register offers a rather 'homogeneous' view of text and the linguistic options that texts take up in context, it is clear that actual language use displays more structure: when we describe the linguistic details of texts in close detail, it is rare that an entire text exhibits precisely the *same* range of stylistic options. More often we can locate particular phases or segments of a text showing a relatively homogenous range of stylistic options and other segments of the same text that show different options being taken up. Therefore, a single linguistic text, or linguistic event, may appeal to several distinct registers while it is unfolding and yet still be seen as a coherent example of a single 'type' of text. It is this feature of texts that has presented, and continues to present, the greatest problems for approaches to register, text types and style. Since texts need not be homogeneous, simple 'labels' for registers or genres are rarely appropriate. We will see this below in current work on classifying web-based genres, where the problem is made considerably worse by multimodality.

The theoretical construct that was introduced in systemic-functional linguistics to deal with this 'higher' level structuring and organisational integrity across stylistically distinct textual contributions was genre. Within this view, texts and communicative events belonging to some genre are seen as staged sequences of purposive actions, where each stage can take on a distinctive register. This established a fundamental link between observable patterning of collections of linguistic features, or styles, and patterns in the social activity unfolding: distinct stages of a social activity (e.g., selecting an item in a market or shop, fixing the price, etc.) co-occur with and are signalled by particular 'styles' of language use.

The first explicit representation of genre in this sense within the systemic-functional model was Hasan's (1978) *Generic Structure Potential*, or GSP. In this account, a particular *contextual configuration* gives rise to a particular text structure, whose individual elements manifest specific linguistic properties. The text structure is defined by the particular GSP associated with the context. This specifies precisely which structural elements are necessary for a text to be considered to be an example of a particular genre, which elements are possible but not obligatory, the relative ordering of these elements (preceding, following, interspersed), the particular *semantic functions* to be achieved by each element and, last but by no means least, the corresponding *linguistic features* of semantics, grammar and lexis that may be used for those functions' achievement.

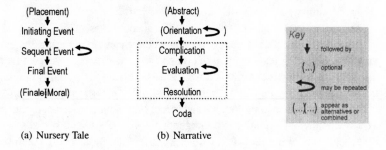

(a) Nursery Tale   (b) Narrative

Figure 5.3   Graphical representation of the genre structures of Hasan (1984) for nursery tales and of Labov and Waletzky (1978) for narrative

One of the first examples of a characterisation of a genre developed by Hasan within this framework was that of the 'nursery tale' (Hasan 1984), the GSP of which is shown in Figure 5.3(a). Here we can see how this genre 'predicts' that recognisable elements will occur in a particular sequence, that one of these (the placement) may be omitted, that one (the sequent event) may be repeated and that the finale and the moral may be mixed or interspersed with one another.[3]

Hasan's discussion of the nursery tale made contact with several other approaches to textual organisation being pursued at that time, most significantly Labov and Waletzky's (1978) work on the structure of narratives. Figure 5.3(b) shows the narrative structure they propose in the same format as used for Hasan's GSP. In both approaches we see clearly the view of

---

[3] Analogies and forerunners of this account can accordingly be found in, for example, Propp (1968), Mitchell (1957) and others. We will not pursue the historical development further here; for more detail, see Martin and Rose (2007).

genres as "staged, goal-oriented social processes" that has subsequently become a cornerstone of approaches to genre in general (Swales 1990, Martin 1992, 1993).

Given the abstractness of the stages proposed within generic structures, it is understandable that much of Hasan's (1984) discussion actually centres on the *motivation* for distinguishing particular elements from others. That is, it is important—particularly from a linguistic perspective—to be able to find *evidence* that one particular structure holds rather than another; it is not sufficient to simply assert that some interpretation is 'plausible' or apparently the case. Hasan, Labov and Waletsky, and others approaching the issue of text description linguistically were therefore obligated to find linguistic evidence for the distinctions they were proposing. This then becomes the main criterion for establishing distinct categories. If, for example, a genre structure proposes that there is an orientation element in stories, then there should be linguistic features of grammar and lexis that reliably distinguish this element from, for example, the elements of the complication of those stories (cf. Figure 5.3).

It is this acceptance that distinctions may only be proposed if there is sufficient evidence *on the basis of linguistic patterning* for the presence of distinct elements that, on the one hand, places the investigation of genres and genre structures on a firm empirical foundation and, on the other, distinguishes the linguistically-motivated approach to genres from other, more interpretative approaches. It is also the step that is crucial for us here. When we move to multimodal documents, we also need to be able to find concretely identifiable empirical evidence to motivate particular structures and interpretations rather than others. Only then do we have a foundation sufficiently firm for further theory building.

Theory building also needs to proceed with respect to a sufficiently broad range of data. In linguistic genre analysis this has already proved its worth—just as it has in other areas of linguistics (and science at large). Martin and Plum (1997), for example, were able to develop a finer description of narrative genres by teasing apart distinct generic structures on the basis of more precise characterisations of the linguistic features found across genre stages. By close analysis, they discovered that the 'central' portion of narratives—shown within a dotted box in Figure 5.3(b)—manifests distinctive linguistic variation corresponding to several distinguishable *subgenres*. Not all of these are appropriately termed 'narratives' in the traditional sense, although they are nevertheless descriptions of chronological series of events. These more specific genres include *recounts*, which simply relate what occurred, *procedures*, which give somewhat anonymous instructions for activities to be carried out, *anecdotes*, which tell a story to make a point, as well as the classical *narratives* themselves, which need not only to tell what happened but also to make it interesting—typically by setting up a complication which needs to be resolved. Each of these stages calls for *distinct collections of linguistic features* that allows it to be recognised and distinguished from the others.

Adopting an empirical foundation for genre investigation has therefore opened up the way for significant growth in our knowledge about genres and their structures. The resulting *genre families*, collections of more or less closely related genres, offer a clear illustration of the importance of pursuing fine-grained and empirically motivated analytic detail (cf. Christie and Martin 1997). But this is only possible when sufficiently accurate analytic tools are applied.

5.1.2   Genre as social action

Whereas the view of genre within the socio-semiotic perspective was anchored in the systemic-functional linguistic tradition, with its origins in anthropology and functional linguistics, the view found in the other approach to genre we discuss developed within a quite different intellectual climate. Within North American linguistics, the Chomskyan paradigm had already driven approaches to language as a social phenomena outside of the 'mainstream' to surface in parallel strands such as ethnomethodology (Garfinkel 1967) and work such as that of Hymes (Hymes 1974), both of which had strong roots in sociology and sociolinguistics. Interest in genre at that time was therefore not primarily a 'core' linguistic one.

Outside of linguistics, however, active traditions from literary theory and rhetorical studies contributed to the formation of the *New Rhetoric* (cf. Freedman and Medway 1994), which provided a setting within which explicit treatments of genre could grow. Here, language events were most readily seen as instantiating particular *social activity types* and these were then later assimilated to the notion of genre. Detailed linguistic description of the kind pursued for grammar and semantics was not a central part of this work and so remained very much on the edge of the account as genre studies in this tradition gained momentum.

Researchers in the North American and New Rhetoric traditions of genre generally cite Miller (1984) as the crystallisation point that brought notions of genre and social action together. Miller argued that those disciplines where the term 'genre' had traditionally been employed had not yet produced usable definitions. Many of the issues contributing to this problem continue in genre theory to the present day, and include concerns over the nature of taxonomising and the value (or lack thereof) of relating texts to fixed and allegedly over-rigid notions of some ideal form. Miller's position on these issues, and on the value of genre as such, is that:

> "an understanding of genre can help account for the way we encounter, interpret, react to, and create particular texts. ... [G]enre study is valuable not because it might permit the creation of some kind of taxonomy, but because it emphasizes some social and historical aspects of rhetoric that other perspectives do not."
>
> (Miller 1984, p151)

To further these aims Miller takes the vital step that is incorporated in all those approaches that build on her work: i.e., that a sound definition of genre needs to rely not on the form of a discourse but on the social action that is being achieved through the use of that discourse. Recurring social situations give rise to recurring problems that can be approached through recurrent communicative solutions. These recurrent communicative solutions can then themselves be recognised as such by virtue of their recurrent form—but it is the social action that drives the account.

A description of genre in Miller's terms then picks out one particular dimension for discourse classification:

> "a classification based in rhetorical practice and consequently open rather than closed and organized around situated actions (that is, pragmatic, rather than syntactic or semantic)."
>
> (Miller 1984, p155)

Moreover, as a signpost for which practices will be found, she takes the 'de facto' genres that are already named and recognised in our societies as a good indication of just what genres will need to be described. A position also taken up by Swales (1990) in his standard introduction to the field.

This view of genre is one way of taking the actual practices and classifications of those using genres seriously. Genres are related to situations but those situations are themselves abstractions; they are social constructs that are maintained and created through action, including the genres that accompany them. A discourse of a particular genre is not then simply a reflection of an objectively defined situation, but is instead one of the ways in which an abstract social type of situation is signalled and maintained through communicative acts. Here Miller draws on other approaches that emphasise the constitutive role of language use, including ethnomethodology (Garfinkel 1967) and Halliday (e.g., Halliday 1978), allowing genre to take its place within a hierarchy of kinds of meaning, ranging from behaviour at one end through to culture and ideology at the other (cf. Miller 1984, p162).

Defining genre in this way allows Miller to set out some criteria by which classes of discourse can be accepted as genres or not. They will clearly tend to show similarity of form, but most importantly they also have to function as bearers of meanings for the culture they are embedded within. This is similar to the relation seen by Martin (1992) between genre and ideology in the socio-semiotic tradition: different cultures will activate or use repertoires of different genres. Moreover, Miller holds that such entities do not support a treatment in terms of taxonomies, because genres "change, evolve, and decay" (p163).

A further move in this tradition relevant for the view of genre under development here is that of Bazerman (1994). Bazerman draws on the connection between social organisation and distinctive styles of discourse in order to argue for entire collections of genres that stand in systematic relationships. He characterises genres as actions, adopting further aspects of speech act theory, and argues that certain kinds of texts, particularly those that are intended to fulfill particular functions (such as filing a patent, which he discusses as one detailed example of genre change over time) can be considered as complex speech acts, quite analogous to speech acts formulated within single sentences.

Then, just as utterances rarely, if ever, occur in a vacuum and are generally components of larger scale 'conversations', Bazerman sees certain genres similarly. A text in a particular genre may require texts to have preceded it in other genres and certain other texts to follow: for example, court rulings, reports and legal decisions may each belong to their own genres but it is the entire ensemble of interlinked generic acts that make the social subsystem involved work. Seen more generally, Bazerman therefore invites an interpretation of society as a whole as a *system of genres*. The genres available at particular points in the network define the options for behaviour that a society provides for its members. Such larger groupings of genres are now receiving study within a variety of frameworks; they are termed *macro-genres* by Martin (e.g., Martin 1994, 2002), and *genre chains* and *genre networks* by Swales (2004, pp18–25).

Finally, the development arising out of the North American genre-as-action context that is probably the most significant for multimodal theorising at present is the research programme initiated by Yates and Orlikowski (1992). Yates and Orlikowski propose genre as a powerful means of investigating organisational practice and, in particular, *changes* in organisational practice over time. This approach has proved particularly influential for work on the genres of the new media, web-based genres and so on. Yates and Orlikowski begin by emphasising the essential role that communication plays in all organisations. Communicative genres, and their structuring and inter-relationships, then offer an incisive method for characterising organisations and their structure.

This framework represents a fruitful combination of several strands of research including, on the one hand, approaches to genre from rhetoric (cf. Simon 1978, Harrell and Linkugel 1978 and Chapter 4) and, on the other, the sociologically sophisticated model of *structuration* developed by Giddens (1984). Miller, as we have seen, had already defined genres as "typified actions based in recurrent situations" (Miller 1984, p159) and had moved 'situation' to be an essentially socially constructed, and hence semiotic, entity. This, taken together with structuration, provides a particularly important role for genre to play. Under this account, genre is understood in terms of a dual structure where genre both structures the stream of social practices and is shaped by that stream.

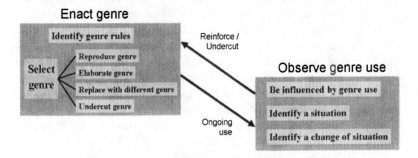

Figure 5.4   Characterisation of the cyclic process of genre change according to Yoshioka and Herman (2000); used by permission

The development of organisations over time is then addressed by Yates and Orlikowski by charting how the *genres* of those organisations change. Social practices in an organisation are given structure by the genre repertoires available to the organisation (Orlikowski and Yates 1994), and so changes in those genres also correspond to changes in those organisations' practices and structure. In other words, using a genre to structure a communication serves both to *reproduce* the genre and, whenever changes are introduced into the communication, to *modify* the genre.

This has led both to detailed analyses of changing document genres and to theories of just how such genre change occurs. One general model of the process is set out in Yoshioka, Herman, Yates and Orlikowski (2001), summarised graphically in Figure 5.4. Here we see how genres are selected and used, which can lead to a situation being identified and, conversely, how changes in situations can lead back to motivate elaborations, changes or even rejections of the originally associated genres. The model also corresponds well to the view of change in the socio-semiotic perspective: the system provides the possibilities for instantiation that may be taken up and each instance of language produced in turn feeds back to either maintain or alter the system (Lemke 1988*a*, 1993, Kress 1993).

Yates and Orlikowski (1992) provide a detailed illustration of their approach to genre change over time drawing on the *business memo*. This distinctive form appears to have emerged as a progressive response to the need to manage intra-organisational communication and memory as companies grew beyond small groups with small numbers of management hierarchies. At first, the already existing genre of business letters was employed for this situation; this was then adapted by a reduction in formal language and other linguistic markers of a greater shared context of interpretation. Memos also began serving more as records of company-internal decision making and policies. This additional role as 'organisational memory' created further requirements for the administration and storage of the memos exchanged— requirements partly satisfied by new systems of document storage. The introduction of 'vertical filing', for example, led to a functional requirement that the subject matter, date, addressee, and originator of a memo be clearly and quickly identifiable; this is an example of a consumption constraint being exercised on form. In addition, the need to produce such documents in ever larger quantities, more quickly and reproducibly, was supported by the introduction and subsequent widespread use of the typewriter.

This technological change established production constraints that also served to shape the forms of the emerging memo genre. Underlining and capitals supported the use of subheadings for structural layout in memos and, subsequently, the introduction of tab stops further supported and encouraged the use of tabular information displays (Yates and Orlikowski 1992, p314). By 1920 this form was then established as a virtual canvas in its own right, one which continues in use to this day—perhaps in vestigial form even in the 'one-line table' discussed for our original Gannet example in Chapter 2.

Yates and Orlikowski go on to show how the memo form has contributed significant aspects of the 'email' genre as well. In the context of electronic mail systems:

> "System designers embedded the structural features of the memo heading into the new medium. In this case, computers rather than people routed the messages, so the fields of the memo heading were designed to be readable by computers (as well as humans). A typical memo layout for the fields was not required by computers, so its widespread adoption shows that designers (whether implicitly or explicitly) retained elements of an existing and familiar genre in moving to a new medium."
>
> (Yates and Orlikowski 1992, p316)

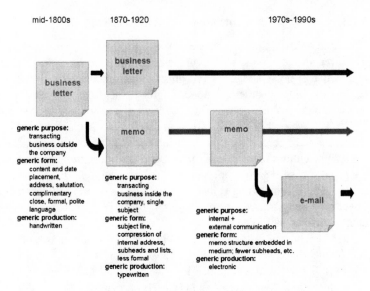

Figure 5.5   *Graphical representation of the development of the memo genre as discussed by Yates and Orlikowski (1992, p315)*

This is another good example of the power exercised by the virtual canvas. We summarise Yates and Orlikowski's discussion graphically in Figure 5.5. This suggests more readily the way that genres split and grow and also includes reference to the production modes employed in the genres. All of the genres involved here continue to develop; indeed, in certain respects the email genre is already dividing in numerous ways, ranging from the (almost) recognisable genres of spam messages to variants that are encroaching on the traditional preserves of the non-digital business letter.[4]

As we will suggest in detail with respect to our own examples below, changes such as those reported here for the business memo can be tracked even more effectively when we have a sufficiently detailed characterisation of the features that will change. We see the distinct layers of description given by the GeM model and the correlations that we can set up between these layers for particular genres as providing a particularly good foundation for such explorations.

---

[4] Strengthened in some places by legislation: for example, there is a European Union regulation that all business communication, including emails, should carry appropriate legal information concerning the contact details of the originating business, who is legally 'in charge', and so on. This regulation is gradually finding its way into corresponding national legislation.

5.1.3   Genre: the need for fine-grained descriptions

The standard definition of genre given by Swales (1990) still generalises well over all the approaches discussed so far: a genre is a class of communicative events that share a recognisable communicative purpose, that exhibit a schematic structure supporting the achievement of that purpose, and which show similarities in form, style, content, structure and intended audience (Swales 1990, p58). Swales also follows Miller in privileging 'folk' labels for genres: i.e., the terms and classifications that are actually named in a culture. By virtue of the recognition of a genre, language users are given access to particular schemes of interpretation for the social activities in progress (including verbal activities and their record in documents). These properties are assumed by most of the 'camps' involved in the genre debates that we have seen.

There are, however, some differences in precisely which aspects of 'style' and 'content' are considered indicative of a genre's schematic structure. For example, in Swales' (1990, p140–142) account genre structure is divided into 'moves' and 'steps' and is closely associated with broad 'rhetorical strategies', analogous to those found in traditional rhetoric. A similar relation between genre moves, or stages, and rhetorical organisation is proposed by both Lemke (1988*b*) and Thibault (1990, pp106–108). In other approaches, for example in Hasan's model of generic structure and approaches derived from it, there is a particularly strong expectation that generic stages will correlate with fine-grained lexical, grammatical and semantic differences. For both rhetorical organisation and notions of 'style' and 'content' in terms of linguistic features, generic phases are recognised by finding segments of text over which the variation of features selected is significantly less than that theoretically possible. Constraint on variation is then considered as a significant symptom for an associated genre phase.

The kind of information appealed to in approaches of the North American school appears, in contrast to this, to be more linguistically *ad hoc* or opportunistically selected. This can be revealing of distinct genres but is not necessarily so. As an example, the 'form criteria' established in order to find genre distinctions and developments in one investigation of the use of email within a 'virtual community' reported by Orlikowski and Yates (1994) show rather little systematic organisation; a selection of these features is given in Table 5.1. Although, on the positive side, we can already see features relevant for a multimodal view of the documents analysed, rather more problematic is the loose, pre-theoretical nature of these features. In particular, the characterisation of *linguistic* detail that is assumed in linguistic-based analyses of genre is not at all present. As mentioned

Definition of coding category

Message includes all or part of a previous message
Message includes graphical elements
Message includes a single main heading
Message indicates informality and colloquialism
Message includes lists in the body of the text
Message includes nonstandard grammar or punctuation
Message includes an opening salutation or phrase
Message includes a closing remark or signature
Message emphasises some words or phrases

Table 5.1   Extract from Orlikowski and Yates's definition of coding criteria for their investigation of genres deployed within an extended email-mediated organisational effort (Orlikowski and Yates 1994, p552).

above, incorporating broader ranges of linguistic features has already been found to aid genre identification significantly—even largely automatic identification (cf. Kessler, Nunberg and Schütze 1997)—and so its absence here can only weaken the accounts possible.

We see this as a major contributor to some of the problems that Yates and Orlikowski raise with respect to the degree of detail desirable in genre descriptions:

"undue proliferation of genres may also weaken the usefulness of the concept. ...If ...such cataloguing were extended to every industry, it would result in endless lists of genre comparable to the exhaustive (and exhausting) model letter books common in the 19th century. [] Thus there is a tension between too broad and too narrow a definition of genre."   (Yates and Orlikowski 1992, p305)

We do not accept this tension at all; the situation is actually the same for any linguistic analysis. The question is simply one of how fine an analysis needs to be for a specific analytic purpose. This decision should rest with the analyst and not be imposed *a priori* by the *framework*: the framework employed should be able to support analytical resolution of any granularity that is appropriate for the kinds of research questions raised. We should not, therefore, build into the definition of genre itself a preference for, or an avoidance of, particular resolutions.

Crucial for an effective answer to the problem is the capability to define whether and in what ways one genre might be more 'specific' than another. The experiences of linguistically based investigations of genre lead us to expect that the more detail that is available to us, the more refined our views of individual genres and their interrelationships will become. The discovery of genre families mentioned above is a clear example of how this can work to good effect. Drawing on such detail is one way by which we can avoid our study of genre collapsing into the simple catalogues of genres that Yates and Orlikowski warn against.

The serious attention given to the value of linguistic form found in strongly linguistic-based approaches is then not equally available to the accounts deriving from the North American School of genre. But we consider this to be crucial for turning genre into a usable construct. Fine linguistic detail is a prerequisite for fine-grained genre classification since only then do we achieve sufficient detail (i) to allow predictions to be made and (ii) to reveal more genres than superficially available by inspection or folk-labelling within a given discourse community. When we turn to the even less well understood areas involved in multimodal genre, a fine-grained specification employing a greater degree of linguistic sophistication and systematicity in the *kinds of forms* that can be used for evidence for or against the recognition of a genre category is even more important.

5.2   The move to multimodal genre

The previous section has presented how genre has been developed as a theoretical notion for analysing text. We argued that the most important theoretical property that makes an account of genre usable for empirical study is its potential to function *predictively*. Knowing the genre to which a text belongs leads to particular predictions concerning the form, function and contents of that text. This link between form and genre is a crucial feature that distinguishes linguistically-motivated approaches to genre from non-linguistic approaches. In this section, we discuss moves that have been made to extend existing accounts to include *multimodal* configurations in addition to texts alone. In taking this move, maintaining and extending the ability to function predictively is a, perhaps the, major challenge.

We will also address approaches to multimodal genre that have not been concerned primarily with text. This includes notions of document types from design, of particular classes of document based on visual organisational features, as well as results that have been obtained in automating document class recognition in the document analysis community. We will argue that these diverse orientations to genre usefully converge in, and can be improved by, the theoretical account of genre we are pursuing.

The section concludes with a brief discussion of one current area of concern in multimodal genre where a lack of an appropriate theoretical foundation is leading systematically to problems of application: this is the area of the so-called *cybergenre* (cf. Shepherd and Watters 1998), which is currently receiving considerable, and increasing, attention. We will argue that current efforts to characterise the kinds of documents found on the World-Wide Web are seriously handicapped by a relatively simple notion of genre that has only been extended minimally from traditional, non-multimodal conceptions of register and style.

5.2.1 Multimodal moves within linguistic and rhetorical approaches to genre

To the extent that the approaches to genre that we have discussed so far have addressed phenomena of multimodality, we will see in this subsection the problems that such extensions cause. This will allow us to set out more clearly just where a more developed treatment of multimodal genre has to start. As above, we begin with the systemic-functional approach and then move on to the social action perspective.

We have already discussed several applications of the systemic-functional linguistic approach to multimodal documents in previous chapters and so it will come as no surprise to see that there have been similar attempts to extend the systemic-functional notion of genre to deal with multimodality also. This development is one specialisation of the general assumption that is always made when extending SFL multimodally—i.e., that some artefact is subject to similar functional pressures to those that affect language and so will exhibit similar organisational properties (cf. Kress et al. 2000, p44). This applies equally to genre and its use multimodally.

We have seen in the previous sections, for example, that SFL attributes genres with a very particular social significance. As Kress emphasises in his account, the term *genre*

> "is best used to describe one aspect of textual organisation, namely that which realises and allows us to understand the social relations of the participants in the making, the reception and the reading/interpretation of the text."
>
> (Kress 2003, p96)

Kress and van Leeuwen then claim that since both verbal and non-verbal artefacts—and, indeed, social practices—can be indicative of social relations, then genre must also be a useful category to apply regardless of mode.

SFL approaches to multimodal genre have also focused on issues of change over time. One detailed example of the combination of issues of change and issues of multimodal genre is Baldry's (2000) analysis of two 'genres' of scientific text over the past 100 years: texts in plant biology and in economics. Baldry suggests that combining the contribution of various modalities can be seen as a *social achievement* of the relatively recent past, an achievement motivated by the greater possibilities of *meaning compression* that the combinations afford. Combining meanings is thus claimed to become increasingly effective as a means of communicating complex abstract meaning configurations.

Baldry illustrates this with contrastive examples of the use of tables in writings from the 19th century and the current use of time-graphs in the *Economist*, a 'genre' (and magazine) also addressed at length by Royce (1999, 2007). We saw in Chapter 2 that the table is often used as an example in this kind of discussion because it stands with feet in both camps: its organisation and content has traditionally been textual (and numeric), while its tabular organisation makes the first moves away from linearity to meaningful spatial configurations. Tables thus open up a semiotic mode in which the two dimensions of space on the page combine for carrying meanings. Baldry then points to a difference between tables and diagrams and discusses how, for example, graphs allocate a range of additional meanings to the two spatial dimensions of the page. With graphs one of the spatial dimensions is commonly used for time: this is then a convention mapping time to spatial extent.[5]

Whereas discussions of this kind show well how a particular range of conventions has emerged and developed over time, we need ways of tracking such changes for entire documents. We propose that the layers of the GeM model are one good way of doing this. This is necessary because restricting attention to tables and graphs does not yet provide a sufficient basis to deal with the most extensive move into multimodality that can be observed in recent documents—the use of the entire page as a two dimensional canvas for distributing meaningful contents that we introduced in the previous chapter as *page-flow*.

Page-flow is of central importance for advancing the treatment of multimodal genre because it is the primary 'resource' that multimodal genre builds upon. In early books, diagrammatic and tabular material was generally directly integrated into the text flow. Then, with the move towards more modern texts, the units separate out—driven in part by print technology constraints (separate treatments of text and diagram) and by interlinked professional constraints (distinct professions for text and diagram). Documents of this kind then contain explicit cross-references to figures and tables via document deixis and cross-modal cohesion, but the *spatial* relationships are

---

[5]Further descriptions of the internal make-up of tables and graphs have been given by Winn (1987), by Royce (2007, pp73–74), and by Guo (2004), who develops characterisations both of schematic drawings building on O'Toole (1994) and of statistical graphs building on O'Halloran (2004a). Also relevant here are studies such as Lefèvre, Renn and Schoepflin (2003) and Hentschel (2002).

not brought into play to take up semiotic work beyond framing. In more recent pages still, this has changed completely. We need for these a separate explicit account of the *spatial* composition of pages as a whole. This development is equally visible in all document types analysed, including those discussed by Baldry, but has not yet received the central attention as a distinct semiotic mode that it requires.

When page-flow is deployed as a semiotic resource, issues of reading paths also become paramount because the spatial extension provides, indeed encourages, alternatives. Bringing reading paths explicitly into the process of meaning-making has also been proposed as a way of achieving a more 'dynamic' construction of genre. This is relevant for the analysis of many kinds of documents, but is particularly prominent in discussions of web-pages and similar 'new media' artefacts. We have seen that one common property proposed for traditional genres is that they unfold in particular text-determined stages. But when a multimodal document does not rely on text-flow to constrain the reading paths that are sensible, linear characterisations of genre are difficult; this is exactly analogous to our discussion of the problems of moving beyond the linear view of rhetorical organisation discussed with respect to Rhetorical Structure Theory in the previous chapter.

One proposal for maintaining the notion of genre in the face of dynamic, non-linear artefacts considers, on the one hand, genres to present relatively stable semiotic configurations for interpretation, and reading paths, on the other, to dynamically *select* those stages that a reader is piecing together. The genre remains a linear, staged-activity, but the stages, rather than being pre-given by the text, are instead constructed by the reading path (cf. Lemke 2002, van Leeuwen 2005). This suggests a further set of resources by which a reader/user can 'make sense' (quite literally) of the documents that they encounter. Only if elements can be picked out from a document in such a way that they can be interpreted as stages of some genre will a 'coherent' reading be perceived. Lemke (2005) suggests that this may also offer an effective mechanism for the creation of *new* genres, whenever stages selected as a sequence are found to be recurrently useful. Under this view:

> "the text *itself* is no longer a staged, goal oriented process. It is an environment for such processes, and must be analysed as a kind of map, a spatial structure allowing a number of trajectories, or as the layout of a building, a spatial structure designed to facilitate a range of specific activities."
>
> (van Leeuwen 2005, p85)

For this, we need to analyse both the visual 'input'—the document as the reader/user encounters it—and how readers/users proceed to interact/use the document. This perspective leads us to "study, not the structuring of the text, but the structuring of the reading (using) process." (van Leeuwen 2005, p84) Clearly, there is much to do in this area and we are still very much at the beginning in terms of researching the kinds of meanings and meaning-making activities that are involved.

It is important, however, not to loose sight of this explicit separation of, on one hand, the text and, on the other, readers' interaction with texts. This is necessary in order to locate more clearly how the resources deployed in individual texts/artefacts *themselves* contribute to, or confound, interpretations. Particularly in analyses of web-pages, for example, it is crucial that we can focus on how the resources deployed in the artefact construct intended paths for the reader, regardless of whether any particular reader follows them or not. Moreover, although the construction of dynamic reading paths is made easier in the context of the World-Wide Web, it is by no means unique to that context. Readers can always construct dynamic reading paths combining materials. Without a firm analytic hold of the 'documents themselves', therefore, the object of study is in danger of dissolving since we are not able to characterise precisely just what each individual document, or page, brings to the interpretation process. The more precisely we can describe what reader/users find on the pages with which they interact, the better position we will be in for specifying genre.

When we turn to the work deriving from the New Rhetoric tradition, we also find significant approaches that directly take up issues of multimodality. We have already seen above, for example, how in Yates and Orlikowski's account there was a basic assumption from the outset that the forms that characterise genres may well involve non-linguistic manifestations. Genres should, Orlikowski and Yates argue, be seen in terms of socially significant practices characterised by a recognised communicative purpose and common aspects of form (Orlikowski and Yates 1994, p543)—but those forms may be drawn from any of the media involved. Something of the breadth of this consideration of genre is made clear in their following description:

> "A genre also typically has some characteristic aspect(s) of form. Form refers to the readily observable features of the communication, including structural features (e.g., text formatting devices, such as lists and headings, and devices for structuring interactions at meetings, such as agenda and chairpersons), communication medium (e.g., pen and paper, telephone, or face to face), and language or symbol system (e.g., level of formality and the specialised vocabulary of corporate or professional jargon)."   (Orlikowski and Yates 1994, p544)

This is particularly interesting in that it represents one of the few theoretical accounts of genre which have not begun from a position of 'monomodality'. Orlikowski and Yates also incorporate directly the relationship between genre and technology that we suggested in the introduction to be crucial; we saw this above in their characterisation of the development of business memos.

This rather broad starting point for discussing genres together with their emphasis on tracking change is one reason why Orlikowski and Yates's approach has been particularly influential for research on new, 'emergent' genres in contexts such as that of the World-Wide Web (cf. Crowston and Williams 1997). Here it is recognised that the ability to 'classify' web-documents according to some scheme promises to be of considerable benefit for providing more structured and focused access to the sheer quantity of documents available. The view of genre built upon in these web-based studies is, however, quite restricted—as we will set out in more detail later in this chapter.

In conclusion, the extension of genre to treat multimodal linguistic artefacts has evidently been found quite natural in almost all research traditions that work explicitly with a notion of genre. With seemingly little theoretical problematisation, the everyday use of genres of various literary forms has been taken over and used in otherwise quite technical analyses of multimodal documents. We therefore have genres of websites—such as homepages (Roberts 1998), genres of technical manuals (Hartley 1994), of non-linear hypertexts (Shepherd and Watters 1998), of e-mail messages (Gruber 2000), of magazine covers (Tseng 2001, Held 2005), of patents (Bazerman 1994), of newspapers (Blum and Bucher 1998) and many more. But despite this fashionability of multimodal analysis, without an overall framework for placing any such documents alongside other multimodal offerings, insightful *explanatory* analyses of the meanings on offer will remain illusive.

5.2.2 Moving in on genre from the visual

There have also been approaches to classifying the kinds of multimodality exhibited in documents that begin with the visual composition itself, i.e., with the *form* of the visual representations found. Such approaches do not typically begin by asking what purpose the document is serving, going on to investigate what texts and text-accompanying features may be observable, but instead go directly to the visual resources deployed. Links can be found between particular visual genres and particular kinds of uses, but this has been systematised only to a very limited degree.

Such approaches again come from a variety of disciplines and have rather different aims.

The interaction between classifications of visual form and *design*, for example, has been approached in at least two ways. First, there is an empirical-historical concern with ascertaining just what design attributes have been mobilised in artefacts at various stages in their history. This is a kind of broad 'stocktaking' of what has been done. It is perhaps surprising to note that such information is not at all widely available. Partly as a consequence of the traditional lack of attention given to the non-verbal aspects of documents, other contributions to their design have often been neglected. Second, there is a further step that draws more on the essential *function* of genre in establishing expectation frameworks for interpretation.

There are also beneficial interactions to be explored between classifications of visual form and automatic document analysis, where the aim is one of automatically providing appropriate genre 'labels' for documents.

We address each of these contributions to a visually-based notion of genre in turn.

Proposals from design

In order to ascertain the possibilities for visual form that have been taken up over time, it is useful to characterise more abstractly just how documents are structured visually. To this end, Twyman (1979) proposes a schema that classifies pages according to 28 categories of visual composition. In one sense, we can see these categories as a set of candidates for 'visual genres'. The categories are defined in terms of an intersection of two dimensions. The first dimension is concerned with the 'modes' of information portrayal mobilised in a page, which Twyman groups into the following four frequently occurring combinations:

- verbal and numerical,
- pictorial,
- pictorial, verbal and numerical,
- schematic.

The second dimension is concerned with how readers are led by a document's composition to access the information presented in particular orders. This Twyman characterises in terms of the *degree of linearity* imposed.

Pure linear presentations are rare since they must attempt to ignore the physical boundaries of the canvas making up the page. They can only be approximated—for example, by writing in spirals. The most common compromise between the logical linearity of text and the physical canvas constraints used to carry that text is then the category of 'linear interrupted', which respects line and shape boundaries but otherwise unfolds linearly. Normal typographic rendering of print in lines and columns is an example, but any canvas or virtual canvas shape may impose constraints similarly. In all Twyman sets out seven possibilities of varying degrees of linearity. These categories, together with examples taken from Twyman (2004), are illustrated for his first mode, verbal and numerical, in Figure 5.6.

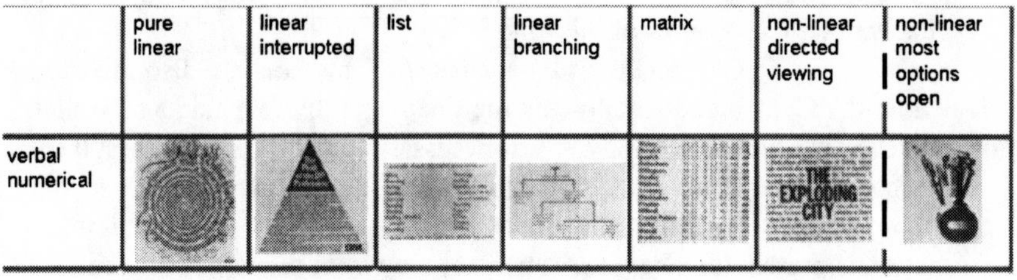

	pure linear	linear interrupted	list	linear branching	matrix	non-linear directed viewing	non-linear most options open
verbal numerical							

Figure 5.6   The verbal and numerical row of Twyman's schema of 'graphic language' together with examples from Twyman (2004); used by permission

Twyman (2004) shows that the actual situation is somewhat more complex than his original schema suggested in that (i) there are some further arrangements that can be discriminated and (ii) many document pages involve *combinations* of the more 'pure' forms illustrated in the schema itself. Although it is the combinations that are of particular interest for our account here, it is nevertheless advantageous to have a clear account of the range of forms that contribute to these combinations also.

We introduced further work of the Reading School valuable for establishing just what document attributes combine in particular genres in Chapter 2. It is worthwhile mentioning this again here because there is a considerable overlap with the particular goals that we are pursuing in this chapter. This work has had a long-term commitment to investigating empirically just what kinds of visual features and combinations are actually encountered in 'naturally occurring' visual artefacts. One of its main concerns is to define frameworks appropriate for classifying the attributes observed in such artefacts so that more general descriptions of entire classes of documents can be found (cf. Walker 1982, Norrish 1987).

Walker's solution for this is a detailed classification of the typographical attributes of documents that goes beyond narrow typographical concerns of font or type face to include *spatial* characteristics (word spacing, line increment, margins, etc.), *graphic* characteristics (underlining, capitalisation patterns, etc.), and *physical* attributes (produced with a typewriter, the paper used, and so on). These all form part of a *Verbal Graphic Language* (VGL) which has served as a basis for exploring the generic features of a variety of genres. Walker (1982), for example, describes some characteristics of hand-written letters, Norrish (1987) applies and extends the technique to a range of printed genres, and Waller (1987*a*, Table 9.1, p291) sets out an overview of the contrasting attributes of instructions for domestic appliances, holiday brochures and traffic signs. This general technique is well suited to tracking fine-grained changes in genres over time and current work is continuing to uncover genre properties of this kind.[6]

As we saw in Chapter 3, visual attributes of this kind are also included within the GeM model. Following the line begun by Twyman and Waller, however, we also showed how it was necessary to go beyond typographical attributes, particularly so as to take in overall spatial properties of layout and composition over and above that concerned with how the verbal information is presented. Characterisations of the visual properties of elements as well as of their relative locations on the page may make equally valuable contributions to specifications of genre: only by including these can we begin to capture genre-conditioned aspects of page-flow.

In some respects, there is also an overlap between the concerns of genre and approaches that try to characterise *visual style*. At this level of analysis, we still find ourselves between register and genre proper. Dondis, for example, sets out a classification scheme for style that he characterises as: "the visual synthesis of the elements, techniques, syntax, inspiration, expression and basic purpose." (Dondis 1972, p128) For this, he proposes a collection of dimensions for positioning visual artefacts in general, providing examples of 19 'techniques for visual communication'. These are defined in terms of the following scales: balance *vs.* instability, symmetry *vs.* asymmetry, regularity *vs.* irregularity, simplicity *vs.* complexity, unity *vs.* fragmentation, economy *vs.* intricacy, understatement *vs.* exaggeration, predictability *vs.* spontaneity, activeness *vs.* passiveness, subtlety *vs.* boldness, neutrality *vs.* accent, transparency *vs.* opacity, consistency *vs.* variation, realism *vs.* distortion, flatness *vs.* depth, singularity *vs.* juxtaposition, sequentiality *vs.* randomness, sharpness *vs.* diffusion, and continuity *vs.* episodicity (Dondis 1972, pp111–127).

---

[6]Walker (2003) reports on a project investigating the generic visual-verbal properties of children's educational publications based on a collection of texts from 1830 to 1960; see http://www.kidstype.org/The project/Describing book design/corpus.html. (N.B. "The project" and "Describing book design" in this web address are written with spaces between the words.) A similar project investigating text/image relations in contemporary children's books is also underway at Sydney: http://www.arts.usyd.edu.au/research/projects/seahfm/linguistics.shtml.

Although this list is not intended to be exhaustive, it does go some way towards providing a lattice for positioning distinctive visual styles. Dondis characterises, for example, the techniques of *expressionism* as exhibiting exaggeration, spontaneity, activeness, complexity, boldness, variation, distortion and several more, whereas *primitivism* exhibits exaggeration, spontaneity, activeness, simplicity, economy, flatness, irregularity, and so on. The poles of the scales that Dondis proposes are intended to represent cases that are sufficiently clear to be reliably recognised, although the extent to which this can be extended for finer characterisations is unclear.

There is also work that attempts to theorise explicitly a notion of specifically *visual* genre in a way that includes the social dimension of genre. One detailed approach of this kind is the framework developed by Kostelnick and Hassett (2003). Kostelnick and Hassett present a rich and varied collection of examples that reveal both how design practice has changed over time and how interpretation needs to be carried out with respect to particular user communities—very much analogous to the discourse communities explored in linguistic approaches to social variation in language and genre. To this end, they classify several resources deployed in multimodal documents according to their conventional, community-specific interpretation. These resources include conventions such as italics for book titles or emphasis, multiple levels of headings within a text, superscripts for footnotes, justified text for formal documents, lines between cells in tables, frames around pictures and charts, page borders, and many more (cf. Kostelnick and Hassett 2003, p16; adapted from Kostelnick 1988 and Kostelnick 1989). These techniques are grouped into three broad categories: *textual, spatial* and *graphic*, and are ranged across a spectrum running from *small-scale* to *large-scale*.

Unfortunately for our present concerns, Kostelnick and Hassett focus directly on interpretation and do not pay very much attention to how the units that participate in these conventions are to be identified; this is analogous to most of the approaches from design that we described in Chapter 2 above, i.e., the parts of the documents being analysed are not themselves problematised. Kostelnick and Hassett then focus on the role of conventionality in design and visual meaning by already *combining* design element and interpretation. This makes it difficult to track combinations of genres since elements and their interpretations are not allowed to follow trajectories of development independently of one another. As we will see below, the ability to follow forms and interpretation separately is necessary for 'picking apart' the manifold contributions to any particular instantial genre. Nevertheless, Kostelnick and Hassett's research clearly demonstrates how a good account of genre, however we finally come to achieve this, is necessary to understand users' interpretations of the documents they encounter. The importance of such *generic expectations* brought about by convention when dealing with multimodal artefacts cannot be over-estimated.

Proposals from automatic analysis

Arising out of the school of thought mentioned above that genre is not amenable to precise formalisation, it is sometimes suggested that it makes limited sense to attempt detailed and explicit characterisations of genres, particularly multimodal documents. But, in fact, there is good evidence that substantial detail can be extracted from such artefacts—and this can be used to drive considerably more refined genre characterisations than are currently available.

Within the automatic document analysis tradition, for example, the task of classifying documents according to their visual appearance in order to assign them to particular categories has received close attention for many years. This research is relevant for us here because significant progress has been made in 'clustering' visually related documents together into families of similar documents. Such families consist of documents exhibiting similarities of 'style', both linguistically and visually.

With respect to linguistic similarity, statistical techniques of various kinds have now been applied with considerable success. This is closely related to research into linguistic register as introduced above (cf. Biber 1988), extending this to apply to linguistic genre classification (cf. Kessler et al. 1997). There is, however, little differentiation here of 'style', 'register' and 'genre'—the main focus is on providing labels for families of similar documents. The term 'genre' is used when those labels correspond to existing categories such as 'legal text', 'fictional', 'editorial' and so on.

Similar techniques have now also been applied to visual similarity (e.g., Hu, Kashi and Wilfong 1999, Cesarini et al. 2001, Diligenti, Frasconi and Gori 2003, Mao et al. 2005). Approaches here take data consisting of a collection of layout structures, often based on some variant of the XY-trees that we saw in Section 2.4, and organise that collection into specified classes according to the closeness of the structural relations exhibited. Members of the same class are considered to be visually similar; members of distinct classes are visually dissimilar. The fact that some good quality (i.e., reliable) clustering results are being achieved indicates that there is indeed a considerable degree of visual generalization to be drawn on. Although a visual difference *per se* may or may not correspond to a genre difference, the ability to find visual similarities is already a good first step. Considerably more work will need to be carried out to ascertain just how visual similarity and judgements of genre membership relate. This will no doubt feed in future into more developed accounts of multimodal genre.

We see very similar results and methods being applied in the context of automatic recognition and classification of documents found on the World-Wide Web. Doermann et al. (1997) argue that classifying web documents according to their basic intended function will provide considerable benefits. They accordingly propose several broad categories of distinct web-based families of documents that we can consider as genre 'dimensions' or facets (see below). For example, one distinction involves a separation of documents according to 'use' and to 'type'. Use-related categories include documents for reading, documents for browsing, and documents for searching. Each of these can be correlated with particular indicative sets of document features; for example:

> "In a searching document, no more than 25% of the text blocks should have more than five lines. There should be no image components, and few or no graphic components." (Doermann et al. 1997, p1080)

Collections of descriptive criteria of this kind show a broad similarity with notions of genre, serving to associate realisational features of documents with generic purpose. We will see further applications of this kind of approach for web-page classification in the section following.

Doermann et al. (1997, p1080) go on to observe, however, that criteria of this kind cannot be expected to perform well on documents with complex structures. This is again strikingly similar to the state of affairs in linguistic approaches to classifying text types. Attempts to find 'dominant' text functions to generate predictions about the features of a text have not in general been successful because texts are diverse and can be satisfying multiple functions. This is one of the primary motivations for applying a more differentiating view of genre and its realisation—i.e., accepting that texts, and particularly multimodal texts, may exhibit a range of distinct styles across the structural elements that they involve.

There are accordingly proposals in this tradition for processing documents in order to capture their constitutive layout elements (cf. Chapter 2). This can then be taken further by assigning those layout elements distinguishing *functional* labels. Doermann et al., for example, define:

> "...a level of document organization, which can be regarded as intermediate between the geometric and semantic levels, that relates to the efficiency with which the document transfers its information to the reader. We refer to this level as the *functional* level." (Doermann et al. 1997, p1078)

This additional layer characterises the particular communicative roles played by the logical structure elements of a document's pages and so is already very similar to the *generic stages* defined by Hasan's Generic Structure Potentials and related approaches (cf. Figure 5.3 above).

Just as is the case with generic stages, this assignment of functional value also depends crucially on the type of document analysed. For example, we might be able to recognise some short block of text separated by whitespace from its surroundings, identifying many features of the block purely on the basis of its appearance. In the context of the page as a whole, however, that text block will take on further particular roles—such as the *caption* of a figure, or the *by-line* of a news article, or a *label* (or *callout*) in a diagram. Allocating these functional values requires knowledge not only of the geometric and physical properties of a block but also knowledge of the document type, i.e., the genre. Given such information a system may then predict what kinds of functional parts are expected.

Eglin and Bres (2004) formulate a model of functional document analysis for assigning functional labels of this kind automatically. In this account, documents are first decomposed into textual and non-textual elements using filters of various kinds as described in Chapter 2. A range of features are extracted from the visual properties of these elements, including visibility, salience, and position with respect to other elements. This information is taken as the basis for functional labelling. The labels themselves are drawn from a classification hierarchy of families of related functionalities. The main divisions of this classification define three families: titles, intermediate, and paragraphs. A subsequent process then attempts to provide hierarchical structure for the elements discovered, and this can in turn help to further constrain functional labelling and to correct misclassifications.

Eglin and Bres have applied the framework to a range of documents, including newspapers. We show in Figure 5.7, therefore, how our example newspaper page from above might appear if analysed according to this framework. Although the classification is not yet fine enough to reach the standard terms and categories used in newspaper design, the similarities that this functional analysis shows to Hasan and others' generic stages is already suggestive.

Characterising both generic structures and the particular constraints holding on elements of those structures is certain to become increasingly important for all kinds of genre recognition—both of traditional print documents and in new media. Among these, web-pages in particular form a challenging area where a strong and well theorised notion of genre is critical. In the subsection following, we suggest that many problems currently discussed with respect to web-based genres in fact arise from weaknesses in the the-

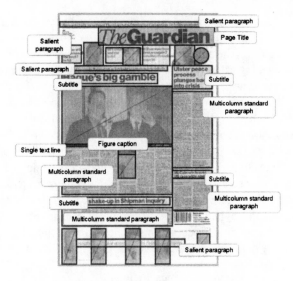

Figure 5.7   Constructed analysis of an example newspaper page following the style of
description of Eglin and Bres (2004)

oretical foundation adopted for genre rather than in the complexity of the documents being analysed. Most problematic is the tendency not to draw on those properties of genre central to its definition—particularly in relation to structure—and to collapse 'genre', 'register', 'style' and similar notions together.

5.2.3   Cybergenres: a brief critique

Several research communities are currently applying notions of genre in the context of the World-Wide Web. In fact, the treatment of web documents is currently one of the fastest moving areas of application for notions of genre that we can find—presumably motivated by the increasingly dominant role that web-based information has taken on in modern life. For approaches to genre that draw on linguistics, this is a natural development: whether the artefacts analysed are on the web or printed is of little concern, one would expect the same analytic frameworks to find broadly similar application. For other approaches, the technological basis of the web has been a major driving force and, as we saw in the previous section, practical issues of web-page classification, clustering for information delivery and retrieval, user evaluation and automatic information extraction play more of a defining role.

For most authors applying genre to the new media one particular aspect of electronic documents is placed firmly in the foreground: that is, their support of *hypertext*. The ability to explicitly link documents together and to provide technological support for following those links is commonly seen as the crucial 'new' component of new media. This was already the case well before the emergence of the World-Wide Web, going back to what is commonly cited as the 'first' work on hypertext, that of Bush (1945).[7]

This aspect is taken up in one of the most well-known and influential positions on genre within the new media, that of Shepherd and Watters's (1998) introduction of the *cybergenre*. Rather than 'simply' being read like normal book pages, web-pages offer opportunities for interaction more reminiscent of interactive computer systems. Shepherd and Watters accordingly propose that cybergenres be differentiated from traditional genres by a component explicitly reflecting this additional 'functionality'. They formalise this by defining 'non-digital genres' in terms of the pair:

$$< \text{content, form} >$$

in contrast to cybergenres, which they define with the triple:

$$< \text{content, form, functionality} >$$

They thus build into their account a distinctive and defining role for the *medium* of the documents encountered, providing at the same time a place for characterisations of a user's *interaction* with the web document.

A number of developments of this kind have now been made. For example, a similar line of argument follows in Askehave and Nielsen's (2005) proposals for extending the notion of genre developed by Swales (1990) to new media by incorporation of a sensitivity to the medium of the web. They propose what they describe as a 'two-dimensional' genre model, in which the generic properties of a web-page are characterised both in terms of a traditional *text* perspective and in terms of the *medium* (including navigation). They motivate this by means of a discussion of a proposed 'homepage' web-genre thus:

> "This duality inherent in homepages may best be described by conceptualising the homepage as a front door with a door sign. The door sign indicates the name of the residents (i.e., the 'content' of the house) while the door itself is the gateway (the medium) which enables guests to enter the house and visit the residents inside."   (Askehave and Nielsen 2005)

---

[7]We will not follow up this history of the medium in any detail here; for further information and many references, see Conklin (1987), Landow (1991, 1994, 1997).

The traditional part of their model continues to rely on Swales' view of genre which, as we saw above, analyses genres at the levels of purpose, moves, and rhetorical strategies. The new part extends this by defining two 'modes' that users take up in their interaction with new media documents: users may adopt either a 'reading mode' or a 'navigation mode'. When content is being read, readers 'zoom in' on content and the traditional genre model applies; when, however, users are moving around the document, they 'zoom out' to use the medium to navigate in the virtual space provided by the document. Askehave and Nielsen argue that hyperlinks and their use constitute an essential extension brought about by the medium; the traditional genre model they situate solely within the reading mode.

A related direction is followed in Crowston and Williams's (1999) empirical study characterising distinct genres in terms of the types of links found on a page—i.e., whether the links point to the same document, to the same website, etc. This inclusion of the linking structure of web-pages shows some similarities to the inclusion of a navigation and 'access' layer in our framework. We do not believe, however, that this is usefully restricted to be solely a feature of web-pages. Indeed, accepting a defining role for medium among the constituents of genre has traditionally been controversial (cf. Yates, Orlikowski and Okamura 1999, p100).

Medium is most commonly associated with aspects of form and Crowston and Williams (1997, 2000) argue, following Yates and Orlikowski, that it is the communicative function and intent that is critical for defining genres, not the 'physical form' of the supporting artefact. Thus, whether a document appears as a 'brochure, booklet or a flyer' should not necessarily be indicative of different genres.[8] But the usage of the term 'genre' nevertheless shows extreme variation. Some researchers even talk of photographs and diagrams as being different 'genres', which goes to an opposite extreme and makes medium criterial.

The precise relationship between physical form, the affordances of that form, and genre is therefore complex. There are many cases where the physical form provides or prevents particular deployments of resources, visual or verbal, from being effective: and in precisely these cases the physical form and a genre definition will need to interact. Moreover, although the tendency to avoid questions of medium has certainly been encouraged

---

[8]In the list of web genres found in Crowston and Williams' study, their description of the characteristics of those genres is accordingly given predominantly in terms of function and purpose (e.g., *meeting minutes*: "the record of the proceedings at a meeting of an assembly, corporate body, society, company, committee, or the like"); this stands somewhat in conflict to their observation that they could often assign genres for web-pages in languages that they did not themselves speak (§ 3.2): the visual side is still clearly under-represented therefore.

by monomodal considerations of text, this is far from the case in socio-semiotic constructions of genre such as those offered by Kress and van Leeuwen (2001) and Kress (2003), where artefactual properties are considered crucial. Significantly, this development has again been proposed for *all* documents, not just those of the 'new' media, and so it is beneficial to return to a consideration of this, rather broader, starting point when theorising web-based genres also.

Many studies, however, have already begun characterising the genres found in documents on the World-Wide Web, usually adopting informal labels for perceived document purposes. Crowston and Williams (1997) report a classification of 100 randomly selected web-pages in which each page was coded according to a hierarchically organised collection of genre labels. The acceptance of a hierarchy follows from Yates and Orlikowski's notions of genre 'specificity' mentioned above. The genre labels themselves were predominantly familiar from non-digital publications, with the addition of some characterised as novel, such as the *hotlist*, webserver statistics, and search engines. But of the pages sampled, 80 appeared to belong to familiar genres, leading Crowston and Williams to comment:

> "Perhaps our biggest surprise was just how mundane our sample was. The 100 pages in our pilot sample did not include anything particularly radical..."
>
> (Crowston and Williams 1997, § 6).

This reaffirms the proposals of Orlikowski and Yates (1994, p547) and others before them that, in novel situations, people adopt and adapt existing genres thereby reproducing them in the new situations of use. It is difficult, for several reasons, to move beyond the realms of established genres—even in the new media.

In a similar study, Shepherd and Watters (1999) characterised a random selection of 96 websites according to properties drawn from their content-form-functionality definition of genre. They used these properties to assign web-pages to a list of rather general genre labels, consisting of homepage (personal and corporate), brochure, resource, catalogue, search engine and game (cf. Table 5.2). After mapping Crowston and Williams' much finer set of genre categories to their own, they suggest that there has been a substantial change in the genres found on the web over the short time period spanned by the two studies: they remark on a significant increase in homepages and a corresponding decrease in 'resource' pages.

But the extent to which such claims are accurate or revealing is questionable. As we can see from Table 5.2, the actual attributes appealed to are very broad and may be subject to a range of variation without being strongly predictive of genre. When it is as straightforward to include a search facil-

Cybergenre	Content	Form	Functionality
Homepage	information about person or company	● introduction ● hierarchical ● images ● animated images	● browsing ● e-mail
Brochure	products and services	● shallow hierarchy ● high-impact visual	● browsing ● e-mail
Resource	subject-specific information	● hierarchical ● images ● video ● audio	● browsing ● e-mail ● search ● discussion ● interaction
Catalogue	products and services	● hierarchical ● images	● browse ● e-mail ordering ● search

Table 5.2 Selection of the results of Shepherd and Watters' analysis of 96 websites according to their content, form and functionality scheme

ity on a web-page as to leave it out (as has almost become the case), we can expect such a functional element to appear whenever the author thinks of including it. Functionalities currently listed in the table as corresponding to specific cybergenres may then spread rapidly across genres, losing any predictive power they might have fleetingly enjoyed concerning genre membership.

Moreover, for the majority of simple websites—such as those sampled both by Shepherd and Watters and by Crowston and Williams—the forms supported by the web are actually extremely limited. The constraints imposed by their use of straightforward web technology constitute a sufficiently strong straightjacket to keep attempts at innovation within familiar channels. The parallel with arguments made elsewhere concerning the consequences of introducing new technology is striking. With the emergence of print technology, for example, instead of immediately opening up a wealth of new possibilities as sometimes assumed, the immature technology actually served to *restrict* variability. Much previously existing use of illustration, colour and their integration with text then went missing until the technology had, in a sense, caught up again with the demands and challenges of design (cf. Twyman 1986 and Waller 1987*a*, pp248–251 for further discussion and references).

This should be taken as a word of caution for the currently exploding 'study of websites' being undertaken in multimodal linguistics: there are useful and interesting aspects of websites to investigate, but they are found exceedingly rarely directly on the surface in terms of novel design and new genres. To what extent the web-page has moved beyond technological dependence to support semiotically interesting meaning-making possibilities is an open question, a question that is not addressed adequately simply by assuming it to be the case.

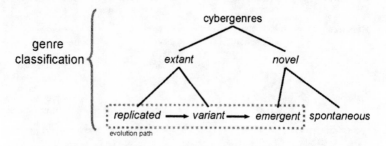

Figure 5.8   Cybergenres and their development according to Shepherd and Watters (1998)

Shepherd and Watters (1998) also propose an abstract characterisation of how genres on the World-Wide Web develop; this is shown in Figure 5.8. They define an 'evolution' path for cybergenres by which initially non-digital genres tend to be simply recreated in digital form: these are the *replicated* genres on the lower left of the diagram. These subsequently pick up additional functionalities supported by the web leading to *variants* on the original replication. This can then extend further to support completely new uses and new genres, described in the diagram as *emergent*. Alternatively, totally new genres can be produced spontaneously, supported by the new functionalities and very rapid distribution possibilities that the web opens up.

Although appealing, this characterisation does not yet do justice to the 'technological straightjacket' imposed by the new medium. It is far more difficult to simply 'replicate' existing genres than might have been thought. This fact contributes both to the dominance of 'familiar' (or *replicated*) genres on the World-Wide Web and to the claimed low degree of *variety* of genres on the web. The range of genres available is still being restricted because the technological limits channel documents into a narrower range of options than a technologically mature medium might support. This manner of genre 'coercion' needs to receive far closer attention. It is probably the most frequent style of 'adopting and adapting' genres that occurs during the emergence of web-based genres.

We can see this in the examples that Shepherd and Watters themselves offer. As illustrations of replicated documents they include early examples of 'electronic newspapers', which tended to be simply versions of print

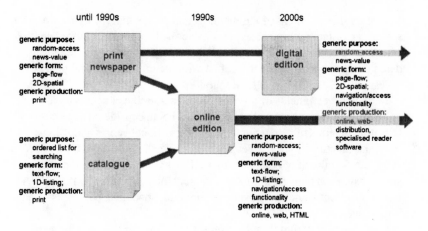

Figure 5.9   Development of parallel distinct online news genres

newspapers with extra facilities. However the documents that they refer to were actually experimental results from research projects in the early 1990s (cf. Ashton and Cruickshank 1993, Haake, Hüser and Reichenberger 1994), which were not at all the electronic newspapers that then arrived on the web *en masse* from newspaper companies. As we discussed above, these actual electronic newspapers were, and often remain, strongly influenced by the weak technological basis provided by the web and were not able to 'replicate' the original non-digital genres at all. It is only with the very much more recent *digital editions* alluded to above that replication has become remotely possible.

An arguably more accurate characterisation of the development process in this case, therefore, is one in which an originating document type is approximated applying a different technological and material basis. This difference may coerce the originating genre into another, more or less related, genre that preserves some aspects of the original while replacing others. The originating newspaper genre here was therefore coerced so that what was produced was not a newspaper but a 'catalogue' of news items with little use of spatial composition for organising meaning and access structure. Shepherd and Watters present the emergence of digital editions as a process of 'evolving back' to the print genre (§ 2.3); we would suggest instead that we have here the emergence of an *additional*, more accurate replication of the *originating* genre for which the supporting technology is only now becoming available. We show this graphically in Figure 5.9 in the style used in Figure 5.5 for our illustration of Yates and Orlikowski's (1992) discussion of the development of the memo genre. In the current figure we see something of the tension created in the intermediate 'online edition' genre, where the generic purpose of providing random-access to news items ordered by news-value stands in conflict with the one-dimensional text-flow access enforced by HTML's catalogue-like tables.

To track developments of this kind, we again need characterisations that go more finely into the details of the genres being considered. The characterisation in terms of <content, form> for traditional genres and <content, form and functionality> for webgenres is misleading. *Any* genre may need to have a functionality component specified and it is not then a matter of simple extension to relate this to the functionalities supported by the web. A true replication would carry over the same functionalities, but this is often impossible.

Many kinds of 'faithful replication' of genres according to the schemes seen so far must therefore be seen as far from faithful. Simply preserving folk-labels across the genre coercion that has occurred can obscure important differences. We need instead to allocate genre on the basis of the documents themselves rather than on claims of their lineage. Only then can we see more clearly the contributions made when genres, and specific aspects of genres, combine. In terms of the metaphor used in the introduction to this book, a loose genre classification that privileges intended 'purpose' can easily swamp (for the analyst) the signals that the document itself might be sending. In Figure 5.10 we illustrate the difference in modelling approach that this entails between the cybergenre view and that presented here.

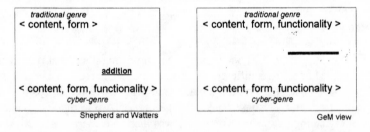

Figure 5.10   *Contrasting Shepherd and Watters (1998) view of cybergenres with the approach proposed within the GeM model*

There is very much more to be said concerning appropriate ways of approaching the issue of genres and the application of the construct to the digital context. Most important for our current purposes, however, is the consideration that a more appropriate definition of genre does *not* in fact open up a divide between 'digital' and 'non-digital' artefacts. We emphasised already in the introduction of the book that the GeM view follows Kress and van Leeuwen in assigning a central role to the 'materiality' of *all* multimodal documents. Traditional views of genre that focused exclusively on texts typically overlooked the 'functionality' contribution of the artefacts themselves because this was not sufficiently foregrounded by their linguistic starting point. When we move to web-based documents, and the self-evident fact that one must 'interact' with the document in order to reach it at all, then this component of genre is no longer to be ignored. But, when examined more closely, we find similar examples of precisely the same phenomena for all multimodal documents.

Anchoring genres in both societal context and time as we propose reduces the likelihood of characterising any cybergenre as an entirely 'new' class of genres, thereby providing additional ammunition for arguments that have been made against an alleged 'new media revolution' (cf., e.g., Manovich 2001, Hocks and Kendrick 2003). As Shepherd and Crowston write, the replicated, variant and emergent genres should preserve aspects of their original content-form mappings as a useful design feature. We go further and suggest that technological limitations and design practices both combine to restrict innovation in this, as well as in every other, medium. Much of what is currently seen as 'novel' or 'new' on the web is then actually caused by it not being possible to track originating configurations of genre components in sufficient detail. And it is to this, more general task that we now return.

5.3   Representing genre

We need now to set out how we can begin to represent genre in a way that can drive empirical inquiry and organise empirical results concerning potential genre descriptions and inter-relationships. This section sets out those approaches to representing genre that have been proposed previously in the literature. We briefly discuss the merits and limitations of these approaches, and propose some working methodological assumptions for taking us further. At the current state of the art, there is no adequate general solution to the problem of representing genres available; the best we can do, therefore, is to establish the kinds of properties that any such solutions are going to require and to provide a framework within which we can move towards this.

Traditionally, genres have been represented in isolation or in terms of loose collections of more or less 'similar' genres. To make an account of genre maximally predictive and useful for organising empirical results, we need to find better ways of bringing out both the individuality of individual groups of genres and their distinctiveness with respect to others. A common starting point is to make a working assumption similar to the following:

> "we posit that genres are enacted through rules, which associate appropriate elements of form and substance with certain recurrent situations. We call these rules *genre rules.*"
>
> (Yates and Orlikowski 1992, p302)

This sets up the necessary connection between situation and particular regularities of form, but does not yet allow us to make strong statements about the relationships between genres. How, in particular, do we identify, explicitly express, and 'bundle' genre rules into useful groupings?

We discuss two basic modes of representation proposed for modelling genre: the *typological* and the *topological*. Typological views of genre can be represented as classification networks; topological accounts must be characterised in terms or dimensions of variation. In both cases, the question of *instantiation* is difficult—i.e., how do we relate features and classifications of genre to particular configurations of generic stages and how can we relate generic stages to two-dimensional spatial layouts? These issues must be raised, although we are not yet able to provide fully developed solutions.

A further approach midway between the typological and topological currently receiving some attention adopts a genre representation built on *facets* (cf. Crowston and Kwaśnik 2004). In this approach, adopted primarily from the use of faceted classification in library science, genre is considered as a multidimensional construction combining aspects both of the documents described and the purposes for which they are being taken up. The approach is related to the typological in as far as it attempts to provide a classification system for genre that goes beyond a simple listing of genre labels. A faceted classification consists of a collection of 'ways of viewing' an artefact together with a classificatory breakdown according to each of these views. Crowston and Kwasnik suggest as examples of facets views such as document 'source', 'content', 'structure', 'graphics', 'length', and 'language level'. Under each of these the document receives a classification: for example, the 'language level' might be 'everyday' or 'scholarly', the 'structure' might be 'artistic layout', 'includes references', 'includes subject lines' and so on. This deals with multidimensionality as a kind of 'pre-network' that characterises independent dimensions without requiring them to be brought together in any way.

One of the proposed benefits of adopting a faceted classification is that it moves the account beyond hierarchies in which genres need to be forced under a single organising principle. As we shall see, however, this limitation does not really apply in the case of proper typological representations, since these support, indeed encourage, multidimensional, or 'simultaneous', axes of classification. There is then still a need for further closer comparisons of the typological approaches developed within linguistics and faceted approaches as now proposed in web-based genre research. A further claimed benefit is their sensitivity to new and emerging genres—that is, a faceted classification is intended to be dynamic. This moves us more towards the kind of variability that we will see discussed below within topological approaches.

Methodologically we can see the facet-based approach to developing collections of semi-independent classification systems as a good practical way of gathering information about genres. This may subsequently serve to drive stronger theorising. The ability to simply place facets alongside one another without requiring them to be mutually consistent allows distinct properties of genres to be added as required. Nevertheless, as this develops further, it will be necessary to find stronger statements than the rather loose classification categories illustrated so far and many issues remain concerning just what facets are going to provide the most useful bases for further research and classification.

5.3.1 Genre typology 類型学

One way in which collections of genres, or *genre families*, have been represented in linguistic-based approaches to genre is by adopting the method developed within systemic-functional linguistics for representing all levels of linguistic description: i.e., through networks of choice. This already moves us several steps beyond simple taxonomies in that it is not genres that are placed in relationships to one another—e.g., as one genre might be a more specific subgenre with respect to another—but *classificatory features* for genres. Networks of choice define the conditions under which collections of features may be selected and each resulting collection describes a genre. The conditions may be more or less complex but generally involve at least logical conjunction and logical disjunction of features.

This is most straightforward when genres are assumed to exhibit strong framing. Generic structures are then produced that are similar to constituent structures in grammar. Part of the original network that Martin (1992) proposes for the factual genre family that we mentioned in Section 5.1.1 above is shown in Figure 5.11. Here we can see successive abstract descriptive choices running from left to right: each choice may lead on to further, more 'delicate' discriminations. A genre is then described in terms of the 'features' collected on one complete traversal of the possibilities that the network offers. Underneath each feature in the network we can see the names of corresponding genres. Thus, for example, an EXPLANATION genre is produced when the features 'activity-structured', 'generalised', 'explain', and 'resolve' are selected.

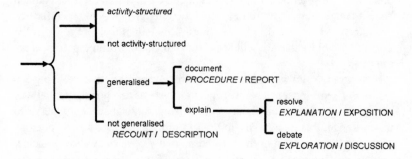

Figure 5.11   Network for classifying members of the factual genre family (Martin 1992, p564). Genre names are shown for the choices of 'activity structured' (in italics) and 'not activity structured' (in regular type).

The relationships *between* genres making up a genre family are captured within this style of representation by the features that are shared by two or more distinct genres. Each feature shared between genres represents an aspect of their organisation, realisation and motivation that is common. Capturing these generalisations is in fact the main motivation for selecting one organisation of a network rather than another. In the present example, we can see that one broad distinction made is between those factual genres that are activity structured, i.e., those which take their generic staging from the chronological ordering of the activities that are being described, and those which are not so structured. We can relate this to faceted-based approaches by regarding this as one of several perspectives considered relevant for factual genres—multiple perspectives correspond to network 'simultaneity', represented by the right-facing brace in the figure.

Systemic-functional networks also require a detailed description of genre *structures* and how these relate to the features in the classification network. And here we still face difficulties. While it is possible for each individual genre to specify its 'generic structure' as we have seen above (cf. Figure 5.3) and to offer particular further constraints on the likely linguistic forms employed within the identified stages, we do not know how to effectively generalise across the structures of *distinct* genres in a network representation such as that shown here. This is relatively well understood for similar linguistic descriptions of grammar, but for genre structures we are largely in unknown territory. The network style of representation therefore has the advantage that it applies well known techniques of linguistic description, but for genre there are few detailed family descriptions that have gone any way towards specifying more than programmatic constraints on the kinds of structures required and their possible linguistic realisations. There are considerable theoretical issues to be addressed here, even for 'monomodal' verbal genres.

If such a framework were to be applied to the multimodal case, the primary change to be made lies naturally in the linearity of the generic structure produced. Since the *features* of the network describe genres as such, they do not yet commit to any particular dimensionality of the structures that are required. The network organisation can therefore remain unchanged. The realisation in one-dimension assumed by traditional genres must, however, be replaced by realisation in, at least, two dimensions. To achieve this, we need to consider the levels of abstraction that might be appropriate for expressing spatial realisations for layout. Since the human perceptual system is as unlikely to work with absolute values in this domain as in any other, we can no doubt rule out from the start specifications that invoke 'absolute' positions, such as coordinate systems or exact measurements. Much more likely are proportionalities of various kinds (as in the Golden Ratio discussed in Section 2.5.1 above), semiotically constructed views of space (such as Kress and van Leeuwen's (1996) characterisation of layout in terms of given/new, ideal/real, and centre/margin, etc.: Section 2.2.2), or our own proposals of layout structure and area models from Chapter 3.

Relevant here are approaches to automatic page generation that already work in terms of qualitative spatial descriptions of page elements. Particularly well developed approaches to this aspect of the page generation problem are offered by *intelligent multimedia layout managers* (IMMLM: Graf 1996). In such systems layout itself is seen as a communicative resource to be manipulated, thereby echoing the modern document design tenet of functional design (cf., e.g., Schriver 1997). Graf describes this as 'intent-based layout', where layout is achieved by providing a

> "non-overlapping arrangement of multimedia items of constant size on a plain layout space as well as the determination of graphical and typographical attributes regarding aesthetical and functional criteria."

This arrangement must appropriately signal the logical organisation of the content being communicated while simultaneously obeying spatial and typographical requirements to be satisfied by the final product. The resulting layout should then lead its users to understand precisely that logical grouping of the information on the page that was intended. This also relates to

TITLE	*above*	TEXT1
TITLE	*full page width*	
TEXT1	*left of*	PIC1
TEXT1	*align-top*	PIC1
CAPTION	*below*	PIC1
TEXT2	*below*	TEXT1

qualitative spatial constraints

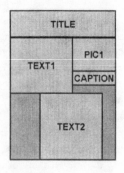

Figure 5.12   An example of spatial layout constraints and a possible page solution

our discussions of the relation between layout and rhetorical organisation in the previous chapter.

The standard solutions currently explored for intelligent layout systems of this kind all involve the notion of *spatial constraints* on layout and work by applying increasingly sophisticated mechanisms for *constraint satisfaction*. Such mechanisms automatically search for solutions to problems that satisfy as many of a set of specified constraints as possible. For layout, therefore, we need constraints that directly express properties to be met by a successful layout. A range of approaches for specifying and resolving such constraints are now on offer (cf. Weitzman and Wittenburg 1994, Schlieder and Hagen 2000, Lok and Feiner 2001).

Building on an example given in Lok and Feiner's (2001) review of automated layout techniques, we might then have a set of constraints given for document parts such as those shown to the left of Figure 5.12. These constraints describe the spatial relationships that need to be respected in a resulting page. There are clearly several possible solutions that satisfy the constraints given and so criteria for evaluating and selecting between those alternatives are also important; one possible, but not particularly attractive, solution is shown to the right of the figure.

Systems of this kind are now producing increasingly sophisticated page layouts. However, a significant set of issues remains concerning just how we can *find* the constraints that must be considered in the layout process. Graf, for example, proposes a set of 'layout relevant design parameters', which includes a catalogue of 'document types', such as technical manuals, overheads, scientific publications, newspapers and magazines and directories, a list of design conventions, such as reading direction, ordering, grids, horizontal *vs.* vertical alignment, etc., resource limitations, such as colour, space, time and expense restrictions, and optimisation criteria, such as space minimisation, graphics-text balancing, and user adaptivity. Applying these constraints allows more effective and acceptable designs to be achieved—even applying a simple grid-based set of constraints would already substantially improve the solution shown to the right of Figure 5.12 above, for example, by enforcing alignment and spacing.

This suggests a beneficial complementarity with the framework presented here for genre. Information obtained concerning the spatial layout of the elements on the page provides a valuable further addition to multimodal genre specifications. When regularly occurring placements, or constraints on relative placement, can be identified for a document type, we begin to form genuinely multimodal statements of genre structure. Graf's inclusion of document types in his framework already moves significantly in this direction. Appropriate genre specifications may therefore provide a source of constraint on layout that has not been effectively theorised so far within automatic layout approaches. And, conversely, the constraint languages provided for specifying layout may also provide an appropriate form of specification for expressing the spatial generalisations that we find in our empirical analyses of document types.

5.3.2 Genre topology 结构

Although suitable for 'well-behaved' genres that are clearly distinguishable from one another, the genre network approach is less straightforwardly compatible with genres which share commonalities and differences to varying degrees. We suggested above that the ability to move across continua of variation may be necessary for capturing the genre space that we require. Proposals for representations from this perspective have also been made applying a straightforward spatial interpretation from topology. A topological space of genres is then simply one in which each genre is characterised as being either nearer or more distant from other genres along a number of dimensions of comparison. Clearly, two genres might simultaneously be close along one dimension of comparison, while remaining distant along another. The dimensions of comparison give the dimensions of the genre space. This is straightforward to represent in two and three dimensions, since we can rely on our natural capabilities for imagining and perceiving everyday space; for higher number of dimensions of simultaneous comparison, intuitive visualisation is difficult although the general principle should still be clear.

One abstract example of the utility of considering genres in this way is discussed by Lemke (1999). Lemke proposes that one level of analysis useful for discriminating genres involves 'rhetorical strategies' (cf. Chapter 4 and above). However, if we characterise genres by the sets of rhetorical strategies that they mobilise, we may well find relationships among those genres of the kind depicted in Figure 5.13. This suggests that genres may differ or resemble each other according to the rhetorical strategies that they employ. In the figure, the three A-genres all use rhetorical strategy 2 to a similar extent and vary according to their use of rhetorical strategy 1; conversely, the three B-genres use strategy 1 similarly but vary according to their use of strategy 2.

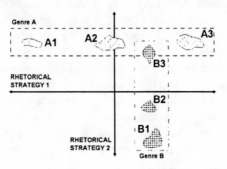

Figure 5.13   Example of overlapping genres adapted from Lemke (1999)

This leads to interesting issues of genre *identity*—for example, to what extent is genre B3 also a candidate for inclusion among the A-genres— and of genre *variability*. We might consider the entire genre space here as analogous to a kind of 'vowel space' as studied in phonology and phonological change where the vowels of a language can 'move around' the space over time, pushing others in particular directions in order to maintain distinguishability, merging, dividing and so on (cf. Aitchison 2001, pp183–197). All of these issues are currently wide open when raised with respect to genre.

How genres characterised in this way can be related to particular generic structures is, however, even more unclear than it was in the case of the typological approach to genre. This issue has not been taken up from the topological perspective at all and so we do not know what happens *structurally* when we move around such a genre space. There are several possibilities. It may be the case that after moving sufficiently far away from the 'centre' of one genre region and towards another, the structure of a genre abruptly (in the sense of catastrophe theory) adapts, moving from one generic structure to that of the other. Alternatively, the constraints imposed on a generic stage from the first genre may be successively weakened or 'mixed' with the constraints from the second genre while, simultaneously, the structure of the first genre gradually deforms to the structure of the second genre. These kinds of possibilities require dynamic models of change and transition and represent an exciting and very new research direction in their own right. At present we do not know how this will develop—but, again, without empirical exploration of the genres that we can find, there will be little to base such models on.

5.4 The multimodal genre space

As we have seen above, most accounts of genre currently see genre in terms of historically and culturally situated social action. Therefore, since one of our main concerns is providing an analytic framework that is able to span multimodal documents across time and contexts of use, the organising framework offered by genre shows considerable promise. We have stressed that it is important here to pursue a notion of genre that admits of fluidity and change while still imposing sufficient constraint to retain predictive value when semiotic modes combine.

Once we have the means for describing genres in this way, we will be able to address a further motivation for focusing on genre: we should aim not only to have an account of genres that exist, or have existed, but also to suggest properties for genres that *do not (yet) exist*. This is only possible when we are able to place 'individual', extant genres against a backdrop of the general possibilities for genres involving the kind of artefact we are studying. Lemke's (1999) view of *genre topology* introduced above is one proposal for using genre in precisely this way. Another is Crowston and Kwasnik's approach to genre systematisation in terms of facets: this is similarly intended to "*identify gaps and missing items*" (Crowston and Kwaśnik 2004, p3; italics in original, page number refers to electronic version).

A sketch of the *boundaries* of such a space is shown in Figure 5.14: here we see four regions identified; proceeding from the upper-right clockwise around the boundary we have (i) linear-interrupted text, respecting the rules of typography and print, (ii) photographic, respecting 2D-projection in perspective, (iii) pure schematic, using space, form and connection, and (iv) drawing, respecting principles and conventions of schematised graphic representation. Moving away from the boundaries, the affordances and design principles of these cases are progressively blended giving rise to many of the document page types we have seen so far. We also need to fold in the issues of structure that we have raised. The kinds of structure we assume are given by the particular modes of 'semiotic development' discovered. For

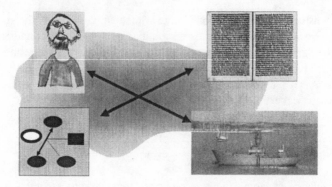

Figure 5.14 *The genre space and some recognisable regions lying along its boundary: (i) linear-interrupted text, (ii) 2D photographic, (iii) pure schematic, and (iv) drawing*

example, linear-interrupted documents rely on the *text-flow* mode, while newspapers and similar documents rely on *page-flow*.

Throughout the empirical work that led to the account proposed in this book, we have been attempting to get a better sense of which particular regions of the genre space are populated with actual document types. The motivation for this is that we believe that it will be of considerable benefit for multimodal document analysis if we can map out a detailed overview of the space of genre possibilities. Many suggestions in this area remain at the present time impressionistic and insufficiently unsubstantiated. Kress and van Leeuwen (1996, p203), for example, claim that the centre-margin visual form is 'relatively uncommon'. This is taken up unchallenged in Unsworth (2001, p107). We find, however, that it is very common *for a particular communicative purpose*: whenever that purpose is found, there will be a disposition to employ this kind of representation. Describing it as rare is then questionable.

Figure 5.15 shows two examples of this kind of organisation taken from different documents: one from our travel guide of Paris analysed in Section 3.3.1 above, the other from a booklet of instructions on how to use a telephone similar to that analysed in Section 4.4.2. These pages resemble one another (with respect to centre-margin) but are also quite different in other respects. Charting precisely how such documents vary gives us useful indications of how other documents will also vary.

There is also considerable variation to be accounted for *within* this area of genre. This is the important sense in which we consider genre a *space* with particular dimensions of organisation. Although we do not yet know

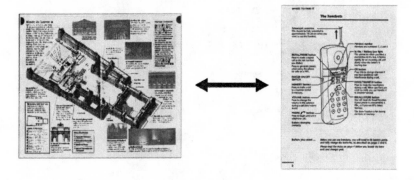

Figure 5.15 Two example documents that share a centre-margin organisation but which vary considerably in other respects

the precise dimensions for such a space, it is to be expected that empirical analysis will be able to successively fill in details and to show paths within the space along which users of documents judge documents to be similar or different to one another. For example, we see in both the Louvre and telephone cases a use of a spatial configuration to organise information, in one case the spatial configuration is the Louvre, in the other it is a telephone handset. However, in the former case, the information presented is not an exhaustive labelling of parts, it is indicating points of interest. Within the added information, the resources deployed for the Louvre again utilise text, photographs and graphics, whereas for the telephone, they are restricted to the typographical mode. Relating these distinct realisations to generic purposes adds in the information necessary to provide a motivated interpretation for the visual rhetorical relations involved: one elaborates, the other identifies. This allows us to track independently how distinct types of document deploy semiotic resources for these two particular communicative tasks—a level of detail that would not be available to us if we simply stopped at the 'page'.

Two further dimensions of variation are shown in Figure 5.16. This begins on the left of the figure with Twyman's linear-interrupted case without visual adornment and moves to include, by the upper route, tables and, by the lower route, pictorial material. Our Gannet page on the right-hand side of the figure includes both pictorial content for the Gannet and, as we argued in Section 3.2, a typographically rendered table.

A final illustrative dimension of variation is suggested in Figure 5.17, reflecting examples of the much discussed issue of 'non-linearity' or underdetermined reading paths. The starting point on the left of the diagram is

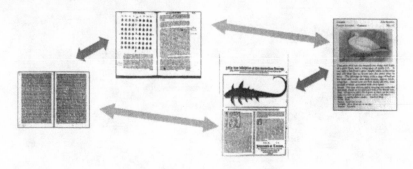

Figure 5.16   *Documents that all remain within broadly typographical, linear-interrupted genres ('text-flow')*

again our archetypal linear-interrupted page. From there we move on to a more complex Gannet page that we will see more of below; this page already exhibits page-flow characteristics by employing diverse informational 'chunks' concerning the Gannet without imposing a 'preferred' reading order on them—even though they all concern the Gannet in some way. Next we come to a magazine, which again includes separated information chunks, some of which are to be read in a certain order and others not, but which is no longer focused solely on a single topic. And finally, on the right of the chain, we reach a newspaper, where there are many chunks that can be read about many different topics and without any necessary order imposed: i.e., an archetypal page-flow document.

Figure 5.17   *Documents ranging from single entry points to multiple entry points (non-linear directed viewing)*

Placing these examples together and, in some cases, re-using the same examples in different dimensional contexts echoes the suggestions made abstractly for Lemke's topographical space in Figure 5.13 above. This shows that there are many simultaneously varying dimensions to be considered.

It also makes the point that staying within intuitive genre labels, such as, for example, 'newspaper' or 'guide book', is far from optimal precisely because it creates artificial boundaries that the dimensions of variation manipulated within genres do not necessarily respect. The ability to trace trajectories of similarity across superficially different genres is essential in order to understand change.

5.5   Illustrations of genre: tracking change

In this final section, we show the notion of genre that we have proposed at work in relation to two sets of loosely related documents. We will see, first, how the documents can be assigned to similar and contrasting genres and, second, how tracking these kinds of documents over time starts to reveal generic trajectories of change. That is, particular aspects of the genres to which these documents belong have over time followed a common trajectory in the genre space with demonstrable and predictable consequences for how their documents appear. Although we will not set this out in any detail, it needs to be emphasised once again that the analyses we present draw on all aspects of the GeM model introduced so far—decomposition into parts, spatial layout, rhetorical organisation and so on—in order to characterise the genres involved. Setting each of these component analyses out in full would, however, lengthen the exposition considerably.

5.5.1   Field guides across time

The first set of examples selected fills in details of the isolated Gannet examples that we have taken at various places in the book so far, placing them in their generic developmental context. The pages span the years 1924 to 1996 and are taken from the following books: *British Birds: Description of All but the Rarest Species, their Nests and Eggs* (London & Edinburgh: Jack and Nelson, 1924, p115), *Observer Book of Birds* (Warne, 1972, p22), *Collins Gem Birds* (HarperCollins, 1994, p21), and *Collins Wild Guide: Birds of Britain and Ireland* (HarperCollins, 1996, p24). We have seen two of these pages before but we set them out here together for ease of comparison in Figure 5.18. Our present analysis treats all four pages as a sequence across time: each one is representative of the book from which it is taken and of a range of further related publications from its period. The main purpose of analysis in this section is then to reveal the particular trajectories of change exhibited in the examples and to relate these trajectories to aspects of genre. Genre statements are made by combining descriptions from the distinct levels provided by the GeM model to bring out mutual 'constraints' or co-occurrences. This allows us to *compare* documents and document pages in a more principled manner and in a way which goes within the particular *bundles* of resource deployments making up any particular genre.

In order to provide an anchor point 'outside' of the documents to get us started with our comparison, it is useful to consider the basic information that the documents are communicating. This is relatively straightforward in the present case because that is one of the primary functions of the genre in any case—to communicate some specific information about the birds in question. For this, we can sketch the content structure (cf. Table 1.2 in the introduction) as suggested graphically in Figure 5.19. The information and its structure is present in more or less detail in each of the pages being analysed. Each page addresses aspects of the bird's appearance, differentiated according to young and mature stages, of the bird's behaviour, including nesting and its eggs, and of the bird's location, in terms of geographical regions where the bird is found and the types of locations (cliff-tops, open sea, etc.) the bird generally frequents. We will use this structure to talk about how the documents differ with respect to their selection and grouping of this information as well as that information's realisation in a variety of expressive resources.

As a first stage in grouping and selection, we can note that the pages are very similar rhetorically. As would be expected from their 'top-level' generic purpose—to describe particular birds so that they can be recognised in the field and to give some background on their lifestyle and habits—we can observe considerable overlap. In essence, we have a pattern of rhetorical ELABORATION and BACKGROUND relations presenting the information of the content structure. We will not show the individual rhetorical structure analyses here therefore.

Layout structures for the Gannet pages

As would probably be expected, we begin to find considerably more variation in the layout structures of the pages. If we focus on the area model component of the layout structure (cf. Section 3.2.3), we see a steady progression in complexity. Figure 5.20 shows the area models for the four pages side-by-side for comparison. The 1924 page does not really have an area model: it is simply text-flow with drawings inserted wherever they can fit in the approximate vicinity of their associated sections (i.e., a qualitative constraint). Within this text-flow, sections are separated by loosely centered headings in italics; individual sections are introduced by a bold section number (as a separate 'text-sentence', cf. Section 2.5.3) and a bold bird name, grammatically integrated into the rest of the first 'sentence'. The

(a) 1924   (b) 1972

(c) 1994   (d) 1996

Figure 5.18 Four Gannet pages

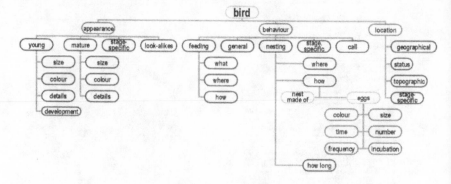

Figure 5.19   Generalised content structure for the Gannet pages

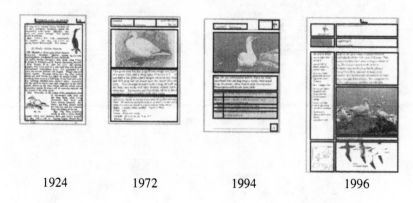

Figure 5.20   The area models for the four Gannet pages

main areas of the content structure are then associated with paragraphs and are realised primarily typographically. We will return to these realisations again in a moment.

The next page, our original Gannet example taken from 1972, then takes some limited steps towards a more developed area model in the sense of an approximate horizontal grid; we discussed this and its relationship to the layout structure for the page in detail in Chapter 3 (cf. Figure 3.6). In this case, there is little beyond a broad segmentation of the page into header, drawing, background textual information and an itemised list of particular content aspects (nest, eggs, etc.) still presented typographically as a single sequence within a text-flow. We refer to this latter collection of elements as a 'secondary level' of content items. Most of the bird pages appear to make at least this degree of differentiation, between detailed background information about the life-cycle of the birds and particular additional features of the species in question, presumably related to features of the bird and its environment useful for recognition and expected of this genre by its consumers.

The next in sequence is from 1994. Here we see an interesting further development because it is almost identical with that from 1972 *apart from* its explicit presentation of its secondary level of content items as a table. Since we consider tables as already having moved out of the text-flow model, we show them as proper components of the area models associated with their pages. The layout structure is then similar to the previous case, with the extension that identified rows, columns and cells are explicitly anchored in the lower part of the area model of the page. These cells are also distinguished typographically: the 'subheading' cell shows their content bold and right-justified, the 'content' cells use regular font and are only left-justified. The entire subarea is also separated by whitespace from the preceding text block, increasing the framing of the secondary information further.

This contrast between the 1972 and the 1994 pages with respect to their deployment of an area model is shown in more detail in Figure 5.21. Whereas in the earlier page, an entire subtree of the layout structure is simply assigned to a broad area of the page and typographical constraints then carry the further layout structure, in the later page the particular subelements of the layout structure corresponding to the header and content information is explicitly assigned to the individual cells of the table of the area model. The figure shows just the first two rows to avoid clutter in the diagram, but the general procedure should be obvious.

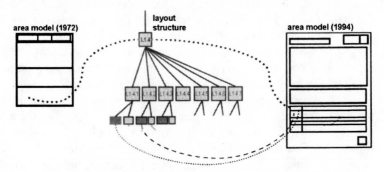

Figure 5.21   The contrasting associations of a common layout structure with the area models of the 1972 and 1994 Gannet pages

A further development with respect to the 1972 page can be seen in the right-justified layout elements at the top of the page. These include for the first time in our sequence an explicit visual *icon*, which shows the group of birds to which this entry belongs: "Gannets and Cormorants". In this document, these icons are always placed in the top *outer* corner of the page and so provide an effective additional visual access mechanism into the document. This is a further reason for breaking them out as separate sub-areas in the area model compared to the superficially similar information presented textually in the earlier page.

Although already providing considerably more visual entry points into the information of the page, the 1994 page has still not completely escaped its text-flow origins, however. This may be due partly to the rather small physical format of the book (8.2×11.6cm), which does not provide very much 'space' to exploit—i.e., a canvas constraint. The material is generally arrayed vertically down the page and this extends inside the individual lines of the material making up the table. This leads to a visual ambiguity whenever both a subheading and its associated content runs over at least two lines:

> **Range &** Breeds colonially on cliffs on N and W coasts,
> **habitat** dispersing to winter at sea.
> **Nest** Mound of seaweed on bare rocky ledge.

The visual discrimination is insufficient to show whether we have three table rows or the intended two rows, where the first row has two text lines. We need, as with many of the examples discussed in this book, to interpret the textual content also to ascertain, first, that the first line of the subheader ends with an ampersand and the second line does not begin with a capital letter and, second, that the second line of the content grammatically extends the first. This could have been indicated visually by more framing, with whitespace, framing lines or framing blocks of some kind.

With the slightly larger page dimensions of the 1996 document, the designers have been able to leave the text-flow model for the page entirely. Although the content, rhetorical and layout structures remain generally similar to the earlier pages, the assignment of layout structures to areas on the page uses far more of the two-dimensional surface on offer. As the area model indicates, there are essentially two columns available for positioning information. The right-hand column contains the general information concerning the bird, the section header, the scientific names, and a photograph. The secondary content information, however, receives its own text block in the left-hand column. The left-hand column also contains other information, such as geographical distribution, size, months when observable and so on, sometimes duplicating information visually that is presented textually in the right-hand column. In addition, the right-hand column is also used to give information about the visual appearance of the bird at different stages of maturity.

The deployment of presentational modes across time

We have suggested informally that a major difference between the earliest page and the most recent is the tendency to present a considerable diversity of information in a variety of modes. Particularly interesting for tracking the genre development, however, is the precise choice of presentational modes for content items and how this choice has changed over time. We will follow this through briefly here drawing attention to the ways in which content elements with differing functions are selected for the information being presented.

The shift in visual genre that has occurred is made most clear with the oldest text. Bird entries in this 1924 book are not given a separate page and so the distinction between entries relies on the title (bold, indented, and the same point size as body text). The organisation appears visually to be a straightforward textual exposition, although as we shall see in a moment this is not actually the case. The pictures are also not strongly aligned with their entries, nor do they appear in a consistent position in each entry. This is particularly clear in the intrusion of the Shag drawing and caption at the right-hand top of the page into the space used for describing Gannets. This far from optimal solution is then compensated for by giving the *section number* to which the figure refers as well as the figure number in the caption of the drawing so as to avoid possible confusion with the Gannet. This is, in fact, an interesting reversal of the usual relationship that we find between text and figures in such genres: rather than the text referring to a figure, the figure-caption refers to its text!

This is also a convincing acknowledgement of the fact that readers can be expected to access the document via the visual material even when the document as a whole is clearly organised around strict text-flow. Only when the figure is 'included' *spatially* within the textual entry that it illustrates do we find captions as they are found today: the drawing of the Gannet, for example, has the caption "Fig. 105". Although the text does not refer to this at all, its position as a graphical insert with the text wrapping around it has evidently been considered a sufficient 'reference'. In general, connections between elements are not as polished in the older text as they are in the 1996 book. For example, in the newer text, 'look-alikes' are listed in the same place on every page, and the reference to appearance makes it clear what the purpose of the comparison is. In the older text, this information, '(See No. 177)', comes after the description of the Gannet's size, so it may be presumed that this reference is meant to enable size comparison between the Gannet and entry 177, which is the Cormorant.

This is not to suggest, however, that the entry lacks organisation: on the contrary, there is a strong generic structure for each bird. First, there is the bird's name, specialised family name (English and Latin), Resident Status, and where it is found (given as a list). Minimal structuring information is given in the form of the graphically undifferentiated subheading 'Breeding Places'. The list that then follows is much more detailed than that in the later texts—for example, in the 1996 page the information about location is covered less specifically by a map. The rest of the older text, despite appearing visually as a piece of continuous prose, is in fact composed entirely of a *description list*, i.e., a list with item headings. Following the list of the locations in which the bird is found, the entry goes on to describe the bird itself as follows:

> *Bird.* Length 33in. (see no. 177.) Bill strong, straight, with hook, and of a pale lead-blue with deeper slate-coloured longitudinal lines. . .
> *Nest.* Generally on the ledges of precipitous sides of sea-washed isles, such as the Bass Rock (Scotland). . .
> *Egg.* One. Blue, covered or nearly so with a white chalky deposit which soon becomes dirty and yellow stained. Av. size, 3.06 x 1.96 in.

In the whole text, there are only two syntactically complete sentences: 'In breeding dress there is a buff tinge on the head and neck' and 'Laying begins March-May'. The visual appearance of continuous prose is therefore in stark contrast to the actual organisation of this entry. Apart from the italicised and indented list labels Bird, Nest, and Egg, and some horizontal space between these labels and the beginning of their associated text, it is only the *content* of the list (finite ellipsed simple present tense property ascriptions) that indicates the list status of the information.

The dominant organization of the page, then, is a series of slots for different sorts of information, one or two of which are given head or subhead status, with the remainder differentiated positionally and by content. This represents a very low level of graphical differentiation per function. Note, too, that there is no differentiation in fonts or sizes: only italic, bold, and plain text within the same font family are used. Punctuation does not mark rhetorical relations consistently, as the labels Bird, Nest and Egg (arguably introducing informative elaborations) are marked with a full stop, rather than the colon that might now be expected (cf. the 1996 text's list entries in the ID FACT FILE textblock), but the same rhetorical relation, the elaboration of nest material within the Nest entry, *is* introduced here with a colon:

... Bull Rock and Little Skellig (Ireland). Material: sea-weed, grasses from the isle top, and any material from the surface of the sea.

Functionally distinguished information is then present, but the modal resources selected for discriminating among these functions is restricted to the narrowly typographical.

The purpose here of course is not to use contemporary expectations about layout to criticise texts like the 1924 text, but simply to point to the far lower degree of graphical differentiation of functions that is present, even in comparison to that from 1972. The general prediction that the further one goes back in time within the genre, the less use will be made of page-flow is naturally supported. Somewhat more interesting is the fact that we can also observe a much increased tendency in the most recent book for information to be presented not only in more modes, but in *multiple* modes. That is, information is presented from several modal perspectives within the same page layout.

We can suggest graphically how this has increased over the three more recent pages as shown in Figure 5.22. This picks out the fragment of the content structure concerned with the bird's appearance and identifies for each content item which presentational modes were selected for its realisation. Each different shade of grey represents a distinct mode, and each duplication of a content item (shown by duplicating the corresponding node in the graph) represents the situation where a given content item is presented on the same page in different modes. White, unfilled content nodes are not explicitly presented in their respective pages at all. Thus, for example, we can see that in the 1972 page there is only one area of multiple presentation: that concerning the size, colour and details of appearance of the mature bird. This is accounted for entirely by the co-presence of text and drawing.

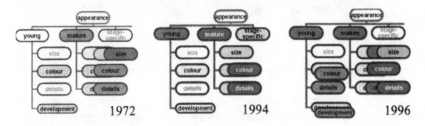

Figure 5.22 Modal presentations of a fragment of the Gannet content structure across time

Moving to the 1996 page, we see that most of the presented content items are presented in more than one 'mode'. The size, for example, is presented in three distinct realisational forms: as an icon augmented with text (upper left-hand corner), as an explicit 'header' for an item in an itemised list (in the 'ID fact file' column on the left), and in the qualitative textual information 'larger than any gull'. This takes up the obvious duplication achieved by combining text and a drawing and extends this into other modes of semiotic presentation.

We can survey this modal deployment more systematically by bringing together all of the distinct presentational modes found on the pages analysed and counting up how many times they are utilised for distinct items of the content structure. The results are summarised in Figure 5.23, where we can see for each Gannet page how the information presented within it is distributed across presentational modes.[9] In the Gannet page from 1972, for example, we can see that most information is presented either in description lists (i.e., an itemised list with an explicit label instead of a bullet), in running text, or in a drawing. This is the same in the 1994 page, apart from the use of a photograph instead of the drawing. In contrast, the 1924 page does not really make a strong distinction between description lists and running text in that the descriptions become so long that they resemble running text (apart from the lack of full sentences). All information is presented in this form or in the drawing. In contrast to these, the 1996 page shows an explosion of resources across all of the types of information portrayed.

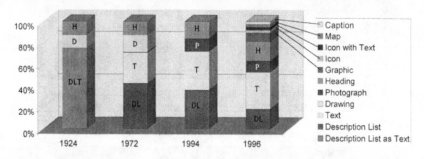

Figure 5.23   Mode distribution across the four Gannet pages. 1924 employs 3 modes, 1972 and 1994 each employ 4 modes, and 1996 employs 9 modes.

This, in combination with the allocation of content items to presentational modes suggested above, clearly documents the increase both in presentational forms and in the use of those forms to present a multifaceted decomposition of the information being given. Each of the modes presented, e.g., text, graphic representation, table, etc., is used to form particular groupings of the content items shown. This moves the entire presentational artefact

---

[9]For further discussion of this aspect of these pages, see Delin and Bateman (2002).

more towards the multidimensional classification well established for newspapers: there is no single dimension of 'newsworthiness' for the information presented concerning Gannets, distinct groupings of information are available for the reader depending on what particular mode or combination of modes are followed.

Across time, this course of development becomes very clear. This is suggested visually in the graph shown in Figure 5.24. This presents a different view of the data of the previous figure, constructing a more developmental rather than snapshot view of how the Gannet pages have changed over time. The vertical axis in this case shows the absolute number of content items realised in each mode rather than the overall distribution. Of course, to a certain extent this view is artificial in that we only have four data points—the continuous connections between these points cannot therefore be taken too seriously at this time. Nevertheless, with the accumulation of further data points from related pages that we advocate being carried out for any more complete analysis of this genre, it should be possible to reach a more refined view of this general kind.

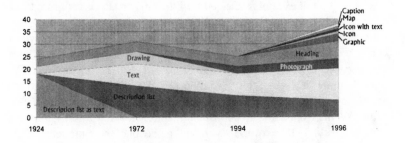

Figure 5.24   *Mode distribution across the four Gannet pages shown as a continuous development. Here we can see how the initial combination of text and description list in 1924 divides into the separate text blocks and description lists of the later texts, and how the role of drawings is taken over later by photographs. The headings present in the 1924 page are maintained throughout.*

With the analogy just drawn to newspapers, we should also consider one final aspect of the layout of these pages in more detail. The move from text-flow to page-flow is itself significant. As suggested in Figure 5.21 and the area models shown there, it is only in the most recent page that there is any substantial use of page-flow at all. Thus, not only are there many more presentational resources being mobilised in the 1996 page, these are also distributed around the page much more freely, drawing on the potential of the page-flow model to provide rhetorically distinguishable areas of the page. This goes together with the explosion of presentational modes possible—it would hardly be possible, after all, to combine this range of presentations sensibly within a text-flow.

Particular content elements are then distributed across particular kinds of presentational modes, partly by convention established (at least) for the book under discussion and partly by suitability (geographical distribution is more naturally carried by a continuous representational form such as a map), and these presentational modes are themselves associated with particular regions made available within the area model for this genre. The icon containing size information is placed, as noted above, in the upper left-hand corner, the graphic showing the development of the young bird to the adult is shown in the bottom of the right-hand column, and geographic distribution map is shown lower left (cf. also Figure 2.17 from Chapter 2 above), and so on.

5.5.2   Wildlife fact files across time

The second set of examples selected for illustrative analysis for genre takes us back to the pages of the information sheets on animals and wildlife that we analysed for their rhetorical structure in Section 4.4.1 of the previous chapter. Here again, we will focus now on how these documents have changed over time rather than on their internal rhetorical organisation. We draw on three versions of this 'encyclopedia': the *Wildlife Fact File*, which appeared in 1990, the *Wildlife Explorer* from 1997, and the series *Discovering Wildlife* from 2002; all published by International Masters Publishers Ltd. Interestingly these overlap with, and go beyond, the more recent Gannet pages that we examined above.

In each version, entries for individual animals are presented on a single sheet of paper with holes punched on the left-hand side for collecting together in a looseleaf folder. The page is folded vertically slightly off-center to make a four-page double-sided 'document'. The front-page, formed by folding the complete page back towards the punch holes, contains a large picture of the animal described with more or less further information depending on the edition. The back-page thus formed is a 'fact file' analogous to the field guide pages analysed in the previous subsection; the tiger examples used in Section 4.4.1 above were taken from this page of the document. The center-pages make up in all cases a single double-paged spread providing more detailed background information about the animal in question. Figure 5.25 shows the back-page 'fact file' entries for the Nile Crocodile.[10]

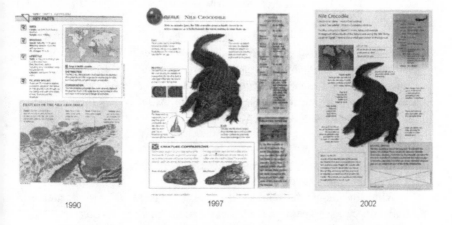

Figure 5.25   Three fact file entries for the Nile Crocodile; used by permission

Interestingly, the middle page from 1997 shows many similarities with our Gannet page from 1996. It has clearly already moved to a page-flow layout: information in the form of an inset table is presented in a column running down the right-hand side of the page and there is a further inset at the bottom of the page comparing similar appearing related species. Since the front-page of the sheet already shows an attractive and attention-getting picture of the crocodile, the central graphic here can concentrate on giving information as we discussed with respect to the tiger page in Section 4.4.1.

The earlier page, from 1990, is a simpler form that is nevertheless already page-flow in design. It is made up of three strongly framed elements: one describing the geographical distribution (which in the 1997 version has moved to the front-page of the document), one picking out some particular features of the animal graphically, and a complex itemised list giving isolated facts such as the animal's size, breeding habits, 'lifestyle' and so on. This list is, in fact, somewhat over-complex for the information it presents. An enlarged portion of one entry of this list is the following:

---

[10]The pages and extracts that we show here from the two older editions are based on scans of the corresponding pages; the pages and extracts taken from the most recent edition have been created from the original QuarkXpress files kindly provided by the publisher. For copyright reasons these differ slightly from the published versions: for example, photographs are not reproduced and some fonts are replaced. These changes do not effect our discussion, although the reproduced pages are not therefore of the same quality as the published versions.

SIZES
Length: Up to 6m from head to
tip of tail
Weight: Up to 1000kg.

The list includes two levels of embedding: the first is doubly signalled by the large icon of a snake and the bold capitals of the category ('sizes'), and the sublevel is shown by bold attribute names separated by a colon from the values of those attributes. The icon of a snake, repeated for each top-level item in the list, indicates repeatedly that the crocodile is a reptile. This double structure with redundant labelling disappears in the later versions, where we simply have attributes and their values listed in a table. It is assumed that readers can work out for themselves that 'weight' has something to do with 'size' and the additional access information grouping attributes by similarity is omitted.

Within the geographical information presented there is also a reduction in 'redundancy', seen perhaps from today's perspective, of the presentational style. In the older page, the map of the world, shaded according to the areas where the crocodile is found, is also given the caption, or legend: "Range of the Nile Crocodile". It could be asked what else shaded regions on such a map could indicate and, accordingly, this information no longer appears in the 2002 version: here there is shading without explanation.[11]

The newest page also shows a continuation of some trends that are already observable in the 1996 Gannet page and the 1997 wildlife page. One of these is the *expansion* of the semiotic resources carried by combinations of icons, graphics and text. Information that was previously carried in text and, perhaps, in a simple form by an icon, is here moved to an entire system of icons that permits more differentiated expression of the intended content.

In the 1994 Gannet page, for example, there is a navigation element carried by the outline of a bird depicted in the upper left of the page (cf. Figure 5.18(c)); different bird outlines indicated the major sections in the book. In the 1996 edition the same icon (now shown upper left: cf. Figure 5.18(d)) is shown augmented by an indication of the bird's size: "87–100 cm". Similarly, earlier indications of the bird's location across the year that were presented in text ("wintering at sea", "resident", etc.) are captured in the 1996 page in a compositional 'icon' showing an idealised calendar with the months where the bird is present shaded in (shown just below the previously discussed icon). Finally, the lower part of the page shows the maturation

---

[11] This is not always without loss of information: in some of the older maps, use was made of multiple shadings to capture, for example, migratory habits of birds. This requires explanation in a legend. Such information is not then given in the newer version.

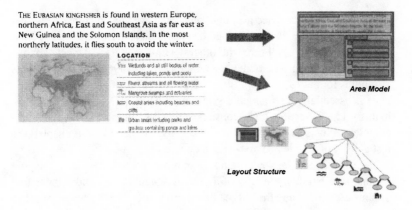

THE EURASIAN KINGFISHER is found in western Europe, northern Africa, East and Southeast Asia as far east as New Guinea and the Solomon Islands. In the most northerly latitudes, it flies south to avoid the winter.

Figure 5.26   *Composite layout presenting information about the distribution of the King-fisher and its layout structure*

of the bird as a sequence of drawings—thereby moving information previously only given in textual form into an *image-flow* component of the page.

This process is taken still further in the 2002 animal page. The information concerning geographical distribution, previously given by the shaded map, is now taken up by a more complex layout element that combines a textual description of both the geographic locations and the *types* of location (swamps, ponds, etc.), a shaded map (without caption), and a table that itself combines attributes represented by icons and values expressed textually. An example of this complex layout element is shown in Figure 5.26. Moreover, even the simplest icons begin to do more work: in the top right-hand corner of the newest fact file pages, for example, we find a further composite icon that expresses *comparative* size. This is presented on each page without explanation at that point—its interpretation is admirably clear in any case:

Again, this shows a nice combination of conventional images, profiles referring by similarity of form to the 'current' animal being described on the page, and compositional meaning expressing rhetorical comparison or contrast.

Finally, we can show that the move from text-flow to page-flow has also been continued still further in the animal fact files. This is no doubt in part due to the extra space available on these pages when compared to the more limited space in the field guides—which in turn makes additional connections, as we shall see, with other document genres. We noted above the strongly framed area model that applied for the 1996 Gannet page. This also holds for the 1997 fact files: as can be seen above for the crocodile, the page is essentially a rectangular grid with a header. One of the 'modules' in this grid (cf. Section 2.5.1) consists of the drawing of the crocodile, with complex callouts as discussed for the tiger page in the previous chapter; the rest consist of a table and text-with-picture combinations.

In the 2002 fact file, however, a further move has taken place. The layout of this page is a combination of a grid-like organisation and a more free organisation following the outline of the crocodile. The top of the page has a generically imposed grid structure that extends across both the location information just shown for the Kingfisher and the 'Statistics' table given on the right. The upper portion of the page then provides strong structure for direct access to particular classes of information. The remainder of the page does not have a generically imposed grid structure of this sort and so is more supportive of 'random' access. Its organisation is closer to that of the Louvre page that we discussed in detail in Chapter 3. The outline of the central drawing gives a non-rectangular area model for positioning both the callouts that are most closely and explicitly connected to the drawing and the various satellite text blocks providing further information.

These satellites are themselves differentiated typographically in order to define several classes of information, precisely as was the case with the Louvre. To the upper-left of the drawing we find what is, in effect, an extended caption presenting an orienting summary, or abstract, of the information that is elaborated upon in the callouts. To the lower-left there is a framed text inset with a typographically distinct heading asking 'Myth of Fact?'. To the lower-right is a further framed box, with both a distinct typographical heading and a coloured background, presenting text and pictures concerning 'related species'. Finally, as with the Louvre, the callouts are positioned on an 'inner' circuit nearest to the drawing while the other textual insets occupy positions as satellites on an 'outer' circuit.

This is shown graphically in Figure 5.27 for one further animal fact file: the 2002 version of our old friend, the Gannet. On the left of the figure, we see the layout structure shown over the original page; on the right of the figure just the layout structure. The relation to the Louvre layout structure should be obvious. In both the cases of the Louvre and of the 2002 animal fact files we see a marked reduction of rectangular page-flow. Images on the page instead provide the guide lines for defining the spatial zones used.

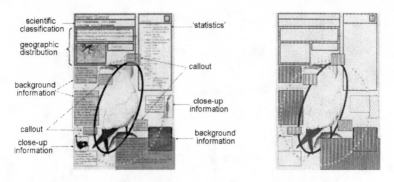

Figure 5.27 Layout grid for the 2002 animal fact sheet for the Northern Gannet

This can be seen equally in the development of the 'inside' pages of the fact files. The 1990 edition employs a clear 6-column spread, with picture-plus-caption combinations taking up multiple columns and bold red framing lines separating text 'sections'. The rigid layout sometimes causes the captions for photographs to be situated some way away from the photographs themselves, requiring 'explanatory' page-internal document deixis of the form: "Above", "Below", "Far left", etc. In the 1997 edition this has changed considerably. The inside pages have a much more 'open' 8-column spread with considerable whitespace. Text blocks run over 2 columns. The pages are divided into 'sections' much more clearly and the overall layout impression created is of four layout 'blocks', each containing its own pictures, text and captions, with strong framing lines and boxes and distinguishing icons.

With the 2002 edition this has, again, changed completely. There is now little use of any kind of grid structure. The text sections are individual text blocks that can be moved freely on the spread. Their actual position is generally determined by the outline of a large realistic full-colour photograph of the animal at issue. Edges of the text blocks that come into contact with the photographs are justified to follow the profile of the photograph, weakening still further the sense of any rectangular blocks. The segmentation of these blocks is nevertheless maintained by extensive whitespace framing.

This progression is shown in the three examples given in Figure 5.28. The first two spreads in the figure show a straightforward grid organisation; the latter shows instead free positioning of blocks of text around the space created by the central image.[12] The genre here has clearly moved away

---

[12]This space is shown by the guide-lines defined by the designer for controlling text-flow, visible here from the underlying QuarkXPress rendition.

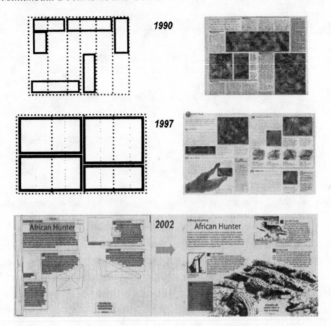

Figure 5.28   Contrasting layout organisation taken up by the central spreads of the three editions of the animal fact files. As with all of these examples, the photographs have been replaced for copyright reasons.

from the column-based organisation of the early 1990s to the much freer positioning observable in the last example. In the middle, there is a period of much clearer framing that already used the grid of the page as a scaffold for positioning very clearly demarcated units. In the last example, this demarcation of units has been taken over by the attribute that is most clearly available for page-flow—the space of the page itself.

5.6   Discussion and conclusion

In this chapter we have shown possible definitions and uses for a multimodal genre space. To achieve this, we have argued that a linguistically motivated approach to genre offers much that is supportive of a move into multimodality. It is in these traditions that accounts of genre have gone furthest beyond the loose classifications or clarificatory schemes for discursive analysis. Again, we see the overall empirical orientation of our approach making itself felt: we seek to discover and characterisation genres in ways that are (a) empirically motivated and (b) predictive concerning how genres are formed and used. That is, for our purposes, and to make genre a useful tool for analysis in the area of multimodality, we need to develop a theoretical construct which allows us to make predictions concerning the form and content of multimodal documents. These predictions will relate particular purposes that are to be achieved with a document and aspects of that document's contexts of use to details of the document's selected realisational strategies—i.e., what selection of modal resources it makes and how these resources are related to the meanings that they are to carry. This needs to be more than a loose framework for discussion, however, if it is to serve any significant role in our overall model of multimodal documents.

But to populate this space we need considerably more empirical analysis: the particular properties of documents, identified in terms of the parts and their distinctive attributes specified in terms of the GeM model's presentation layers, gives us a way of proceeding. Characterising documents that we find in terms of these properties and relating them to documents, or groups of documents, that have already been analysed can progressively build up a multidimensional space of genres. This work is still very much in its infancy, but is a prerequisite for taking multimodal analysis further. Only when we have a much richer characterisation of the organisation of the genre space and the documents that inhabit it, will be able to make really strong predictions about multimodal documents, their functions and possible developments.

We have illustrated something of how this empirical analysis can proceed by using the GeM model to discuss the relationships of two related genres as they have developed over time. This analysis revealed that certain generic trends can be observed operating over both of the genres analysed. Moreover, this has also related aspects of these genres to other texts discussed: particularly the example of the Louvre tourist guide from Chapter 3. This shows clearly how it is necessary to break genre down into particular aspects of the presentational forms mobilised in multimodal documents to track these across the boundaries that might be suggested by a more superficial genre labelling.

When tracking such genre developments over time, further questions are raised concerning the identity of the genres tracked themselves. For example, the earliest Gannet text that we examined, taken from 1924 has more in common with a contemporary encyclopedia entry than with modern texts like those from 1994 and 1996. What has taken place is that the genre itself has shifted its definition, along with the kinds of uses that people expect to make of such texts. While we may not now be happy to accept the older text as a usable field guide (it looks more like a 'book-for-reading' than a quick field reference to the contemporary eye), it is clear from the foreword that the author's intention was for users to recognise birds, rather than to use the book as a reading resource:

> "THE object of this book is to make as easy as limits of space permit the recognition of all the British species... The descriptions have been written with an eye to the requirements of the non-specialist observer... they should prove adequate for practical purposes."

This, then, sounds like a field guide, although our more graphically-oriented contemporary expectations would lead us into difficulties differentiating important information sufficiently quickly.

What we must conclude is that we cannot simply compare texts on the basis of the assumption that they constitute a single time-extended genre: there are other variables at work. Genres must be described independently of the particular use that a culture makes of them. Genres do not merely 'reflect' convention: each instance of a particular genre helps create convention and hence generic expectation. Our surprise perhaps that the 1924 text could be anything other than a reference book reflects how far the genre has moved since then. A sophisticated model of genre must reflect genres as bundles of features within the genre space that change their allegiances over time. Our decompositions of both the individual presentational modes found in our example documents and the use made of layout as such within page-flow documents show that certain developments among such bundles are generic and reoccur across distinct document types.

This kind of analysis therefore allows us to be much more discriminating when making statements about the increased use of multimodality in recent times. We can indeed see an increase in the use of some kinds of multimodality, even though multimodal deployments of resources in 'documents' can be seen from almost any historical period—Craig and Barton (1987), for example, suggest that the first 'documents' combining illustrations and text can be found in Egyptian writings from around 1400 BC. But the precise *types* of increase can now be described far more finely with the help of a detailed account of just what multimodality is achieving on any page. Moreover, we can begin placing these trajectories of change as dimensions of our developing genre space, in order to locate and compare an ever broader range of documents.

6

Building Multimodal
Document Corpora:
the State of the Art

Throughout our discussion in this book so far we have emphasized that entire collections of multimodal documents should be analysed. For more reliable interpretations of the elements and configurations found in our documents, we always need to see our documents against the background provided by relevant 'co-generic' documents. Unravelling the properties of multimodal document genres must be seen as one of the main challenges for multimodal analysis at this time.

To find such properties, multimodal analysis must move on from informal, interpretative and suggestive analyses towards an empirically-based discipline that allows hypotheses concerning the function and form of multimodal documents to be derived and explored. Here, the adoption of the methods of *corpus-based linguistics* is a crucial step. Such methods need to be made usable for multimodal analysis and so, in this chapter, we set out more explicitly both what this involves and how it is supported by our framework.

We begin by briefly characterising corpus-based linguistics as such, including its principles and methods. We then sketch the current state of the art in *linguistic* corpora—this brings in some of the important technical issues that we need for corpus work in general, in particular, the adoption of *multilayered views* of corpora. Finally, we show how this state of the art is now being extended to deal with multimodal artefacts and where our model fits in with this. We will see that the analyses of multimodal documents developed in this book map directly into a multilayered corpus representation that is particularly suitable for multimodal corpus construction.

6.1   Corpus-based linguistics

Corpus-based linguistics starts with the collection of, usually quiet large, bodies of naturally occurring linguistic data—written, spoken, signed, etc. These 'corpora' are then used to search for patterns of co-occurring linguistic phenomena. The patterns found in turn feed the construction of hypotheses that seek to explain why the data is patterned as it is. The methodological cycle then ends with explicit testing of the hypotheses by making *predictions* concerning what patterns occur under what circumstances and testing this against the patterns actually occurring in the corpus.

Although corpus-based linguistics has long been presented as a beneficial way of approaching language studies (cf. Sinclair 1991, Francis 1993), it is only relatively recently that it has taken its proper place as an essential linguistic method. It is generally advantageous to have larger collections of data so that the phenomena in which one is interested occur sufficiently frequently as to provide enough to work with. But when those collections start containing millions, tens of millions, hundreds of millions and more words, even finding the patterns that one is interested in becomes a significant problem. Appropriate tools are therefore essential.

The increase in the use of corpus-based methods accordingly owes much to the ready availability of sufficiently fast computers and the very large storage capabilities necessary for storing corpus information in usable forms. Just what constitutes a 'usable form' is itself, however, a significant question. One could consider all of the information in the World-Wide Web that is stored as textual data as one extremely large corpus (which is, in fact, now a very active research area in its own right); but there are then several significant limits to what one can *do* with that corpus. Linguistics works by looking for increasingly complex reoccurring patterns; using computational tools with large corpora demands that those patterns can be expressed in ways that the computational search engines provided can interpret. If a corpus only contains words (as would be the case for the textual part of most World-Wide Web documents), then it is already quite difficult to search for the more subtle patterns that might be significant for the linguist.

One simple illustration of this is the following. If we are seeking all occurrences of the modal verb 'can' in order to explore how it is being used in different social situations or by differing social groups, for example, we might try to ask a web search engine to retrieve all instances of the word 'can'. Unfortunately, we then receive alongside the cases that we do want all the (for this particular question irrelevant) instances of the noun and (non-modal) verb 'can' too. When we are dealing with a few hundred cases, this might not be a problem; but when we are examining thousands of cases, this imprecision comes to represent a considerable overhead—so much so that ruling out the irrelevant cases reduces the effectiveness of using the corpus at all. When we move to more sophisticated patterns, such as, for example, an investigation of the contexts in which some grammatical construction is used rather than another, then we need to be able to search for the constructions directly rather than particular words or sequences of words: this can be a difficult undertaking.

To move beyond these problems, modern corpora provide direct support for investigation by *annotating* their contained data. This adds information whose purpose is to directly support the formulation of queries. That is, not only will a corpus contain the bare textual information, it will also contain information about the root form of the words used, their word classes (thus enabling a question exclusively about modal 'can'), and possibly some grammatical structures or other information in addition. The provision of corpora viewed as collections of texts is thus giving way to *annotated corpora*, which contain additional information for framing more exact linguistic questions.

One of the key steps in making this corpus method possible is precisely the definition of appropriate formats and annotation forms. We have explained that corpus-based research is all about searching for reoccurring patterns; the more the format of stored data can be made to support the activity of searching for patterns, then the more valuable that corpus becomes for analysis. This is where our discussion of corpora and their further development of multimodal corpora then really starts: just what formats and annotation forms are appropriate for providing useful resources for scientific inquiry.

There are several further issues to be considered when designing corpora. Common requirements include, for example, 'balance', 'representativeness' and quality. Corpora are usually constructed for specific purposes and, as such, may need to cover particular types of language. They should also generally meet standards appropriate for their use: allowing just any text into a corpus without regard of its origin can skew the data and reduce the value of the corpus as a whole. Although these points are important, we cannot discuss them here and refer instead to standard introductions to corpus linguistics, such as McEnery and Wilson (2001) and Biber et al. (1998).

6.2   The origin and representation of annotated corpora

To support corpus-based research, then, we require organisations of the data that support, rather than hinder, scientific inquiry. The development of annotated corpora has been one of the most important steps made towards this. In the earlier days of corpus construction, however, such annotation was achieved on a case-by-case basis. When we contrast corpora of this kind, we see some very different representational techniques at work. In this section we show some of these earlier approaches and use them to motivate the move towards standardised annotations that is now more representative of the state of the art.

6.2.1   Annotated corpora: early days

Consider, as an illustration, the contrast shown between Figure 6.1 and Figure 6.2; the former is an extract from one of the earliest corpora to find wide-scale use, the Lancaster-Oslo-Bergen (LOB) corpus, while the latter is from the more recently produced SUSANNE corpus (Sampson 1995). The LOB corpus was the result of a cooperation between the University of Lancaster, the University of Oslo, and the Norwegian Computing Centre for the Humanities at Bergen and was developed between 1970 and 1976 (Johansson, Leech and Goodluck 1978). It was subsequently annotated to show part of speech information (verb, noun, etc.) by means of a so-called *tagset* (Johansson, Atwell, Garside and Leech 1986). This is a more or less complex classification scheme that identifies classes of individual words. Each word in the corpus therefore receives a corresponding tag. We can see in the first line of Figure 6.1, for example, that 'stubbed' has been assigned the tag VBD (a past-form of a verb) and 'her' the tag PP (personal pronoun).

```
P05    32    ^ Joanna_NP stubbed_VBD out_RP her_PP$
              cigarette_NN with_IN
P05    32    unnecessary_JJ fierceness_NN ._.
P05    33    ^ her_PP$ lovely_JJ eyes_NNS were_BED
              defiant_JJ above_IN cheeks_NNS
P05    33    whose_WP$ colour_NN had_HVD deepened_VBN
P05    34    at_IN Noreen's_NP$ remark_NN ._.
```

Figure 6.1   Extract from the Lancaster-Oslo-Bergen (LOB) corpus

In order to be useful for linguistic inquiry, such tags need to go into rather more detail than the handful of parts-of-speech seen in school grammars, but the general approach is nevertheless straightforward. Clearly, in order to find either the original text or to use the part-of-speech information, par-

```
J04:0230c NN1u resonance      resonance      .Ns:s102]
J04:0230d VBZ  is             be             [Vzu.
J04:0230e VVGv becoming       become         .Vzu]
J04:0230g RR   increasingly   increasingly   [R:h.R:h]
J04:0230h VVNt used           use            [Vn.Vn]
J04:0230i II   in             in             [P:p.
J04:0230j NN2  investigations investigation  [Np.
J04:0240a IO   of             of             [Po.
J04:0240b NN1n structure      structure      .Po]Np]P:p]Fa:c]S]
J04:0240c YF   +.             -              .
```

Figure 6.2   Extract from the SUSANNE corpus (slightly abbreviated)

ticular support software is necessary—although we will not go into details here, how this would work in principle should be relatively clear.

The form of the SUSANNE corpus is already far more complex. It is organised as a table with the original text making up just one column of the entire data set. The first column gives a unique identifier for each word in the corpus, analogously to our base units (cf. Chapter 3), and the second column again provides specialised 'part-of-speech' tags. These are quite distinct to the tags used in the LOB corpus and are also considerably more detailed, indicating several significant subclasses. The fourth column contains the base form of the word used—this makes it straightforward, for example, to search for all uses of the word 'become' (including 'becoming', 'became', etc.). And the final column goes a stage further in sophistication and includes some detailed descriptions of the *grammatical* structures in the corpus. The form of this information is also particular to the SUSANNE corpus and groups words together by opening and closing square brackets, each pair of which is labelled by a grammatical category. We can see in the second and third line, for example, how 'is' and 'becoming' are grouped together into a single phrase of type VZu and, in lines 6–9, how 'in investigation of structure' is a single prepositional phrase of type P:p with further *internal* structure within this: i.e.,

$$[_{\text{P:p}} \text{ in } [_{\text{Np}} \text{ investigation } [_{\text{Po}} \text{ of structure}]]]$$

These structures can become arbitrarily complicated and provide a detailed phrase structure analysis of the sentences in the corpus.

This level of detail makes available considerable information useful to the linguist searching for interesting linguistic patterns. But it also requires a different set of tools for dealing with the information of the corpus that is stored in this form. Moreover, such richly annotated data is correspondingly more expensive to produce: the technology for creating particularly the information of the last column automatically is only now beginning to become reasonably accurate and still requires time-intensive, and hence expensive, manual checking.

The LOB and SUSANNA corpora together show clearly the diversity of representations adopted and something of the additional information typically added to a corpus to make it more useful for linguistic investigation. Many such corpora have now been developed, each with its own style of annotation Since no particular style was clearly better than another, designers of individual corpora typically took very different decisions when constructing their corpora. Each corpus adopted its own formatting conventions and its own tagsets, requiring users of more than one corpus to be familiar with a range of incompatible classification schemes. As a consequence, the tools developed for asking queries and examining results for one corpus were not in general re-usable for any others.

More recently, the design of corpora has moved towards establishing standards and guidelines both for the kinds of information maintained and the form in which that information is represented. This supports a greater re-usability of tools and helps users to transfer their skills across different corpora. The first stage of this development involved separating out more clearly the basic data stored in a corpus and information about that data, i.e., the annotations. This is an important step to make information easier to process and manipulate. We can see this problem with the LOB corpus example of Figure 6.1: it is not clear to a reader, and hence to a computational tool for using the data, what aspects of the corpora correspond to the original data and which are added information. This is partially addressed in the SUSANNE corpus by allocating the basic data to its own column: however, the remaining tags are still adopting very much their own conventions and a tool written for this corpus is not usable for corpora following other designs.

6.2.2   Applying XML to corpus design

We have seen precisely this problem from a very different perspective in Chapter 2 above. There we saw that the general task of 'adding' information to a textual document in a way that maintains a clear distinction between that text and its presentational form has been a particular concern of the publishing industry for a long time. Whereas with corpora the extra information to be added is linguistic annotations of some kind, in publishing it was information concerning formatting or layout attributes, or notes of differences between editions, etc. Despite this difference, many of the same issues arise and the solution that has been reached for both aims is virtually the same. Just as in the publishing industry, the additional information necessary for making corpora usable is now being expressed in terms of *standardised mark-up.* Extensive descriptions of current approaches to such linguistic mark-up are available in the introductions to corpus linguistics mentioned above and we will not be concerned with the particular kind of mark-up employed here in any detail. Relevant for us is the general path that this course of development has taken and its current extensions to include multimodality. Just as with the representation of documents for publishing and then electronic use, linguistic corpora went through a stage of being represented in the Standard Generalised Mark-up Language (SGML) followed by a general move to the Extensible Mark-Up Language (XML) that we also introduced in Chapter 2. When considering corpus annotation, however, there are several central mechanisms of XML that are of considerable importance and which we need to introduce in more detail. We pick out three of these here for the purposes of defining multimodal corpora.

The first is the ability to explicitly define particular 'languages' or 'dialects' of XML: the most commonly known such dialect is XHTML—the XML version of HTML. Corpus designers also now draw on this capability for defining their corpora. Any particular corpus design can be specified as a variant of XML—that corpus can then be processed by any software that knows about XML. This represents a significant saving in time and costs for developing corpus software and has the natural corollary that data prepared in different corpus efforts can be more readily re-used across different projects. Adopting the generic design decisions inherent in XML automatically renders initially quite distinct corpora compatible.

The second is the following: once a 'dialect' of XML has been defined in this way, there are tools that *automatically check* whether any particular specification conforms to that dialect or not. The particular mechanisms that provide this capability are *Document Type Descriptions* (DTDs) and, more recently, *XML Schema.* Checking data for conformity with a DTD or schema is called *document validation.* It is by no means straightforward to guarantee that any sizeable collection of information in fact contains no errors even of a formal, structural kind: and this is the kind of service that a DTD or XML-Schema provides. Standard XML-parsers check documents for conformity with their specified dialect so that at least formal errors (such as misspelled tags, inconsistent or incorrect structures, missing tags, etc.) can be avoided. Locating and removing errors of this kind automatically is a considerable help for ensuring quality and usability. Moreover, as we will see more of below, corpus annotation creates complex webs of interlocked information and it is virtually impossible to maintain such bodies of information by hand.

The third mechanism is the possibility that XML provides of 'moving around' within complex XML documents and for searching for parts of those documents that meet particular criteria. This latter set of mechanisms supports the 'transformations' of XML that we mentioned in Chapter 2 above as a central part of the XML-based publishing chain (cf. Figure 2.19). Such transformations primarily work by locating particular elements according to specified criteria, examining their attributes, and building some new piece of XML structure as a result. As we shall return to in more detail below, this already provides a way both of querying XML-based corpora and of building generic and re-usable tools for working with them.

With the increase in sophistication of XML and the tools for its support, there has also been considerable motivation to agree on standardisation dialects of XML for the purpose of annotation. One of these is a development that began with the *Text Encoding Initiative* (TEI) of the Association for Computational Linguistics, the Association for Literary and Linguistic Computing, and the Association for Computers and the Humanities (Sperber-McQueen and Burnard 2002, 2007). The TEI defines guidelines for specifying machine-readable texts and was subsequently built upon by one of the European Union 'Expert Advisory Groups on Language Engineering Standards' (EAGLES) in order to provide specialised guidelines particularly for corpus construction. This enables corpus designers to prepare and construct corpora more systematically and in ways supportive of re-use within a broader research community.

These specialised guidelines, called the Corpus Encoding Standard (CES: Corpus Encoding Standard 2000), set out several layers of increasingly demanding mark-up that corpora should adopt for expressing their additional information. Thus, whereas the TEI specifies the form of machine-readable documents in general, the CES provides particular details about the content of the additional information that needs to be represented when building corpora. Software designed for corpus processing can now be specifically tailored to the more precise specifications given in the CES while still maintaining very broad applicability—i.e., applicability to any corpus that is (provably, via the given DTDs) *CES-conformant*. The increasing acceptance of XML has naturally also led to the latest versions of the Corpus Encoding Standard being given in XML (XCES: Ide, Bonhomme and Romary 2000).

The adoption of XML across the board is now allowing both corpus designers and users to employ state-of-the-art display and data manipulation tools as they become available. As the information content of a corpus expands, the corpus documents themselves come to look less and less like the original texts they represent: the corpus is no longer intended to be read directly by a human reader. The point of providing additional information is, after all, to make it easier for computational tools to be developed that support linguists in their search for linguistic patterns. The user's *view* of the corpus is therefore always to be mediated by appropriate tools. XML makes the provision of such tools very much easier than hitherto—increasingly powerful concordance and corpus-search programs based on XML are immediately applicable to any corpus represented in an XML-conformant fashion. The benefits of standardisation in this area are therefore very tangible and are set to significantly improve the design and use of linguistic corpora in all areas.

As suggested in Chapter 2, the basic organisation of a document written in XML is very simple. Information is structured by means of tags in the same way as is information for web pages in HTML. A piece of information is marked with a certain tag by enclosing it within an opening tag and a closing tag; when, for example, marking a body of text according to XCES as a single paragraph, we use the 'p' tag: the opening 'p' tag is written as `<p>` and the closing 'p' tag as `</p>`. An example of an annotated fragment of text adapted from the CES documentation is given in Figure 6.3. On the left of the figure we see a rendering of a fictitious edition of Charlotte Brontë's *Jane Eyre*, where the division into two areas represents two consecutive pages of the book. On the right of the figure we see an XCES-conformant version of the text employing the tags of the basic TEI level of mark-up (depicted in bold face to make them stand out somewhat although this is *not* part of the actual data!). This illustrates use of the paragraph tag and the quotation tag ('q') in particular and gives an indication of how explicit structure is imposed on raw text.

We also see here one of the reasons why such mark-up is of interest to researchers into literary editions: the page numbering, in particular the page division, is also indicated in the XCES mark-up with the page-break tag pb:

```
<pb edition="1934" n="435"/>
```

This mark-up makes use of a particular variant of the XML syntax for expressing an 'empty' tag—i.e., there is no separate closing page-break tag, the form 'closes itself', so to speak. This is used for adding single pieces of information into an XML document without necessarily spanning any content of the marked-up document; we will see this technique employed in several of our examples below.

More importantly here is how this tag can be seen to associate increasingly complex information with the text by using *attributes* that take particular *values*. In this case, we have two attributes specified for the tag, the edition that the page break refers to and the page number, n, in that

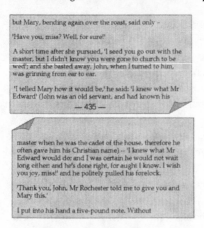

but Mary, bending again over the roast, said only -

'Have you, miss? Well, for sure!'

A short time after she pursued, 'I seed you go out with the master, but I didn't know you were gone to church to be wed'; and she basted away. John, when I turned to him, was grinning from ear to ear.

'I telled Mary how it would be,' he said: 'I knew what Mr Edward' (John was an old servant, and had known his

— 435 —

master when he was the cadet of the house, therefore he often gave him his Christian name) -- 'I knew what Mr Edward would do; and I was certain he would not wait long either: and he's done right, for aught I know. I wish you joy, miss!' and he politely pulled his forelock.

'Thank you, John. Mr Rochester told me to give you and Mary this.'

I put into his hand a five-pound note. Without

```
but Mary, bending again over the roast,
said only &dash; </p><p><q>Have you,
miss? Well, for sure!</q> </p><p><q>A short
time after she pursued, <q>I seed you go
out with the master, but I didn't know
you were gone to church to be wed</q>;
and she basted away. John, when I turned
to him, was grinning from ear to ear.
</p><p><q>I telled Mary how it would
be,</q> he said: <q>I knew what Mr
Edward</q> (John was an old servant, and
had known <pb edition="1934" n="435"/>
his master when he was the cadet of the
house, therefore he often gave him his
christian name) &dash; <q> I knew what Mr
Edward would do; and I was certain he
would not wait long either: and he's done
right, for aught I know. I wish you joy,
miss!</q> and he politely pulled his
forelock.</q> <p><q>Thank you, John. Mr
Rochester told me to give you and Mary
this.</q></p><p><p>I put into his hand a
five-pound note. Without
```

Original Text from a fictitious 1934 edition of *Jane Eyre*

XCES-conform version

Figure 6.3   Example of XCES-conformant annotation adapted from the TEI Guidelines

edition. In general, there could by any number of such page break tags scattered around the document, each referring to *different* editions. More sophisticated treatments can include information about additions or changes made between editions and so on, each with their own particular attributes indicating origin, date and any other information that the editions expert might require.

We can then go on to query such text collections directly in terms of their *logical* structure (cf. Section 2.4) rather than contingent features of the original. If we had to use originals, then some editions might use a single quotation mark for direct quoted speech whereas others use a double quotation mark, perhaps with distinguished open and closing quotes, and this would need to be known and considered when, for example, searching for quotations. In contrast, the CES specification allows us simply to look for quotations via the q tag no matter how the quotations are represented in any particular text or edition.

The core functionalities that XML provides for manipulating and transforming XML structures already support mechanisms for formulating queries of this kind. The most significant component of XML for this purpose is called *XPath*. XPath is a special way of locating elements in any XML structure. A simple example of its use is the following. Assume that we want to locate all pages numbered '435' from all editions of *Jane Eyre* in an appropriate editions corpus. We can find these by making an

XPath 'interpreter' carry out the following search instruction, written as an 'XPath expression':

```
//pb[@n="435"]
```

This says: find any element that has the tag pb and which also has the value '435' for its page-number attribute n. This would give us the marked segment of our XCES-conformant example shown in Figure 6.3 above, and also the corresponding portions of any other edition with the same value for its n-attribute. This mechanism already provides a very general and power-ful method for extracting information from any XML-organised sources of data. Moreover, as part of the XML specification, we are already beginning to find XPath interpreters being integrated into standard and freely available software, such as web-browsers.

Texts maintained in the structured XML form become increasingly useful the more annotation that they contain. Clearly, if information is not explic-itly present, it is correspondingly more difficult to look for it. The general trend in corpus-related work is therefore for ever more information to work its way into explicit standardised mark-up rather than being left as 'content' in the text. The CES itself suggests several levels of annotation—the first, and minimal level, is as suggested in Figure 6.3, while the higher levels re-quire basic linguistic information to be marked-up as well, such as sentence boundaries and part-of-speech information as indicated above. It is these latter levels which brings us closer to the information content of linguistic corpora.

Most large corpora are now represented in XML. Information previously maintained in *ad hoc* representations has mostly been translated into equiva-lent XML representations so that both the coding scheme (e.g., the tagsets) and the structure of the corpus are standardised and can employ widely available XML processing programs. As an example, a translation of the third line of Figure 6.2 above drawn from the SUSANNE corpus concern-ing the word 'becoming' could look as follows:

```
<w id="J04:0230e" pos="VVGv" lemma="become">becoming</w>
```

This makes liberal use of tag attributes to associate additional information with the annotated word, including the unique identification code, the part-of-speech information and the base form of the word. The precise attributes that are allowed and the kinds of values that they may take is again specified formally in a Document Type Description, which allows formal validation for this information also.

With this structured information in place, we can provide a further illus-tration of using XPath that moves us on towards the traditional kind of uses made of linguistic corpora. For example, we can readily look for all words in the corpus with a particular part-of-speech without employing any more sophisticated or corpus-specific software. The XPath expression:

```
//w[@pos="VVGv"]
```

is all that is necessary to return a list of all words of class 'VVGv'—whatever that class may be: clearly the use of XML and XPath does not help us determine just what this particular corpus-specific tag might mean. For this we need to consider further issues of corpus standardisation, which is not our focus here.

6.2.3   Annotation problems with complex data

Whereas the use of XML represents a major advance for the design of large-scale corpora, there are nevertheless problems with capturing the required linguistic (or other) information in ways which remain faithful both to the structure of that information and to the requirements imposed by XML. As long as the (largely formal) requirements of XML are met, standard tools can be used for processing the data; this is extremely beneficial because of the already very large and growing community of XML users and developers. When data does not conform to the XML specification, it can no longer be processed by the available generic tools and its use is restricted.

An appropriate analogy is the use of HTML for web-pages: as long as someone uses standard HTML, then they know that anyone using a standard browser will be able to see the information they are offering; as soon as they depart from HTML, their potential audience is cut dramatically. Linguistic corpora that do not adopt XML techniques suffer a similar fate. They simply cut themselves off from a rapidly developing set of tools and techniques for maintaining consistence and for pulling out information under specified conditions for inspection. It is therefore highly desirable to find representation solutions that work within the XML standards or which explicitly contribute to those standards' extension.

The main problem encountered when attempting more sophisticated linguistic annotation is that of *intersecting hierarchies*. One of the basic formal requirements of XML is that tags must 'nest properly'. That is, when representing structured data, the structures must properly fit inside each other—there can be no overlapping or intersecting boundaries. This is not only a problem with linguistic annotation, there are many text annotation applications where it is inappropriate to force the structures that are to be represented to nest one within the other.

A good example of this problem is given by Durusau and O'Donnell (2002), taken again from the area of annotation for literary editions. A simple TEI-conformant mark-up of the linguistic content of a document might require a decomposition into identified sentences; this would use a sequence of <S> and matching closing </S> tags. A further simple TEI-conformant mark-up might want to indicate the division into pages that an edition employs. Whereas as in our example above we simplified the situation for the purposes of the exposition by only indicating page *breaks*, an annotation more in the spirit of structured representations would prefer using sequences of <page>...</page> tags to indicate directly which information is contained within the confines of single pages. Only then can we really make the most use of the structured query possibilities provided by XPath.

Now, however, consider an annotation for a machine-readable version of the literary work that wants to capture the page breaks *and* the linguistic divisions simultaneously. This cannot be done straightforwardly with XML precisely because the linguistic division into sentences and the division into pages do *not* necessarily 'nest' one within the other. Since these levels of information have no logical relationship to one another, there is no reason why the structures imposed by the two kinds of division should be related in any way.

The simplest way of capturing this information might appear to be as suggested in Figure 6.4. But this is not 'legal' XML: as shown to the right of the figure the structures defined by the <S>-tags and the <page>-tags do not 'properly nest'. The first sentence tag is not closed before its enclosing page tag is closed. Allowing such non-nesting structures vastly complicates the machinery necessary for checking document conformance and is generally rejected as a viable option.

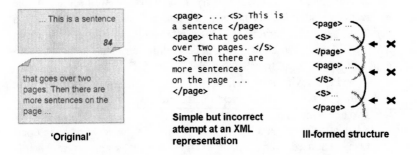

Figure 6.4   Example of a common mark-up situation and an ill-formed XML attempt at its representation

Although this might appear to be an artificial problem induced by the apparatus adopted, it is in fact rather a good illustration of the valuable role of formalisation: the fact that allowing non-nesting structures would result in very much more complex machinery gives us a hint that perhaps this is not the right way to do things. Indeed, why should a single document contain such incompatible kinds of information? Imagine that we take the example further and wish to add in other information: for example, the pages extents of differing editions (each of which may have an arbitrary relationship to the page extents of others), or the intended (or actually used) intonational phrasings of the sentences if the text is to be spoken (as in a play). Each of these structures is compatible and simple when considered in isolation, but may relate in complex ways to the others.

A solution for this problem that has now established itself in the machine-readable corpus community is that of *stand-off annotation* in the style proposed by Thompson and McKelvie (1997). The idea is straightforward, although its realisation in standard XML involves some more technical machinery. Essentially, stand-off annotation recognises the independence of the differing layers of annotation and separates these *both* from the original data *and* from each other. Thus, rather than having a single marked-up document where the annotations are buried within the data, which is in certain respects not so different from the original LOB corpus solution that we started with in Figure 6.1 above, we instead separate off the annotation information into independent annotation layers—hence the phrase 'stand off'. Each individual layer is a well-formed XML file and contact is made with the original data only indirectly by referring to particular elements. This solves the problem of intersecting hierarchies because *within any single XML file* there is no intersecting hierarchy; there is only the single hierarchy of the particular annotation layer that that file captures.

The additional technical complexity involved is that we need to be able to access the individual elements of the data in order to bind them into a variety of annotation structures. This can be achieved most simply within XML by giving each element a unique identifying label, as in the word annotation in the XML translation of the SUSANNE corpus example shown above, and employing *cross-references*. We show this in a simplified form in Figure 6.5, where a single text document shown on the left is divided into two annotation layers on the right.

The situation illustrated takes the first pair of sentences from the document fragment used as an example in Figure 6.3 but assumes further that in this edition there is a page break immediately following the fragment: "... Have you, miss? Well,". This information is captured by breaking the original document into the set of 'basic level' annotation units shown here on

XML 'base' file

```
<w id="u-01">Have<w>
<w id="u-02">you</w>
<punc type="comma" id="u-03">,</punc>
<w id="u-04">miss</w>
<punc type="question" id="u-05">?</punc>
<w id="u-06">Well</w>
<punc type="comma" id="u-07">,</punc>
<w id="u-08">for</w>
<w id="u-09">sure</w>
<punc type="exclamation"
        id="u-10">!</punc>
```

XML file for page breaks

```
<page id="page-01" from="..." to="u-07"/>
<page id="page-02" from="u-08" to="..."/>
```

XML file for sentences

```
<s id="s-01" from="u-01" to="u-05"/>
<s id="s-02" from="u-06" to="u-10"/>
```

Figure 6.5   Example of stand-off annotation

the left of the figure, consisting of words ('w' tags) and punctuation ('punc' tags). Each of these receives a unique identifying label as the value of its 'id' attribute.

The two layers of stand-off annotation shown on the right of the figure then use these labels to define structures over the base document as follows.

The first page—given its own identifying label of 'page-01' in the first stand-off layer—is shown running *from* some base unit that we cannot see in the figure up *to* the unit labelled 'u-07'. The second page then runs from unit 'u-08' onwards. In a complete annotation all of the units would have received identifying labels and so the cross-references would be complete; here we have omitted the labels of the units outside of the example. All of these tags are 'empty' in the sense we introduced above for the page-break tag: they contain no elements and simply function to provide additional information via their attributes and values. The second stand-off layer shows precisely the same kind of information but for sentences.

Each individual layer is now a well-formed XML file and so there is no problem with distinct hierarchies failing to respect one another. The crossing hierarchies have been moved out of the XML structure of the mark-up documents and are only recoverable indirectly by following the cross-references. This example already contains, therefore, the basis for an *open-ended* set of annotation layers, each of which adds in further information to the base material. This also shows the main technical motivation for our definition of the base layer of the GeM model as set out in Chapter 3. The base layer provides just the functionality for constructing other layers of interpretation as illustrated with this simple case in the current figure.

The utility of this method relies crucially on the effectiveness of computational software for dealing with richly structured information of this kind. The fact that the entire framework is XML-conformant then becomes particularly important. Tools for writing inquiries that interrogate data structured in this way are being refined and extended extremely quickly. This is because the main users of XML-structured data are not linguists or researchers at all, but standard commercial providers of information that previously would have been maintained in databases, such as sales catalogues of online companies, stock-lists, personnel data, and so on. Because of this very practical and economic demand, methods for using such data are already finding their way into the standardly available web-browsers—this virtually guarantees that it will soon be possible for annotated corpora to be navigated and manipulated using widely available and familiar tools rather than the complex, corpus-specific schemes and software of the past.

Moreover, a working group of the International Organization for Standardization (ISO TC37/SC4) is now focusing specifically on producing recommendations for corpus and annotations standards. As a contribution to these efforts, a specific *Linguistic Annotation Framework* (LAF: Ide, Romary and de la Clergerie 2003) is currently under development to take on the tasks of the next generation of annotated data, including multimodal corpora. This will also serve to increase dramatically the sheer breadth of information available for investigation. Within this standardisation effort, distinct working groups are focusing on distinct levels of information—we can consider, therefore, the layers of the GeM model as potential future contributions to this ongoing development.

6.3   The move to multimodal corpora

The technical details described in the previous section provide the foundations necessary for the move to *multimodal* corpora. Some of the first developments in this area were pursued in order to support research drawing on instances of spoken language obtained in natural contexts of use. Since it is clear that interpretation is significantly improved if, in addition to the speech, other information, such as gestures, gaze, proximity and so on, is also maintained, this led naturally to *multimodal linguistic corpora* containing collections of speech and video information. Here in addition to a traditional 'transcription' of what is being said by the participants in an interaction, we find synchronised recordings of both the sound and visual context of that interaction. This allows researchers to avoid possible inaccuracies or theoretical bias arising in transcription by providing access to the actual recordings of spoken language, also organised in such a way as to support investigation and theory-building. This area is currently booming and there are substantial efforts aimed at standardising and exchanging both data and tools (cf. Dybkjaer, Berman, Kipp, Olsen, Pirrelli, Reithinger and Soria 2001, Martin, Kühnlein, Paggio, Stiefelhagen and Pianese 2005).

These extensions of the traditional notion of the corpus can be characterised in a similar way: they all move from text-based data to *time-based* data. This works by designating a particular temporally sequenced track as the 'reference' track and all other phenomena are then related back to the elements of that reference track using the kind of stand-off annotation mechanism just introduced. For time-based data, the reference track is naturally the speech or video signal, since both of these are anchored in time and automatically provide orderings for their elements.

Current guidelines for corpus design, particularly multimodal corpora involving speech and video, therefore make significant use of stand-off annotation in order to provide entire sets of annotation 'tracks', or 'tiers', in which different aspects of the data being annotated are maintained. For speech data, for example, we might require a syntax track, an intonational track and, if the interaction is multi-party, particular tracks for each speaker. For video data, there might be a music track, a gestural track, a movement track, as well as a language track that itself involves all of the tracks that we might expect for speech data. For all of these demands, stand-off annotation is particularly well suited and is one of the most commonly used techniques.

Some quite sophisticated systems are now used widely for multimodal research. These include, for example, MMAX developed at the European Media Laboratory in Heidelberg for multilevel text-based annotation,[1] ANVIL developed at the University of the Saarland for multilevel video annotation,[2] ELAN originally developed by the Max Planck Institute for Psycholinguistics in Nijmegen for combined text, video and audio annotation,[3] and several more. Each of these work by allowing the user to define 'markables' at various levels of abstraction, or within various tracks or tiers, which can then be marked up in the data by means of graphical user interfaces. All of these systems make extensive use of XML and stand-off annotation. A further system being developed for the analysis of video data is Baldry's Multimodal Corpus Authoring system[4] (MCA) as described in Baldry and Thibault (2005, 2006); it is as yet unclear to what extent this system currently supports evolving multimodal corpus standards.

Despite these advances, for the purposes of corpus design for multimodal *documents* we still face a problem. As we have shown in the previous chapters, the main characteristic of multimodal documents is provided not by temporal organisation, but by *spatial* organisation. Page-flow makes a

---

[1] http://mmax.eml-research.de
[2] http://www.anvil-software.de/
[3] http://www.lat-mpi.eu/tools/elan/
[4] http://mca.unipv.it/

particular kind of use of the two-dimensional area of the page and we need to be able to make sure that our corpora record this aspect of the data. This raises some perhaps surprising difficulties. There is, in fact, still rather little that we can build when considering two-dimensional spatial information as a basis for corpus work. Thus, on the one hand, although we wish to draw on the obvious benefits of corpus-based methods, on the other hand, we are concerned neither with time-based data nor with pure textual data. This leads to a different direction of development for the notion of multimodal corpora as such: *multimodal document corpora*, collections of naturally occurring bodies of multimodal documents, texts and other spatial artefacts.

In certain specialised areas, such as automatic document analysis, document classification and clustering, and information retrieval, multimodal document corpora have already played an important role for some time—examples here include the Oulu MediaTeam Document Database of Sauvola and Kauniskangas (1999), and the University of Washington document databases.[5] Much of this work is driven by the requirement for test data for extending Optical Character Recognition, which is, as we saw in Chapter 2, nowadays very much concerned with recognising document structure and layout. This work provides so-called 'ground truth' layout databases for testing the accuracy of automatic layout recognition and functional annotation. However, whereas this work already contains some information that is useful for our concerns, it has not been oriented to the kind of detail required for exploring the precise combinations of modes of information presentation, comprehension, rhetorical intepretation, literacy issues and so on.

Multimodal document collections that are prepared in this way are gradually emerging—such as in, for example, work by Corio and Lapalme (1998), by Bouayad-Agha (2000) on 'patient information leaflets', by Eckkrammer and colleagues on layperson-oriented medical texts on infectious diseases (the DIALAYMED corpus: Eckkrammer 2004), by Walker and colleagues on the educational materials produced for children (cf. Section 5.2.2 and Walker 2003),[6] by Baldry and Thibault on a variety of printed and online documents (cf. Baldry and Thibault 2005, 2006 and above), as well as our own approach as developed at length in this book (cf., also: Bateman, Delin and Henschel 2002b, 2004). But we will need substantially more efforts in this direction to further the kind of empirically-based genre studies envisioned in our framework. Moreover, the tools necessary for working with large-scale collections of *page-based* multimodal data are

---

[5] http://documents.car.umd.edu/resources/database/
[6] http://www.kidstype.org/

also under-developed; again, there will need to be substantial developments in this area to support empirical work more effectively.

6.4   The GeM model as a corpus annotation scheme

Although tools for processing multimodal page-based corpora are still few and far between, establishing sound guidelines for the organisation of such data is an important first step. One of our main aims in this book has therefore been to set out in detail how precisely we can extend multimodal corpora to include layers of information necessary for document analysis and for pushing further our theories of multimodal meaning-making. To this end, we can see each layer of the GeM model as a stand-off layer of annotation decomposing the documents analysed. The layers themselves are all defined in terms of XML descriptions and so support the kinds of organisation and query mechanisms described above for other kinds of multimodal corpora.

This allows us both to store the information necessary according to the GeM model and to use that information for constructing complex corpus queries that freely combine information from any of the layers of the GeM model. We see the ability to locate patterns that hold *across* distinct layers of the model as an essential precondition for locating genre characteristics. We presented informally in previous chapters how each layer of the model defines a set of units and structures that hold over those units. Here we will specify this organisation in more detail, so that we can see clearly how the individual layers are represented and combined in an XML-conformant manner. This involves in particular defining appropriate attributes and possible values of those attributes for each type of unit introduced. Space precludes us providing an exhaustive account at this point and so we will simply sketch the formalisation that we follow—for the precise definitions of the first version of this corpus scheme, the interested reader is referred to Henschel (2002).

To begin, we have the base units and the layout units introduced in Chapter 3 and relied upon in all our subsequent analyses. The GeM base only *identifies* the base units. This means that the units defined here have only one main attribute, their identification number. Whereas speech-oriented corpora use the time line as their basic reference method, and syntactically oriented corpora use the sequence of characters or words, the GeM annotation scheme focuses on documents and their layout and so needs to take elements arrayed anywhere and in any order across a page, screen or other visually-defined unit of analysis. Each such unit can then be viewed as a layout object on the one hand or as a sign carrying meaning on the other (cf. Figure 3.1 in Chapter 3). We strictly separate these two perspectives in our account.

The *layout base* then specifies layout units by identifying both the base units they are made up of and their layout properties. As we motivated in Chapter 2 and described in more detail in Chapter 3, it is appropriate here to import many of the standardised treatments of typographical properties being developed in the XML community. Other attributes, particularly those concerned with the specification of the spatial relationships involved, are specifically defined by the GeM model via the area model and the hierarchical layout structure.

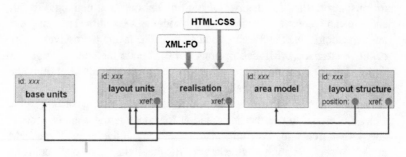

Figure 6.6   The inter-relationships between base units and the components of the GeM layout model

We can see the inter-relationships defined here in Figure 6.6. On the left-hand side of the diagram, we have the base units; then we have layout units defined by collecting together identified base units via a *cross-reference* xref attribute. The layout units are grouped hierarchically (again via cross-reference attributes) in the layout structure, which additionally references areas defined by the area model (via the position attribute). Realisations for identified groups of layout elements are defined, again by cross-referencing, and import from the XML style sheet formatting objects (FO) and the HTML cascaded style sheet (CSS) specifications as suggested in Chapter 2.

Moving on to the semantic perspective, we have (i) base units which contribute directly to the content of the document, these are associated with the RST segments motivated in Chapter 4, (ii) base units which only serve to help the reader navigate through the document, the units associated with navigation elements, and (iii) units which are both. In terms of the inter-connection between components of the GeM model, these layers are more straightforward than the connections within the layout structure. The *RST base* determines which base units (or groups of base units) serve as segments for a rhetorical structure analysis of the document and represents that structure by building a recursive organisation analogous to that shown for the layout structure.

The alignment between the distinct base, layout and RST layers and their information is illustrated schematically in Figure 6.7. Here we see one of our Gannet pages as discussed in Chapter 5 together with extracts from the associated GeM layers. The graphical version of the page is linked directly to the base layer, indicating how the base units are motivated. The layout structure and the rhetorical structure are then each defined independently both of each other and the base layer. The fact that, for example, some span in the rhetorical structure, or that some layout element in the layout structure, corresponds to a given element on the page is then managed by the cross-references, shown graphically in the figure by connecting arrows. Use is also made of cross references *within* layers: for example, within the layout layer, the hierarchical layout structure is related to the area model by cross references (cf. Chapter 3) and, within the rhetorical layer, rhetorical structure is defined over an inventory of rhetorical units by cross-references (cf. Chapter 4). This is shown graphically in the figure by dotted connecting arrows within the boxes representing layers.

The *navigation base* lists the navigation elements and their function within a document. We have not had the opportunity to discuss this aspect of document meaning in any detail in this book and so set out here slightly more of what is involved. Navigation units identify those elements which primarily serve to support the reader in navigating through a document; we can imagine a journey on a two- or more dimensional geographical landscape. Navigation in a document is supported by *pointers*, text pieces or other elements which either tell the reader where the current text, or 'document thread', is continued or point to an alternative continuation or continuations. Such elements may occur in any page-based documents and appear to be a property of the page-flow semiotic mode itself—they are *not*, as sometimes thought, limited to online documents.

The navigation base defines several distinct pointing 'situations'. For example, a *continuation pointer* is used when the layout of an article is broken into two non-adjacent parts. The second part is often printed several pages later than the first part. Continuation pointers are typically pointers that operate with respect to the layout structure. *Branching pointers* are used when a certain piece of information may be appropriately located at more than one physical position in a document. These pointers may then appear at the other places in order to indicate that they were also potential placements but the design has not taken them up; this usage overlaps with

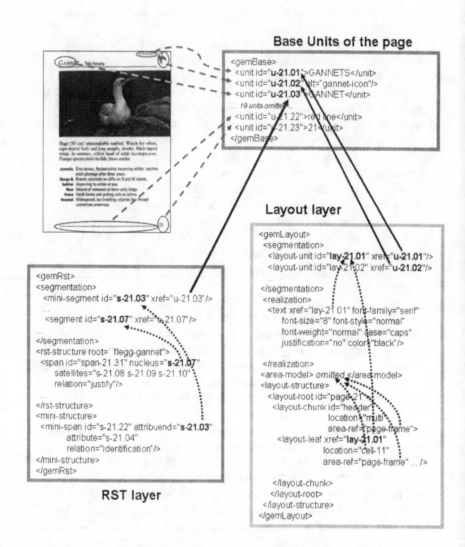

Figure 6.7   *A GeM-style XML representation of a Gannet page showing base, layout and RST layers*

document deixis (cf. Paraboni and van Deemter 2002) in the text mode. A third type of pointer is the *expansion pointer*. This is used when more information is available, but is not central to the writer's goal; an expansion pointer points to this extra information. In print documents, this may be expressed by footnotes, etc.; in online documents, by hyperlinks. Encountering a branching or expansion pointer, the reader has a choice between two alternatives reading paths. With a continuation pointer the reader has only the choice between continuing to read or stopping.

Typical nodes have been identified in the RST structure and in the layout structure to play particular roles when pointers are used: for example, chapter/section headings are names for RST spans and page numbers are names for page-sized layout-chunks, both of which are clearly used for navigation. There are also other name-carrying layout-chunks or RST spans, however; for example: figures, tables, enumerated formulas, and so on. The navigation base of a document lists all these "names" which have been defined in the document to be actually or potentially used in pointers. A pointer (or link) operating on the RST structure connects the current segment with some other RST span—the target RST span—which is located at a different non-adjacent place in the layout. A pointer operating on the layout structure connects the 'containing' layout chunk with another layout chunk which is not adjacent.

To summarise, we can see that the design of the GeM model is multi-layered in that each document receives an analysis according to several independent descriptions. Each of these descriptions forms a layer of annotation in a multimodal corpus. This supports the search for generalizations concerning multimodal documents by allowing examination of whether particular *co-selections* from the independent descriptions can be reliably established. If patterns of co-selection are revealed, we can assume that the theoretically independent choices are in fact constrained so as to preclude or restrict independent choice. We suggest that the controlling variable in such cases will often be locatable in our extended notion of genre. Our multi-layered analyses therefore aim at supporting focused qualitative and quantitative research into the systematically recurring features and patterns of multimodal genres by setting out explicitly the choices that documents have taken up in their design. This then allows us to search for commonalities. More details of the individual layers of annotation in the GeM model, their definition and examples of use can be found in Henschel (2002), Bateman, Delin and Henschel (2002*a*) and Bateman et al. (2004).

6.5　Conclusions and recommendations

We have argued throughout this book that an extension of linguistically informed modes of analysis offers an invaluable vantage point for multimodal analysis. We believe that it is indeed now time to apply linguistic constructs and methodologies in an investigation of meaning-making generally and of multimodal documents in particular. But one of the corollaries of broadening our area of concern in this way is that we need to deal with systems which are manifestly meaning-making (e.g., photographs, diagrams) but for which we lack the rich battery of investigative tools that we now have for linguistic entities.

Linguistic research is being driven furthest where there is a close coupling of theory and data. When the data-basis is too weak, or is not sufficiently strongly linked to the claims that a theory makes, then theory can run wild and the claims it makes are not clearly, if at all, testable; when there is a good link between theoretical claim and data then theory-construction is more constrained and, consequently, more productive. Precisely this close coupling between data and theory-construction is not yet a strong feature of 'multimodal linguistics' despite increasing calls for this move to be made (cf. Kaltenbacher 2004, Bateman et al. 2004, Baldry and Thibault 2005).

For multimodal documents, appropriate models and techniques for this are still largely lacking. A substantial set of problems is raised by the fact that the object of study is not linear, either temporally or in terms of the principles for its consumption; moreover, its multichannel nature makes it difficult to reconcile and peg together the methods of recording, transcription, analysis and annotation that have been developed separately for each mode. This makes empirical study and validation of theory particularly problematic: we have not had the "orderly arrangement of the objects upon which we must turn our mental vision" (cf. Descartes 1701, Rule V) and, partly as a consequence, analysis has remained overwhelmingly impressionistic.

In order to provide a solid empirical basis for investigating questions of meaning making in multimodal documents, we need in the future to construct extensive collections of data organised in a manner that supports this inquiry. The GeM model is intended as one such representational form, drawing on experiences gained with traditional linguistic corpora. We consider developing multimodal corpora in the style described in this chapter as an essential contribution to the establishment of a broader and more objective basis for hypothesis formation, theory construction and verification for all aspects of multimodal documents.

7

Conclusions and Outlook:
What Next?

On our journey so far, we have seen how we can draw on what is known about document design, perception, production and analysis in order to construct a layered approach to fine-grained multimodal document analysis. We have illustrated the main layers that we have developed, showing how these can be used together to draw out similarities and differences across a range of page-based multimodal documents.

Each of these layers takes on a particular aspect of a complete document description. The layout structure lets us identify precisely the components of a document's pages and the spatial arrangements of those components that may be drawn upon to carry meaning. The rhetorical structure layer provides a framework focusing on how various configurations of spatially distributed layout elements can be mobilised in the service of overarching communicative goals. It also shows us places where the deployed resources do a less than optimal job at indicating rhetorical purpose. We then saw how we could begin to formalise the notion of genre in a manner appropriate for dealing with multimodal documents. Here the information of the other layers is brought together in order to reveal how documents are made up of bundles of presentational modes tied to communicative goals by conventional practice and historical development. Finally, we considered the issue of how such detailed analyses are to be managed, placing them within multimodal document corpora that can stand as a foundation for further, more rigorously empirical studies of a broader range of documents.

The range of documents that we have examined in this book has clearly been very limited. We motivated at some length in the introduction just why we considered it important to focus attention narrowly rather than attempting an immediate generic account of multimodality 'as such'. Restricting

our area of concern to just one kind of artefact—i.e., page-based static multimodal documents—has allowed us to be very specific about fine-grained
detail in our analytic framework. However, even within the confines of
static, page-based documents, we have still only scratched the surface of
the variety on offer. Indeed, especially now following our account of genre,
we can see that most of the documents for which we have presented analyses are actually more or less closely related in several respects. Nevertheless, our claim here is that our more restricted and focused attention has
allowed us to push further beneath the surface of the documents we have
considered. Further aspects of the static, page-based document can now be
addressed and this will already move us towards consideration of a broader
range of multimodal artefacts. The following three directions are illustrative of some of the ways that our account prepares the ground for future
work.

First, even though we have described the documents that we analyse as
'static', there are already places where dynamic considerations are present.
Aspects of image-flow, temporal unfolding and, particularly, causation can
be significant in our interaction with, and interpretation of, even static images. This is, in fact, a long-standing topic in the visual arts, where the
question of how movement and time can be captured in static paint-based
media has been addressed in considerable detail (cf., Gombrich 1982*b*). It
is also supported by more recent brain studies, where static images of appropriate kinds can be shown to involve dynamic processing (cf. Bertamini
2002, Kourtzi and Kanwisher 2000). In addition, Coventry and Garrod
(2004, pp100–109) show convincingly how so-called *dynamic-kinetic rou-
tines* are activated even during the processing of static images to predict
how particular actions depicted would continue.

Bringing this evidence together, it appears that we 'see' even static images in terms of the forces apparently being applied to objects and to the
consequences of those forces for the subsequent movements of any objects
and materials shown. These limited but significant aspects of movement
present in static images may then be picked up rhetorically and used as part
of the combined multimodal message of a page. It is therefore important
to bring them into our account in a controlled fashion. Importantly, when
embedded in the context of a static page, we can examine these additional
meanings in a more constrained environment than would be available if we
were analysing, for example, an embedded video sequence. We can use this
constraint for focusing more closely on the relations between the *implied*
movement in the image and the other elements on the page.

Second, even though we have described our documents as page-based,
and hence essentially two-dimensional, there are places where the third

spatial dimension is also already relevant. As we mentioned very briefly in Chapter 3 (Section 3.2.3), this is seen particularly in layouts that create 'layering' effects, where one portion of the page may appear to stand in front of another, obscuring it. As is well known from perceptual studies and the resulting principles of perception (cf. Table 2.1), the human reader of such layouts will most naturally assign a three-dimensional layering to their interpretation of the layout—even on the flat page. This effect can be strengthened in various ways, ranging from using drawings and pictures that show their contents in perspective to typographical effects of shadowing, highlighting, etc. Again, starting from the two-dimensional area model, we already have a good basis for extension into three-dimensional artefacts that employ layout in this extended fashion. Just as we extended the notion of the modular grid to the more developed account of the area model within our layout layer, we can similarly extend previous proposals for using such grids for three dimensions—for example, in Müller-Brockmann's (1985, pp141–149) discussion of grids for exhibition spaces—to pursue a three-dimensional extension of the area model.

And third, even though the static page is present 'all at once', showing itself as a complete spatial layout, we have also seen places where this simultaneity is considerably reduced. Whenever, for example, we have a portion of the page that deploys *image-flow* as its presentational mode, a different scheme of reading applies. This mode employs the linearity of space as a 'substitute' for time. Reading the images of the image-flow often corresponds to temporal development. Such presentations are then ideally suited to instructions which have to be performed one at a time, or to staged developments that are to be interpreted as chronologically ordered. An example of this latter is the graphic at the bottom of our 1996 Gannet page discussed in Chapter 5 (Figure 5.18), where we find successive images of the Gannet moving from its immature appearance to its adult form.

We have suggested that the 'logic' of image-flow is rather different to that we have identified for page-flow. Instead of rhetorical relations, we find relations of temporal succession, of alternative perspectives, and of focusing operations of various kinds; as mentioned in Chapter 4 (Section 4.5), this has been described in considerable detail for comics and other cases of 'sequential visual art' by McCloud (1994). There are here also, therefore, many opportunities for extension. Moreover, the combinations of mode this commonly employs leads into a particularly complex area of our genre space.

We can readily find, for example, progressions from 'pure' image-flow to diagrammatic representations of various kinds. One illustration of this is given in Figure 7.1, based on the tiger page discussed in Chapter 4 (Sec-

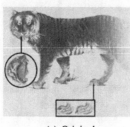

(b) Image-flow version

The tiger is a powerful hunter. Its massive jaws are armed with long canine teeth. Lethal claws retract when walking so that they do not become blunt.

(a) Original   (c) Text-flow version

Figure 7.1   Three versions of the tiger fact sheet image: an extract from the original, a version rendered as pure image-flow, and an 'equivalent' expressed as pure text-flow

tion 4.4.1) above. On the left of the figure, we see the relevant portion of the original page (cf. Figure 4.5). This is a typical page-flow element drawing on the two dimensions of the page. But we can also focus on the connecting links of the 'diagram'—here shown somewhat emphasised—as signalling the intended logical sequence of the images connected. Explicit connections have replaced the simple spatial placement found in image-flow proper.

This technique, along with arrows and other kinds of connectors, is now quite widespread in comics generally—thereby combining diagrammatic components and pure image-flow. We could equally, therefore, render this information in terms of a pure image-flow as shown upper-right in the figure. This illustrates what McCloud (1994, pp70–80) terms *aspect-to-aspect* transition between images, where alternative perspectives are presented and there is no advance of the 'action' of the narrative. This often requires some additional support in an accompanying medium, such as a commentary. And, indeed, the move from linear image-flow to linear text is straightforward in this case—as suggested lower-right in the figure.

As well as providing a finely discriminating net for sorting the modal contributions in page-based, static documents, our account can also throw light on other multimodal artefacts. In fact, when we move beyond the static, page-based document, we find the distinctions that we have set up in this book reoccurring in new configurations. It is a relatively small step, for example, to consider the successive images of an image-flow sequence as *actually* unfolding in time, rather than only simulated through the activity of reading. This is the reason why, as we mentioned in Chapter 4, the semantic relations applicable to image-flow presentations actually overlap considerably with those that have been discussed for film (cf., e.g., Burch 1973, Metz 1974, Branigan 1984, Bateman 2007). This naturally invites a future line of investigation in which our area of concern is extended to dynamic documents also. This will require contact with the already substantial bodies of research and standardisation in the area of video data, which includes the several component standards of the Moving Picture Expert Group (MPEG)[1] as well as XML-related standardisations such as the Synchronized Multimedia Integration Language (SMIL), a World-Wide Web consortium recommendation for describing multimedia presentations,[2] and the earlier, SGML-based, international standard HyTime (Hypermedia/Time-based Structuring Language).[3] Just as was the case with static documents in our discussions in this book, it will be more than interesting to draw upon these results to combine them with the kind of semiotically-layered document model that we have developed here.

Moreover, as soon as film works with techniques such as split screen, there are aspects of page-flow that also become relevant. The utilisation of the two-dimensional spatial configuration of the screen in this way merges seamlessly with the page-based designs we have discussed here. This is also present, in a slightly different form, whenever film employs text—as, for example, in the (critically acclaimed) films of Jean-Luc Godard or in (artistically perhaps less appreciated) TV series such as Batman from the 1960s (KAPOW!, THWACK!). Placing text within the spatial array is a natural invocation of the resources of page-flow. Film is also well known to work with constructions of *space*, which leads us on to further studies of spatial semiotics beyond the page/screen.

The ability of multimodal artefacts to combine differing semiotic modes—either explicitly by framing (such as a newspaper or computer screen shown in a film; or a video embedded within a web-page) or 'implicitly' by virtue of their inherent design—is one of such artefacts' major strengths. To make sense of this complexity it is important to pull apart the very different styles of contributions made by the modes employed. There is no doubt an entire range of semiotic modes waiting to be discovered. Each of them will support particular kinds of meaning-making potential, i.e., their own 'logic'—which is itself a further indication of the importance of proceeding rather more cautiously with multimodal analysis than has often been the case hitherto. Separating

---

[1] MPEG is a working group of the International Organization of Standardization (ISO/IEC JTC1/SC29 WG11; http://www.chiariglione.org/mpeg/). Here particularly relevant for our concerns will be MPEG-7, an ongoing effort to provide a standard for describing multimedia content.

[2] The latest SMIL recommendation can be found at http://www.w3.org/TR/SMIL/; further information is available at http://www.w3.org/AudioVideo/.

[3] http://www.hytime.org/

these contributions so that they can receive the detailed descriptions necessary to show how they work will not be possible if they are simply lumped together as, for example, 'dynamic' phenomena.

Achieving a more discriminating position is precisely what the framework set out in this book is intended to encourage and, for all of these prospective areas, we see this framework as one way of establishing a more solid foundation for empirical research. Despite the current explosion in semiotically-based 'multimodal' studies, the results obtained are still too often presented in idiosyncratic ways, with little constraint on the style of analysis carried out, the methodologies adopted, and the kinds of conclusions drawn.

In a recent survey of the more established field of visual communication, Barnhurst, Vari and Rodríguez (2004) distinguish three broad areas of work, pursued by largely disjoint research communities: *visual rhetoric*, looking at visual persuasion (cf. Chapter 4), *visual pragmatics*, concerned with the practices of production and the reception of visual artefacts (most closely related to our artefact and consumption constraints), and *visual semantics*, which focuses more on the intrinsic form and structure of communicative visual artefacts. Although the approach taken in this book is most closely connected to visual semantics, we consider it equally essential not to lose sight of the use of visual form in rhetorical organisations, nor of the practical consumption/production of visual artefacts. The multiple layers of the GeM model are intended precisely to *combine* such contributions within a single, coherent model. This places us in a better position for moving towards a more rigorously motivated and, above all, evaluable understanding of how such multimodal documents function.

The main task for the immediate future must therefore be to undertake analyses of the kinds proposed in this book with respect to a more representative sample of multimodal documents. This will help to populate the genre space and to uncover its organising dimensions.

Carrying out such a programme of research is certain to reveal gaps in the framework that we have presented, leading naturally to evaluation, extension, and re-application. Such cycles constitute a tried and tested methodology and there are few grounds at present to doubt its efficacy when applied to multimodal analysis. In any case, some framework of the kind presented here will be essential for achieving a sound, empirically-motivated scheme of analysis that can support the fine-grained description required. As we have seen, even the static, page-based document has considerably more complexity than might have been thought. Achieving a sufficiently firm foundation for further development is, then, not a step to be passed over too lightly.

Bibliography

Aitchison, J. (2001) *Language change: progress or decay?*, 3rd edn, Cambridge University Press, Cambridge.

Ames, S. (1989) *Elements of Newspaper Design*, Praeger, New York.

Amouzadeh, M. and Tavangar, M. (2004) 'Decoding pictorial metaphor: ideologies in Persian commercial advertising', *International Journal of Cultural Studies* 7(2), 147–174.

André, E. (1995) *Ein planbasierter Ansatz zur Generierung multimedialer Präsentationen*, Vol. 108, Infix, St. Augustin.

André, E. and Rist, T. (1993) The design of illustrated documents as a planning task, *in* M. T. Maybury, ed., 'Intelligent Multimedia Interfaces', AAAI Press/The MIT Press, Menlo Park (CA), Cambridge (MA), London (England), pp. 94–116.

Arens, Y. and Hovy, E. H. (1990) How to describe what? towards a theory of modality utilization, *in* 'The Twelfth Annual Conference of the Cognitive Science Society', Lawrence Erlbaum Associates, Hillsdale, New Jersey, pp. 487–494.

Arnheim, R. (1974) *Art and visual perception: a psychology of the creative eye*, University of California Press.

Arnheim, R. (1982) *The power of the center*, University of California Press, Berkeley, CA.

Asher, N. and Lascarides, A. (2003) *Logics of conversation*, Cambridge University Press, Cambridge.

Ashton, E. and Cruickshank, G. (1993) The newspaper of the future: a look beyond the front porch, *in* 'Proceedings of the 14th National On-line Meeting', pp. 11–16.

Askehave, I. and Nielsen, A. E. (2005) What are the characteristics of digital genres? – genre theory from a multi-modal perspective, *in* 'Proceedings of the 38th Hawaii International Conference on System Sciences'.

Baker, S., Rogers, R., Owen, A., Frith, C., Dolan, R., Frackowiak, R. and Robbins, T. (1996) 'Neural systems engaged by planning: a PET study of the Tower of London task', *Neuropsychologia* 34, 515–526.

Baldry, A. P. (2000) English in a visual society: comparative and historical dimensions in multimodality and multimediality, *in* A. P. Baldry, ed., 'Multimodality and multimediality in the distance learning age', Palladino Editore, Campobasso, Italy, pp. 41–89.

Baldry, A. and Thibault, P. J. (2005) Multimodal corpus linguistics, *in* G. Thompson and S. Hunston, eds, 'System and corpus: exploring connections', Equinox, London and New York, pp. 164–183.

Baldry, A. and Thibault, P. J. (2006) *Multimodal Transcription and Text Analysis*, Textbooks and Surveys in Linguistics, Equinox, London and New York.

Barnhurst, K. G., Vari, M. and Rodríguez, Ígor. (2004) 'Mapping visual studies in communication', *Journal of Communication* 54(4), 616–644. doi: 10.1111/j.1460-2466.2004.tb02648.x

Barthes, R. (1977a) *Image – Music – Text*, Hill and Wang, New York.

Barthes, R. (1977*b*) The rhetoric of the image, *in* 'Image–Music–Text', Fontana, London, pp. 32–51.

Bateman, J. A. (1998) Automatic discourse generation, *in* A. Kent, ed., 'Encyclopedia of Library and Information Science', Vol. 62, Marcel Dekker, Inc., New York, pp. 1–54. (Supplement 25).

Bateman, J. A. (2007) 'Towards a *grande paradigmatique* of film: Christian Metz reloaded', *Semiotica* **167**(1/4), 13–64.

Bateman, J. A. and Delin, J. L. (2006) Rhetorical Structure Theory, *in* K. Brown, ed., 'The Encyclopedia of Language and Linguistics', 2nd edn, Vol. 10, Elsevier, Amsterdam, pp. 588–596.

Bateman, J. A., Delin, J. L. and Henschel, R. (2002*a*) A brief introduction to the GEM annotation schema for complex document layout, *in* G. Wilcock, N. Ide and L. Romary, eds, 'Proceedings of the 2nd Workshop on NLP and XML (NLPXML-2002) — Post-Conference Workshop of the 19th International Conference on Computational Linguistics (COLING-2002)', Association of Computational Linguistics and Chinese Language Processing, Academica Sinica, Taipei, Taiwan, pp. 13–20.

Bateman, J. A., Delin, J. L. and Henschel, R. (2002*b*) XML and multimodal corpus design: experiences with multi-layered stand-off annotations in the GeM corpus, *in* 'Proceedings of the LREC'02 Workshop 'Towards a Roadmap for Multimodal Language Resources and Evaluation'', Las Palmas, Canary Islands, Spain. http://www.elsnet.org/dox/lrec2002-bateman.pdf

Bateman, J. A., Delin, J. L. and Henschel, R. (2004) Multimodality and empiricism: preparing for a corpus-based approach to the study of multimodal meaning-making, *in* E. Ventola, C. Charles and M. Kaltenbacher, eds, 'Perspectives on Multimodality', John Benjamins, Amsterdam, pp. 65–87.

Bateman, J. A., Delin, J. L. and Henschel, R. (2007) Mapping the multimodal genres of traditional and electronic newspapers, *in* T. D. Royce and W. L. Bowcher, eds, 'New Directions in the Analysis of Multimodal Discourse', Lawrence Erlbaum Associates, pp. 147–172.

Bateman, J. A. and Henschel, R. (2006) Generating text, layout and diagrams appropriately for genre, *in* I. van der Sluis, M. Theune, E. Reiter and E. Krahmer, eds, 'Proceedings of the Workshop on Multimodal Output Generation MOG 2007', Centre for Telematics and Information Technology (CTIT), University of Twente, pp. 29–40.

Bateman, J. A., Kamps, T., Kleinz, J. and Reichenberger, K. (2001) 'Constructive text, diagram and layout generation for information presentation: the DArt$_{bio}$ system', *Computational Linguistics* **27**(3), 409–449.

Bateman, J. A. and Zock, M. (2003) Natural language generation, *in* R. Mitkov, ed., 'Oxford Handbook of Computational Linguistics', Oxford University Press, Oxford, chapter 15, pp. 284–304.

Bazerman, C. (1994) Systems of genres and the enactment of social intentions, *in* A. Freedman and P. Medway, eds, 'Genre and the new rhetoric', Taylor and Francis, London, chapter 5, pp. 79–104.

Bell, A. (1998) The discourse structure of news stories, *in* A. Bell and P. Garrett, eds, 'Approaches to Media Discourse', Blackwell, Oxford, pp. 64–104.

Bernhardt, S. (1985) Text structure and graphic design: the visible design, *in* J. D. Benson and W. S. Greaves, eds, 'Systemic Perspectives on Discourse, Volume 1', Ablex, Norwood, New Jersey, pp. 18–38.

Bertamini, M. (2002) 'Representational momentum, internalised dynamics, and perceptual adaptation', *Visual Cognition* **9**, 195–216.

Bertin, J. (1983) *Semiology of graphics*, University of Wisconsin Press, Madison, Wisconsin.

Biber, D. (1988) *Variation Across Speech and Writing*, Cambridge University Press, Cambridge.

Biber, D., Conrad, S. and Reppen, R. (1998) *Corpus Linguistics: investigating language structure and use*, Cambridge University Press, Cambridge.

Bloor, M. and Bloor, T. (2007) *The Practice of Critical Discourse Analysis*, Hodder Arnold, London.

Blum, J. and Bucher, H.-J. (1998) *Die Zeitung: Ein Multimedium. Textdesign – ein Gestaltungskonzept für Text, Bild und Grafik*, UKV, Konstanz.

Bouayad-Agha, N. (2000) Layout annotation in a corpus of patient information leaflets, *in* M. Gavrilidou, G. Carayannis, S. Markantonatou, S. Piperidis and G. Stainhaouer, eds, 'Proceedings of the Second International Conference on Language Resources and Evaluation (LREC'2000)', European Language Resources Association (ELRA), Athens, Greece. http://www.itri.bton.ac.uk/projects/iconoclast/Papers/lrec00.ps

Bouayad-Agha, N., Power, R. and Scott, D. (2000) Can text structure be incompatible with rhetorical structure?, *in* 'Proceedings of the International Natural Language Generation Conference (INLG-2000)', Mitzpe Ramon, Israel, pp. 194–200. http://www.itri.bton.ac.uk/projects/iconoclast/Papers/inlg00.ps

Bouayad-Agha, N., Scott, D. and Power, R. (2000) 'Integrating content and style in documents: a case study of patient information leaflets', *Information Design Journal* **9**(2), 161–176. http://www.itri.bton.ac.uk/projects/iconoclast/Papers/ITRI.pdf

Branigan, E. (1984) *Point of view in the cinema: a theory of narration and subjectivity in classical film*, Mouton, Berlin.

Bransford, J. and Johnson, M. (1972) 'Contextual prerequisites for understanding: Some investigations of comprehension and recall', *Journal of Verbal Learning and Verbal Behavior* **11**(6), 717–726.

Bryan, M. (1988) *SGML: An author's guide to the Standard Generalized Markup Language*, Addison-Wesley Publishing Company.

Bunt, H. and Beun, R.-J., eds (2001) *Cooperative Multimodal Communication*, number 2155 *in* 'Lecture Notes in Artificial Intelligence', Springer, Berlin.

Burch, N. (1973) *Theory of film practice*, Secker and Warburg, London, chapter 1: 'Spatial and temporal articulations', pp. 3–16. Translated by Helen R. Lane.

Burford, B., Briggs, P. and Eakins, J. P. (2003) 'A taxonomy of the image: on the classification of content for image retrieval', *Visual Communication* **2**(2), 123–161.

Bush, V. (1945) 'As we may think', *Atlantic Monthly* **176**, 101–108. http://www.theatlantic.com/doc/194507/bush

Cesarini, F., Lastri, M., Marinai, S. and Soda, G. (2001) 'Encoding of Modified X-Y Trees for document classification', *Proceedings of the Sixth International Conference on Document Analysis and Recognition (ICDAR'01)* pp. 1131–1136. http://doi.ieeecomputersociety.org/10.1109/ICDAR.2001.953962

Cesarini, F., Marinai, S., Soda, G. and Gori, M. (1999) 'Structured document segmentation and representation by the modified X-Y tree', *Proceedings of the Fifth International Conference on Document Analysis and Recognition (ICDAR'99)* pp. 563–566. http://doi.ieeecomputersociety.org/10.1109/ICDAR.1999.791850

Christie, F. and Martin, J. R. (1997) *Genre and institutions: social processes in the workplace and school*, Cassell, London.

Conklin, J. (1987) 'Hypertext: an introduction and survey', *IEEE Computer Magazine* **20**(9), 17–41.

Corio, M. and Lapalme, G. (1998) Integrated generation of graphics and text: a corpus study, *in* M. T. Maybury and J. Pustejovsky, eds, 'Proceedings of the COLING-ACL Workshop on Content Visualization and Intermedia Representations (CVIR'98)', Montréal, pp. 63–68.

Corpus Encoding Standard (2000) 'Corpus Encoding Standard. Version 1.5'. Available at: http://www.cs.vassar.edu/CES.

Coventry, K. R. and Garrod, S. C. (2004) *Saying, seeing and acting. The psychological semantics of spatial prepositions*, Essays in Cognitive Psychology series, Psychology Press, Hove, UK.

Coventry, K. R., Lynott, D., O'Ceallaigh, R. and Miller, J. (2008) 'Happy is up and sad is down; the facial emotion-spatial congruity effect', *Psychonomic Bulletin and Review* .

Craig, J. and Barton, B. (1987) *Thirty centuries of graphic design: an illustrated survey*, Watson-Guptil Publications, New York.

Crowston, K. and Kwaśnik, B. H. (2004) A framework for creating a facetted classification of genres: addressing issues of multidimensionality, *in* 'Proceedings of the 37th Hawaii International Conference on System Sciences', IEEE, Big Island, Hawaii.

Crowston, K. and Williams, M. (1997) Reproduced and emergent genres of communication on the World-Wide Web, *in* 'Proceedings of the 30th Annual Hawaii International Conference on System Sciences', Vol. VI, IEEE Computer Society Press, Los Alamitos, CA, pp. 30–39. http://doi.ieeecomputersociety.org/10.1109/HICSS.1997.665482

Crowston, K. and Williams, M. (1999) The effects of linking on genres of web documents, *in* 'Proceedings of the 32nd Annual Hawaii International Conference on System Sciences (HICSS'99)', IEEE Computer Society Press, Los Alamitos, CA.

Crowston, K. and Williams, M. (2000) 'Reproduced and emergent genres of communication on the World-Wide Web', *The Information Society* **16**(3), 201–215.

Crystal, D. (1979) Reading, grammar and the line, *in* D. Thackray, ed., 'Growth in reading', Ward Lock, London.

Crystal, D. and Davy, D. (1969) *Investigating English Style*, Longman, London.

Danlos, L. (2007) Strong generative capacity of RST, SDRT and discourse dependency DAGS, *in* A. Belz and P. Kühnlein, eds, 'Constraints in discourse', John Benjamins, Amsterdam.

de Beaugrande, R. (1980) *Text, discourse, and process*, Ablex Pub. Corp., Norwood, New Jersey.

Dehaene, S., Bossini, S. and Giraux, P. (1993) 'The mental representation of parity and number magnitude', *Journal of Experimental Psychology: General* **122**(3), 371–396.

Delin, J. L. and Bateman, J. A. (2002) 'Describing and critiquing multimodal documents', *Document Design* **3**(2), 140–155. Amsterdam: John Benjamins.

Delin, J. L., Searle-Jones, A. and Waller, R. (2006) Branding and relationship communications: the evolution of utility bills in the UK, *in* S. Carliner, J. Verckens and C. de Waele, eds, 'Information and Document Design', John Benjamins, Amsterdam, pp. 27–59.

Descartes, R. (1701) Rules for the direction of the mind, *in* 'Descartes Philosophical Writings', Thomas Nelson and Sons Ltd., London, pp. 153–180. Published 1954. Translated by Elizabeth Anscombe and Peter Thomas Geach.

Diligenti, M., Frasconi, P. and Gori, M. (2003) 'Hidden tree Markov models for document image classification', *IEEE Transactions on Pattern Analysis and Machine Intelligence* **25**(4), 519–523. http://doi.ieeecomputersociety.org/10.1109/TPAMI.2003.1190578

Djonov, E. N. (2007) 'Website hierarchy and the interaction between content organization, webpage and navigation design: A systemic functional hypermedia discourse analysis perspective', *Information Design Journal* **15**(2), 144–162.

Doermann, D., Rosenfeld, A. and Rivlin, E. (1997) The function of documents, *in* 'Proceedings of the 4th International Conference on Document Analysis and Recognition', Vol. 2, Ulm, Germany, pp. 1077–1081.

Dondis, D. A. (1972) *A Primer of Visual Literacy*, The MIT Press, Cambridge, Massachusetts.

Dori, D., Doermann, D., Shin, C., Haralick, R., Phillips, I., Buchman, M. and Ross, D. (1997) The representation of document structure: a generic object-process analysis, *in* 'Handbook of Optical Character Recognition and Document Image Analysis', World Scientific Publishing Company, chapter 17, pp. 421–456. http://citeseer.ist.psu.edu/dori96representation.html

Dorn, R. (1986) *How to design and improve magazine layouts*, Nelson-Publishers, Chicago.

Durand, J. (1987) Rhetorical figures in the advertising image, *in* J. Umiker-Sebeok, ed., 'Marketing and semiotics: new directions in the study of signs for sale', Mouton de Gruyter, Berlin/New York/Amsterdam, pp. 295–318.

Durusau, P. and O'Donnell, M. (2002) Concurrent markup for XML documents, *in* 'Proceedings of XML Europe', Atlanta, Georgia.

http://www.idealliance.org/papers/xmle02/dx_xmle02/papers/03-03-07/03-03-07.html

Dybkjaer, L., Berman, S., Kipp, M., Olsen, M. W., Pirrelli, V., Reithinger, N. and Soria, C. (2001) Survey of existing tools, standards and user needs for annotation of natural interaction and multimodal data, International Standards for Language Engineering (ISLE): Natural Interactivity and Multimodality Working Group Deliverable D11.1, NISLab, Odense University, Denmark; IMS, Stuttgart University, Germany; ILC, Pisa, Italy; DFKI, Saarbrücken, Germany. http://isle.nis.sdu.dk/reports/wp11/

Dyson, M. C. (2004) 'How physical text layout affects reading from screen', *Behaviour and Information Technology* **23**, 377–393.

Eckkrammer, E. M. (2004) Drawing on theories of inter-semiotic layering to analyse multimodality in medical self-conselling texts and hypertexts, *in* E. Ventola, C. Charles and M. Kaltenbacher, eds, 'Perspectives on Multimodality', John Benjamins, Amsterdam, pp. 211–226.

Egan, D. and Schwartz, B. (1979) 'Chunking in recall of symbolic drawings', *Memory and Cognition* **7**, 149–158.

Eglin, V. and Bres, S. (2004) 'Analysis and interpretation of visual saliency for document functional labeling', *International Journal on Document Analysis and Recognition (IJDAR)* **7**, 28–43. DOI: 10.1007/s10032-004-0127-2

Elam, K. (2004) *Grid Systems: Principles of Organizing Type*, Princeton Architectural Press, Princeton.

Epstein, J. (1981) 'Informing the elderly', *Information Design Journal* **2**, 215–235.

Fairclough, N. (1989) *Language and power*, Longman, London.

Fairclough, N. (1992) *Discourse and Social Change*, Polity Press, Cambridge.

Feiner, S. K. (1988) A grid-based approach to automating display layout, *in* 'Proceedings of the Graphics Interface', Morgan Kaufman, Los Angeles, CA, pp. 192–197.

Feiner, S. K. and McKeown, K. R. (1993) Automating the generation of coordinated multimedia explanations, *in* M. T. Maybury, ed., 'Intelligent Multimedia Interfaces', AAAI Press/The MIT Press, Menlo Park (CA), Cambridge (MA), London (England), pp. 117–138.

Fix, U. and Weillmann, H., eds (2000) *Bild im Text – Text und Bild*, Winter, Heidelberg.

Forceville, C. (1996) *Pictorial metaphor in advertising*, Routledge, London.

Fowler, A. (1982) *Kinds of literature*, Oxford University Press, Oxford.

Fowler, R., Hodge, B., Kress, G. and Trew, T. (1979) *Language and control*, Routledge and Kegan Paul, London, Boston and Henley.

Francis, G. (1993) A corpus-driven approach to grammar: principles, methods and examples, *in* M. Baker, G. Francis and E. Toginini-Bognelli, eds, 'Text and technology: In honour of John Sinclair', Benjamins, Amsterdam, pp. 137–156.

Freedman, A. and Medway, P. (1994) Locating genre studies: antecedents and prospects, *in* A. Freedman and P. Medway, eds, 'Genre and the new rhetoric', Taylor and Francis, London, chapter 1, pp. 1–22.

Gaede, W. (1981) *Vom Wort zum Bild: Kreativ-Methoden der Visualisierung*, Langen-Müller/Herbig, Munich. 2nd edn, 1992.

Garfinkel, H. (1967) *Studies in Ethnomethodology*, Prentice-Hall, New York.

Ghyka, M. (1977) *The geometry of art and life*, Dover Publications, Mineola, NY. originally published 1946.

Gibson, J. (1977) The theory of affordances, *in* R.Shaw and J.Brandsford, eds, 'Perceiving, Acting, and Knowing: Toward and Ecological Psychology', Erlbaum, Hillsdale, NJ, pp. 62–82.

Giddens, A. (1984) *The constitution of society: outline of the theory of structuration*, Polity Press, Cambridge.

Glenberg, A., Wilkinson, A. and Epstein, W. (1982) 'The illusion of knowing: failure in the self-assessment of comprehension', *Memory and Cognition* 10(6), 597–602.

Goldfarb, C. F., ed. (1990) *The SGML Handbook*, Clarendon Press, Oxford.

Gombrich, E. (1982a) *The image and the eye: further studies in the psychology of pictorial representation*, Phaidon, Oxford.

Gombrich, E. (1982b) *The image and the eye: further studies in the psychology of pictorial representation*, Phaidon, Oxford, chapter Moment and movement in art, pp. 40–62.

Graf, W. H. (1996) Towards a reference model for intelligent multimedia layout, *in* G. Faconti and T. Rist, eds, 'Proceedings of the ECAI '96 Workshop 'Towards a Standard Reference Model for Intelligent Multimedia Systems''.

Gregory, M. (1967) 'Aspects of varieties differentiation', *Journal of Linguistics* 3, 177–198.

Gregory, M. (2001) Phasal analysis within communicative linguistics: two contrastive discourses, *in* P. H. Fries, M. Cummings, D. Lockwood and W. Spruiell, eds, 'Relations and functions within and around language', Open Linguistics, Continuum Press, London.

Gregory, M. and Carrol, S. (1978) *Language and Situation: Language varieties and their social contexts*, Routledge and Kegan Paul, London.

Gross, A. G. (1996) *The rhetoric of science*, 2nd printing edn, Harvard University Press, Cambridge, MA.

Gruber, H. (2000) Scholarly email discussion list postings: A single new genre of academic communication?, *in* L. Pemberton and S. Shurrille, eds, 'Words on the web: Computer-mediated communication', Intellect Ltd., Exeter, pp. 36–43.

Guo, L. (2004) Multimodality in a biology textbook, *in* K. L. O'Halloran, ed., 'Multimodal discourse analysis: systemic functional perspectives', Open Linguistics Series, Continuum, London, pp. 196–219.

Haake, A., Hüser, C. and Reichenberger, K. (1994) 'The Individualized Electronic Newspaper: An example of an Active Publication', *Electronic Publishing* 7(2), 89–111.

Habel, C. and Acartürk, C. (2006) On reciprocal improvement in multimodal generation: co-reference by text and information graphics, *in* I. van der Sluis, M. Theune, E. Reiter and E. Krahmer, eds, 'Proceedings of the Workshop on Multimodal

Output Generation MOG 2007', Centre for Telematics and Information Technology (CTIT), University of Twente, pp. 69–80.

Halliday, M. A. K. (1978) *Language as social semiotic*, Edward Arnold, London.

Halliday, M. A. K. and Hasan, R. (1976) *Cohesion in English*, Longman, London.

Halliday, M. A. K. and Matthiessen, C. M. (2004) *An Introduction to Functional Grammar*, 3rd edn, Edward Arnold, London.

Harrell, J. and Linkugel, W. (1978) 'On rhetorical genre: an organizing perspective', *Philosophy and Rhetoric* **11**, 262–281.

Hartley, J. (1994) *Designing Instructional Text*, 3rd edn, Nichols, East Brunswick, NJ.

Hasan, R. (1973) Code, register and social dialect, *in* B. Bernstein, ed., 'Class, Codes and Control: applied studies towards a sociology of language', Routledge and Kegan Paul, London, pp. 253–292.

Hasan, R. (1978) Text in the Systemic-Functional Model, *in* W. Dressler, ed., 'Current Trends in Text Linguistics', de Gruyter, Berlin, pp. 228–246.

Hasan, R. (1984) 'The nursery tale as a genre', *Notthingham Linguistic Circular* **13**, 71–102. Reprinted as Hasan (1996).

Hasan, R. (1996) The nursery tale as a genre, *in* C. Cloran, D. Butt and G. Williams, eds, 'Ways of saying, ways of meaning: selected papers of Ruqaiya Hasan', Cassell, London, pp. 51–72.

Hegarty, M. (1992) 'Mental animation: Inferring motion from static displays of mechanical systems', *Journal of Experimental Psychology: Learning, Memory and Cognition* **18**, 1084–1102.

Hegarty, M., Carpenter, P. and Just, M. (1991) Diagrams in the comprehension of scientific text, *in* R. Barr, M. Kamil, P. Mosenthal and P. Pearson, eds, 'Handbook of reading research. Volume 2', Longman, New York, pp. 641–668.

Held, G. (2005) 'Magazine covers – a multimodal pretext-genre', *Folia Linguistica* **XXXIX**(1–2), 173–196.

Henschel, R. (2002) GeM annotation manual, Gem project report, University of Bremen and University of Stirling. http://purl.org/net/gem

Henschel, R., Bateman, J. A. and Delin, J. L. (2002) Automatic genre-driven layout generation, *in* 'Proceedings of the 6. Konferenz zur Verarbeitung natürlicher Sprache (KONVENS 2002)', University of the Saarland, Saarbrücken, pp. 51–58.

Hentschel, K. (2002) *Mapping the spectrum: techniques of visual representation in research and teaching*, Oxford University Press, Oxford and New York.

Herskovits, A. (1998) Schematization, *in* P. Olivier and K.-P. Gapp, eds, 'Representation and processing of spatial expressions', Lawrence Erlbaum Associates, Mahwah, New Jersey, pp. 149–162.

Hocks, M. and Kendrick, M., eds (2003) *Eloquent images: word and image in the age of new media*, MIT Press, Cambridge, MA.

Hofinger, A. and Ventola, E. (2004) Multimodality in operation: language and picture in a museum, *in* E. Ventola, C. Charles and M. Kaltenbacher, eds, 'Perspectives on Multimodality', John Benjamins, Amsterdam, pp. 193–210.

Hollis, R. (2006) *Swiss Graphic Design: The Origins and Growth of an International Style, 1920-1965*, Yale University Press, New Haven, CT.

Holsanova, J., Rahm, H. and Holmqvist, K. (2006) 'Entry points and reading paths on newspaper spreads: comparing a semiotic analysis with eye-tracking measurements', *Visual Communication* 5(1), 65–93.

Hovy, E. H. (1993) 'Automated discourse generation using discourse relations', *Artificial Intelligence* 63(1-2), 341–385.

Hu, J., Kashi, R. and Wilfong, G. (1999) Document classification using layout analysis, *in* 'Proceedings of the 10th International Workshop on Databases and Expert Systems Applications', Florence, Italy.

Hurlburt, A. (1978) *The Grid: A modular system for the design and production of newspapers, magazine, and books*, Van Nostrand Reinhold Company, New York.

Hurst, M. (2006) 'Towards a theory of tables', *International Journal of Document Analysis* 8(2), 123–131.

Hüser, C., Reichenberger, K., Rostek, L. and Streitz, N. (1995) 'Knowledge-based editing and visualization for hypermedia encyclopedias', *Communications of the ACM* 38(4), 49–51.

Hutt, A. (1973) *The changing newspaper: typographic trends in Britain and America 1622-1972*, Gordon Fraser, London.

Hymes, D. H. (1974) *Foundations in sociolinguistics: an ethnographic approach*, University of Pennsylvania Press, Philadelphia.

Hyon, S. (1996) 'Genre in three traditions: implications for ESL', *TESOL Quarterly* 30(4), 693–722.

Ide, N., Bonhomme, P. and Romary, L. (2000) XCES: An XML-based encoding standard for linguistic corpora, *in* M. Gavrilidou, G. Carayannis, S. Markantonatou, S. Piperidis and G. Stainhaouer, eds, 'Proceedings of the 2nd International Conference on Language Resources and Evaluation (LREC 2000)', European Language Resources Association (ELRA), Athens, Greece. http://www.cs.vassar.edu/~ide/papers/xces-lrec00.pdf

Ide, N., Romary, L. and de la Clergerie, E. (2003) International standard for a linguistic annotation framework, *in* 'Proceedings of the HLT-NAACL'03 Workshop on the Software Engineering and Architecture of Language Technology'. http://citeseer.ist.psu.edu/article/ide03international.html

International Organization for Standardization (1986) *ISO 8879-1986 (E). Information processing – Text and Office Systems – Standard Generalized Markup Language (SGML). First edition – 1986-10-15*, International Organization for Standardization, Geneva.

Ito, Y. and Hatta, T. (2004) 'Spatial structure of quantitative representation of numbers: Evidence from the SNARC effect', *Memory and Cognition* 32(4), 662–673.

Ittelson, W. H. (1996) 'Visual perception of markings', *Psychonomic Bulletin and Review* 3(2), 171–187.

Itti, L. and Koch, C. (2001) 'Computational modelling of visual attention', *Nature Reviews: Neuroscience* pp. 194–203.

Jacobs, C., Li, W., Schrier, E., Bargeron, D. and Salesin, D. (2003) Adaptive grid-based document layout, *in* 'SIGGRAPH '03', ACM Press, New York, NY, USA, pp. 838–847. http://doi.acm.org/10.1145/1201775.882353

Johansson, S., Atwell, E., Garside, R. and Leech, G. (1986) *The Tagged LOB Corpus: User's Manual*, Norwegian Computing Centre for the Humanities, Bergen.

Johansson, S., Leech, G. and Goodluck, H. (1978) *Manual of Information to Accompany the Lancaster-Olso/Bergen Corpus of British English, for Use with Digital Computers*, Department of English, University of Oslo, Oslo.

Johns, A. M., ed. (2002) *Genre in the classroom: multiple perspectives*, Lawrence Erlbaum Associates, Marwah, NJ.

Kalantzis, M. and Cope, B., eds (2000) *Multiliteracies: Literacy Learning and the Design of Social Futures*, Routledge, London.

Kaltenbacher, M. (2004) 'Perspectives on multimodality: From the early beginnings to the state of the art', *Information Design Journal* 12(3), 190–207.

Keller-Cohen, D., Meader, B. and Mann, D. (1990) 'Redesiging a telephone bill', *Information Design Journal* 6, 45–66.

Kessler, B., Nunberg, G. and Schütze, H. (1997) Automatic detection of text genre, *in* 'Proceedings of the 35th. Annual Meeting of the Assocation for Computational Linguistics and the 8th. Conference of the European Chapter of the Association for Computational Linguistics (ACL-EACL97)', Association for Computational Linguistics, Madrid, Spain, pp. 32–38.

Kitis, E. (1997) 'Ads–*part of our lives:* linguistic awareness of powerful advertising', *Word and Image* 13(3), 304–313.

Knieper, T. and Müller, M. G., eds (2001) *Kommunikation visuell. Das Bild als Forschungsgegenstand – Grundlagen und Perspektiven*, Herbert von Halem Verlag, Köln.

Knox, J. S. (2007) 'Visual-verbal communication on online newspaper home pages', *Visual Communication* 6(1), 19–53.

Koffka, K. (1935) *Principles of Gestalt Psychology*, Harcourt-Brace, New York.

Köhler, W. (1947) *Gestalt psychology*, Liveright, Liverpool.

Kong, K. C. (2006) 'A taxonomy of the discourse relations between words and visuals', *Information Design Journal* 14(3), 207–230.

Kosslyn, S., Koenig, O., Barrett, A., Cave, C., Tang, J. and Gabrieli, J. (1989) 'Evidence for two types of spatial representations: hemispheric specialization for categorical and coordinate relations', *Journal of Experimental Psychology: Human Perception and Performance* 15, 723–735.

Kostelnick, C. (1988) 'A systematic approach to visual language in business communication', *Journal of Business Communication* 25(3), 29–48.

Kostelnick, C. (1989) 'Visual rhetoric: a reader-oriented approach to graphics and designs', *Technical Writing Teacher* 16, 77–88.

Kostelnick, C. and Hassett, M. (2003) *Shaping Information: The Rhetoric of Visual Conventions*, Southern Illinois University Press.

Kourtzi, Z. and Kanwisher, N. (2000) 'Activation in human MT/MST by static images with implied movement', *Journal of Cognitive Neuroscience* 12, 48–55.

Kress, G. (1993) Genre as social process, *in* B. Cope and M. Kalantzis, eds, 'The powers of literacy: a genre approach to writing', University of Pittsburgh Press, Pittsburgh, pp. 22–37.

Kress, G. (2003) *Literacy in the New Media Age*, Routledge, London.

Kress, G., Jewitt, C., Ogborn, J. and Tsatsarelis, C. (2000) *Multimodal teaching and learning*, Continuum, London.

Kress, G. and van Leeuwen, T. (1996) *Reading Images: the grammar of visual design*, Routledge, London and New York.

Kress, G. and van Leeuwen, T. (1998) Front pages: the (critical) analysis of newspaper layout, *in* A. Bell and P. Garrett, eds, 'Approaches to Media Discourse', Blackwell, Oxford, pp. 186–219.

Kress, G. and van Leeuwen, T. (2001) *Multimodal discourse: the modes and media of contemporary communication*, Arnold, London.

Labov, W. (2001) *Principles of linguistic change, Volume 2: social factors*, Blackwell, Oxford.

Labov, W. and Waletzky, J. (1978) Narrative analysis, *in* J. Helm, ed., 'Essays on the verbal and visual arts', University of Washington Press, Seattle, pp. 12–44. (Proceedings of the 1966 Spring Meeting of the American Ethnological Society).

Landow, G. P. (1991) Hypertext, hypermedia and literary studies: the state of the art, *in* P. Delany and G. P. Landow, eds, 'Hypermedia and literary studies', MIT Press, Cambridge, MA, pp. 3–50.

Landow, G. P. (1997) *Hypertext 2.0: the convergence of contemporary critical theory and technology*, 2nd edition edn, John Hopkins University Press, Baltimore and London.

Landow, G. P., ed. (1994) *Hyper / Text / Theory*, John Hopkins University Press, Baltimore and London.

Laspina, J. A. (1998) *The visual turn and the transformation of the textbook*, Lawrence Erlbaum Associates, Mahway, NJ.

Lassen, I., Strunck, J. and Vestergaard, T., eds (2006) *Mediating ideology in text and image*, John Benjamins, Amsterdam.

Le Corbusier (1951) *The Modulor: a harmonious measure to the human scale universally applicable to architecture and mechanics*, Faber and Faber, London. Originally published in French in 1948.

Lee, D. Y. (2001) 'Genres, registers, text types, domains, and styles: clarifying the concepts and navigating a path through the BNC jungle', *Language Learning and Technology* 5(3), 37–72. http://llt.msu.edu/vol5num3/lee

Lefèvre, W., Renn, J. and Schoepflin, U., eds (2003) *The power of images in early modern science*, Birkhauser Verlag, Basel, Switzerland.

Lemke, J. L. (1983) 'Thematic analysis: systems, structures, and strategies', *Semiotic Inquiry* 3(2), 159–187.

Lemke, J. L. (1988a) Discourses in conflict: heteroglossia and text semantics, *in* J. D. Benson and W. S. Greaves, eds, 'Systemic Functional Approaches to Discourse', Ablex, Norwood, NJ, pp. 29–50.

Lemke, J. L. (1988*b*) 'Genres, semantics and classroom education', *Linguistics and Education* **1**(1), 81–100.

Lemke, J. L. (1993) 'Discourse, dynamics, and social change', *Cultural Dynamics* **6**(1-2), 243–276.

Lemke, J. L. (1998) Multiplying meaning: visual and verbal semiotics in scientific text, *in* J. Martin and R. Veel, eds, 'Reading science: critical and functional perspectives on discourses of science', Routledge, London, pp. 87–113.

Lemke, J. L. (1999) Typology, topology, topography: genre semantics. MS. University of Michigan. http://www-personal.umich.edu/~jaylemke/papers/Genre-topology-revised.htm

Lemke, J. L. (2002) 'Travels in hypermodality', *Visual Communication* **1**(3), 299–325.

Lemke, J. L. (2005) 'Multimedia genre and traversals', *Folia Linguistica* **XXXIX**(1-2), 45–56.

Lentz, L. (2005) 'Eye-tracking and information design', *Information Design Journal* **13**(3), 255–261.

Lentz, L. and Pander Maat, H. (2004) 'Functional analysis for document design', *Technical communication* **51**(3), 387–399.

Lim, V. F. (2004) Problemising 'semiotic resource', *in* E. Ventola, C. Charles and M. Kaltenbacher, eds, 'Perspectives on Multimodality', John Benjamins, Amsterdam, pp. 51–64.

Lok, S. and Feiner, S. (2001) A survey of automated layout techniques for information presentation, *in* 'Proceedings of Smartgraphics '01', Hawthorne, NY. citeseer.ist.psu.edu/lok01survey.html

Lowe, R. (1993) 'Diagrammatic information: techniques for exploring its mental representation and processing', *Information Design Journal* **7**, 3–18.

MacDonald-Ross, M. and Waller, R. (2000) 'The transformer revisited', *Information Design Journal* **9**(2-3), 177–193.

Mandell, L. and Shaw, D. (1973) 'Judging people in the news—unconsciously: Effect of camera angle and bodily activity', *Journal of Broadcasting* **17**, 353–362.

Mann, W. C., Matthiessen, C. M. I. M. and Thompson, S. A. (1992) Rhetorical structure theory and text analysis, *in* W. C. Mann and S. A. Thompson, eds, 'Text Description: Diverse Analyses of a Fund Raising Text', John Benjamins, Amsterdam, pp. 39–78.

Mann, W. C. and Thompson, S. A. (1985) Assertions from discourse structure, *in* 'Proceedings of the Eleventh Annual Meeting of the Berkeley Linguistics Society', Berkeley Linguistic Society, Berkeley.

Mann, W. C. and Thompson, S. A. (1986) 'Relational propositions in discourse', *Discourse Processes* **9**(1), 57–90.

Mann, W. C. and Thompson, S. A. (1988) 'Rhetorical structure theory: Toward a functional theory of text organization', *Text* **8**(3), 243–281.

Manovich, L. (2001) *The language of the new media*, MIT Press, Cambridge, MA.

Mao, S., Nie, L. and Thoma, G. (2005) Unsupervised style classification of document page images, *in* 'Proceedings of the IEEE International Conference on Image Processing (ICIP)', Vol. II, Genova, Italy, pp. 510–513. http://archive.nlm.nih.gov/pubs/mao/ICIP05Mao.pdf

Marsh, E. E. and White, M. D. (2003) 'A taxonomy of relationships between images and text', *Journal of Documentation* **59**(6), 647–672.

Martin, J.-C., Kühnlein, P., Paggio, P., Stiefelhagen, R. and Pianese, F., eds (2005) *LREC 2006 Workshop on Multimodal Corpora: From multimodal behaviour theories to usable models*.

Martin, J. R. (1984) Language, register and genre, *in* F. Christie, ed., 'Children Writing: reader', (ECT Language Studies: children writing), Deakin University Press, Geelong, Vic., pp. 21–30.

Martin, J. R. (1992) *English text: systems and structure*, Benjamins, Amsterdam.

Martin, J. R. (1993) A contextual theory of language, *in* W. Cope and M. Kalantzis, eds, 'The Powers of Literacy: a genre approach to teaching literacy', (Critical Perspectives on Literacy and Education), Falmer, London, pp. 116–136. Also published by University of Pittsburgh Press (Pittsburgh Series in Composition, Literacy, and Culture), Pittsburgh.

Martin, J. R. (1994) 'The macro-genre of the page', *Network* **21**, 29–52.

Martin, J. R. (2000) Close reading: functional linguistics as a tool for critical discourse analysis, *in* L. Unsworth, ed., 'Researching language in schools and communities: functional linguistic perspectives', Cassell, London, pp. 275–302.

Martin, J. R. (2001) Language, register and genre, *in* A. Burns and C. Coffin, eds, 'Analysing English in a Global Context: a reader', Teaching English Language Worldwide, Routledge, Clevedon, pp. 149–166.

Martin, J. R. (2002) A universe of meaning - how many practices?, *in* A. M. Johns, ed., 'Genres in the Classroom: multiple perspectives', Lawrence Erlbaum Associates, Mahwah, NJ, pp. 269–278.

Martin, J. R. and Plum, G. (1997) 'Construing experience: some story genres', *Journal of Narrative and Life History* **7**(1-4), 299–308. (Special Issue: Oral Versions of Personal Experience: three decades of narrative analysis; M. Bamberg Guest Editor).

Martin, J. R. and Rose, D. (2003) *Working with discourse: meaning beyond the clause*, Continuum, London and New York.

Martin, J. R. and Rose, D. (2007) *Genre relations: mapping culture*, Equinox, London and New York.

Martin, J. R. and Stenglin, M. (2007) Materializing reconciliation: negotiating difference in a transcolonial exhibition, *in* T. D. Royce and W. L. Bowcher, eds, 'New Directions in the Analysis of Multimodal Discourse', Lawrence Erlbaum Associates, pp. 215–238.

Martin, J. R. and Wodak, R., eds (2003) *Re/reading the past. Critical and functional perspectives on time and value*, Benjamins, Amsterdam.

Martinec, R. (2005) Topics in multimodality, *in* J. Webster, R. Hasan and C. M. Matthiessen, eds, 'Continuing Discourse on Language: A Functional Perspective', Vol. 1, Equinox, London and New York.

Martinec, R. and Salway, A. (2005) 'A system for image-text relations in new (and old) media', *Visual Communication* **4**(3), 337–371.

Matthiessen, C. M. (2007) The multimodal page: a systemic functional exploration, *in* T. D. Royce and W. L. Bowcher, eds, 'New Directions in the Analysis of Multimodal Discourse', Lawrence Erlbaum Associates, pp. 1–62.

Matthiessen, C. M. I. M. and Bateman, J. A. (1991) *Text generation and systemic-functional linguistics: experiences from English and Japanese*, Frances Pinter Publishers and St. Martin's Press, London and New York.

Maybury, M. T. (1993) *Intelligent Multimedia Interfaces*, AAAI Press and MIT Press, Cambridge, Massachusetts.

McCloud, S. (1994) *Understanding comics: the invisible art*, HarperPerennial, New York.

McConkie, G. W. and Currie, C. B. (1996) 'Visual stability across saccades while viewing complex pictures', *Journal of Experimental Psychology: Human Perception and Performance* **22**(3), 563–581.

McEnery, T. and Wilson, A. (2001) *Corpus Linguistics*, Edinburgh Textbooks in Empirical Linguistics, 2nd edn, Edinburgh University Press, Edinburgh.

Meier, B. P. and Robinson, M. D. (2004) 'Why the sunny side is up: Associations between affect and vertical position', *Psychological Science* **15**, 243–247.

Meng, A. P. K. (2004) Making history in *from colony to nation*: a multimodal analysis of a museum exhibition in Singapore, *in* K. L. O'Halloran, ed., 'Multimodal discourse analysis: systemic functional perspectives', Open Linguistics Series, Continuum, London, pp. 28–54.

Messaris, P. (1997) *Visual Persuasion: the role of images in advertising*, Sage, Thousand Oaks, CA.

Messaris, P. (1998) 'Visual aspects of media literacy', *Journal of Communication* **48**(1), 70–80. doi: 10.1111/j.1460-2466.1998.tb02738.x

Messaris, P. and Moriarty, S. (2005) Visual literacy theory, *in* K. Smith, S. Moriarty, G. Barbatsis and K. Kenney, eds, 'Handbook of visual communication. Theory, methods and media', Lawrence Erlbaum Associates, Mahwah, NJ, pp. 479–502.

Metz, C. (1974) *Film language: a semiotics of the cinema*, Oxford University Press and Chicago University Press, Oxford and Chicago. Translated by Michael Taylor.

Meyrowitz, J. (1986) Television and interpersonal behavior: Codes of perception and response, *in* G. Gumpert and R. Cathcart, eds, 'Inter/media: Interpersonal communication in a media world', 3rd edn, Oxford University Press, New York, pp. 253–272.

Miller, C. R. (1984) 'Genre as social action', *Quarterly Journal of Speech* **70**, 151–167. Reprinted as Miller (1994).

Miller, C. R. (1994) Genre as social action, *in* A. Freedman and P. Medway, eds, 'Genre and the new rhetoric', Taylor and Francis, London, chapter 2, pp. 23–42.

Mitchell, T. F. (1957) 'The language of buying and selling in Cyrenaica: a situational statement', *Hesperis* **44**. (Reprinted in T.F. Mitchell, *Principles of Neo-Firthian Linguistics*, London: Longman, 1975, pp31-71).

Moen, D. R. (1989) *Newspaper Layout and Design: a team approach*, 2nd. edn, Iowa State University Press, Ames, Iowa.

Müller-Brockmann, J. (1985) *Grid systems in graphic design: a visual communication manual for graphic design*, Hastings House, New York.

Müller, M. G. (1997) *Politische Bildstrategien im amerikanischen Präsidentschaftswahlkampf 1828–1996*, Akademie Verlag, Berlin.

Muntigl, P. and Gruber, H. (2005) 'Introduction: approaches to genre', *Folia Linguistica* **XXXIX**(1–2), 1–18.

Naumann, A., Waniek, J. and Krems, J. (2001) Knowledge acquisition, navigation and eye movements from text and hypertext, *in* U.-D. Reips and M. Bosnjak, eds, 'Dimensions of Internet Science', Pabst, Lengerich, pp. 293–304.

New London Group (2000) A pedagogy of multiliteracies designing social futures, *in* M. Kalantzis and B. Cope, eds, 'Multiliteracies: Literacy Learning and the Design of Social Futures', Routledge, London, chapter 1, pp. 9–38.

Nielsen, J. (2000) *Designing web usability: the practice of simplicity*, New Riders Publishing, Indianapolis, Indiana.

Nielsen, J. (2006) 'F-shaped pattern for reading web content', *Jakob Nielsen's Alertbox*. http://www.useit.com/alertbox/reading_pattern.html

Nielsen, J. and Loranger, H. (2006) *Prioritizing Web Usability: the practice of simplicity*, New Riders Publishing, Berkeley, CA.

Norman, D. A. (1988) *The design of everyday things*, Doubleday Press, New York.

Norris, S. (2004) Multimodal discourse analysis: a conceptual framework, *in* P. LeVine and R. Scollon, eds, 'Discourse and technology: multimodal discourse analysis', Georgetown University Press, Washington, D.C., pp. 101–115.

Norrish, P. (1987) *The graphic translatability of text*, number 5854 *in* 'British Library Research and Development Report', Department of Typography and Graphic Communication, Reading.

Nunberg, G. (1990) *The Linguistics of Punctuation*, number 18 *in* 'CSLI Lecture Notes', Center for the Study of Language and Information, Stanford.

O'Halloran, K. L. (1999*a*) 'Interdependence, interaction and metaphor in multisemiotic texts', *Social Semiotics* **9**(3), 317–354.

O'Halloran, K. L. (1999*b*) 'Towards a systemic functional analysis of multisemiotic mathematics texts', *Semiotica* **124**(1/2), 1–29.

O'Halloran, K. L. (2004*a*) *Mathematical Discourse: Language, Symbolism and Visual Images*, Continuum, London and New York.

O'Halloran, K. L. (2004*b*) On the effectiveness of mathematics, *in* E. Ventola, C. Charles and M. Kaltenbacher, eds, 'Perspectives on Multimodality', John Benjamins, Amsterdam, pp. 91–118.

O'Halloran, K. L., ed. (2004*c*) *Multimodal discourse analysis: systemic functional perspectives*, Open Linguistics Series, Continuum, London.

Okun, O., Doermann, D. and Pietikäinen, M. (1999) Page segmentation and zone classification: the state of the art, Technical Report LAMP-TR-036, CAR-TR-927, CS-TR-4079, MDA9049-6C-1250, Language and Media Processing Laboratory, University of Maryland. http://lampsrv01.umiacs.umd.edu/pubs/TechReports/LAMP_036/LAMP_036.pdf

Ollerenshaw, A., Aidman, E. and Kidd, G. (1997) 'Is an illustration always worth ten thousand words?. effects of prior knowledge, learning style and multimedia illustrations on text comprehension', *International Journal of Instructional Media* **24**(3), 227–238.

Ong, W. J. (1982) *Orality and literacy : the technologizing of the word*, Methuen, London.

Orlikowski, W. J. and Yates, J. (1994) 'Genre repertoire: the structuring of communicative practices in organizations', *Administrative Science Quarterly* **39**(4), 541–574.

O'Toole, M. (1990) 'A systemic-functional semiotics of art', *Semiotica* **82**, 185–209.

O'Toole, M. (1994) *The language of displayed art*, Leicester University Press (Pinter), London.

Paltridge, B. (1997) *Genre, frames and writing in research settings*, John Benjamins, Amsterdam.

Paraboni, I. and van Deemter, K. (2002) Towards the generation of document-deictic references, *in* K. van Deemter and R. Kibble, eds, 'Information sharing: reference and presupposition in language generation and interpretation', CSLI Publications, pp. 333–358.

Phillips, B. and McQuarrie, E. (2004) 'Beyond visual metaphor: a new typology of visual rhetoric in advertising', *Marketing Theory* **4**(1/2), 113–136.

Power, R. (2000) Mapping rhetorical structures to text structures by constraint satisfaction, Technical Report ITRI-00-01, ITRI, University of Brighton.

Power, R., Scott, D. and Bouayad-Agha, N. (2003) 'Document structure', *Computational Linguistics* **29**(2), 211–260.

Propp, V. (1968) *The morphology of the folktale*, University of Texas Press, Austin, Texas. Originally published in Russian in 1928.

Reichenberger, K., Rondhuis, K., Kleinz, J. and Bateman, J. A. (1995) Effective presentation of information through page layout: a linguistically-based approach., *in* 'Proceedings of ACM Workshop on Effective Abstractions in Multimedia, Layout and Interaction', ACM, San Francisco, California. http://www.cs.uic.edu/~ifc/mmwsproc/reichen/page-layout.html

Reiter, E. and Dale, R. (2000) *Building Natural Language Generation Systems*, Cambridge University Press, Cambridge, U.K.

Roberts, G. (1998) The home page as genre: a narrative approach, *in* 'Proceedings of the 31st Annual Hawaii International Conference on System Sciences', Vol. 2, IEEE Computer Society Press, Los Alamitos, CA, pp. 78–86. http://csdl.computer.org/comp/proceedings/hicss/1998/8236/02/82360078.pdf

Roberts, L. and Thrift, J. (2002) *The designer and the grid*, Rockport, Gloucester, MA.

Rorty, R. (1979) *Philosophy and the Mirror of Nature*, Princeton University Press, Princeton.

Roth, W.-M., Bowen, G. and McGinn, M. (1999) 'Differences in graph-related practices between high school biology textbooks and scientific ecology journals', *Journal of Research in Science Teaching* **36**, 977–1019.

Royce, T. D. (1999) Visual-verbal intersemiotic complementarity in The Economist Magazine, PhD thesis, University of Reading, United Kingdom.

Royce, T. D. (2007) Intersemiotic complementarity: A framework for multimodal discourse analysis, *in* T. D. Royce and W. L. Bowcher, eds, 'New Directions in the Analysis of Multimodal Discourse', Lawrence Erlbaum Associates, pp. 63–110.

Royce, T. D. and Bowcher, W. L., eds (2007) *New Directions in the Analysis of Multimodal Discourse*, Lawrence Erlbaum Associates, Mahwah, NJ.

Rubin, E. J. (1921) *Visuell wahrgenommene Figuren: Studien in psychologischer Analyse*, Gylendalske Forlag, Copenhagen. Original publication in Danish, 1915.

Rutledge, L., Bailey, B., van Ossenbruggen, J., Hardman, L. and Geurts, J. (2000) Generating Presentation Constraints from Rhetorical Structure, *in* 'Proceedings of the 11th ACM conference on Hypertext and Hypermedia', pp. 19–28. http://www.cwi.nl/~media/publications/ht00.pdf

Sacerdoti, E. (1977) *A Structure for Plans and Behavior*, Elsevier North-Holland, Amsterdam and New York.

Safeyaton, A. (2004) A semiotic study of Singapore's Orchard Road and Marriot Hotel, *in* K. L. O'Halloran, ed., 'Multimodal discourse analysis: systemic functional perspectives', Open Linguistics Series, Continuum, London, pp. 55–82.

Samara, T. (2002) *Making and breaking the grid: a graphic design layout workshop*, Rockport Publishers, Gloucester, MA.

Sampson, G. (1995) *English for the computer*, Oxford University Press, Oxford.

Sarkar, S. and Boyer, L. (1993) 'Perceptual organization in computer vision: a review and a proposal for a classificatory structure', *IEEE Transactions on Systems, Man, and Cybernetics* **23**(2), 382–399.

Sauvola, J. and Kauniskangas, H. (1999) *MediaTeam Document Database II, a CD-ROM collection of document images*, University of Oulu, Finland, Oulu, Finland. http://www.mediateam.oulu.fi/downloads/MTDB/

Schill, K., Umkehrer, E., Beinich, S., Krieger, G. and Zetzsche, C. (2001) 'Scene analysis with saccadic eye movements: top-down and bottom-up modeling', *Journal of Electronic Imaging* **10**(1), 152–160.

Schlieder, C. and Hagen, C. (2000) Interactive layout generation with a diagrammatic constraint language, *in* C. Freksa, W. Brauer, C. Habel and K. Wender, eds, 'Spatial Cognition II - Integrating Abstract Theories, Empirical Studies, Formal Methods, and Practical Applications', Springer, Berlin, pp. 198–211. http://link.springer-ny.com/link/service/series/0558/tocs/t1849.htm

Schriver, K. A. (1997) *Dynamics in document design: creating texts for readers*, John Wiley and Sons, New York.

Scott, D. and Power, R. (2001) Generating textual diagrams and diagrammatic text, *in* H. Bunt and R.-J. Beun, eds, 'Cooperative Multimodal Communication', Lecture Notes in Artificial Intelligence, Springer, Berlin. ftp://ftp.itri.bton.ac.uk/reports/ITRI-01-01.pdf

Sefton, P. M. (1990) Making plans for Nigel (or defining interfaces between computational representations of linguistic structure and output systems: Adding intonation, punctuation and typography systems to the PENMAN system), Technical report, Linguistic Department, University of Sydney, Sydney, Australia. Bachelor's Honours Thesis.

Seppänen, J., ed. (2006) *The power of the gaze: an introduction to visual literacy*, Peter Lang, New York.

Shepherd, M. and Watters, C. (1998) The evolution of cybergenres, *in* 'Proceedings of the 31st Annual Hawaii International Conference on System Sciences', Vol. 2, IEEE Computer Society Press, Los Alamitos, CA, pp. 97–109. http://csdl.computer.org/comp/proceedings/hicss/1998/8236/02/82360097.pdf

Shepherd, M. and Watters, C. (1999) The functionality attribute of cybergenres, *in* 'Proceedings of the 32nd Hawaii International Conference on System Sciences', IEEE, Big Island, Hawaii.

Simon, H. (1978) "genre-alizing" about rhetoric: a scientific approach, *in* K. Campbell and K. Jamieson, eds, 'Form and genre: shaping rhetorical action', Speech Communication Association, Falls Church, VA, pp. 33–50.

Simon, J. R., Acosta Jr., E., Mewaldt, S. P. and Speidel, C. R. (1976) 'The effect of an irrelevant directional cue on choice reaction time: Duration of the phenomenon and its relation to stages of processing', *Perception and Psychophysics* **19**, 16–22.

Sinclair, J. M. (1991) *Corpus, Concordance, Collocation*, Oxford University Press, Oxford.

Sless, D. (1996) 'Better information presentation: satisfying consumers?', *Visible Language* **30**(3), 246–267.

Solso, R. (1994) *Cognition and the visual arts*, MIT Press, Cambridge, MA.

Sperber-McQueen, C. and Burnard, L. (2007) TEI P5: Guidelines for electronic text encoding and interchange, Technical report, The TEI Consortium. Online documentation. http://www.tei-c.org/release/doc/tei-p5-doc/html/index.html

Sperber-McQueen, C. and Burnard, L., eds (2002) *TEI P4: Guidelines for Electronic Text Encoding and Interchange*, 4th edn, Oxford. http://www.tei-c.org/P4X/

Spillner, B. (1980) 'Über die Schwierigkeit semiotischer Textanalyse', *Die Neueren Sprachen* **79**(6), 619–630.

Spillner, B. (1982) 'Stilanalyse semiotisch komplexer Texte', *Kodikas/Code. Ars Semeiotica* **4/5**(1), 91–106.

Spiro, R. J. (1980) 'Prior knowledge and story processing: Integration, selection and variation', *Poetics* **9**(1–3), 313–328.

Stock, O. (1993) ALFRESCO: Enjoying the combination of natural language processing and hypermedia for information exploration, *in* M. T. Maybury, ed., 'Intelligent Multimedia Interfaces', AAAI Press and MIT Press, Cambridge Massachusetts, pp. 197–224.

Stöckl, H. (1997) *Textstil und Semiotik englischsprachiger Anzeigenwerbung*, Peter Lang, Frankfurt am Main.

Stöckl, H. (1998) '(Un-)chaining the floating image. Methdologische Überlegungen zu einem Beschreibungs- und Analysemodell für Bild/Textverknüpfung aus linguistischer und semiotischer Perspektive', *Kodikas/Code. Ars Semeiotica* **21**, 75–95.

Stöckl, H. (2004*a*) *Die Sprache im Bild — Das Bild in der Sprache: Zur Verknüpfung von Sprache und Bild im massenmedialen Text. Konzepte - Theorien - Analysemethoden*, Walter de Gruyter, Berlin.

Stöckl, H. (2004*b*) In between modes: language and image in printed media, *in* E. Ventola, C. Charles and M. Kaltenbacher, eds, 'Perspectives on Multimodality', John Benjamins, Amsterdam, pp. 9–30.

Straßner, E. (1999) Kommunikative and ästhetische Leistungen von Bild und Sprache im Plakat, *in* J.-F. Leonhard, H. W. Ludwig, D. Schwarze and E. Straßner, eds, 'Medienwissenschaft. Ein Handbuch zur Entwicklung der Medien und Kommunikationsformen. 2. Teilband', de Gruyter, Berlin, pp. 1783–1788.

Swales, J. M. (1990) *Genre Analysis: English in academic and research settings*, Cambridge University Press, Cambridge.

Swales, J. M. (2004) *Research Genres. Exploration and applications*, Cambridge University Press, Cambridge.

Taboada, M. T. and Mann, W. C. (2006*a*) 'Applications of Rhetorical Structure Theory', *Discourse Studies* **8**(4), 567–588.

Taboada, M. T. and Mann, W. C. (2006*b*) 'Rhetorical Structure Theory: looking back and moving ahead', *Discourse Studies* **8**(3), 423–459.

Thibault, P. J. (1990) Questions of genre and intertextuality in some Australian television advertisements, *in* R. R. Favretti, ed., 'The Televised Text', Pàtron, Bologna, pp. 89–131.

Thibault, P. J. (2001) Multimodality and the school science textbook, *in* C. T. Torsello-Taylor, G. Brunetti and N. Penello, eds, 'Corpora Testuali per Ricerca, Traduzione e Apprendimento Linguistico', Unipress, Padua, pp. 293–335.

Thompson, H. S. and McKelvie, D. (1997) Hyperlink semantics for standoff markup of read-only documents, *in* 'Proceedings of SGML Europe '97'.

Tiemens, R. (1970) 'Some relationships of camera angle to communicator credibility', *Journal of Broadcasting* **14**, 483–490.

Tschichold, J. (1996) *The Form of the Book: Essays on the Morality of Good Design*, Classic Typography Series, Hartley and Marks Inc. Originally published in German in 1948.

Tseng, C. (2001) Words and images–a multimodal discourse analysis of contemporary news magazine covers, M.A. Hons thesis, Department of English, Communication and Philosophy, University of Wales, Cardiff.

Tufte, E. (1997) *Visual explanations: images and quantities, evidence and narrative*, Graphics Press, Cheshire, CT.

Tversky, B., Kugelmass, S. and Winter, A. (1991) 'Cross-cultural and developmental trends in graphic productions', *Cognitive Psychology* **23**, 515–557.

Twyman, M. (1979) A schema for the study of graphic language, *in* P. A. Kolers, M. E. Wrolstad and H. Bouma, eds, 'Processing of Visible Language', Vol. 1, Plenum, New York and London, pp. 117–150.

Twyman, M. (1982) 'The graphic presentation of language', *Information Design Journal* **3**(1), 2–22.

298   *Bibliography*

Twyman, M. (1986) Articulating graphic language: a historical perspective, *in* M. Wrolstad and D. Fischer, eds, 'Towards a new understanding of literacy', Praeger, New York, pp. 188–251.

Twyman, M. (2004) Further thoughts on a schema for describing graphic language, *in* 'Proceedings of the 1st International Conference on Typography and Visual Communication (2002)', University of Macedonia Press, pp. 329–350.

Unsworth, L. (2001) *Teaching multiliteracies across the curriculum: changing contexts of text and image in classroom practice*, Open University Press.

van Hooijdonk, C., Krahmer, E., Maes, A., Theune, M. and Bosma, W. (2006) Towards automatic generation of multimodal answers to medical questions: a cognitive engineering approach, *in* I. van der Sluis, M. Theune, E. Reiter and E. Krahmer, eds, 'Proceedings of the Workshop on Multimodal Output Generation MOG 2007', Centre for Telematics and Information Technology (CTIT), University of Twente, pp. 93–104.

van Leeuwen, T. (1991) 'Conjunctive structure in documentary film and television', *Continuum: journal of media and cultural studies* **5**(1), 76–114.

van Leeuwen, T. (1993) 'Genre and field in critical discoure analysis: a synopsis', *Discourse and Society* **4**(2), 193–225.

van Leeuwen, T. (2004) Ten reasons why linguists should pay attention to visual communication, *in* P. LeVine and R. Scollon, eds, 'Discourse and technology: multimodal discourse analysis', Georgetown University Press, Washington, D.C., pp. 7–19.

van Leeuwen, T. (2005) Multimodality, genre and design, *in* S. Norris and R. Jones, eds, 'Discourse in Action – Introducing Mediated Discourse Analysis', Routledge, London, pp. 73–94.

van Leeuwen, T. and Kress, G. (1995) 'Critical layout analysis', *Internationale Schulbuchforschung* **17**(3), 25–43.

Van Mulken, M. (2003) 'Analyzing rhetorical devices in print advertisements', *Document Design* **4**(2), 114–128.

Van Mulken, M., Van Enschot, R. and Hoeken, H. (2005) 'Levels of implicitness in magazine advertisements: an experimental study into the relationship between complexity and appreciation in magazine advertisements', *Information Design Journal + Document Design* **13**(2), 155–164.

vander Linden, K. (2000) Natural language generation, *in* D. Jurafsky and J. Martin, eds, 'Speech and Language Processing: an introduction to speech recognition, computational linguistics and natural language processing', Prentice-Hall, New Jersey, chapter 20, pp. 763–798.

Ventola, E. (1984) 'The dynamics of genre', *Nottingham Linguistics Circular* **14**.

Ventola, E. (1987) *The Structure of Social Interaction: A Systemic Approach to the Semiotics of Service Encounters*, Frances Pinter, London.

Walker, S. (1982) 'Describing graphic language: practicalities and implications', *Information Design Journal* **3**(2), 102–109.

Walker, S. (2001) *Typography and language in everyday life: prescriptions and practices*, Longman, London.

Walker, S. (2003) Towards a method for describing the visual characteristics of children's readers and information books, *in* 'Proceedings of the Information Design International Conference', Recife, Brazil. (CD-ROM).

Waller, R. (1980) Graphic aspects of complex texts: typography as macropunctuation, *in* P. A. Kolers, M. E. Wrolstad and H. Bouma, eds, 'Processing of Visible Language', Vol. 2, Plenum, New York and London, pp. 241–253.

Waller, R. (1987*a*) The typographical contribution to language: towards a model of typographic genres and their underlying structures, PhD thesis, Department of Typography and Graphic Communication, University of Reading, Reading, U.K. http://www.robwaller.org/RobWaller_thesis87.pdf

Waller, R. (1987*b*) Using typography to structure arguments: a critical analysis of some examples, *in* D. Jonassen, ed., 'The Technology of Text', Vol. 2, Educational Technology Publications, Englewood Cliffs, NJ, pp. 105–125.

Waller, R. (1990) Typography and discourse, *in* R. Barr, ed., 'Handbook of reading research', Vol. II, Longman, London, pp. 341–380. Reprinted 1996; Erlbaum (Mahwah, NJ).

Waller, R. (1999) Making connections: typography, layout and language, *in* R. Power and D. Scott, eds, 'Proceedings of the AAAI Fall Symposium on Using Layout for the Generation, Understanding, or Retrieval of Documents', American Association for Artificial Intelligence, Cape Cod, MA. Technical Report FS-99-04.

Waller, R. and Delin, J. L. (2003) 'Cooperative brands: the importance of customer information for service brands', *Design Management Journal* 14(4), 63–69.

Ware, C. (2000) *Information Visualization: Perception for Design*, Morgan Kaufmann Publishers, San Francisco.

Weitzman, L. and Wittenburg, K. (1994) Automatic presentation of multimedia documents using relational grammars, *in* 'Proceedings of the Second ACM International Conference on Multimedia (Multimedia '94)', ACM Press, New York, pp. 443–452.

Wilson, P. T. and Anderson, R. C. (1986) What they don't know will hurt them: The role of prior knowledge in comprehension, *in* J. Orasanu, ed., 'Reading Comprehension: From Research to Practice', Erlbaum, Hillsdale, New Jersey, pp. 31–48.

Winn, W. (1987) Charts, graphics and diagrams in educational materials, *in* D. Willows and H. Houghton, eds, 'The Psychology of Illustration. Vol. 1. Basic Research', Springer, New York, pp. 152–198.

Winn, W. (1989) The design and use of instructional graphics, *in* H. Mandl and J. R. Levin, eds, 'Knowledge acquisition from text and pictures', number 58 *in* 'Advances in Psychology', Elsevier, Amsterdam, pp. 125–144.

Winn, W. (1991) 'Learning from maps and diagrams', *Educational Psychology Review* 3(3), 211–247.

Wolf, F. and Gibson, E. (2005) 'Representing discourse coherence: a corpus-based study', *Computational Linguistics* 31(2), 249–287.

Wright, P. (1970) 'Presenting information in tables', *Applied Ergonomics* 1, 234–242.

Wright, P. (1980) Usability: the criterion for designing written information, *in* P. A. Kolers, M. E. Wrolstad and H. Bouma, eds, 'Processing of Visible Language', Vol. 2, Plenum, New York and London, pp. 183–206.

Wright, P. (1995) 'Evaluation, design and research: empirical contributions to the beginnings and ends of the design process', *Information Design Journal* **8**, 82–85.

Wright, P. (1998) Printed instructions: can research make a difference?, *in* H. Zwaga, T. Boersema and H. Hoonout, eds, 'Visual information for everyday use; design and research perspectives', Taylor and Francis, London, pp. 45–66.

Wright, P. and Barnard, P. (1978) 'Asking multiple questions about several items: The design of matrix structures on application forms', *Applied Ergonomics* **9**, 7–14.

Wright, P., Lickorish, A., Hull, A. and Umellen, N. (1995) 'Graphics in written directions: appreciated by readers not by writers', *Applied Cognitive Psychology* **9**, 41–59.

Yarbus, A. (1967) *Eye Movements and Vision*, Plenum Press, New York, NY.

Yates, J. and Orlikowski, W. J. (1992) 'Genres of organizational communication: A structurational approach to studying communicatios and media', *Academy of Management Review* **17**, 299–326.

Yates, J., Orlikowski, W. and Okamura, C. (1999) 'Explicit and implicit structuring of genres in electronic communication: reinforcement and change of social interaction', *Organisation Science* **10**(1), 83–117.

Yoshioka, T. and Herman, G. (2000) Coordinating information using genres, Working Paper CCS WP 214 and SWP 4127, Massachusetts Institute of Technology, Sloan School of Management, Center for Coordination Science, Boston, Massachusetts.

Yoshioka, T., Herman, G., Yates, J. and Orlikowski, W. J. (2001) 'Genre taxonomy: A knowledge repository of communicative actions', *ACM Transactions on Information Systems* **19**(4), 431–456. http://doi.acm.org/10.1145/502795.502798

Author Index

Acartürk, 145, 285
Acosta Jr., 51, 296
Aidman, 32, 294
Aitchison, 224, 279
Ames, 181, 279
Amouzadeh, 144, 279
Anderson, 32, 299
André, 92, 151–153, 159, 279
Arens, 92, 279
Arnheim, 9, 43, 279
Asher, 148, 279
Ashton, 214, 279
Askehave, 210, 279
Atwell, 252, 288
Bailey, 152, 295
Baker, 11, 279
Baldry, 2, 7, 8, 39, 40, 47, 48, 50, 53, 54,
    56, 99, 100, 106, 197, 265, 266,
    272, 279
Bargeron, 85, 288
Barnard, 32, 300
Barnhurst, 278, 279
Barrett, 11, 288
Barthes, 38, 144, 146, 279
Barton, 248, 282
Bateman, 67, 68, 75, 91, 92, 100–102,
    122, 151, 153, 176, 181, 238, 266,
    271, 272, 277, 280, 283, 286, 292,
    294
Bazerman, 7, 10, 190, 201, 280
Beinich, 65, 295
Bell, 181, 281
Berman, 264, 284
Bernhardt, 10, 93, 174, 281
Bertamini, 274, 281
Bertin, 9, 121, 281
Beun, 151, 281
Biber, 14, 184, 206, 251, 281
Bloor, 45, 281
Blum, 40, 201, 281
Bonhomme, 256, 287
Bosma, 30, 298
Bossini, 51, 283
Bouayad-Agha, 94–98, 100, 175, 266,
    281, 294
Bowcher, 38, 295
Bowen, 7, 294
Boyer, 68, 295
Branigan, 277, 281
Bransford, 22, 281

Bres, 208, 209, 284
Briggs, 183, 281
Bryan, 86, 281
Bucher, 40, 201, 281
Buchman, 67, 283
Bunt, 151, 281
Burch, 277, 281
Burford, 183, 281
Burnard, 256, 296
Bush, 210, 282
Carpenter, 32, 286
Carrol, 184, 285
Cave, 11, 288
Cesarini, 73, 74, 206, 282
Christie, 188, 282
Conklin, 210, 282
Conrad, 14, 251, 281
Cope, 7, 288
Corio, 266, 282
Corpus Encoding Standard, 256, 282
Coventry, 51, 274, 282
Craig, 248, 282
Crowston, 201, 211, 212, 218, 225, 282,
    283
Cruickshank, 214, 279
Crystal, 31, 95, 283
Currie, 116, 292
Dale, 92, 294
Danlos, 148, 150, 283
Davy, 31, 283
de la Clergerie, 264, 287
de Beaugrande, 99, 182, 283
Dehaene, 51, 283
Delin, 4–6, 101, 151, 181, 238, 266, 271,
    272, 280, 283, 286, 299
Descartes, 272, 283
Diligenti, 206, 283
Djonov, 65, 283
Doermann, 67, 70, 206, 207, 283, 293
Dolan, 11, 279
Dondis, 6, 204, 283
Dori, 67, 283
Dorn, 37, 65, 82, 283
Durand, 144, 283
Durusau, 261, 283
Dybkjaer, 264, 284
Dyson, 57, 284
Eakins, 183, 281
Eckkrammer, 40, 266, 284
Egan, 116, 284

Eglin, 208, 209, 284
Elam, 80, 284
Epstein, 38, 174, 284, 285
Fairclough, 10, 44, 284
Feiner, 85, 152, 222, 284, 290
Fix, 40, 284
Forceville, 35, 144, 284
Fowler, 44, 182, 284
Frackowiak, 11, 279
Francis, 250, 284
Frasconi, 206, 283
Freedman, 188, 284
Frith, 11, 279
Gabrieli, 11, 288
Gaede, 35, 36, 144, 146, 285
Garfinkel, 188, 189, 285
Garrod, 274, 282
Garside, 252, 288
Geurts, 152, 295
Ghyka, 78, 285
Gibson, 11, 150, 285, 299
Giddens, 190, 285
Giraux, 51, 283
Glenberg, 174, 285
Goldfarb, 86, 285
Gombrich, 9, 274, 285
Goodluck, 252, 288
Gori, 73, 206, 282, 283
Graf, 221, 285
Gregory, 54, 184, 285
Gross, 7, 285
Gruber, 183, 201, 285, 293
Guo, 64, 198, 285
Haake, 215, 285
Habel, 145, 285
Hagen, 222, 295
Halliday, 38, 42, 145, 162, 184, 189, 286
Haralick, 67, 283
Hardman, 152, 295
Harrell, 144, 190, 286
Hartley, 22, 201, 286
Hasan, 145, 183–186, 286
Hassett, 177, 183, 205, 288
Hatta, 51, 287
Hegarty, 32, 116, 286
Held, 201, 286
Henschel, 101, 162, 181, 266, 267, 271,
    272, 280, 286
Hentschel, 198, 286
Herman, 191, 300
Herskovits, 47, 286

Hocks, 217, 286
Hodge, 44, 284
Hoeken, 5, 298
Hofinger, 8, 286
Hollis, 80, 287
Holmqvist, 63, 287
Holsanova, 63, 287
Hovy, 92, 153, 279, 287
Hu, 206, 287
Hull, 22, 300
Hurlburt, 80, 82, 287
Hurst, 99, 287
Hüser, 101, 215, 287
Hutt, 17, 181, 287
Hymes, 188, 287
Hyon, 183, 287
Ide, 256, 264, 287
International Organisation for
    Standardization, 86, 287
Ito, 51, 287
Ittelson, 59, 287
Itti, 65, 287
Jacobs, 85, 288
Jewitt, 38, 46, 47, 197, 289
Johansson, 252, 288
Johns, 183, 288
Johnson, 22, 281
Just, 32, 286
Kalantzis, 7, 288, 289
Kaltenbacher, 13, 38, 272, 288
Kamps, 100, 102, 280
Kanwisher, 274, 288
Kashi, 206, 287
Kauniskangas, 266, 295
Keller-Cohen, 5, 288
Kendrick, 217, 286
Kessler, 194, 206, 288
Kidd, 32, 294
Kipp, 264, 284
Kitis, 40, 288
Kleinz, 67, 68, 100, 102, 122, 280, 294
Knieper, 45, 288
Knox, 48, 181, 288
Koch, 65, 287
Koenig, 11, 288
Koffka, 59, 288
Köhler, 59, 288
Kong, 129, 144, 159, 288
Kosslyn, 11, 288
Kostelnick, 177, 183, 205, 288
Kourtzi, 274, 288

Krahmer, 30, 298
Krems, 64, 293
Kress, 11–13, 36–40, 43–47, 121, 156,
    191, 197, 211, 221, 225, 284, 289,
    298
Krieger, 65, 295
Kugelmass, 51, 297
Kühnlein, 264, 291
Kwaśnik, 218, 225, 282
Labov, 184, 186, 289
Landow, 210, 289
Lapalme, 266, 282
Lascarides, 148, 279
Laspina, 7, 289
Lassen, 45, 289
Lastri, 74, 206, 282
Le Corbusier, 79, 289
Leech, 252, 288
Lee, 183, 289
Lefèvre, 198, 289
Lemke, 2, 5, 10, 39, 54, 99, 100, 144, 178,
    191, 194, 199, 223–225, 289
Lentz, 22, 65, 290
Lickorish, 22, 300
Lim, 121, 290
Linkugel, 144, 190, 286
Li, 85, 288
Lok, 222, 290
Loranger, 22, 293
Lowe, 116, 290
Lynott, 51, 282
MacDonald-Ross, 33, 290
Maes, 30, 298
Mandell, 41, 290
Mann, 5, 20, 146–148, 151, 288, 290,
    297
Manovich, 217, 290
Mao, 74, 206, 290
Marinai, 73, 74, 206, 282
Marsh, 35, 144, 291
Martinec, 38, 144, 159, 291, 292
Martin, 8, 45, 50, 65, 157, 183, 184, 186–
    190, 219, 220, 264, 282, 291
Matthiessen, 42, 75, 103, 148, 162, 286,
    290, 291, 292
Maybury, 151, 282, 292
McCloud, 175, 275, 276, 292
McConkie, 116, 292
McEnery, 251, 292
McGinn, 7, 294
McKelvie, 262, 297

McKeown, 152, 284
McQuarrie, 35, 294
Meader, 5, 288
Medway, 188, 284
Meier, 51, 292
Meng, 8, 292
Messaris, 6, 41, 144, 292
Metz, 277, 292
Mewaldt, 51, 296
Meyrowitz, 41, 292
Miller, 51, 182, 183, 188, 189, 191, 282,
    292
Mitchell, 186, 292
Moen, 181, 293
Moriarty, 6, 292
Müller, 45, 288, 293
Müller-Brockmann, 80, 275, 293
Muntigl, 183, 293
Naumann, 64, 293
New London Group, 7, 293
Nielsen, 22, 65, 210, 279, 293
Nie, 74, 206, 290
Norman, 30, 293
Norrish, 30, 31, 203, 293
Norris, 2, 293
Nunberg, 95, 194, 206, 288, 293
O'Ceallaigh, 51, 282
O'Donnell, 261, 283
Ogborn, 38, 46, 47, 197, 289
O'Halloran, 38, 39, 54, 64, 198, 293
Okamura, 211, 300
Okun, 67, 293
Ollerenshaw, 32, 294
Olsen, 264, 284
Ong, 2, 294
Orlikowski, 190–195, 200, 211, 212, 215,
    217, 294, 300
O'Toole, 8, 9, 21, 22, 38, 121, 198, 294
Owen, 11, 279
Paggio, 264, 291
Paltridge, 183, 294
Pander Maat, 22, 290
Paraboni, 114, 175, 271, 294
Phillips, 35, 67, 283, 294
Pianese, 264, 291
Pietikäinen, 67, 293
Pirrelli, 264, 284
Plum, 187, 291
Power, 94–98, 100, 175, 281, 294, 295
Propp, 186, 294
Rahm, 63, 287

Reichenberger, 67, 68, 100–102, 122, 214, 280, 285, 287, 294
Reiter, 92, 294
Reithinger, 264, 284
Renn, 198, 289
Reppen, 14, 251, 281
Rist, 92, 152, 279
Rivlin, 70, 206, 207, 283
Robbins, 11, 279
Roberts, 80, 201, 294
Robinson, 51, 292
Rodríguez, 278, 279
Rogers, 11, 279
Romary, 256, 264, 287
Rondhuis, 67, 68, 122, 294
Rorty, 8, 294
Rosenfeld, 70, 206, 207, 283
Rose, 50, 183, 186, 291
Ross, 67, 283
Rostek, 101, 287
Roth, 7, 294
Royce, 36, 38, 39, 41, 145, 198, 295
Rubin, 60, 295
Rutledge, 152, 295
Sacerdoti, 152, 295
Safeyaton, 8, 295
Salesin, 85, 288
Salway, 144, 159, 292
Samara, 80, 82, 83, 295
Sampson, 252, 295
Sarkar, 68, 295
Sauvola, 266, 295
Schill, 65, 295
Schlieder, 222, 295
Schoepflin, 198, 289
Schrier, 85, 288
Schriver, 6, 20, 22, 32–34, 53, 58, 59, 65, 76, 80, 83, 118, 119, 144, 156, 174, 221, 296
Schütze, 195, 206, 288
Schwartz, 116, 284
Scott, 94–98, 100, 175, 281, 294, 295
Searle-Jones, 4, 5, 283
Sefton, 121, 295
Seppänen, 6, 296
Shaw, 41, 290
Shepherd, 196, 201, 210, 212–214, 216, 296
Shin, 67, 283
Simon, 51, 144, 190, 296
Sinclair, 250, 296

Sless, 22, 296
Soda, 73, 74, 206, 282
Solso, 41, 296
Soria, 264, 284
Speidel, 51, 296
Sperber-McQueen, 256, 296, 296
Spillner, 39, 145, 296
Spiro, 32, 296
Stenglin, 8, 291
Stiefelhagen, 264, 291
Stock, 152, 296
Stöckl, 36, 40, 145, 158, 175, 296
Straßner, 40, 297
Streitz, 101, 287
Strunck, 45, 289
Swales, 186, 189, 190, 193, 194, 210, 297
Taboada, 151, 297
Tang, 11, 288
Tavangar, 144, 279
Theune, 30, 298
Thibault, 2, 8, 39, 40, 47, 48, 50, 53, 54, 56, 99, 100, 106, 144, 161, 162, 194, 265, 266, 272, 279, 297
Thoma, 74, 206, 290
Thompson, 20, 146–148, 262, 290, 297
Thrift, 80, 294
Tiemens, 41, 297
Trew, 44, 284
Tsatsarelis, 38, 46, 47, 197, 289
Tschichold, 78, 80, 297
Tseng, 201, 297
Tufte, 121, 297
Tversky, 51, 297
Twyman, 24, 29, 30, 103, 118, 132, 183, 202, 203, 213, 297
Umellen, 22, 300
Umkehrer, 65, 295
Unsworth, 226, 298
van Deemter, 114, 175, 271, 294
Van Enschot, 5, 298
van Hooijdonk, 30, 298
van Leeuwen, 11–13, 24, 36–40, 43–45, 47, 121, 144, 157, 199, 211, 221, 225, 289, 298
Van Mulken, 5, 36, 144, 298
van Ossenbruggen, 152, 295
vander Linden, 91, 153, 298
Vari, 278, 279
Ventola, 8, 183, 287, 298
Vestergaard, 45, 289

Waletzky, 186, 289
Walker, 29–31, 118, 203, 204, 266, 298, 299
Waller, 4–6, 17, 24, 33, 83, 99, 119, 178, 179, 203, 213, 283, 290, 299
Waniek, 64, 293
Ware, 59, 61, 62, 299
Watters, 196, 201, 210, 212–214, 216, 296
Weillmann, 40, 284
Weitzman, 222, 299
White, 35, 144, 291
Wilfong, 206, 287
Wilkinson, 174, 285

Williams, 201, 211, 212, 282
Wilson, 32, 251, 292, 299
Winn, 11, 32, 121, 198, 299
Winter, 51, 297
Wittenburg, 222, 299
Wodak, 45, 291
Wolf, 150, 299
Wright, 22, 32, 37, 38, 57, 99, 299, 300
Yarbus, 65, 300
Yates, 190–195, 200, 211, 212, 215, 217, 294, 300
Yoshioka, 191, 300
Zetzsche, 65, 295
Zock, 92, 153, 280

Subject Index

access structure, 104, 242
access, to documents, 100, 104, 108, 114, 130, 132, 136, 140
access, to XML elements, 262
Adobe InDesign, 88
affordance, 11, 156, 181
anecdote, 188
animation, 155
annotated corpora, 251
annotation
  stand-off, 262, 263, 265, 267
annotation language, 75, 251, 252, 254–256, 259–262, 271, 272
annotation standards, 264
annotation tools, 265
applicability conditions, of rhetorical relations, 148, 150
area model, 91, 124, 125, 142, 221, 230, 233, 234, 239
art
  displayed, 8
  sequential visual, 176, 275
aspect-to-aspect, 276
attentional goal, 154
attribute, 257
automatic document analysis, 96, 206
automatic page generation, 75, 85, 101, 221

base layer, 267
Bauhaus, 80
box model, 91
branching pointers, 269
business memo, 192
by-line, 208

callout, 48, 135, 137, 161, 208
camera angle, 41
Canada page example, 55, 59, 71, 81
canvas, 16
canvas constraints, 18, 31
caption, 208
Cascaded Style Sheet, 89, 268
CDA, *see* Critical Discourse Analysis
centred composition, 43
checklist, of document properties, 31
closure, 61
cluster
  Baldry and Thibault, 53

Schriver, 33
co-deployment, 2
cohesion, 145
column grid, 81, 141
communicative goal, 92
composition, 42
  framing, 42
  information value
    centred, 43, 140
    given-new, 43, 140, 221
    ideal-real, 43, 140, 221
    polarized, 43, 140
  salience, 42
conceptual representations, 40
conjunctive relation, 157
constraint satisfaction, 222
consumption constraints, 18, 128, 192
content structure, 19, 76, 230
contextual configuration, 186
continuation pointer, 269
continuity, 61
convention, 177
corpora
  LOB, 252
  multimodal documents,
    see multimodal document corpora
  SUSANNE, 252, 259, 262
corpus-based linguistics, 249
Critical Discourse Analysis, 44
cross-references, 262
CSS, *see* Cascaded Style Sheet
cybergenre, 196, 210

$DART_{bio}$, 100
delicacy, 219
delivery channel, 57
dependence, 36
description list, 236
design features, 22
diagrams, 46, 48, 113, 121, 176, 198, 208, 211, 276
digital edition, 181, 215
discourse structure
  acyclic graph, 159
  tree, 150, 159
document classification, 67
document deictic expressions, *see* document deixis
document deixis, 113, 114, 175, 198, 271

307

document description languages, 85
document functional level, 208
document markup, 96
document parts, 23
    in images, 35, 41
document recognition, 66
document structure
    Baldry and Thibault, 53
    Power, Scott and Bouayad-Agha, 94,
        122
Document Type Description, 255
document validation, 255
dynamic-kinetic routine, 274

elderly, design for, 38
embodied perception, 52
exhibition spaces, 275
expansion pointer, 271
expressionism, 205
eXtensible Markup Language, *see* XML
extraposition, 98
eye-tracking, 63

facet, 218, 220, 225
Fibonacci series, 78
figure-ground, 61
film, 277
flow rule, 127
flowline, 82
formatting objects, 89, 121, 268
framing, 42, 56, 64, 102, 104, 112, 116,
        122, 124, 128, 134, 135, 138, 140,
        168, 171, 181, 199, 219, 233, 234,
        245, 246, 277

Gannet pages, 229, 238
    1924, 230, 235, 237, 238, 247, 248
    1972, 25, 27, 33, 34, 37, 41, 42, 48,
        81, 93, 112, 119, 122, 127, 192,
        232, 233, 237, 238
    1994, 233, 234, 238, 242, 247
    1996, 84, 239, 247, 275
    2002, 244
gaze, 41
GeM model
    area model, 124, 221, 230, 233, 234,
        239
    base layer, 267
    canvas constraints, 18, 31
    consumption constraints, 18, 192
    content structure, 19, 230
    genre structure, 19, 20

layout base, 115, 268
layout structure, 19, 20, 122, 179, 221
linguistic structure, 19
navigation base, 108, 269
navigation structure, 19
pointer, 269
production constraints, 17, 18, 31
rhetorical structure, 19, 20, 139, 143,
        163
RST base, 269
generation system
    DART$_{bio}$, 100
    ICONOCLAST, 94
generic stage, 208
generic structure, 187, 208, 219, 220, 223
Generic Structure Potential, 186, 194,
        208, 220
genre, 9, 18, 20, 178, 190, 223
    expectations, 206
    families, 219
    macro-genre, 190
    network, 219
    rules, 218
    topology, 225
    visual, 203, 205
genre coercion, 214
genre families, 188, 195
genre repertoire, 191
genre structure, 19, 20
genre system, 190
genre theory
    North American School, 188
    Sydney School, 184
genre, types of
    advertisements, 5
    anecdote, 188
    bills, 5
    brochure, 213
    business memo, 192, 216
    catalogue, 213
    comics, 176
    cybergenre, 201
    e-mail, 192, 201
    homepage, 201, 213
    hotlist, 212
    instructions, 114
    letters, 29
    magazine cover, 201
    narrative, 186, 188
    newspaper, 201, 215
        front page, 44

patent, 201
patient information leaflet, 94, 96, 100
procedure, 187
recount, 187
resource, 213
Gestalt laws, 59
Gestalt perception, 59
Gestalt Psychology, 59
given-new, 43, 140, 221
Golden Ratio, 77, 221
Golden Rectangle, 78
good continuation, 58
granularity, 68, 111
graphic articulation, 31
graphic features
extrinsic, 118
intrinsic, 118
graphic translatability, of text, 30
graphical schema, 202
graphology, 95
grid, 74, 76, 176
column, 81, 141, 181
manuscript, 80, 127
modular, 81, 125, 244, 275
grid-based design, 80, 275
GSP, *see* Generic Structure Potential
gutter, 81

hierarchical grid, 82
hotlist, 212
HTML, 86–88, 181
hyperlink, 105, 132
hypertext, 210
Hypertext Markup Language, *see* HTML
HyTime, 277

icon, 234
ICONOCLAST, 94
ideal-real, 43, 140, 221
ideology, 190
illusion of knowing, 174
image-flow, 175, 243, 275
indentation, logical, 97
information design, 5
information extraction, 66
information retrieval, 66
information value, 42
inset, 127, 138, 245
instantiation, 218
intelligent multimedia layout manager, 221

intentional goal, 154
International Organization for Standardization, 264, 277
International Typographic Style, 80
intersecting hierarchies, 260
intersemiosis, 39
intersemiotic metaphor, 54
ISO, 86, 264, 277

kerning, 118

label, 208
LaTeX, 88
layout base, 115, 268
layout constraints, 222
layout structure, 19, 20, 122, 125, 142, 179, 221, 230
layperson, design by, 29
Le Corbusier, 79
leading, 118
library science, 218
linearity, 202
linearity, of language, 98
Linguistic Annotation Framework, 264
linguistic corpora, 14
linguistic structure, 19
literacy
multimodal, 7
visual, 7
LOB corpus, 252
logic, types of, 156, 275, 277
logical document structure, 70
logical indentation level, 97
logical structure, 70, 86, 258

machine-readable document, 96
macro-genre, 190
macro-punctuation, 103, 160
makeup sheet, 82
manuscript grid, 80, 127
margin composition, 43
markup language, 75, 86–88
materiality, of genre, 10
mathematical formulae, 39
meaning compression, 198
mediator composition, 43
menus, 113
metafunction, 39, 40
ideational, 39–41, 51
interpersonal, 39, 41, 162
textual, 42, 162

mini-genre, 53
mini-span, 162, 269
modal density, 2
mode, *see* semiotic mode
modular grid, 81, 125, 275
Modulor, 79
mouse-over behaviours, 113
MPEG, 277
MPEG-7, 277
multiliteracy, 7
multimedia content, 277
multimodal document, 1, 9
multimodal document corpora, 266
   DIALAYMED, 266
   educational materials, 266
   MediaTeam Document Database, 266
   patient information leaflets, 94, 266
   University of Washington
      UW-II, 266
      UW-III, 266
multimodal linguistics, 28, 38, 213
multimodal literacy, 7
multiplying meaning, 2, 54
MXY
   see XY-tree 73

narrative, 156, 188
narrative representation, 40
Natural Language Generation, 75, 92, 143
navigation base, 108, 269
navigation mode, 211
navigation structure, 19, 177
new media, 199, 208, 210, 212, 217
New Rhetoric, 188
news value, 181
NLG
   see Natural Language Generation 92
NLG system, *see* generation system

OASIS, 121
OCR, *see* Optical Character Recognition
Open Document Format, 121
optical centre, of page, 65
Optical Character Recognition, 66
optical illusions, 61

page model, 91
page-flow, 157, 176, 198, 226, 269
paralinguistic, 103
paravisual, 104

part of speech, 252
pdf, *see* Portable Document Format
perception, embodied, 52
perception, Gestalt, 59
phase, 54, 185
Phidias, 77
phonology, 224
photographs, 211
plan operator, 152
point, unit of measurement, 117
pointer, 269
polarized composition, 43, 140
Portable Document Format, 89
pre-attentive, 60, 115
primitivism, 205
procedure, 187
production constraints, 17, 18, 31
proximity, 61
psycholinguistics, 57
punctuation, 95

QuarkXPress, 88, 241

re-purposing, 66
reading comprehension, 57
reading mode, 211
reading path, 64, 70, 199, 227
Reading School, 29, 203
recount, 187
register, 184
relative size, 61
rendering, 75
resolution, 67
resource integration principle, 54
rhetoric, traditional, 144
rhetorical cluster, 33, 76, 93
rhetorical figure, 38
rhetorical relation, 105, 148, 150
   background, 93, 168, 230
   circumstance, 150
   concession, 96
   contrast, 168
   elaboration, 93, 96, 102, 162, 165, 168, 230
   enablement, 132, 150, 165, 172
   evidence, 96
   interpretation, 158
   joint, 93, 96, 160, 165
   motivation, 165
   purpose, 169
   restatement, 159, 169

sequence, 150, 165, 172
rhetorical structure, 19, 20, 132, 139, 143, 163, 230
rhetorical structure layer, 139, 143
Rhetorical Structure Theory, *see* RST
RST, 20, 92, 144, 150, 199
  nucleus, 148
  satellite, 137, 148
  sequentiality assumption, 158
  subnuclear, 162
  text span, 148, 150, 159, 269
RST base, 269

salience, 42
semiotic mode, 1, 106, 157, 175
separator, 102, 112, 127, 140, 171, 234, 245
sequentiality assumption, of RST, 158
SFL, *see* systemic-functional linguistics
SGML, 86, 88, 255, 277
signal processing techniques, 66
similarity, 61
Simon effect, 51
SMIL, 277
SNARC effect, 51
social activity type, 188
social context, 184
space, 277
spatial array, 52
spatial constraint, 222
spatial constraints, on layout, 221
spatial zone, 82, 244
speech act theory, 190
spread, 58, 245
stand-off annotation, 262
Standard Generalised Markup Language, *see* SGML
standardised mark-up, 255
standards, 86
stratification, linguistic, 184
structuration, 191
structure, 145
style, of language, 184
Stylesheet Transformation, 89, 121
subgenre, 187
SUSANNE corpus, 252, 259, 262
symmetry, 61
Synchronized Multimedia Integration Language, 277
systemic-functional linguistics, 38, 40, 184

tables, 32, 34, 99, 100, 104, 122, 130, 160, 198
tags, 87
tagset, 252
technology, 12, 192, 198, 213, 215
text element, 33
Text Encoding Initiative, 256
text linguistics, 39
text span, 148, 150, 151
text-clause, 95
text-flow, 49, 99, 100, 132, 160, 175, 177, 226
text-sentence, 95, 230
tie, cohesive, 145
time-based data, 265
topological, 218
topological-continuous, 162
transcription, 53,
    see annotation language, 272
typographic rules, 129
typological, 218
typological-categorial, 162

usability studies, 22
user-oriented documents, 32

variability, of genres, 224
variation, 184
Verbal Graphic Language, 31, 204
VGL, *see* Verbal Graphic Language
virtual artefact, 16, 80, 83, 181
virtual canvas, 192
visual communication, 278
visual field, 83
visual icon, 130
visual literacy, 7
visual message element, 40
visual pragmatics, 278
visual realisation, 117
visual rhetoric, 278
visual semantics, 278
visual style, 204
visual transitivity frame, 40
VME, *see* visual message element
vowel space, 224

W3C, 88, 277
web browser, 75, 87
whitespace, 42, 72, 73, 102, 122, 128, 135, 168, 208, 233, 234, 245
World-Wide Web consortium, *see* W3C

XCES, 256
XML, 88, 121, 255, 256, 277
XML Schema, 255
XPath, 258, 261
XSL, *see* Stylesheet Transformation

XSL:FO, *see* formatting objects
XY-tree, 71, 123, 124, 206
   modified, 73

Z-pattern, 65

Breinigsville, PA USA
06 July 2010
241206BV00002B/3/P